Going Forth

Stanley Weinstein. New Haven, 2003

STUDIES IN EAST ASIAN BUDDHISM 18

Going Forth

Visions of Buddhist Vinaya

Essays Presented in Honor of Professor
Stanley Weinstein

EDITED BY

William M. Bodiford

A KURODA INSTITUTE BOOK
University of Hawai'i Press
Honolulu

Printed in the United States of America
24 23 22 21 20 19   6 5 4 3 2 1

Library of Congress Cataloging-in-Publication Data
Going forth : visions of Buddhist vinaya / edited by William M. Bodiford.
p. cm.—(Studies in East Asian Buddhism ; no. 18)
Includes bibliographical references and index.
ISBN 0-8248-2787-2 (hardcover : alk. paper)
1. Monasticism and religious orders, Buddhist—Rules.
I. Bodiford, William M., 1955–
II. Series.
BQ6122. G65 2002
294.3'657—dc22
2004006302

ISBN 978-0-8248-8153-5 (pbk.)

The Kuroda Institute for the Study of Buddhism and Human Values is a nonprofit,
educational corporation founded in 1976. One of its primary objectives is to
promote scholarship on the historical, philosophical, and cultural ramifications of
Buddhism. In association with the University of Hawai'i Press, the Institute also
publishes Classics in East Asian Buddhism, a series devoted to the translation of
significant texts in the East Asian Buddhist tradition.

University of Hawai'i Press books are printed on acid-free paper and meet the
guidelines for permanence and durability of the Council on Library Resources.

Designed by University of Hawai'i Press production staff

To Stanley Weinstein

For his tireless dedication
to excellence,
to his students, and to Buddhist studies

Contents

Preface

ALL THE CONTRIBUTORS to this volume completed their Ph.D. training under the guidance of Professor Stanley Weinstein. The fact that we, his students, produced essays that cover such a wide variety of topics and span such a broad range of history testifies to Weinstein's own breadth and depth as a scholar and mentor. Unfortunately, our essays cannot begin to convey Weinstein's persona, his abiding love and respect for Asia and for Buddhism, his deep concern for his fellow man, his devotion to his students, and his personal warmth and strong sense of decency. I remember Weinstein once saying in a seminar that the starting point of Buddhism is the human heart (*Bukkyō no shuppatsuten wa ningen no kokoro* 佛教の出發點は人間の心). For him, the starting point for education also is the human heart, and all of us are richer for it. With respect, affection, and gratitude, we dedicate this volume to Stanley Weinstein.

In preparing these essays for publication, I wanted to ensure clarity and accessibility above all else. I simplified and in many cases severely shortened and streamlined the essays beyond what their authors would have preferred. To the extent possible, I imposed a uniform style, identified people, and added dates to aid nonspecialist readers. Whenever possible foreign words and titles were replaced with English translations; the term or title in the original language usually appears inside parentheses upon first occurrence in each essay. Titles that do not appear in their original language and abbreviations for textual titles are fully identified in the bibliography. Chinese, Japanese, or Korean glyphs are provided for all East Asian technical terms and proper names upon first occurrence within each essay as well as for all East Asian sources in the bibliography. When the orthography for these characters differs in China and Japan I often opted for the Japanese form (e.g., 説 instead of 說). I bear full responsibility for any defects that resulted from my solutions to these editorial challenges.

This volume never would have seen the light of day without the help and support of many people and organizations, a few of whom I must acknowledge by name. First I thank John McRae for organizing a panel at the 1992 annual meeting of the American Academy of Religion in San Francisco where the essays in this volume began to take shape. The essays were further refined during a symposium on Buddhist Vinaya held in Taiwan in 1995 organized by Yifa and generously sponsored by Foguangshan Buddhist Monastery in Gaoxiong, Taiwan. All the contributors join me in thanking them for their support. After 1995 this volume suffered a long period of incubation, not all of which was due to our lack of dedication. Computer software problems, especially those stemming from incompatible operating systems and different methods of representing diacritic marks and Chinese glyphs presented what for a while seemed like insurmountable obstacles. Fortunately, David E. Riggs and James A. Benn came to UCLA, where they took time out from their studies to provide indispensable assistance with computer software conversions. The Council on East Asian Studies at Yale University provided generous financial support without which this volume could not have been published at an affordable price. The volume benefited from numerous suggestions by two anonymous outside readers for the Kuroda Institute. I am especially grateful for the encouragement and advice provided by Peter N. Gregory of the Kuroda Institute, Patricia Crosby of the University of Hawai'i Press, and Stephanie Chun, who copyedited the manuscript. I also wish to thank Mary Mortensen, who prepared the index to the volume, with funding provided by UCLA's Center for Buddhist Studies.

Introduction

WILLIAM M. BODIFORD

> Though the Buddha's discourses *(sūtra)* and advanced
> doctrines *(abhidharma)* may be forgotten, so long as the
> vinaya still exists the Buddha's teachings yet endure
> *(pamuṭṭhamhi ca suttante abhidamme ca tāvade vinaye
> avinaṭṭhamhi puna tiṭṭhati sāsanaṃ)*. (Vin 1.98–99)

THIS PITHY STATEMENT appended to the Theravāda recension of
the vinaya aptly captures a fundamental attitude widely adopted in
all branches of the Buddhist clergy, one with far reaching consequences. On the surface it asserts that of the three main divisions
(tripiṭaka) of Buddhist scriptures (i.e., the discourses teaching mental cultivation, or *samādhi;* the advanced doctrinal treatises teaching the cultivation of wisdom, or *prajñā;* and the vinaya teaching
the cultivation of morality, or *śīla*), survival of the vinaya constitutes the survival of Buddhism. On a deeper level the statement
affirms that the teachings of the Buddha can be conveyed only
through the living presence of a properly constituted religious order
(saṅgha). For the vinaya alone equates the Buddhist religion with
the inauguration and life of that order. In what may be termed a
founding myth, the vinaya tells the story of how the Awakened One
(buddha) Śākyamuni attained awakening, selected disciples to hear
the truth *(dharma)*, brought these chosen ones to the same insight,
then admitted their "going forth" (Skt. *pravrajyā;* Pali *pabbajjā*) into
a new religious order. He then conferred on them the authority to
admit, train, and confirm additional members and finally charged
them with the mission of propagating this new order throughout

1

the world. In identifying properly ordained members of the order as the sole heirs to the religious authority of the Buddha, the vinaya also dictates strict guidelines governing how the order maintains its legitimacy and perpetuates its existence.

Because of the vinaya's status as the founding charter for the entire Buddhist movement, it has played a far broader and deeper role in doctrinal and social aspects of Buddhist religious life than suggested by the usual English-language translations "discipline," "book of discipline," or "behavioral code." Vinaya texts are concerned with establishing not only rules for the disciplined behavior of members of the order, but also social practices that guide a well-organized religious order in the management of its affairs and property, in its interactions with the laity and secular powers, and—most of all—in defining its religious identity by linking the order historically to the Buddha, distinguishing the order from the laity, encouraging the laity to give to the order, and determining the proper procedures for going forth into the order; only by following such prescribed practices do members of the order become worthy recipients of the laity's charity. Through this fundamental agenda ceremonial issues involving lineage, seniority, initiation, purification, repentance, visualization, vows, and ordination acquire profound social, psychological, and philosophical significance in Buddhism. Nowhere is this more evident than in the historical development of Buddhism in China and Japan, which has been characterized by unresolved tensions over attempts to legitimate Buddhist orders according to some kind of vinaya while simultaneously allowing new organizational forms and institutional structures better adapted to the demands of local culture and history to exist.

To understand why this is so—and to place the following essays within a larger context—a brief review of some of the concepts associated with vinaya and their development in East Asia is in order. Depending on context, the word "vinaya" carries a wide range of connotations. First, it refers specifically to the textual scriptures known by the title "vinaya." In the context of these scriptures, it can narrowly denote specific disciplined actions for controlling one's behavior as well as the broader religious aspirations and motivations that underlie that discipline. The specific actions are codified as precepts (i.e., moral standards) and as religious aspirations expressed as vows, in particular the vows to adhere to the precepts that are affirmed as part of the ceremonies for going forth into the order and for complete confirmation *(upasampadā)* as a member of the order. If the ceremonies are performed properly—by a qualified preceptor and applicant, before the appropriate witness—then the applicant not only becomes a member of the order, but also acquires an inner moral fortitude associated with the religious goals of Buddhism. In China this inner aspect became known as the "essence of the precepts" *(jieti* 戒體; J. *kaitai)*. If any of the required ceremonial procedures specified by the vinaya are performed incorrectly, then the essence of the precepts will be lacking and the applicant's membership rendered invalid. In other words, members of the Buddhist order are distinguished from ordinary laypeople not by their outward appearance (e.g., shaved head, robes), their specific behavior, or the quality of their daily morality, but by whether or not the essence of the precepts was confirmed by the proper rituals (Hirakawa 1970, 521–522). This essence can be likened to an inner purity that, theoretically at least, finds outward expression in proper behavior. Buddhists, therefore, commonly describe vinaya not as rules imposed from the outside, but as the manifestation of an inner spiritual quest.

Vinaya in China

How a Buddhist order emerged in China is not clear. Buddhists of some sort probably were active within Chinese borders as early as the first century of the common era, and Buddhist scriptures began to be translated from Indic languages into literary Chinese by the second century. When Dharmakāla (Tankejialuo 曇柯迦羅, or Tanmojialuo 曇摩迦羅), a Buddhist from India, arrived in the Chinese Wei 魏 capital of Luoyang 洛陽 some time during the years 249–253, however, he found so-called Buddhist monks who had ordained themselves simply by shaving their heads and donning Indian-style robes. Moreover, their fasts, confessions, and religious ceremonies had the appearance of traditional Chinese ancestral rites (FT, fasc. 35, T 49:332a; *Song gaoseng zhuan* 宋高僧傳, fasc. 1, T 50.324c–325a). At the time knowledge of the vinaya and the correct rituals for constituting a Buddhist order did not exist in China (Moroto 1990, 287–293). Chinese translated the Buddhist notion of going forth as "leaving one's family" *(chujia* 出家*)* and understood it as requiring the conferral *(shou* 授*)* and acceptance *(shou* 受*)* of precepts (*jie* 戒)—a process that usually is translated into English as "ordination" (i.e., the conferral of priestly status).[1] Yet without the actual vinaya texts to guide them, Buddhists in China lacked more than just knowledge of specific precepts or ordination ceremonies: They also lacked adequate arguments to justify leaving their families (an idea antithetical to basic Chinese values and not legally permitted until the early fourth century [Ogawa 1968, 287]) and to secure the degree of autonomy necessary for the Buddhist order to possess its own property and manage its own affairs (a matter of endless contestation between Buddhists and the Chinese state).

Even the translation of Indic vinaya texts into Chinese (which began in earnest at the beginning of the fifth century) could not fully answer the religious, social, and legal needs of the Chinese Buddhist order. Several new issues presented themselves. First, in short succession the Chinese obtained translations of complete vinaya texts from several different Buddhist communities in India: the *Ten Recitation Vinaya* (of the Sarvāstivāda, trans. ca. 404–409), the *Four Part Vinaya* (of the Dharmaguptaka, trans. ca. 410–412), the *Mahāsāṃghika Vinaya* (trans. ca. 416–418), and the *Five Part Vinaya* (of the Mahīśāsaka, trans. ca. 422–423; Hirakawa 1970, 115–145).[2] How were discrepancies between these different vinayas to be reconciled? Second, the practices described in these translations assumed a warm climate and social customs very different from those of China. Who had the authority to adapt them to Chinese conditions? Third, by this time Buddhists in China were concerned with distinguishing between the self-proclaimed "superior" Buddhism known as Mahāyāna and other forms that Mahāyāna scriptures denigrated as inferior *(hīnayāna)*. Were the spiritual goals, forms of discipline, and religious ceremonies described in these translated vinaya compatible with Mahāyāna or should they be rejected as *hīnayāna?* Fourth, the translated scriptures contained passages that clearly forbade the possibility of ordaining oneself and stated that anyone attempting to join the order merely by shaving his head and donning new robes without proper ritual confirmation was a false monk who should be expelled and forever denied admission to the order (*Five Part Vinaya,* fasc. 17, T 22.118a; *Four Part Vinaya,* fasc. 34, T 22.811c; *Ten Recitation Vinaya,* fasc. 21, T 23.153a; also see Vin 1.62). If these passages were interpreted literally, then the legitimacy of the ordination lineages claimed by the Chinese order of Buddhist monks could be cast into doubt.[3]

A fifth element, the appearance of Mahāyāna precept scriptures, further confused the situation in China. Unlike the vinaya, which constitutes its own division of the Buddhist canon, these scriptures were seen as belonging to the discourse division of the canon, which represents the words of Śākyamuni Buddha *(buddhavacana)*. Three in particular played major roles in East Asian Buddhism. The *Bodhisattva Stage* was originally part of an Indian doctrinal treatise, but it was translated into Chinese (ca. 420) as an independent discourse of the Buddha with all the scriptural authority such a text would imply. The *Brahmā Net Sūtra* (composed ca. 432–460) and the *Bodhisattva Adornments Sūtra* (*Pusa yingluo jing* 菩薩瓔珞經, T no. 656; composed ca. 480) are Chinese Buddhist apocrypha (i.e., indigenous scriptures; Buswell 1990) that gained acceptance in East Asia as authentic accounts of the Buddha's teaching. All three scriptures describe precepts to be observed by bodhisattvas, the followers of the Mahāyāna path. Moreover, they present an approach to the precepts that differs from that found in the vinaya. The scriptures of the vinaya emphasize in concrete detail how members of the order should discipline their behavior; the Mahāyāna discourses describe precepts that are, in some cases, little more than vague exhortations to perform good. In contrast to the vinaya's concern with distinguishing members of the order from the laity and its different sets of rules for men and women, for novices and full-fledged members, the Mahāyāna scriptures present universal precepts to be observed by all sentient beings, whether they are male or female, monastics or laypeople, humans or nonhumans (as long as they can understand human speech). More important, these scriptures describe self-ordination procedures involving rituals of purification and repentance to obtain a vision of the Buddha (or Buddhas). Such rituals provided Chinese with a scriptural justification for dismissing questions regarding the historical legitimacy of the Chinese Buddhist order. Nobuyoshi Yamabe's essay, "Visionary Repentance and Visionary Ordination in the *Brahmā Net Sūtra*," traces the genealogy of these mystical practices in which people sought direct contact with the Buddha to expiate sins and obtain the precepts. His research demonstrates that dreams, visions, revelations, and magical omens played an important part in Mahāyāna precept ceremonies in India, Central Asia, and China. (Hence the *Brahmā Net Sūtra*'s acceptance in China as an authentic sūtra.) From the fifth century down to the present, visionary ordinations remain a constant source of inspiration in East Asian Buddhism, as we will see in several other essays in this volume (e.g., McRae, Groner). Yamabe concludes his essay with an account of a vision quest in contemporary Japan, where this practice still forms part of the ordination procedures followed by some Buddhist priests.

Repentance, the ritual expiation of sins, is a prerequisite for a successful vision quest. The relationship between repentance and the vision quest reflects the common Buddhist motif that our karmic obstructions (i.e., previous sins) are like dust in our eyes, preventing us from seeing the truth. In his essay, "The *Precious Scroll of the Liang Emperor:* Buddhist and Daoist Repentance to Save the Dead," David W. Chappell describes how from a very early period Buddhist repentance rituals grew in popularity in China among both monastics and laypeople (especially government officials) and were incorporated into Chinese Daoism (Taoism) as well. In vinaya texts repentance is described as a private affair, performed by individuals who have violated one of the lesser precepts. In China, however, repentance rituals became major public ceremonies performed to ease the suffering of deceased people and baleful spirits. This is a remarkable example of the kinds of transformations that can occur when the ritual technologies of one cultural landscape reappear in a place with a different cosmological framework. Chappell argues that the development of the new repentance rituals constitutes an important part of the Chinese adaptation of Buddhism and that these rituals also integrated Buddhism into Chinese society by bringing its monastic elites into the service of mainstream society.

Chinese concerns regarding the interpretation of the vinaya eventually were addressed by a scholastic tradition that came to be called the Vinaya (Lü 律; J. Ritsu) school. Buddhists in India and Southeast Asia never developed separate, competing traditions of vinaya studies, but then they never had to confront the difficult interpretative issues mentioned above. In China the Vinaya school ultimately determined that the disciplined behavior and rituals dictated in the translated vinaya represented neither superior (Mahāyāna) nor inferior *(hīnayāna)* Buddhism: Their orientation depends on the spiritual motivations of those practicing the rituals. Moreover, proper ordination rituals based on vinaya are indispensable for creating a properly constituted order capable of fulfilling its role along with *buddha* and *dharma* as one of the three jewels in which all Buddhists take refuge. Although the Vinaya school drew on the entire corpus of translated Buddhist scriptures, it relied primarily on the *Four Part Vinaya* of the Dharmaguptaka for liturgical matters, such as determining the wording and number of the precepts; the ordination procedures used for tonsure lineages and seniority; and the decorum, monastic rituals, and procedures for managing the affairs of the order. In addition to the precepts of the *Four Part Vinaya*, both monastics and laypeople were urged to undergo ordination with the bodhisattva precepts of the *Brahmā Net Sūtra* to encourage Mahāyāna spiritual goals. The Japanese monk Eisai 榮西 (1141–1215; *Kōzen gokokuron* 興禪護國論, fasc. 2, pp. 39–40) characterized this approach as one in which "outward vinaya [discipline] and decorum prevent transgressions, while inward [bodhisattva] compassion benefits others" (*ge ritsugi bōhi, nai jihi rita* 外律儀防非、內慈悲利他).

Although the Vinaya school is known for its scholastic commentaries, it was much more than an academic enterprise. As John R. McRae demonstrates in his essay, "Daoxuan's Vision of Jetavana: The Ordination Platform Movement in Medieval Chinese Buddhism," the pioneer of the Chinese Vinaya school, Daoxuan 道宣 (596–667), relied as much on his dreams and visions of the Buddha as on his scholastic learning. Or, rather, it might be more correct to say that dreams and visions constituted an indispensable part of his scholastic learning. For Daoxuan the Buddha was neither a figure confined to the ancient past nor a philosophical abstraction. The Buddha was a living presence, one who could confirm and expand on the details found in written sources. Daoxuan sought to ensure the legitimacy of the Chinese Buddhist order by creating in China exact replicas of Śākyamuni Buddha's original monastery, the Jetavana Anāthapiṇḍikārāma (known in Chinese as Qihuansi 祇洹寺, or Qiyuansi 祇園寺), within which special platforms were erected for conducting ordination rituals. If Chinese Buddhist ordinations occurred on platforms similar to those used by the Buddha, then clearly they must be as orthodox and reliable as any that had been conducted by the Buddha himself. Daoxuan's ordination platform movement transformed not only Chinese Buddhism but the spiritual landscape of China by presenting a new model for the use of traditional forms to reinvigorate religious life. This provides a key example of another theme that runs through this volume, namely, how vinaya uses the authority of (apparent) conformity to established tradition to promote innovation and adaptation.

Ordination platforms provided the Chinese government with a

new mechanism for controlling the Buddhist clergy because they allowed the authorities to distinguish between orthodox monks who had ascended the platforms for ordination and false monks (*weilan seng* 偽濫僧) who had not. Moreover, by controlling access to ordination platforms, the government could restrict the Buddhist cleric population. As a result of these policies the Buddhist clergy in China consisted of a set number of authorized clerics who had ascended the ordination platforms to take full monastic vows as members of the order and a larger population of privately ordained priests who had either completed the going-forth rituals to become novices (*śrāmaṇera;* Ch. *shami* 沙彌) or ignored vinaya procedures altogether and ordained themselves simply by shaving their heads and donning Buddhist robes. Full-fledged members of the order were allowed to reside in state-sponsored monasteries, while other clerics found refuge in a variety of other sanctuaries or were itinerant (Gernet 1995, 4–11). Ordination platforms also provided the government with a source of income: Since the eighth century, ordination certificates granting wealthy, privately ordained clerics the status of fully ordained monks or nuns were sold. Aside from its religious significance, the government-issued precept certificate was desirable because it exempted its owner from onerous corvée obligations (Gernet 1995, 48–62).

Ordination platforms demonstrate how Buddhism (like all successful religions) became an economic institution involved in the daily lives of people across a broad spectrum of society—from elite government officials to commoners. As such, it was subject to the same kinds of abuses and scandals one expects to find in any large institution. When centralized authority became weak, for example, local officials were tempted to engage in the private sale of ordination certificates for their own profit. A famous case involved a local governor named Wang Zhixing 王智興 (fl. ca. 825). Wang violated an imperial order in the waning days of the Tang dynasty (618–907) by constructing an ordination platform at a Buddhist monastery in the Linhuai 臨淮 area, where he sold ordinations at greatly reduced prices. T. H. Barrett's essay, "Buddhist Precepts in a Lawless World: Some Comments on the Linhuai Ordination Scandal," examines this event from a Rashomon-like variety of perspectives: cultural, historical, political, economic, doctrinal, Chan 禪 (Zen), literary, and Daoist. That one event could resonate so widely demonstrates that the study of vinaya in China demands a comprehensive examination of the wider cultural landscape. It also serves to remind us that the study of vinaya should concern scholars of not only religion, but all fields dealing with traditional Asia.

After the fall of the Tang dynasty and the warfare and chaos that followed, the Song dynasty (960–1279) witnessed a rebirth of Chinese culture and a reassertion of Chinese cultural identity. New technologies, new arts, and new philosophies ruled the day. Chan hagiographers of the Song (as well as modern Japanese scholars) depicted the Chan lineage as a sectarian and uniquely Chinese school of Buddhism that asserted its religious independence by replacing the vinaya with its own distinctive "pure rules" (*qinggui* 清規) for monastic life. Earlier scholars have cited the Song court's designation of major state monasteries as "Chan cloisters" (*chan-yuan* 禪苑) as evidence that a Chan school had gained sectarian and institutional independence from rival "vinaya monasteries." Essays by Yifa and by Morten Schlütter challenge this received interpretation by carefully examining its textual basis and the historical relationships between the vinaya and Song-period developments.

Yifa's "From the Chinese Vinaya Tradition to Chan Regulations: Continuity and Adaptation" demonstrates that the pure rules did not deviate from earlier Chinese monastic norms; they merely summarized established practices based on vinaya texts as interpreted by the Vinaya school. Although they did not break away from the vinaya, these pure rules responded to new developments in the Chinese cultural milieu at the time of their writing. As such, they provide a valuable resource for examining how vinaya practices evolved in China. Schlütter's "Vinaya Monasteries, Public Abbacies, and State Control of Buddhism under the Song (960–1279)" examines the new Song system of classifying Buddhist monasteries. Schlütter's analysis shows that although the terms "vinaya monasteries" and "Chan monasteries" in Song-period documents did carry certain sectarian implications, they are not the ones emphasized by previous scholars. Rather than representing an institutional identity separate from other schools of Chinese Buddhism, the Chan monastic title designated the elite institutions of Chinese Buddhism wherein resided monks and nuns who had been ordained according to the vinaya and who claimed to be the legitimate heirs to the teachings of the Buddha.

Bodhisattva precepts and rituals for bodhisattva ordinations have remained important features of Chinese Buddhism to the present day. Daniel A. Getz's essay, "Popular Religion and Pure Land in Song-Dynasty Tiantai Bodhisattva Precept Ordination Ceremonies," shows how successive generations of Buddhist monks in the Tiantai 天台 (J. Tendai) lineage worked to develop bodhisattva ordination rituals for laypeople (for whom ordination does not imply the conferral of priestly status but induction into a lay brotherhood). This process required the development of cultic practices of popular appeal that addressed the religious aspirations of ordinary people who could not devote all their energies to the Buddhist path. For these (and most) people the Pure Land of Amitābha Buddha, which anyone of pure faith could achieve in the afterlife, offered a soteriological alternative that seemed more accessible than the difficult goal of religious awakening or enlightenment in this life. Thus bodhisattva ordinations came to be seen as a way of promoting Pure Land faith. These rites also addressed traditional Chinese religious concerns, such as prayers to local gods and spiritual benefits for one's ancestors. Vinaya procedures developed initially for those leaving their families behind helped to affirm family bonds as they addressed the religious hopes of those who remained at home.

Vinaya in Japan

In many ways the status of the vinaya in Japan reflects the same kinds of unresolved tensions found in China—but in reverse. The Chinese Buddhist order, emerging without access to the vinaya, had to develop its own interpretation of the vinaya to gain legitimacy and acceptance by the Chinese government. In Japan, however, Buddhist institutions were incorporated into the very first law codes and the Vinaya school was one of the six fields of learning (*rokushū* 六宗) officially promoted by the early Japanese court. In one of the great heroic journeys of all time, the Chinese monk Jianzhen 鑑眞 (688–763; J. Ganjin) and his disciples endured twelve years of hardship and five shipwrecks to travel to Japan where, to the delight and acclaim of the Japanese rulers, they established an ordination platform in the capital of Nara 奈良. Within the confines of that ancient town the Vinaya school remains a living tradition to this day, but mainstream Japanese Buddhism went on to develop in a different direction. In a startling move, the Japanese monk Saichō 最澄 (767–822; Dengyō 傳教) fought for and succeeded in establish-

ing a separate Tendai school of Buddhism that rejected the vinaya
and conducted ordinations based solely on Mahāyāna discourse
scriptures (Groner 2000). As the Tendai school flourished, Saichō's
successors found themselves having to fashion an organized Buddhist order without reliance on the vinaya and even in direct opposition to it (Groner 1987, 1990a).

It is difficult to exaggerate how much Saichō altered the course
of Buddhism in Japan. By rejecting ordinations based on the vinaya
in favor of rituals derived from Mahāyāna precept discourses alone,
Saichō implicitly dismissed any distinction between the laity and
the clergy insofar as the bodhisattva precepts themselves admitted
no such distinction. Many of the bodhisattva precepts seem applica-
ble to both secular and religious lifestyles. Henceforth the conferral
of religious status and ecclesiastical authority became as much a social process as a sacerdotal one. Just as radical in its effects was the
fact that Saichō's new ordinations split the Japanese Buddhist order
into rival factions. The clergy of Nara viewed Saichō's ordinations
as illegitimate, while members of Saichō's breakaway sect rejected
the ordinations practiced in Nara. Monks from one camp were not
recognized or allowed to enter the temples of the other camp. Temple sectarianism became the norm for subsequent Japanese Buddhism. Saichō established his monastic center on Mount Hiei 比叡,
initiating a move away from urban centers like Nara to a rural-
based Buddhism in the mountains, close to the local gods. Finally
Saichō's new sect and ordinations incorporated practices based
on tantric or esoteric (mikkyō 密教) initiation ceremonies, thereby
helping to generate the mixed exoteric-esoteric (kenmitsu 顕密)
Buddhism that prevailed for much of Japanese history.

As mentioned above, the order of monks and nuns constitutes
one of the three jewels to which all Buddhists turn for refuge. In
rejecting the vinaya, Saichō did not intend to disband the Japanese
Buddhist order—however much his critics accused him of doing so.
Rather, Saichō sought to establish a new Mahāyāna order of monks
and nuns that obtained legitimacy directly from Śākyamuni Buddha without reference to the vinaya, which he rejected as hīnayāna.
This issue was never fully resolved. Throughout Japanese history
Buddhists continued to debate the relationship between the vinaya
and their monastic orders, and new vinaya lineages continued to be
introduced from China. In spite of these efforts, Saichō's exclusive
reliance on Mahāyāna precepts always remained the norm for the

majority of Buddhists in Japan. For this reason, many Japanese texts posit a somewhat artificial distinction between vinaya (ritsu), interpreted as external rules (and thus regarded as hīnayāna), and precepts (kai 戒), which imply inner spiritual qualities.

The ritual format of Saichō's new exclusive Mahāyāna ordinations was based on the Brahmā Net Sūtra and its set of fifty-eight bodhisattva precepts (ten major, forty-eight minor) and visionary ordination procedures in which one receives the precepts directly from Śākyamuni Buddha. (See Yamabe's essay for a contemporary account of an ordination procedure.) The religious doctrines that sought to legitimate the use of this procedure for going forth (i.e., monastic ordinations), however, went far beyond anything in the Brahmā Net Sūtra. It is misleading, therefore, to describe the Japanese precept traditions that began with Saichō merely in terms of the Brahmā Net Sūtra without giving full consideration to the other doctrines. Although the details of these doctrines continually evolved at the hands of Saichō's successors without ever achieving a consensus, their mature features can be summarized (Fukuda 1954, 568–649). First, the Mahāyāna precepts advocated by Saichō are Perfect Sudden Precepts (endon kai 圓頓戒); they are attained immediately, in a single instant. The Vinaya school, in contrast, practices a series of step-by-step ordinations (kenju 兼受) in which one first goes forth to receive the precepts of a novice (10 precepts), followed by a separate confirmation ceremony to receive the precepts of a full-fledged monk (250) or nun (348), and finally yet another ceremony to receive the Mahāyāna bodhisattva precepts (58). At each step, the ceremonies differ, the sets of precepts differ, the wording of the individual precepts differs, and the essence of the precepts differs. Sudden precepts are received in a single act (tanju 單受) because each precept embodies all others. They are "perfect" (literally, "round") because they are without deficiency. As the superior (mahāyāna) practice they embrace the entire Buddhist path, taking into consideration all three categories (morality, mental cultivation, and wisdom) of Buddhist learning (sangaku ittai 三學一体). In other words, Perfect Sudden Precepts are not preparatory to anything else because they embody the goal of the Buddhist path. Second, even though the format of these precepts is based on the Brahmā Net Sūtra, their spiritual power derives primarily from the Lotus Sūtra (shōe hokke, bōe bonmō 正依法華、傍依梵網). The central scripture for the Tendai tradition, the Lotus Sūtra reveals the eternal Śākyamuni who proclaims the one vehicle (*ichijō* 一乘; *ekayāna)*, which, in transcending all distinctions between bodhisatt-vas and followers of inferior *(hīnayāna)* forms of Buddhism, saves all beings. Thus the Lotus One-Vehicle Precepts (*hokke ichijō kai* 法華一乘戒) transcend all distinctions between Mahāyāna and Hīnayāna to save everyone. Third, their essence is the true reality of buddhahood (*shinnyo busshō* 眞如佛性) itself. It is eternal and can never be lost, lifetime after lifetime, even if one fails to keep the precepts, which also are known as the Unconditioned Vajra Jewel Precepts (*musa kongō hō kai* 無作金剛寶戒). The precepts of the vinaya, in contrast, last only as long as one's present physical body and only so long as one does not violate them.

My contribution to this volume, "Bodhidharma's Precepts in Ja-pan," examines the nexus between Saichō's Perfect Sudden Precepts and the Zen tradition. Saichō's disciple Kōjō 光定 (779–858) identi-fied Saichō's precepts as the One Mind Precepts (*isshin kai* 一心戒) and described them in tantric terms. More important, he stated that they had been brought from India to China by Bodhidharma (the legendary Zen ancestor), who transmitted them to the founders of the Tendai lineage. Although Kōjō's explanations exerted little influ-ence among subsequent Tendai scholars, they were readily accepted within medieval Japanese Zen circles, where the One Mind Precepts became synonymous with the mind-to-mind (*isshin denshin* 以心傳心) transmission of Zen. Thus many Japanese Zen lineages relied on Chinese monastic pure rules for their standards of proper behav-ior and performed precept ordinations not for their moral content but as a tantric initiation rite that conferred a direct link to the awakened mind of the Buddha. This adherence to a Japanese approach to the precepts contrasts sharply with the role of Zen lin-eages in popularizing many aspects of Song culture in medieval Japan.

The medieval period (ca. eleventh to sixteenth centuries) wit-nessed many major transformations in Japanese society. New agri-cultural technologies, population growth, and foreign trade pro-vided additional sources of wealth, for which both established and new social groups competed. The royal court found its authority challenged by warrior governments and outlaws. The established Buddhist orders of Nara, Mount Hiei, and Kyoto 京都 expanded even as many fledgling Buddhist organizations, such as the Zen lin-eages mentioned above, appeared on the scene. Lawlessness and frequent military campaigns, with their wanton killing and destruction (including the burning of the major Buddhist monasteries of Nara in 1180), sparked renewed interest in morality and the proper role of vinaya in Japanese Buddhism. Some monks promoted strict adherence to the norms of the traditional Vinaya school by either introducing new vinaya lineages from China or revitalizing the standards for ordination in Nara. Others went to the opposite extreme and openly abandoned all pretense of observing any Buddhist precepts.

An example of the latter type is Shinran 親鸞 (1173–1263), the well-known Pure Land teacher who came to be regarded as the founder of the Jōdo Shinshū (Pure Land True Doctrine) denomination. Shinran taught that the Buddha Amitābha alone possessed the spiritual power to save humans from the heavy karmic burden of their sins. Only those who abandoned their own power (self power; *jiriki* 自力) for Amitābha's (other power; *tariki* 他力) could be saved. From this perspective, observing the Buddhist precepts is an exercise in self-power and thus should be avoided. But Shinran's rejection of the precepts did not mean that he discarded basic morality. He taught that people who rely on Amitābha's power are endowed with a spiritual joy and faith, which causes them to lament any intentional or willful wrongdoing (Dobbins 1989, 49–56). Although some scholars have interpreted Shinran's disavowal of all precepts as a logical and inevitable result of Saichō's rejection of the vinaya, his interpretations were by no means universally accepted by Japanese Buddhists.

One monk who called for strict adherence to the norms of the traditional Vinaya school is Eison 叡尊 (1201–1290; Eizon), the subject of Paul Groner's essay, "Tradition and Innovation: Eison's Self-Ordinations and the Establishment of New Orders of Buddhist Practitioners." Eison was the son of a Nara monk, which indicates a lapse in the standards of the Nara Buddhist order in spite of its supposed adherence to the interpretations of the Vinaya school and its ordinations based on the *Four Part Vinaya*. (Refraining from sexual activity is its first precept.) If the monks of Nara had lost the essence of the precepts—and it is clear that they had—then the ordinations they performed would be invalid. Eison sought to create a new ordination lineage based on the *Four Part Vinaya*. But to accomplish this he had to rely on the visionary ordination procedures described in Mahāyāna precept discourses. In other words, to revive the vinaya he employed ritual techniques that the vinaya itself would never have admitted. However, the Vinaya school's interpretation of the *Four Part Vinaya* as being compatible with Mahāyāna teachings provided a way for Eison to justify his methods. Eison's new order of monks (and nuns) demonstrates how the vinaya in Japan, as elsewhere, became a living and mutable document in the hands of its interpreters.

James C. Dobbins examines a third approach to the vinaya, one that stands between the two extremes represented by Shinran and Eison, in his essay, "Precepts in Japanese Pure Land Buddhism: The Jōdoshū." The leaders of the Jōdoshū inherited the same Pure Land traditions as Shinran and advocated the same doctrine of sole reliance on the power of Amitābha Buddha. They therefore felt no inclination to follow the *Four Part Vinaya*. But unlike Shinran they did not reject all precepts outright. Together with Japanese Zen teachers they regarded themselves as the rightful heirs to Saichō's doctrines concerning the Mahāyāna precepts, which they struggled to reinterpret in a way that was compatible with their Pure Land faith. However, the Jōdoshū clerics differed from some of their Zen counterparts in that they never treated precept ceremonies solely as initiatory rites. The precepts are understood and practiced as moral teachings—but as Dobbins points out, their ethical implication is seen more as an unattainable ideal than a practical requirement. Thus Dobbins argues that the Jōdoshū's approach to the precepts was (and is) an ongoing exercise in ambivalence.

The passage of time amplified this ambivalence and spread it to clerics of all denominations as illustrated by the changing attitudes toward vegetarian diets, which Richard M. Jaffe examines in his essay, "The Debate over Meat Eating in Japanese Buddhism." Establishment of the Tokugawa shogunal government in 1603 ushered in a new age of stability and peace during which Buddhist temples were established in every village and neighborhood to help suppress dissent. Buddhist temples promoted education, causing new editions of Buddhist books to be imported from China and printed in Japan. Social changes prompted Buddhists of all backgrounds to reexamine their practices and justify them in light of their own sectarian traditions. In this new atmosphere of sectarian debate, initially clerics in the Jōdo Shinshū tradition of Shinran found themselves on the defensive as rival Buddhists denounced their eating of meat—a practice condoned in many passages in vinaya literature but forbidden in certain Mahāyāna sūtras. In response to these denunciations, Shinshū leaders developed their own Buddhist justifications for meat consumption. Jaffe explains that while opponents of the practice continued to couch their arguments in terms of Buddhist scripture and doctrine, over time the pro-meat advocates began expressing their Buddhism in the rhetoric of social progress. This trend accelerated after the Meiji regime overthrew the Tokugawa in 1868 and adopted anti-Buddhist, pro-Western policies. The introduction of social Darwinism along with Western notions of medicine, hygiene, and nutrition transformed meat eating into a symbol of national strength. Buddhist clerics of all denominations came to see a meat diet as one of the requisites of a modern industrialized civilization.

Tensions between local social imperatives and the ideals of vinaya pulse through the history of Buddhism. Vinaya provides the founding charter for the order, the rationale for the order, and the procedures for perpetuating the order. As such it has been essential for the survival of Buddhism from ancient times down to the present day. The means by which Buddhism survives, however, frequently tells us as much about its fallible followers as its ideals.

Notes

1. In practice, this process overlaps with aspects of ceremonies that in other religions are not necessarily associated with ordination, such as baptism (as a ritual purification and a rite for joining a religious community), christening (as a ritual for assigning a religious name), consecration (as a ritual anointment that confirms a religious status), or initiation (as a ritual admission to the secret traditions or knowledge of a religious order).

2. In addition to these four complete vinayas, Chinese translated many other minor vinaya texts. Almost three hundred years later, during the years 700–713, the Chinese monk Yijing 義浄 (635–713) introduced much of the *Mūlasarvāstivāda Vinaya*, which he translated as a series of eighteen separate texts (T nos. 1442–1459; Hirakawa 1970, 147–145) and passages of which (according to Gregory Schopen) he incorporated into his travel diary (*Nanhai jigui neifa zhuan* 南海寄歸內法傳, T no. 2125) as his own firsthand observations.

3. The Chinese order of Buddhist nuns eliminated any doubts as to its legitimacy in 437 when a group of twelve nuns from Sri Lanka who had traveled to China performed ordination rituals for more than three hundred Chinese women (*Biqiuni zhuan* 比丘尼傳, fasc. 2, T 50.939c; Tsai 1994, 54).

Chapter 1

Visionary Repentance and Visionary Ordination in the Brahmā Net Sūtra

NOBUYOSHI YAMABE

THE *BRAHMĀ NET SŪTRA*, an apocryphal scripture compiled in the mid-fifth century, has long occupied a cardinal position in the practice of bodhisattva precepts in East Asia. In China and Korea eminent monks such as Huisi 慧思 (514?–577), Zhiyi 智顗 (538–597), Wǒnhyo 元曉 (617–686), Fazang 法藏 (643–711), Zhizhou 智周 (668–723), and T'aehyŏn 太賢 wrote or were credited with commentaries on this sūtra (Shirato 1969, 119–122). The *Brahmā Net Sūtra* also defined the tenor of Japanese Buddhism following Saichō's rejection of the traditional precepts of the *Four Part Vinaya* and his advocacy of the full ordination exclusively based on the Mahāyāna precepts (Groner 1990a, 251–280; 2000, 107–246). Considering the highly didactic nature of most of the injunctions in the *Brahmā Net Sūtra*, it is understandable that modern scholars have discussed the sūtra mainly in terms of morality, but this scripture is important within other contexts as well. The present essay analyzes the visionary elements in the *Brahmā Net Sūtra* and other closely related texts on bodhisattva ordination to shed light on the mystical aspect of the practice of bodhisattva precepts.

Materials in Sanskrit and Chinese testify to a variety of visionary aspects of both the bodhisattva precepts themselves and associated rituals of repentance and ordination. Based on information found in these sources, I believe that the practice of Mahāyāna precepts spoke not only to the practitioner's moral conduct, but also to his participation in mystical, visionary experiences. People seem to have believed that Mahāyāna precepts should ultimately be conferred by the Buddha or bodhisattvas in a vision. Of particular importance in this regard are the apocryphal or suspicious visualization texts dating from the fifth century that emphasize the expiation of sins and, as we shall see, provide the foundation for the visionary elements found in the *Brahmā Net Sūtra*.

Visionary experiences played a crucial role more than once in the history of vinaya in East Asia. Notable examples, both discussed in this volume, include Daoxuan's 道宣 (596–667) vision of the ordination platform and Eison's 叡尊 (1201–1290) vision that justified his self-ordination. Visions thus provided crucial legitimization when an attempt was made to establish a new vinaya tradition. The *Brahmā Net Sūtra*, directly or indirectly, exerted significant influence on this practice.

In the following sections I examine passages from several early texts to better understand the visionary elements found in the *Brahmā Net Sūtra*. I begin with a brief description of two instances in which the *Brahmā Net Sūtra* calls for visionary experiences on the part of the practitioner. This is followed by examples of visionary repentance from Indian, Central Asian, and Chinese sources that are similar to those described in the *Brahmā Net Sūtra*. After establishing a close connection between visionary experiences and bodhisattva precepts in these various sources, I conclude with what I believe to be the legacy of this connection in contemporary Japanese Buddhist practice.

Two Passages from the *Brahmā Net Sūtra*

The *Brahmā Net Sūtra* requires visionary experiences on two occasions:

> If a child of the Buddha wishes with good intention to receive the bodhisattva precepts, he can ordain himself in front of the statues of the Buddha and bodhisattvas. He should repent for seven days and, after seeing auspicious signs (*haoxiang* 好相; J. *kōsō*), he will acquire the precepts. If he cannot see auspicious signs, he should definitely see them [even if it takes] fourteen days, twenty-one days, or even one year. Only after seeing the auspicious signs can he receive the precepts in front of the statues of the Buddha and bodhisattvas. If he cannot see the auspicious signs, even if he receives the precepts in front of the statues, he cannot acquire the precepts.... If he cannot find a master who can transmit the precepts, he can receive the precepts in front of the statues of the Buddha and bodhisattvas; but in that case, he must definitely see the auspicious signs. (Fasc. 2, T 24.1006c5–18; cf. de Groot 1893, 56; Groner 1990b, 231)

The two masters [who administer the precepts] must ask [the recipient]: "Have you committed any of the seven obstructions?"[1] They should not allow anyone who has committed the seven obstructions to receive the precepts. If one has not committed them, then they can give him the precepts. If one has broken the ten major precepts, [the masters] should teach him to repent. He should chant the ten major and forty-eight minor precepts in front of the statues of the Buddha and bodhisattvas throughout the six periods of day and night. When he has worshipped the thousand Buddhas of the past, present, and future, he can see auspicious signs. [Even] if [it takes] seven days, fourteen days, twenty-one days, or one year, he must see auspicious signs. Auspicious signs mean that [he sees] the Buddhas come and rub his head, that [he] sees light, flowers, and various extraordinary signs. [Only after seeing such signs] can his transgressions perish. If he does not see auspicious signs, his repentance is fruitless and he cannot receive the precepts in this life. (Fasc. 2, T 24.1008c9–19; de Groot 1893, 75–76)

Visionary experiences are necessary when one is without a master and must ordain oneself and when one has committed serious offenses that require repentance beforehand. As this essay will show, self-ordination and repentance are so closely connected in practice that they can almost be treated as a single set of practices.

Dharmakṣema, Daojin, and Turfan

The circumstances outlined in the two above passages from the *Brahmā Net Sūtra* resemble those described in this excerpt from the *Lives of Eminent Monks* (*Gaoseng zhuan* 高僧傳), compiled by Huijiao 慧皎 (497–554) in about 530:

When Dharmakṣema (Tan Wuchan 曇無讖) was first in Guzang 姑藏, a monk named Daojin 道進 from Zhangye 張掖 wished to receive bodhisattva precepts from him. Dharmakṣema said: "First repent your transgressions." Thereupon [Daojin repented] most earnestly for seven days and nights. On the eighth day, he went to see Dharmakṣema and asked him to give him precepts, but Dharmakṣema suddenly became furious. Daojin further thought: "This must be only because my karmic obstructions have not disappeared yet." He further exerted himself in meditation and in repentance for three years. Then in meditation he saw Śākyamuni Buddha and the great beings (*mahāsattva*) giving him precepts. That same evening, more than ten people who were staying with him dreamt the same scene as was seen by Daojin. Daojin wished

to see Dharmakṣema to report this, but when he was still tens of steps
away, Dharmakṣema stood up in surprise and said: "Excellent! Excellent! You have already acquired the precepts. Now I shall authenticate
it (*zuozheng* 作證) for you." He then explained the aspects of the precepts in front of a statue of the Buddha.

In those days, the monk Daolang 道朗 was renowned in Hexi 河西.
On the same night when Daojin miraculously received precepts, Daolang shared [the same] dream. Thereupon he lowered his seniority
and asked to become Daojin's younger brother in dharma. Thereafter
more than a thousand people received precepts from Daojin. The transmission of this lineage (*fa* 法) continues to this day. Everything derives
from Dharmakṣema's method. (Fasc. 2, T 50.336c19–37a2; cf. Shih
1968, 104)

Dharmakṣema taught Daojin (Fajin 法進, or Faying 法迎) that he
must repent to remove his karmic obstructions before he can be
properly ordained as a bodhisattva. The visionary encounter with
the Buddha and bodhisattvas ("great beings") indicated that his
transgressions had been purified and the ordination accomplished.
Later, the ordination was corroborated by a master (Dharmakṣema)
—in other words, authentication by a human occurs only after the
visionary experience.

As noted by Arthur Wright (1990, 105–106), the account of
Dharmakṣema in the *Lives of Eminent Monks* is largely based on
the *Tripiṭaka Translation Notes* (*Chu sanzang jiji* 出三藏記集), an
annotated catalogue of translated scriptures compiled by Sengyou
僧祐 (445–518) between the years 510 and 518.[2] This particular episode, however, is missing from the *Tripiṭaka Translation Notes*. Its
source was probably the *Lives of Renowned Monks* (*Mingseng zhuan*
名僧傳), compiled by Baochang 寶唱 in southern China and completed in 519 (Wright 1990, 95). According to the *Lives of Eminent
Monks* (fasc. 12, T 50.404a29–b21), Daojin's bodhisattva ordination
took place in Guzang, located in Northern Liang 北涼. By what
route was this account of an event in the north transmitted to Baochang in the south?

Dharmakṣema was active in Northern Liang during the reign of
Juqu Mengxun 沮渠蒙遜 (r. 401–433), so Daojin must have received
bodhisattva precepts from him at about this time. In 439 when the
Northern Wei 北魏 overthrew the Northern Liang, members of the
Juqu clan fled to Turfan and established a short-lived local king-
dom, the so-called Turfan State of the Juqu Clan (Juquzhi Gao-

changguo 沮渠氏高昌國, 442–460). Daojin followed and moved to Turfan. Later, when the region suffered a terrible famine, Daojin asked the ruler Juqu Anzhou 沮渠安周 on several occasions to distribute food to the starving poor people. When the state-supplied stocks of food were almost exhausted, Daojin, instead of asking yet again, cut off pieces of his own flesh, mixed them with salt, and fed them to the people.[3] Moved by his self-sacrifice, Anzhou opened additional granaries and distributed more food. Daojin thus died, leaving behind a disciple, Sengzun 僧遵, who was versed in the *Ten Recitation Vinaya* (*Shisong lü* 十誦律) and who always practiced repentance (also see Funayama 1995, 13–21).

Anzhou's support of Buddhism in and around Turfan is attested in a votive stele from Xoco (Gaochang 高昌) that records his dedication of a shrine to Maitreya and copies of scriptures from Toyok donated by him (Soper 1958, 143; Ōmura 1972a, 177–178). Further, judging from the existence at Toyok of a manuscript of the *Laymen's Precepts Sūtra* (*Youposajie jing* 優婆塞戒經, **Upāsakaśīla Sūtra*) translated by Dharmakṣema, it is likely that the tradition of Dharmakṣema's bodhisattva precepts was indeed transferred to this area. If this is the case, the story of Daojin's repentance was probably transmitted to the people of Turfan who belonged to his lineage, and when this lineage was transmitted to south China, the story followed suit. The link of this story to Turfan (or nearby areas) is important for the sake of our discussion, so let us examine this point more closely.

In this regard, a notable source is the *Pusajie yishu* 菩薩戒義疏, a commentary attributed to Zhiyi on the *Brahmā Net Sūtra* that mentions a bodhisattva ordination manual from Turfan, the so-called *Gaochang ben* 高昌本. Concerning the origin of the Turfan manual, the commentary gives this explanation:

> The Turfan manual is also entitled the manual of Master Xuanchang 玄暢. The original teaching came from the *Bodhisattva Stage* (*Pusa dichi jing* 菩薩地持經) and the method is slightly supplemented. . . . Originally the *Bodhisattva Stage* was translated by Dharmakṣema in Hexi. There was a monk, Daojin, who asked Dharmakṣema to bestow the bodhisattva precepts. Dharmakṣema did not allow this and first made him repent. After [repenting for] seven days and nights, Daojin saw Dharmakṣema and requested him to bestow the precepts. Dharmakṣema became furious and did not answer. Daojin reflected: "This must be only because my obstructive karmas have not disappeared." He

then repented most earnestly for three years. Daojin saw in a dream
Śākyamuni Buddha confer the precepts upon him, and the next day he
went to see Dharmakṣema to report what he had dreamt. When Daojin
was still tens of steps away, Dharmakṣema stood up in surprise and
said: "Excellent! Excellent! You have already obtained the precepts.
Now I shall authenticate it for you." Then he further explained the
aspects of the precepts in front of a statue of the Buddha.

In those days, there was a master, Daolang, who was respected in
the Hexi area. When Daojin miraculously obtained precepts, Daolang
shared the same dream. Thereupon he lowered his seniority and asked
to become Daojin's younger brother in dharma. After this event, there
were more than a thousand people who received precepts from Daojin.

Juqu Jinghuan 沮渠景環, a son of the king of Hexi, Juqu Mengxun, later moved to Turfan.[4] Since Jinghuan had already made Daojin
his master, Daojin also moved there and encountered a famine at Turfan. Daojin saved starving people by cutting his own body while alive,
and thus he died. Daojin's disciple from Turfan, Sengzun, whose sur-
name was Zhao 趙, transmitted the master's method of precepts (*jiefa*
戒法). There was another monk, Tanjing 曇景, who transmitted this
method. Since the teaching came from that region, it is called the Turfan manual.

Toward the end of the Yuanjia 元嘉 era (424–453), there was a
master, Xuanchang, who crossed the border from the state of Wei and
stayed at the gate of Jingzhou 荆州 and Shu 蜀. The method of conferring the precepts was largely the same [as that of the Turfan manual],
but there were slight differences. Therefore there is a separate manual
of Master Xuanchang. This method came from Dharmakṣema and
slightly supplemented the *Bodhisattva Stage*. Apparently the vows of
Dharmakṣema have moved people's hearts, so there are such dupli-
cates. (Fasc. 1, T 40.568b14–c23)

This story is almost identical to the one quoted earlier from the
Lives of Eminent Monks. It is important to note that this story is
clearly associated with the tradition of the Turfan ordination manual and that Xuanchang's manual is stated as being essentially the
same as the Turfan manual. Unfortunately neither of these manuals
is extant, but the author of this commentary seems to have had
direct access to them—or at least to Xuanchang's. For the *Lives of
Eminent Monks* also, a tradition brought to the south in the mid-
fifth century by a person from the north could have been a source
of information. According to the *Lives of Eminent Monks* (fasc. 8,
T 50.377a3–c7), Xuanchang was from Jincheng 金城 (in Hexi),

was ordained in Liangzhou 涼州, and later became a disciple of the renowned meditator Xuangao 玄高. It does not connect Xuanchang to Dharmakṣema's lineage. Nevertheless, according to the commentary above, concerning the bodhisattva ordination, Xuanchang seems to have been linked to the Turfan tradition, and considering his ties to Hexi, this is not unlikely.

One problem with this scenario is that the authenticity of the *Pusajie yishu* commentary has been questioned. According to Satō Tetsuei (1961, 412–415), there are substantial differences between the theoretical discussions found in this text and those in the unquestioned works of Zhiyi. Moreover, the earliest point at which we can confirm the existence of the *Pusajie yishu* is the beginning of the eighth century (see also Groner 2000, 225–227). If the work was composed at this late date, it would be difficult to give much weight to the information it contains. We cannot go into the problem of the authenticity of the entire work here. But concerning the section quoted above, we have reason to believe that it is reliable and represents an even older tradition than the *Lives of Eminent Monks.*

First, let us note that in the *Pusajie yishu* Daojin sees the Buddha in a dream and not while meditating. On this point, there is reason to suspect that this version may be closer to the original tradition, because a medieval Japanese monk Shūshō 宗性 (1202–?) describes the contents of the biography of Fajin (Daojin) in the now-lost *Lives of Renowned Monks* as follows: "In this story Fajin, while sleeping, saw Śākyamuni Buddha and bodhisattvas confer precepts upon him in a forest of sandalwood trees" (*Meisōden shō* 名僧傳抄, Z 2B.7.16d7–8). It is difficult to say whether Huijiao altered the contents of the *Lives of Renowned Monks* himself or based his version of the story on another source. In any case, the *Pusajie yishu* is not quoting from the *Lives of Eminent Monks.* Rather the story from the *Pusajie yishu* retains an older form of the tradition than that found in the *Lives of Eminent Monks.*

Further, it has been pointed out that the basic information contained in the *Pusajie yishu* is confirmed by another bodhisattva ordination manual found in Dunhuang, the *Bodhisattva Ordination Manual for Monastics* (*Chujiaren shou pusajie fa* 出家人授菩薩戒法, Pelliot no. 2196; see Suwa 1971; 1972a, 90–91; 1972b, 348–350; and Funayama 1995, 29–30). The manuscript of this manual is dated 519 (i.e., before the *Lives of Eminent Monks*) and is said

to have been compiled by Emperor Wu 武 of the Liang 梁 dynasty
between 512 and 519, making it one of the oldest and most reliable
records on the early history of bodhisattva ordination in China. According to the manuscript:

> The bodhisattva ordination manuals (*pusajie fa* 菩薩戒法) prevalent
> in the world seem to be based on the two sūtras [i.e., the *Brahmā
> Net Sūtra* and the *Bodhisattva Stage*] and are often supplemented
> by Hīnayāna methods. There are many who composed bodhisattva
> ordination manuals. [There is] a bodhisattva ordination manual com-
> posed by Kumārajīva. [There is another] bodhisattva ordination man-
> ual orally transmitted by Tanjing from Turfan. Kumārajīva used the
> *Brahmā Net Sūtra*. The Turfan Master [Tanjing] made use of the text
> compiled by Maitreya [i.e., the *Bodhisattva Stage*] and also the *Brahmā
> Net Sūtra*. [There was also] a bodhisattva ordination manual composed
> by Xuanchang of the Changsa Temple 長沙寺. (Tsuchihashi 1980b, 847;
> see also Groner 1990b, 236, 239)

This information neatly agrees with that given in the *Pusajie yishu;*
thus Suwa Gijun (1971, 61) infers that the *Pusajie yishu* was partly
based on the *Chujiaren shou pusajie fa* or its sources. It is certain
that the basic information in the *Pusajie yishu* dates back at least
to the early sixth century. Taken together with the aforementioned
testimony of Shūshō, it is clear that, regardless of the authenticity
of the *Pusajie yishu* as a whole, the information contained in the
section quoted here is reliable and represents very old traditions. I
therefore consider the following points to be valid for the sake of
the discussion that follows: (1) a tradition of the bodhisattva ordination primarily based on Dharmakṣema's translation of the *Bodhisattva Stage* was transmitted from the Liangzhou area to Turfan,
and later to south China; (2) the story of Daojin's rigorous repentance was remembered among the people belonging to the Turfan
lineage in association with the foundation of their lineage; and (3)
this story came to Baochang and Huijiao's attention through the
Turfan tradition transmitted to south China.

Self-Ordination and Repentance in the *Bodhisattva Stage*

It is difficult to determine the veracity of the story of Daojin's repentance. The people of the Turfan lineage may have invented it to sol-
emnize the origin of their lineage. Moreover the *Lives of Renowned*

Monks and the *Lives of Eminent Monks* record a fair number of somewhat similar visionary experiences (not all of which seem historical): Daojin's repentance may have been just one such story. In any case, the historicity of the event is not at issue here. What should be noted is that the bodhisattva ordination based on the *Bodhisattva Stage* was associated with a visionary experience and that Daojin's story seems to have had strong ties to the Liangzhou and Turfan areas. This association, however, raises an additional issue. Dharmakṣema's translation of the *Bodhisattva Stage* contains few mystical elements. The sections on repentance and self-ordination in Dharmakṣema's translation are as follows:

[Repentance:] If there is a transgression, one should repent properly. All these transgressions of bodhisattvas should be known as *duṣkṛta* [minor offences]. One should repent properly to a person of either Mahāyāna or Hīnayāna (*Da Xiao cheng ren* 大小乘人) who understands words and can receive the repentance.

If a bodhisattva commits a *pārājika* [major offence] out of vehement passion, he loses the precepts. He must receive them again. If he commits a *pārājika* offence out of moderate passion, he must squat with his palms together in front of three or more people and do the repentance for a *duṣkṛta* offence. He chants the name of the offence he has previously committed and recites the following: "Venerable, please remember me. I, So-and-so by name, have abandoned the bodhisattva vinaya (*pusa pini* 菩薩毘尼). As I have stated, I have committed the *duṣkṛta* offence." The rest is as prescribed in the method of repentance of *duṣkṛta* offenses for monks. If he commits a *pārājika* and other offenses out of minor passion, he should repent in front of one person.

If there is no person upholding the Dharma [to confess to], he should give rise to a pure thought and should recite [in mind]: "I will never commit this transgression again. In future, I will always uphold the moral precepts (*lüyi jie* 律儀戒)." If one acts in this way, one's transgression is expiated.

[Self-Ordination:] If there is no meritorious person from whom to receive the bodhisattva precepts, the bodhisattva should receive the precepts in front of a statue of the Buddha in the following way. He clothes himself neatly, bares his right shoulder, puts his right knee on the ground, bows down with palms together, and recites the following: "I, So-and-so by name, declare to all the Buddhas and bodhisattvas who have attained the great stages in the worlds in the ten directions. I now in front of the Buddhas and bodhisattvas receive all the precepts of bodhisattvas; the moral precepts, the precept for embracing all good

deeds (*she shanfa jie* 攝善法戒), and the precept for saving sentient
beings (*she zhongsheng jie* 攝衆生戒). These precepts were learned by
all past bodhisattvas, will be learned by all future bodhisattvas, and
are being learned by all present bodhisattvas." One repeats the same
phrases for a second and the third time. Having stated so, one should
rise up. The rest is as before. (Fasc. 5, T 30.917a8–28; cf. Tatz 1986,
83–84)

Thus, both repentance and self-ordination are described as purely
human procedures. Unlike the corresponding portions of the
Brahmā Net Sūtra, this text does not require a visionary experience
at all. This is also the case in Xuanzang's 玄奘 (ca. 596–664) translation and the extant Sanskrit text of the *Bodhisattva Stage*. Elsewhere
in the section on the regular ordination from a human master, the
Bodhisattva Stage says that after the ceremony, a vision (*xiang* 相;
nimitta) of the event appears to the Tathāgatas and bodhisattvas
in the ten directions (fasc. 5, T 30.912c16–13a4; Wogihara 1971,
155.1–6). This, however, is entirely different from a vision seen by a
practitioner. Why then did Dharmakṣema or his successors believe
that visionary repentance was necessary as a prerequisite for the
bodhisattva ordination? The *Bodhisattva Ordination Manual for Monastics* indicates that the Turfan tradition was already under the
influence of the *Brahmā Net Sūtra*, so one might argue that the people who invented Daojin's story (if it is a fiction) were inspired
by the stipulations of the *Brahmā Net Sūtra*. This answer, however,
is in a way only a deferment of the solution. According to Mochizuki Shinkō (1946, 457–471) and Ōno Hōdō (1954, 262–284), the
Brahmā Net Sūtra itself was based on Dharmakṣema's translation
of the *Bodhisattva Stage*. Why then did the *Brahmā Net Sūtra* require
visionary experiences for repentance and self-ordination when they
were not required by one of the sūtra's main sources? Were these
visionary elements merely inventions by Chinese people?

Vision and Bodhisattva Precepts in Indian Mahāyāna Scriptures

When we view the aforementioned versions of the *Bodhisattva
Stage* in isolation, we get the impression that bodhisattva precepts
in India were purely a matter of morality with few mystical elements. But of course the *Bodhisattva Stage* is not the only Indian

text that addresses bodhisattva precepts (see Ōno 1954; Shizutani 1974, 118–147). If we take other texts into account, we are left with a very different picture. Also if dreams are included in the category of visionary experience, then it is possible to say that bodhisattva precepts contained visionary elements at a very early stage of Indian Mahāyāna Buddhism. According to a Perfection of Wisdom scripture entitled *Daoxing bore jing* 道行般若經 (the oldest Chinese version of the *Aṣṭasāhasrikā Prajñā-pāramitā*):

> [A bodhisattva who is free from retrogression] himself keeps the ten precepts even in dreams and sees in dreams the ten precepts face to face. (Fasc. 6, T 8.454c2–3)

What is meant by the phrase "sees in dreams the ten precepts face to face" is not entirely clear. Since the Sanskrit text (325.11–12) indicates that the Chinese expression "ten precepts" corresponds to *daśakuśalāḥ karmapathā[ḥ]*, "ten wholesome courses of actions." what the text originally meant may have been simply that a bodhisattva follows good conduct even in dreams.

In the case of the following passage from the *Golden Light Sūtra*, it clearly states that a bodhisattva hears verses for repentance in a dream:

> Then Ruciraketu (Shining Banner) Bodhisattva slept. In his dream, he saw a golden drum made of gold.... There he saw a man in the form of a Brahmin beating the drum and heard the following verses of confession coming out of the sound of the drum. (*Suvarṇabhāsottama Sūtra*, 20.2–9)

This passage however, relates the personal experience of Ruciraketu; the text is not encouraging practitioners in general to have the same experience in their dreams. For our present purposes, this excerpt from the *Ākāśagarbha Sūtra* is more significant:

> If the bodhisattvas hear the name of Ākāśagarbha Bodhisattva and seek his vision, wishing to confess the fundamental transgressions out of the fear of falling into bad destinies; if they pay homage to Ākāśagarbha Bodhisattva and praise his name, the son of a good family [Ākāśagarbha] stands in front of them in his own form, [or] he will stand in [various kinds of] forms, from that of a Brahmin up to that of a girl, according to their fortune. He [Ākāśagarbha] points out the transgressions of that beginner bodhisattva that he has made. He further shows

profound skillful means and the practice in Mahāyāna and eventually establishes him in the stage of nonretrogression. . . .

If [Ākāśagarbha] does not grant direct vision to them, the beginner bodhisattva with offenses seeking for the [vision] should rise up from the seat in the last watch of the night, stand to the east, and offer incense. He should pray to the Sun, son of a god, and say as follows: "Sun, Sun, the merciful one, the fortunate one, the lofty one, protect me in the Jambudvīpa with your mercy. Quickly wake up Ākāśagarbha, the merciful one, with my words. Show me in a dream the means by which I [may] confess my transgression and [by which] shall attain the wisdom of means in the noble Mahāyāna. Then he should sleep in a bed. When the Sun rises in this Jambudvīpa, there will be an encounter here with Ākāśagarbha Bodhisattva. In a dream, he stands in front of the beginner bodhisattva, in his [very] own form, and shows [him] the fundamental transgression according to the means of Mahāyāna. He further shows him the wisdom of means, by which the beginner bodhisattva attains the *samādhi* called "retention of the aspiration for the [supreme] enlightenment" and is firmly established in Mahāyāna. (*Ākāśagarbha Sūtra* quoted in *Śikṣāsamuccaya*, 64.14–65.12; also see T 13.652c22–63a17)

In this text, Ākāśagarbha in the vision reminds the practitioner of the transgressions he should confess and leads him to successful repentance. The juxtaposition of visions experienced in an awakened state and in a dream is an old tradition of Mahāyāna visualization and can be seen in the *Samādhi of Direct Encounter with the Buddha* (*Pratyutpanna-samādhi Sūtra* in Harrison 1990, 32). By the time of the *Ākāśagarbha Sūtra*, the tradition of Mahāyāna visualization seems to have been closely linked to another old tradition of Mahāyāna Buddhism: repentance.

Upāli's Questions Sūtra on Determining the Meaning of Vinaya

The texts quoted thus far indicate that the practice of bodhisattva precepts, and of repentance in particular, contained visionary elements already in India. It would be reasonable to suspect then that the visionary elements in the *Brahmā Net Sūtra* and Daojin's stories from the *Lives of Eminent Monks* and the *Pusajie yishu* can also be somehow traced back to Indian traditions, even though these texts were clearly written in China. In this regard, the most important text is the *Upāli's Questions Sūtra on Determining [the Meaning] of Vinaya* (*Vinaya-viniścaya Upāli-paripṛcchā Sūtra;* see Python 1973, 1–4; Pagel 1995, 428–429). According to this sūtra (sec. 22 ff), if a bodhisattva commits the five heinous crimes, ten unwholesome deeds, or other serious offenses, he must repent day and night in the presence of the thirty-five Buddhas. His repentance consists of taking refuge in the three jewels, chanting the names of the thirty-five Buddhas, confessing all his transgressions committed in previous lives, and transferring any merits he has acquired to the supreme awakening. If his repentance is successful:

> There Buddhas, the Blessed Ones, show themselves directly to the [bodhisattva] all of whose evils are purified this way, in order to liberate sentient beings. [The Buddhas] show various secondary [bodily] marks and forms to mature confused and immature common beings.... A bodhisattva cannot purify the transgression as the cause of regret by [resorting to] all those belonging to the Vehicles of Auditors (*śrāvaka*) and Solitary Buddhas (*pratyekabuddha*), so he removes the regret of transgressions and attains *samādhi* by upholding and praising the names of these Buddhas, the Blessed Ones, and by reciting the *Triskandhaka-dharmaparyaya* scripture day and night. (*Upāli's Questions Sūtra*, sec. 27–32; also see Omaru 1985, 435–436; 1984, 380–381)

Having a vision is clearly taken as an indication of successful repentance, which, as we have seen, is one of the cardinal elements of the *Brahmā Net Sūtra* and Daojin's story.

We should recall here that the passages from the *Brahmā Net Sūtra* and the stories of Daojin are all concerned with repentance and ordination (or self-ordination). We should further recall that the sections on repentance and self-ordination of the *Brahmā Net Sūtra* have corresponding sections in the *Bodhisattva Stage,* and that Daojin's ordination was obviously based on Dharmakṣema's translation of the *Bodhisattva Stage.* Clearly the *Bodhisattva Stage* is the key text in the present investigation. Our problem is that the *Bodhisattva Stage* has few mystical elements that could possibly account for the visionary elements in the *Brahmā Net Sūtra* and the Daojin stories.

In this regard, it is important to note that the *Upāli's Questions Sūtra,* which is a visionary text, was closely linked to the *Bodhisattva Stage* in India. This can be established in several ways.

First, the text of the *Bodhisattva Stage* itself seems to have presupposed the *Upāli's Questions Sūtra*. Compare this passage from the Sanskrit text of the *Bodhisattva Stage* with the one that follows from the *Upāli's Questions Sūtra:*

> As has been also stated by the Blessed One, one should understand that a transgression of a bodhisattva is mostly brought about by hatred, not by lust. (182.6–7)

> If, Upāli, a bodhisattva who has set out in the Mahāyāna [career] commits transgressions as many as the grains of the sand in the Gangā River associated with lust, and if he commits a [single] transgression associated with hatred, from the point of view of the Vehicle of Bodhisattva *(bodhisattvayānaṃ pramāṇīkṛtya)*, the more serious transgression of these two is the one associated with hatred. For what reason? Upāli, hatred conduces to the abandonment of sentient beings, but lust to embrace them. (sec. 42)

Second, we should take into account a Sanskrit manuscript from Nepal that combines elements derived from the *Bodhisattva Stage* and the *Upāli's Questions Sūtra*. This manuscript (copied in the twelfth century according to Dutt 1931, 261–262) was edited and published by Nalinaksha Dutt under the title *Bodhisattvaprātimokṣa Sūtra*. Although the title *Bodhisattva-prātimokṣa* is supported by the text itself (Dutt 1931, 285.8), as Dutt himself points out, the manuscript does not contain precepts *(prātimokṣa)* as such but rather represents a Mahāyāna ordination manual combined with some theoretical discussion. According to Fujita Kōkan (1983, 96), the first portion (ordination manual) is actually a full copy of the *Formula for Bodhisattva Precepts* (Tibetan *Byang chub sems dpa'i sdom pa'i cho ga;* Sanskrit *Bodhisattva-saṃvaravidhi;* Peking no. 5404) by Byang chub bzang po (Bodhibhadra, fl. ca. 1000). Fujita argues that the *Formula for Bodhisattva Precepts* is a combination of sections taken from the *Bodhisattva Stage* and the *Formula for Giving Rise to the Aspiration for Awakening* (Tibetan *Byang chub tu sems bskyed pa'i cho ga;* Sanskrit *Bodhicittotpādavidhi;* Peking nos. 5361, 5405) attributed to Nāgārjuna. On the other hand, the second theoretical portion of the *Bodhisattva-prātimokṣa Sūtra* is based on the *Upāli's Questions Sūtra* (sec. 33–44).

The existence of this combined manuscript indicates that in India the textual traditions of the *Bodhisattva Stage* and the *Upāli's*

Questions Sūtra were closely linked. In other words, I suspect that in practice the apparently rational-looking *Bodhisattva Stage* was used in conjunction with a more mystical, visionary text, the *Upāli's Questions Sūtra*. Considering that, it becomes particularly important that a version of the *Upāli's Questions Sūtra*, including the visionary portion translated above, is incorporated as the introductory section to Guṇavarman's translation of the *Bodhisattva Stage* (*Pusa shanjie jing* 菩薩善戒經, fasc. 1, T 30.961b13–20), which was completed at Jianye 建鄴 (the capital of the Southern Dynasties) in 431 (regarding this translation, see *Tripiṭaka Translation Notes*, T 55.12b14–19, and *Lives of Eminent Monks*, T 50.340c29–41b10). The one-fascicle version of Guṇavarman's translation, which was originally fascicle five of the full text, even bears the subtitle: "Upāli's Questions: The Method of Bodhisattva Ordination" (*Youboli wen pusa shoujie fa* 優波離問菩薩受戒法, T 30.1013c; see Ōno 1954, 194–195). Not surprisingly Guṇavarman's translation of the *Bodhisattva Stage* mentions visionary experience in the section on self-ordination:

> The recipient … then in a quiet place worships the Buddhas in the ten directions. Facing east, he puts his right knee on the ground in front of a statue, puts his palms together, and says as follows: "… Now I have no master, so the Buddhas and bodhisattvas in the ten directions are my masters." He repeats the same phrase for the second and the third time. Then the Buddhas and bodhisattvas in the ten directions make [an auspicious] sign and show it (*zuoxiangshi* 作相示) [to the recipient]. [If such a thing happens] one should know that the precepts have been successfully obtained.
>
> The Buddhas and bodhisattvas in the ten directions tell the assemblies: "So-and-so in this world has truly received the bodhisattva precepts. I have now conferred the precepts out of mercy. Now this person has no master, so I have become his master. I now keep him in my mind; he is my dharma disciple." At that moment, [the recipient] stands up and worships the Buddhas in the ten directions. This is the self-ordination. (Fasc. 1, T 30.1014a4–21)

Ōno (1954, 194–204) claims that "Guṇavarman's translation" of the *Bodhisattva Stage* is in fact a Chinese alteration of Dharmakṣema's translation with the *Upāli's Questions Sūtra* added to the beginning of the text. According to Naitō Tatsuo (1962, 130), however, the *Upāli's Questions Sūtra* attached to Guṇavarman's *Bodhisattva*

Stage differs substantially from the oldest Chinese version of the
Upāli's Questions Sūtra (the *Jueding pini jing* 決定毘尼經), the only
chronologically possible source for Chinese alterations to Dharmakṣema's translation. Naitō suggests that the introductory section of
Guṇavarman's translation derives from an independent version
of the *Upāli's Questions Sūtra* that reflects another stage of textual development in India. Okimoto Katsumi (1972, 131; 1973,
374–375) further notes a similar combination of the *Bodhisattva
Stage* and the *Upāli's Questions Sūtra* in the Nepalese *Bodhisattva-
prātimokṣa Sūtra* and argues for the authenticity of Guṇavarman's
translation. His argument is convincing. Since we confirm that the
Bodhisattva Stage and the *Upāli's Questions Sūtra* were combined in
two separate traditions, one in China and the other in Nepal, we
should infer the existence of a tradition of combining these two
texts in India. The structure of Guṇavarman's translation of the
Bodhisattva Stage may well reflect the actual practice of bodhisattva
ordination in India. If this is the case, it would not be too surprising
that the tradition of Dharmakṣema's translation of the *Bodhisattva
Stage*, which on first examination does not appear to have visionary
elements, came to be associated with visionary repentance.

Be that as it may, apparently the combination of the *Bodhisattva
Stage* and the *Upāli's Questions Sūtra* as seen in Guṇavarman's translation had a significant effect on the subsequent development of
self-ordination in China (especially in the south). The *Ākāśagarbha
Visualization Sūtra* (*Guan Xukongzang pusa jing* 觀虛空藏菩薩經)
provides a clear example of this influence:

> If a lay bodhisattva has violated the six grave dharmas [i.e., six grave
> precepts],[5] or if a monastic bodhisattva has broken the eight grave
> prohibitions,[6] according to the Blessed One's former teaching in the
> vinaya, these sinners should be definitely expelled [without possible ex-
> piation] like a broken big stone. Now in this sūtra, he says that the
> greatly compassionate Ākāśagarbha can eliminate various sufferings and
> teaches a spell *(dhāraṇī)* to remove transgressions.... The Blessed One
> has great compassion; his vow [to save sentient beings] is boundless,
> and he does not abandon anybody. He, in the *Sūtra on Profound Merits*
> (*Shen gongde jing* 深功德經), teaches a method to cure transgressions
> called the *Determination [of the Meaning] of Vinayas* (*Jueding pini* 決定
> 毘尼; *Vinaya-viniścaya*). There are thirty-five Buddhas with great com-
> passion to save the world whom you should pay homage to.... In a
> dream, or in meditation, [Ākāśagarbha] stamps a seal on that person's

forearm with the seal on a *maṇi* gem. The seal has the characters "removal of sin." Having obtained those characters, one enters a monastery and [may participate in?] the lecture of precepts as before. If a layman obtains these characters, he can become a monk. Even if he cannot obtain these characters, [Ākāśagarbha] will make a voice appear in the sky saying. "The transgression has disappeared. The transgression has disappeared." If there is no voice in the sky, he will see Ākāśagarbha Bodhisattva in a dream.... Thus he spends another twenty-one days in repentance. Then a wise man should gather familiar people. He chants the names of the thirty-five Buddhas, Mañjuśrī, and the bodhisattvas of this eon and makes them witnesses. He announces the ceremonial act *(jiemo* 羯磨; *karman)* according to the ordination method I have already taught. Owing to the power of this asceticism, all sinful karma is permanently removed. (T 13.677b15–c23)

Since this is the *Sūtra on the Visualization of Ākāśagarbha,* as one can expect from the title, the influence of the *Ākāśagarbha Sūtra* is naturally noticeable. I would like to point out, however, that the cult of the thirty-five Buddhas is clearly based on the *Upāli's Questions Sūtra* (as is shown by the explicit reference), and that the six grave precepts for laypeople and the eight grave precepts for monastics correspond to the same system of precepts found in Guṇavarman's *Bodhisattva Stage* (fasc. 1, T 30.1015a17–18). Visionary elements are also present, although the characters for "removal of sin" and so forth should be regarded as Chinese elements. Furthermore, the last part (chanting and the "ceremonial act") seems to refer to a ritual of self-ordination after an austere practice of repentance. This text was clearly influenced by the combination of the *Bodhisattva Stage* and the *Upāli's Questions Sūtra.*

The *Samantabhadra Visualization Sūtra* (*Guan Puxian pusa xingfa jing* 觀普賢菩薩行法經) seems to belong to the same line of texts:

At that time, if a practitioner wishes to receive the bodhisattva precepts, he should put his palms together, stay in a deserted space, universally worship the Buddhas of the ten directions, repent sins, and manifest his own transgressions. Then he says: "Buddhas, the Blessed Ones, are always in the world, but because of my karmic obstructions, I cannot see Buddhas clearly even though I believe in Mahāyāna. Now I take refuge in the Buddha.... Now may Śākyamuni Buddha be my preceptor. May Mañjuśrī be my teacher. May Maitreya confer the Dharma

on me. May the Buddhas of the ten directions be my witnesses. May
virtuous bodhisattvas be my company." ... Then he should swear to receive the six grave precepts by himself. Having received the six grave
precepts, one should follow unobstructed pure practice (*wuai fanxing*
無礙梵行). One gives rise to the aspiration to save [the sentient beings]
widely, and one receives the eight grave precepts.... Whether one is
monastic or lay, one does not need a preceptor, witnesses, nor need he
follow the ceremonial act. (Fasc. 1, T 9.393c11–34a4)

Visionary elements are less evident here than in the previous
text. Nevertheless, the idea that karmic obstructions hinder vision
is found in many kindred visualization texts and clearly presup-
poses visionary practice. The combination of visionary elements
and the six or eight grave precepts would be traced back to Guṇavarman's *Bodhisattva Stage,* in other words, to the combination of
the *Bodhisattva Stage* and the *Upāli's Questions Sūtra* (cf. Mochizuki
1946, 285–286, 296). The ten grave precepts of the *Brahmā Net
Sūtra* are considered a combination of the six grave precepts for
lay bodhisattvas and the eight grave precepts for monastic bodhisattvas (see Ōno 1954, 266–267). If so, it is very likely that the self-
ordination of the *Brahmā Net Sūtra* was also related to this line of
development and not only to Dharmakṣema's translation of the
Bodhisattva Stage.

Visionary Experience as Purification in Central Asian Texts

To approach our problem from a slightly different angle, let us ask
the following question: Why is a visionary experience required in
the context of repentance? Most likely, a vision was considered
proof of spiritual purification. In other words, the underlying concept must have been that one's transgressions block one's visual
sense and prevent one from seeing the Buddha. Only after these
transgressions are expiated can one see the glorious body of the
Buddha. Such an idea is expressed in a passage from the *Ocean-
like Samādhi of Buddha Visualization Sūtra* (*Guanfo sanmei hai jing*
觀佛三昧海經):

If one gives rise to polluted, evil, and bad thoughts, or if one has
broken the Buddha's precepts, he sees an image [of the Buddha] as
pure black, like a man of charcoal.

Among the Śākya clan, five hundred people saw the Buddha's physical body like that of a man of charcoal. Among the assembly of monks, there were one thousand people who saw the Buddha's physical body like that of a man of red clay. Among the laymen, there were sixteen who saw the Buddha's physical body like legs of black elephants. Among the laywomen, there were twenty-four people who saw the Buddha's physical body like dense ink. . . . "We cannot see the Buddha's physical body because of our former transgressions." . . . When they repented to the Buddha, their spiritual eyes opened, and saw the Buddha's magnificent and refined physical body, like light from Mount Sumeru illuminating the ocean. (Fasc. 3, T 15.660a28–c26)

In this connection, we should further note that visionary repentance opens the way to an even more mystical experience: a visionary consecration *(abhiṣeka)*. This passage from the *Meditation's Secret Essence Sūtra (Chan miyaofa jing* 禪秘要法經) shows the link between repentance and consecration:

A person with heavy karmic obstructions sees only the Buddha's mouth moving but cannot hear the sermon. Like a deaf person, he has no wisdom from listening. In that case, he should further practice repentance. Having repented, he prostrates with his whole body and cries to the Buddha. He practices various meritorious deeds spending a long time, and only after that can he hear the Buddha's sermon. Even though he hears the sermon, he cannot understand the meaning. Then he sees that the Blessed One pours water from a jar on the practitioner's head. The color of the water turns into pure diamond color and enters the top of the head. The color is then diversified into blue, yellow, red, and white. Various polluted signs also appear there. The water enters the top of the head, descends straight through the body, and goes out of the heels of the feet. [The water then] flows into the ground, and the ground instantly becomes luminous. (Fasc. 2, T 15.256b20–28)

Judging from the context, probably this water symbolically purifies past transgressions. The "various polluted signs" perhaps represent a materialization of the spiritual pollution that is washed away by the water. The "auspicious signs" mentioned in the *Brahmā Net Sūtra* may originally have been an antonym of "polluted signs."

As I have discussed elsewhere (Yamabe 2000, 230–240), both the *Ocean-like Samādhi of the Buddha Visualization Sūtra* and the

Meditation's Secret Essence Sūtra seem to have close ties to Central Asia, more specifically to the Turfan area. They are more or less contemporary to Daojin, so it is likely that they reflect the atmosphere of Daojin's time in and around Turfan. It is this atmosphere that lies behind the story of Daojin's visionary repentance transmitted by the people of the Turfan lineage.

Conclusions

In this paper, I have tried to clarify the origins of the visionary elements in the *Brahmā Net Sūtra* and the story of Daojin by tracing them back to relevant sources. In a way, however, this may have been a futile attempt. The associations between repentance or ordination and visionary experience are so ubiquitous that it is almost impossible to pinpoint a single source. Nevertheless, it is clear that Bodhisattva precepts had visionary elements already in India, as is seen in the *Ākāśagarbha Sūtra* and the *Upāli's Questions Sūtra*. Although the *Bodhisattva Stage*, which organized the method of bodhisattva ordination and repentance, does not require visionary experience in these contexts, this text seems to have been used in conjunction with the visionary text the *Upāli's Questions Sūtra*. In China, Guṇavarman's version of the *Bodhisattva Stage* followed the tradition of combining these two texts, and it was the visionary self-ordination found in Guṇavarman's version that defined the keynote of the subsequent development of self-ordination—at least in south China. In Central Asia also, as we have observed, repentance seems to have been closely linked to visionary practice.

In a way, it is frustrating that we cannot decisively identify the direct source of the visionary elements in the *Brahmā Net Sūtra* and Daojin's story. In another way, however, this is a very satisfying result. As I suggested in the beginning of this paper, receiving bodhisattva precepts was not just a matter of morality; it involved highly mystical (even magical) practices. At least it is certain that many people had an image of precepts as such. Rather than any single textual source, it must be this popular image of bodhisattva precepts that indeed explains the existence of visionary elements in the *Brahmā Net Sūtra* and Daojin's story of repentance.

Finally I would like to point out that the visionary ordination based on the *Brahmā Net Sūtra* and the *Samantabhadra Visualization Sūtra* is still a living tradition in the Japanese Tendai school.

Even today, the monk who aspires to enter the twelve-year seclu-
sion as chaplain (*jishin* 侍眞, or *rissō* 律僧) of Jōdoin, the mauso-
leum of Saichō and the most sacred place on Mount Hiei, must
practice austerities to acquire auspicious signs *(haoxiang; J. kōsō)*
and attain the vision of the Buddha as prescribed by the *Brahmā
Net Sūtra*. Horizawa Somon 堀沢祖門, one of the former chaplains
who completed such a rigorous practice, describes his experience
in some detail (Horizawa 1984, 70–86; 1994, 6–11). The remainder
of this essay summarizes his description.

   In the center of the hall, large scrolls depicting Śākyamuni Buddha and the bodhisattvas Mañjuśrī and Maitreya are hung, and a
pair of tall lamps are kept lit day and night. An incense burner, a
basket of anise leaves, and a bell are arranged in front of the scrolls,
and the *Three Thousand Buddhas' Names Sutra* (*Sanqian foming jing*
三千佛名經) lies open in front of the practitioner. The practitioner
repeats full prostrations, chanting the names of the three thousand
Buddhas. After each prostration, he offers incense and a leaf, and
rings the bell once. This practice continues until he obtains a vision
of the Buddha. During that period, he cannot interrupt his prostrations except for meals, to go to the toilet, and for short periods of
rest on a chair.

   At first the monk undertakes the practice with every expectation
of seeing the Buddha. Horizawa compares the practitioner's mentality at this stage to that of a mountain climber: One keeps going,
expecting to see the Buddha at the top. His hopes, however, are repeatedly disappointed, and he suffers deep frustration and skepti-
cism. He keeps asking himself: "How can the Buddha appear? How
can one see auspicious signs? It is simply impossible." In such a
state of mental confusion, the act of prostration itself becomes a
task of enormous difficulty. The monk's body becomes as heavy as
lead, and he needs to use all of his strength merely to raise himself
up. Around midnight, his mind grows even more confused, and at
times he cannot even tell what he is doing. Horizawa remarks that
he often had to slap his face or head to remind himself that he was
practicing prostrations.

   After a month or two, the monk abandons all his hopes: he can
no longer expect anything from the Buddha but continues his prostrations merely as practice without hope. After about three months
of such practice, it finally happened. Horizawa describes the experience as follows:

While I was dozing at midnight, suddenly the Buddha appeared from the darkness. Enormously shocked, I woke up at once. Even after I woke up, however, the Buddha was still clearly visible. As is stated in the line: "One worships the Buddha with open or closed eyes," the auspicious signs must be visible whether the eyes are open or closed.

Even though the hall dimly lit by only two lamps, the Buddha was clearly visible as if he had escaped from the surrounding darkness. He was about one meter tall. Standing in the air at about two or three meters from the floor, four or five meters ahead of my seat, he was looking at me. As if he had just emerged out of the colorfully painted scroll, all the details of the Buddha were clearly visible, and his garments were even slightly waving. Without any words, the Buddha just gazed at me. (Horizawa 1994, 10)

Horizawa immediately went to his master, who at one time also had the same experience, and received his confirmation. Only after this visionary experience was Horizawa able to receive the bodhisattva precepts from a human master (Horizawa 1984, 73–74, 85; 1994, 6–7, 11). In the Daojin story, Dharmakṣema explained the precepts to Daojin in front of a statue (probably as part of the ordination ritual) only after Daojin had received the precepts from the Buddha in a vision. The present Tendai system, which requires a visionary experience before the human ritual can take place, faithfully preserves the same structure. As we have seen, visionary repentance can be traced back to India through Chinese apocryphal texts. I believe it is significant that such an old practice is still followed in present-day Japan, if only by a very limited number of people.

Notes

A more extensive version of this paper is available in Japanese. (See Yamabe 2000.)

1. The *Brahmā Net Sūtra* (fasc. 2, T 24.1008c2–3) defines the seven obstructions as shedding the blood of a Buddha, patricide, matricide, killing a preceptor (*heshang* 和尚; *upādhyaya*), killing a teacher (*esheli* 阿闍梨; *ācārya*), causing a schism in a *saṅgha* that performs official acts (*karman*) and turns the Dharma Wheel, and killing a noble person (*shengren* 聖人).

2. Huijiao wrote (fasc. 14, T 50.419a18–19) that his biographies were based on existing sources and that nothing new was added (*Jie sanzai zhongji, jin zhi xiaoju yichu. Gu shu er wuzuo* 皆散在衆記，今止削聚一處。故述而無作).

3. Perhaps this deed was inspired by the story of Mahāsenā, who gave her own flesh to an ailing monk, in the *Ten Section Vinaya* (fasc. 26, T 23.185c12–23). Daojin's biography states that he had a disciple familiar with this text, so it is likely that Dao-

jin was also familiar with the story. He might also have been influenced by the many stories of self-sacrifice in the *Jātakas*.

4. Funayama (1995, 20) suggests that "Juqu Jinghuan" is a contamination of "Maoqian" 茂虔 and "Anzhou" (both sons of Juqu Mengxun).

5. These are prohibitions of (1) killing; (2) theft; (3) telling a lie; (4) adultery; (5) telling the faults of monks, nuns, laymen, and laywomen; and (6) selling liquor (*Youposaijie jing* 優婆塞戒經, fasc. 3, T 24.1049a28–b24).

6. These are prohibitions of (1) killing, (2) theft, (3) sex, (4) telling a lie, (5) praising oneself and disparaging others, (6) stinginess in donation and teaching, (7) anger, and (8) staying with people who slander the Mahāyāna teaching (*Pusa shanjie jing* 菩薩善戒經, fasc. 1, T 30.1015a4–16).

Chapter 2

The Precious Scroll of the Liang Emperor

Buddhist and Daoist Repentance to Save the Dead

DAVID W. CHAPPELL

While staying in the inner chambers of the palace, [Emperor Wu 武, r. 502–549] heard the sound of a disturbance outside. Upon investigation, he saw a large serpent crawling over the palace. With flashing eyes and gaping mouth, it faced the emperor, who was frightened, but there was no escape. He lost control and stumbled, but then stood up and said to the serpent: "My imperial palace is a severely restricted area and not a place for all kinds of snakes to live...."

But in a human voice the snake said to the emperor: "This snake is Empress Chi 郗 from the past. Your handmaiden in life was envious of the [emperor's concubines in the] six palaces and my nature became bitter and cruel. Once my anger arose it produced a raging fire. My arrows shot out to ruin things and hurt people, and when I died these wrongs were used to accuse me and turn me into a snake.... I implore the emperor for the sake of peace and for old times' sake to save the virtue of your handmaiden...."

The emperor heard her plea and ... the next day at a great assembly of monks in the palace, the emperor explained the reason for calling the meeting and asked them what was the very best way to remove this suffering.

Master Baozhi 寶誌 [418–514] replied: "It cannot be done by venerating the Buddha, but by means of repentance and purification with great sincerity." (T 45.922b21–c8)

40

THE PREFACE to the *Cibei daochang chanfa* 慈悲道場懺法, a ten-fascicle repentance ritual attributed to Emperor Wu of the Liang 梁 kingdom and commonly known today as the *Precious Scroll of the Liang Emperor* (*Lianghuang baochan* 梁皇寶懺), says that for several months after the death of Empress Chi, memorial rites were constantly performed by Emperor Wu. Nevertheless, during the day sadness would suddenly overcome him, and at night he was restless and could not sleep. Then one day he encountered a large snake with flashing eyes that announced that it was the Empress Chi who had been turned into a snake because her cruel jealousy in life had brought harm to others. She told of her great suffering and misery in her new form and pleaded for the emperor's help. After being advised by an assembly of monks, the preface says that the emperor compiled and performed an elaborate repentance ritual. As a result of his actions the empress returned to the emperor in the form of a lovely lady to report that the ritual had been successful and that she had been reborn in heaven.

Stories of retribution in the afterlife as payment for wrongdoing in this life were common in India and China, but using Buddhist repentance rituals to ease the suffering of the dead was unusual. There are many Chinese stories about the return of the dead in some new form, especially if the deceased had been unjustly treated, and it was not uncommon for the dead to be manifested as a snake.[1] Because family obligations continued beyond the grave, spirits also returned when they had great suffering to seek support from family members, who would be haunted if they did not help. All medieval Chinese lived with this sense of connection and responsibility toward the dead and could relate to Emperor Wu's dilemma. Indian Buddhists also believed in ghosts, retribution, rebirth, rituals to earn merit to help relatives, and repentance, but it seems to be a Chinese innovation to connect Buddhist repentance rituals with easing the sufferings of deceased relatives. This connection was not made in India but became a dominant feature of Chinese Buddhism.

Shioiri Ryōdō (1964, 584–585) observes the remarkable fact that Chinese pilgrims with the most extensive and detailed travel records—namely Faxian 法顯, who traveled in 399–413; Xuanzang 玄奘 in 629–645; and Yijing 義淨, who entered India in 671—reported only two Buddhist repentance rituals during their many years in India and Southeast Asia. By comparison, Chinese Bud-

dhist repentance rituals are especially prominent as regular public ceremonies; more than one-fourth of the ritual texts collected
among contemporary Chinese Buddhist practitioners by Kamata
Shigeo (1986) are repentance texts.[2] These ceremonies pervade the
Chinese Buddhist liturgical year and constitute a major bond between the monastic elite and the laity, between the worlds of Buddhism and Chinese society, between the visible and the invisible.
The ghost story of Empress Chi may help us understand what
made Buddhist repentance rituals so prevalent in China in contrast
to their scarcity in India.

The source of the ghost story of Empress Chi is unknown, but
the story itself is widely circulated among Chinese Buddhists today.
Although the first mention of a ten-fascicle ritual and the ghost
story does not appear until half a millennium after the death of
Emperor Wu, the scriptural contents of the ritual came from texts
available around the time of the emperor.[3] What is certain, however, is that Chinese became convinced that Buddhist repentance
ceremonies could relieve the suffering of family members, living
and deceased, and that the present popularity of the ghost story is
an expression of this central feature of Chinese Buddhist religious
life.[4] By studying Emperor Wu's repentance ritual this essay will explore how and why Buddhist repentance rituals came to be a central and distinctive feature of Chinese Buddhism.

Fortunately Kuo Li-ying (1994) recently completed an excellent
review of many Buddhist repentance practices from the fifth to the
tenth century based on Chinese sources that show the standard
range of Indian models of Buddhist repentance. She does not ana-
lyze the *Cibei daochang* repentance text attributed to Emperor Wu,
however, nor does she deal with repentance for relatives. Although
she refers to Daoist practices of repentance to cure illness and for
family members (pp. 9–11), she limits herself to Buddhist materials.
By contrast, in seeking to understand Emperor Wu's ritual in its
Chinese cultural context, this essay will compare it to a ten-fascicle
Daoist text with a similar title, the *Repentance Ritual of the Great
Compassion Training Site of Taishang, Who Disperses Calamities
and the Nine Gloomy Hells* (*Taishang cibei daochang xiaozai jiuyou
fachan* 太上慈悲道場消災九幽法懺, HY 543; hereafter shortened to
Taishang cibei daochang), which has existed since the Tang dynasty.
The influence of Daoism on Chinese Buddhist repentance rituals,
and of Buddhism on Daoist repentance rituals, is a largely unex-

plored subject, so comparisons between the Buddhist and Daoist *Cibei daochang* will be a preliminary step in that direction.

In this essay I will attempt to show that the story of the ghost of Empress Chi that became attached to the Buddhist *Cibei daochang* repentance ritual expresses a new role for repentance in the Buddhist tradition and is a clear case of the sinification of Buddhism. Although Indian Buddhist repentance rituals were infrequent, and often private, Chinese Buddhist repentance rituals were very popular and elaborate among both monastics and the laity. By addressing the worst fears of Chinese culture (being reborn as a ghost, animal, or hell-dweller or being haunted by such beings), these rituals enabled practitioners to transform their fears into harmony and happiness. On the other hand, by reflecting the core kinship patterns of Chinese culture, they also transformed and reintegrated society by bringing the Buddhist and Daoist elites into the service of mainstream society while encouraging the common people to practice compassion beyond kinship ties. In sum, these repentance rituals localized Buddhism in China and broadened Chinese understanding to include concern for all beings everywhere.

Buddhist Repentance in India and China

The Buddhist monastic order was defined by vinaya guidelines to prevent trouble and increase conditions leading to enlightenment and freedom from karma and rebirth. Rules are not meant to be broken, but they inevitably are, and repentance was a way for practitioners to become reinstated as members of the monastic community. Repentance acknowledged and expressed regret for a fault; confession of the fault to others showed a desire to change and return to the order of monks. Some precepts were too serious to allow reinstatement if they were broken and others were too small to require confession, but for a particular group the vinaya required verbal confession for reinstatement. This process became a regular part of monastic practice (Kuo 1994, 29–35).

Repentance practices also developed outside the vinaya among the laity. Although monastic confession reinforced inner reform and monastic solidarity, the laity prayed to be released from the bad karma of wrong actions committed in this and previous lifetimes. These prayers sometimes were just expressions of inner longing; at other times they were addressed to supermundane Buddhas

as requests for help. Other kinds of repentance were not for break-
ing rules but to reject harmful habits of perception that tended
toward attachment ("meditative repentance"). Still other repentance
practices identified and rejected false understanding ("philosophical repentance") (Chappell 1990, 253–258). The great vinaya master
Daoxuan 道宣 (596–667) grouped the causes of repentance into
three categories: violations of monastic codes; violations of phe-
nomena (immoral behavior); and violations of principle (wrong
attitudes, perceptions, and understanding; T 40.96a.28–29; cf. Kuo
1994, 59–79). In all cases, repentance in Indian Buddhism involved
rejecting a ruinous way of life for oneself but had no necessary implications for others, and certainly not for deceased family members. The preface to the *Cibei daochang chanfa* shows Chinese Buddhists using repentance not just as a personal and individual way to
recover purity by rejecting wrong actions as defined by the Indian
Buddhist tradition. Something new is added. Repentance had somehow entered into a drama involving ghosts as a form of social misery and family responsibility in the visible and invisible worlds. The
popularity of repentance rituals in China in contrast to India seems
connected to this new role, which has yet to be explored.

Divine Litigation: The Chinese Background

In traditional China, relations with the dead were based on not only
compassion for the deceased, but also fear of possible reprisal for
the wrongs of relatives and neighbors. Based on the *baojia* 保甲 system, everyone in a group was punished for the crimes of its individual members. This ancient system had various forms and was revived by Emperor Xiao Wen 孝文 (r. 471–498) in north China just
before the reign of Emperor Wu. Although the folktale of Emperor
Wu does not accuse him of causing Empress Chi's jealousy (by having other court ladies), he does take responsibility for her release.

Legal action to save the dead in the other world appears in
China several centuries before the appearance of Buddhist and
Daoist communities.[5] Just as punishment could extend to the living
from relatives in other realms, as either a complaint from the deceased or a shared responsibility, so litigation, repentance, vows,
and appeals for mercy also could extend beyond oneself to pacify
and free kin in other realms. Litigation before the Director of Fate
(*si ming* 司命) would not have worked for Emperor Wu, however,
because there was no mistake: Empress Chi was guilty of wrong-

doing. Also, release through enlightenment would not have been possible for Empress Chi because life as a snake obstructed Buddhist practice. The only hope for Emperor Wu was to appeal for mercy. And that is exactly what Emperor Wu's repentance ritual does. After quoting various scriptures that describe the dreaded consequences of committing specific evil deeds, the *Cibei daochang chanfa* affirms our shared culpability:

> Now today in this sanctuary, this great congregation with the same karma (*tongye* 同業), just like that described in the scriptures, has a great likelihood of experiencing these dreadful things. We may already have done these crimes, or [in the future] delusion may return without our knowing. In this way we will commit wrongs that are endless and boundless and will receive painful retribution in future places.
>
> Now today with the most sincere heart and with our five limbs touching the ground [in prostration] we bow our heads and implore you, with utmost shame and repentance for the wrongs we have already committed, we confess and reject and eliminate them. For the wrongs that we have not yet done, from now on we will be pure and make this vow to all the Buddhas of the ten directions:
>
> Namo Maitreya Buddha ... Śākyamuni ... Avalokiteśvara Bodhisattva.
>
> Namo Buddha, Namo Dharma, Namo Saṅgha.
>
> Great Compassionate and Great Merciful Ones, save, protect, and lift us up, cause all living beings to immediately attain liberation, cause all living beings to have their hellish, ghostly, and animal karma extinguished, cause all beings to never again receive evil retribution, cause all beings to abandon the suffering of the three lower rebirths, and all attain the ground of wisdom, and cause them to attain the place of peace and ultimate happiness. (T 45.934b.9–c.2)

Although the prayer of confession at the beginning is individualized, the plea for universal mercy at the end is not; it is on behalf of all beings throughout time and space. Also, the purpose of the individual confession does not seem to be relief from one's guilt or that of others or building a stock of merit for oneself or others. Rather, it appears to be a method of demonstrating sufficient sincerity that makes the plea for salvation worthy of consideration. Salvation is not achieved through wisdom and nonattachment or a cosmic arithmetic of merits and demerits, but through the exercise of divine power, through the intercession of the Great Compassionate Ones.

Universal mercy may sound like an impractical dream, but in

China more than anywhere else in the world, such sweeping amnesty was actually practiced. For over two thousand years China had a legal tradition whereby the government regularly issued a general amnesty for most criminals. Amnesty began in the Han dynasty (206 BCE–220 CE), and was rekindled in the Tang (618–906) and the Song (960–1279). Brian McKnight finds that during these three dynasties covering a thousand years, general amnesties took place at least every two years:

> In medieval China, on the average of once every two years or less, the state opened up its judicial doors, returning to society almost all of the criminals in its grasp and preventing forever the prosecution of those who had succeeded in eluding it. The docket was cleared, the jails were emptied, the open cases were closed—all in a manner without precedent elsewhere in the world. (McKnight 1981, 72)

The Chinese court had enormous power to not only impose judgment, but also exercise leniency. The imagination reels before stories of cruelty by Chinese emperors in medieval times, but the thoroughness and frequency of amnesty in China are equally breathtaking.

Using this court-bureaucracy model, Chinese Buddhist repentance rituals would have differed greatly in meaning from Indian Buddhist confession in a monastic community, or enlightened release from attachment to self or objects of perception, or removal of karma by balancing individual debts with deeds that produced good karma. Repentance for Chinese could imply a social procedure on behalf of oneself and others to move higher authorities to issue a general amnesty freeing the dead to move on to a better condition and the living from the threat of otherworldly reprisals. Several factors were involved, including following the proper procedures and being earnest in one's plea. The emphasis on being emotionally overcome with repentance in Chinese instructions on rituals is strikingly different from Indian vinaya requirements. Several examples of elite Buddhist leaders who expressed great emotion are given by Daniel Stevenson (1987): Tiantai Zhiyi 天台智顗 (538–597) describes a devotee with "tears of grief streaming down his face" (p. 410) and instructs that in the Lotus *samādhi* the devotee should confess aloud with "streaming tears of remorse" (p. 501); Fazhao 法照 in meditation cries "tears of grief" (p. 418); and Shandao 善導 (613–681) adds a postscript to his *Hymns in Praise of Birth* (*Wangsheng lizan jie* 往生禮讚偈) to say:

> Superior confession is performed with such intensity that blood seeps from the eyes and pores. When confession is of the middling degree the body becomes hot. Sweat pours from the pores; blood oozes from the eyes. The lowest degree of confessional fervor is attended by heat and tears. (p. 411)

Although Shandao admitted that these outer manifestations of remorse were not essential as long as one's inner intention and resolve were genuine, the traditional Chinese practice of wailing at funerals shows that public emotion was frequently displayed out of a sense of duty, in spite of the distrust of emotion in elite Confucian circles.

The many ghost stories in Chinese culture illustrate how the living were terrified that deceased family members, suffering at the hands of an otherworldly bureaucracy, would haunt them by sending illness and disaster into their midst. But thanks to the frequency of general amnesty in China, there was room for hope that pleas for mercy to authorities in the other world might eventually release family members from their bondage (and protect the living from reprisals). Based on the bureaucratic pattern of Chinese society, it was crucial that these appeals be made in the most impressive way through the proper channels and to the highest authorities. Law was determined by the judgment and mercy of a divine ruler. Consequences for certain crimes could be dissolved—not by the Indian Buddhist solution of awakening to the impermanence of things and self or by dissolving the distinctions of good and evil through enlightenment, but only by confessing with visible remorse one's crimes and those of one's relatives and by throwing oneself on the mercy of the court. This same soteriological structure can also be found in Daoism.

Repentance in Early Daoism

Charles Benn has vividly illustrated the extreme forms of mortification and fettering of the body recommended in the medieval Daoist Mud and Soot Retreat (*tutan zhai* 塗炭齋). Penitents were required to smear mud on their brows, tie their hair to the altar railings, have their hands tied behind their backs, lie facedown on the ground, and strike their heads on the earth for six hours during the day and six hours at night as they repented and sought forgiveness of sins. As Benn (1998, 1) writes: "The penitents expressed their contrition by placing themselves in the most abject state—binding their hands like condemned criminals, undoing their hair like madmen, soiling their faces like beggars, and beating their brows on the ground like lackeys" (cf. *Wushang biyao* 無上秘要, HY 1130, fasc. 50; also summarized by Lagerway 1981, 156–158, and Maspero 1981, 381–386).[6] Why did they go to such extremes? Daoist repentance was emotional because it was so consequential. In addition to the fate and happiness of the practitioner, the remission of sins and future well-being of family members, living and dead, near and remote, known and unknown, were at stake:

> For three days and three nights … [such-and-such family] has carried out repentance to obtain pardon, so that the hundred thousand ancestors, relatives and brothers, already dead or who will later die, including the person of So-and-so (who is performing the ceremony), shall be without evil throughout several Kalpas. (Maspero 1981, 382)

Repentance involved saving oneself and one's family over many generations. No wonder that it led to a frenzy of desperation, causing participants to roll on the ground, lament loudly, and cover themselves with mud.

It is difficult to understand the significance of Buddhism in China without also studying Daoism to see both the context and role of Buddhism in Chinese society. This is especially true for the study of repentance, which became an arena where elite and commoner were equally engaged. Most scholarship has focused on elite Buddhism because it is accessible in texts, especially repentance in Tiantai (Kuo 1994, 80–107; Stevenson 1987). Popular Buddhism was usually not organized and preserved because it was deemed uncontrollable and dangerous by the government.[7] There was one place, however, where popular Buddhist practices had a chance to organize, textualize, and be preserved—namely, Daoism. The full story of Chinese Buddhism cannot be known without studying the Buddhist practices that were adopted by, or from, Daoism.

Communal Daoism dates from 142 CE, when Zhang Daoling 張道陵 allegedly received revelations from a divinized Laozi, Taishang

Laojun 太上老君, who appointed Zhang as the first heavenly master (*tianshi* 天師). Early Tianshi Daoism was territorial and members were divided into districts (*zhi* 治) or parishes led by religious leaders called libationers (*jijiu* 祭酒).[8] After the dispersal of the community from Sichuan in the third and fourth centuries, Tianshi Daoism survived as a guild of religious specialists who assigned members to celestial districts. Libationers continued to play an official role in representing their constituents before the gods of the celestial bureaucracy to (1) ensure that their names were recorded, (2) check the records of their deeds, and (3) intercede by pleading for leniency to protect them from destructive demons and vengeful ghosts who brought sickness, disaster, and death. The earliest records of Tianshi Daoism noted that sickness was cured by rituals of repentance in which the libationer priests "were responsible for praying for the sick. The ritual of prayer was that the sick person's name was written down, along with a statement of confession of his or her sins" (Nickerson 1997, 232).[9]

Unlike the earlier practice of confessing specific wrong deeds and popular religion's reliance on mediums to pinpoint wrong actions that were the cause of ailments, the Tianshi priesthood developed more general petitions to the gods. These petitions embraced not only wrongs in this lifetime, but also other more invisible sources of illness and misfortune, such as wrong deeds committed by distant ancestors that could cause a vengeful spirit to initiate a divine lawsuit against the living. Rejecting animal sacrifices for propitiating the gods and demons as heterodox, Tianshi priests claimed to bring relief through their authority over the gods based on divinely revealed registers (*lu* 錄) that enabled the libationers to petition and instruct the gods to protect their members in generalized petitions, such as:

> Now seven generations of ancestors are long ago and far away, and the descendants cannot fathom them. Who among them might be (or have been) good or evil cannot be known in detail. Now, having no object of knowing the affair [behind the suit], instead we respectfully set forth the multitude of items, listing all of them.[10]

This general petition over seven generations then lists scores of injuries that the ancestors may have committed that might become the basis for a wronged spirit to bring about a lawsuit against the living and cause sickness or trouble in the present. Because no specific remedy is necessary to correct the wrongdoing, no specific injury need be identified. Peter Nickerson gives several examples of how the ritual petitions of Master Red-Pine reject the need for detailed information about specific ghostly influences or invisible energies. The celestial officials who respond to the Daoist ritual petition will dispatch civil and military authorities from heaven who will cure any and all problems:

> The auspicious is difficult to preserve, and he [the supplicant] fears that the springs of the underworld await him. Thus he can only single-mindedly take refuge with the Great Dao, respectfully providing all the ritual pledges, displaying and offering them to the numinous officials of the five directions, and today announcing to your servant, beseeching that I deliver a petition to the Celestial Bureaux to redeem his life. Your servant does not understand the Descrying of Vapors ... I [can] only take up this request, respectfully prostrating myself on the earth, and submitting this single petition, [thus] reporting to my superiors in the Celestial Bureaux.... Find out which of his or her wrongs and mortal sins are recorded in the Black Register—I beg that you remove them. If there are disasters, let them be eliminated. If there are illnesses, let them be cured. Let the withered bloom anew, the dead live again. (Nickerson 1994, 54–55)

The Tianshi Daoists based their religious authority and effectiveness not on discerning and manipulating local powers and rivalries, but on a literary tradition of revealed registers and talismans that empowered their priests to plead to the celestial authorities that sins be forgiven. As a result, argues Peter Nickerson, the Tianshi Daoist priests promoted a more general and authoritative source of protection and renewal than was available from local diviners, shamans, mediums, and healers.

Although these ritual incantations may have seemed abstract and detached for the plaintive, they had the advantage of being secure and authoritative—and not dependent on the vagaries of local mediums or changing circumstances. They also had the advantage of providing assurance beyond one's immediate control. The incantations rectified one's present life, which was known, and controlled forces that were unknown: misdeeds by distant ancestors that could prompt recrimination against the living and random disaster brought by unrelated and anonymous destructive demons and energies. As a result, Tianshi Daoism pushed the arena for repentance, confession, and petition beyond the realm of the visible world and into the invisible world of demons, ghosts, and ancestors. Acts of restitution were directed even beyond these forces to invoke a celestial hierarchy of gods and heavenly officials, and finally the Supreme One (Taiyi 太一), the Most High Taishang Laojun, the personification of the unfathomable Dao.

How did Tianshi rituals avoid becoming abstract and empty for practitioners when the petitions appealed to a remote source of power and confessed only general sins? By requiring a profundity of feeling. A certain solemnity was provided by the manner in which the ritual was conducted and by the location: Petitions took place in a sacred area maintained by the priest, a "quiet room" (*jingshi* 靜室) that could be a separate room or building kept meticulously clean of animals and ritual pollution. Lu Xiujing 陸修淨 (406–477) gave detailed instructions for such a room (Nickerson 1996, 355) that evoke the concern for cleanliness in Buddhist Tiantai repentance rituals (Stevenson 1987, 477–478). Also, the Tianshi priest was to kowtow and slap his own face several times in penance. Tao Hongjing 陶弘景 (456–536) added that if the situation was desperate, the officiant might tear off his headgear and weep (Nickerson 1997, 232). But as we have seen in the Mud and Soot Ritual, the behavior of the penitents could go to even further extremes.

In his study of medieval Chinese Buddhist rituals, Daniel Stevenson (1987, 436–437) persuasively demonstrates the "existence of a common liturgical legacy that cuts across the bounds of individual sectarian and cult interests and functions as an integrative basis for Chinese Buddhist devotion as a whole." Stevenson found that repentance/confession is at the heart of the liturgical sequence, although the source of this emphasis is uncertain. Evidence for the increasing role of repentance within Indian Mahāyāna Buddhism can be found in Chinese translations of Mahāyāna scriptures; at least sixty-one of them contain repentance materials (Shih Ta-rui 1998). Stevenson (1987, 437), however, argues that the cohesiveness found in the Tiantai, Shanshi Pure Land, and Three Stages repentance rituals "has little to do with the scriptural sources themselves, but is informed by a living tradition of devotion quite apart from them." What is this "living tradition of devotion" that gives such primacy to repentance?

Many Daoist scriptures have repentance as their central theme. K. M. Schipper lists only 31 repentance texts out of 1,476 in his *Concordance du Tao-tsang* (1975, 209), but repentance was a central feature of every ceremonial fast (*zhai* 齋). A more accurate reading is given by Ren Jiyu (1991, 1,273–1,278) who lists 145 repentance and *zhai* texts out of 1,473. Thus texts focusing on repentance constitute almost one tenth of the *Daozang*. Yoshioka Yoshitoyo (1983, 1:391–411) suggests that the Buddhist *Cibei daochang chanfa* had influenced the Daoist *Taishang cibei daochang* given the similarity of their names. But when Shioiri Ryōdō (1977, 505–509) compared these two texts, as well as an earlier Chinese Buddhist ritual of 494 CE, the *Jingzhu zi jingxing famen* 淨住子淨行法門 (found in *Guang Hongmingji* 廣弘明集, T 52.306b–321b), he did not find direct copying among the three texts, only some parallel structures. Regardless of which text came first, their shared themes show that repentance is not a feature exclusive to either tradition but is a "common liturgical legacy" central to Chinese religious life that permeates both Buddhism and Daoism.

The Great Compassion of Lord Lao

The *Taishang cibei daochang* has forty-three sections in ten scrolls.[11] Although it is uncertain when the text first appeared, it was accepted as a normative Daoist ritual at least by the mid-Tang, at the height of the imperial support of Daoism under Emperor Xuanzong 玄宗 (r. 713–756) (Barrett 1996, 47–71; Benn 1977); its preface is by Li Hanguang 李含光 (683–769), the thirteenth master of the Mao Shan Shangqing 茅山上清 line (Hu 1995, 98b; Min and Li 1994, 540a). The preface says that the text was sent down as a revelation by Taishang 太上 (Laojun 老君, i.e., Lord Lao) to the Daoist Immortal Ge Xuan 葛玄 (164–244) when he resided in Shangyu prefecture of the Tiantai mountain range (*Tiantai shangyu shan* 天台上虞山).[12] The large number of Buddhist terms in the text, however, confirms a later origin. It is also worth noting that the text is associated with Mount Tiantai 天台山 because the major Chinese Buddhist repentance rituals originated there.

The Daoist *Taishang cibei daochang* is a smoothly written text that carefully integrates its different features without redundancy. Although it shares many of its themes and terminology with the Buddhist *Cibei daochang* text, the two are organized very differently. The main body of the text devotes most of its attention to meditation and internal purification practices (secs. 6–21, scrolls 2–5) in preparation for outer moral behavior (secs. 22–26, scrolls 5–6), including attending to family responsibilities (secs. 27–30, scroll 7), saving those in hell (secs. 31–35, scroll 8), caring for the nation, and saving all living beings (secs. 36–38, scroll 9). Clearly this concern with inner purification methods reflects many elements in Tiantai Buddhist repentance rituals, such as the Lotus *samādhi* and the Fangdeng 方等 *(vaipulya) samādhi* (Kuo 1994, 80–127; Stevenson, 1987, 468–596). But more important for our purposes is the connection between repentance and the work of saving others, especially family members and hell-dwellers, which is a goal highlighted in its opening vows.

Although groups of vows permeate the Buddhist text, the Daoist text has only one short set of vows at the very beginning (HY 543, Ce 冊 1.3b–4b). Unlike the first set of Buddhist vows that focuses on attaining individual purity and wisdom (T 45.929c25–931a13), the ten Daoist vows begin with a concern to save all beings: "from this day forward to establish every kind of good practice to transform every being in the six paths of rebirth and the four kinds of birth so that they will equally and forever transcend the various kinds of defiled realms." The next nine vows cultivate celibacy, spiritual friends, teachers, worship, and so on, ending with a vow to save those oppressed by demons and ghosts. These are followed by wishes that those of the three vehicles (a Daoist version of the Lotus teaching from Mount Tiantai?) grow in their wisdom and vow to seek rebirth as human relatives and teachers "so that we may meet together in this sanctuary to become companions of the truth." After rejecting angry and envious attitudes, the section ends with an appeal for compassionate achievement as a kinship community:

> If one sees the gloomy prisons and sicknesses of orphaned souls, then give rise to a mind of compassion, a mind of deliverance, a mind of the Dao, a true mind … and vow that fathers and mothers, the six relations, and all relatives of the past, present, and future shall see those in this generation all together being peaceful and happy: Those who are gone will not be born in the three evil rebirths (of hell, ghosts, and animals), those of the future will not be tied to heavy sins, but all together at this time may we give rise to the fruits as presented in these vows. (HY 543, Ce 1.3b–4b)

Such pledges, concerned with saving orphaned souls as well as relatives to build a harmonious and universal community of faith in the present, constitute a statement of purpose. They make clear early on that the ritual is not just for traditional family and clan members, but is a voluntary religious ceremony in which participants promise to undertake a special mission that unites them in a new community—one without the social differentiation of Confucianism.[13] The entire ritual is an elaboration and application of these vows. Although revered as a Daoist ritual text, the *Taishang cibei daochang* is clearly influenced by Mahāyāna values. It begins with a vow to save all beings, and Buddhist technical terms are sprinkled throughout: six paths, four kinds of birth, successive rebirths, leaving home (celibacy), field of merit, cultivating compassion, transcending one's human self, finding an enlightened master, three vehicles, three jewels, and so on.[14] Thus we can say that the Daoist ritual does include the conventional family and Chinese state morality, but extends itself with heroic and all-embracing ideals of a cosmic community that are akin to Mahāyāna Buddhism.

Robert Hymes (1996, 53) does not find "any scholarship on the place and role of vows or promises in secular Chinese life at any period," but vows permeate Chinese culture. The bodhisattva vows of Mahāyāna Buddhism provided ritual models for Daoist vows.[15] Taking the three refuges and being ordained as a monastic are vows to maintain Buddhist morality, but Mahāyāna monastics supplemented these by adding the heroic vows to save all beings. In cultures with a professional clergy, vows also provide "an alternative channel of direct communication and exchange for a lay population, a way of establishing contact that works around" (p. 53) and could replace professional rules (such as the vinaya) as an alternative structure for religious life. The Daoist ritual seems to follow this pattern.

Most of the *Taishang cibei daochang* is devoted to personal cultivation in preparation for the end of the ritual when salvation of others becomes paramount. The section most relevant to Empress Chi's plight as a snake is scroll eight, sections 31–34 (Ce 8.15a–19b), which deals with saving the suffering from rebirth in hell and as hungry ghosts and animals. The ritual leads the congregation through repentance for each of these three evil rebirths. Regarding those who dwell in hell, the repentance master says:

> I now worshipfully repent and arouse a mind that reaches out to all these [hell-dwellers], so that by relying on the power of good, the power of the Dao, the power of merit, I vow that all those who belong to the officials of hell will all together transcend and rise beyond suffering and progress gradually to become a heavenly immortal. As the same family (*tongqin* 同親) may they attain the Dao, and in accord with cause-and-effect may they change their human body so that the many kinds of poison can all be extinguished by them. (15b7–16a1)

Similarly, after describing various kinds of hungry ghosts, the repentance master declares:

> I now worshipfully repent and arouse a mind with unlimited expediencies, and by the power of merit, the power of discussing difficult ideas, the power to save others, I vow that these hungry ghosts and their whole household (*yijie juanshu* 一切眷屬) all will attain rebirth endowed with a human appearance and body and be able to provide different flavors of food and drink in response to one's thought. (16a3–6)

And finally, after noting different animals and insects (including those that lack consciousness and those that are not free), the repentance master says:

> All those who move in various ways, now on this day by the power of the sanctuary, the power of the ritual of repentance, by the power of merits, may they attain rebirth as a human.
>
> I, Repentance Master So-and-so, prostrate myself and make a pledge (using a nonanimal sacrifice, peacefully and reflectively) for fear lest I sink down because of the consequences of my actions. Now by repenting may all beings be liberated. (16a10–b4)

These passages clearly reveal a connection between repentance and rescuing others from being reborn as animals, ghosts, and hell-dwellers. The many sections (6–21) concerned with purification prepare the mind to connect with suffering beings in other realms and include them in the process of repentance. Orphaned souls and unknown sinners are among those receiving benefits. The whole ritual involves the reconstitution of a community of beings. By affirming that all beings are related and belong, whether in this world or the next, whether human, animal, ghost, or hell-dweller, the ritual aspires to create a shared human endeavor, a sanctified family in the sanctuary of the great compassion of Taishang.[16]

But who saves these beings? The "power of merit" is invoked to save beings in each of the three lower rebirths; it is not transferred and is only one of several powers, which include the power of goodness, of the Dao, of the discussion of difficult ideas, of saving others, of the sanctuary, and of the repentance ritual. The powers themselves do not seem to save, but they do change how practitioners understand themselves and their connections to others and make the petitioner worthy of being heard. In some theories of salvation, the transfer of merit employs a simple economic model that involves the transfer of good karma to cancel out the debts of bad karma and redeem beings from evil rebirths. This ritual is a process not only of merit-making, the transfer of merit, or repentance, but "worshipful repentance" (lichan 禮懺)—repentance that makes the practitioner worthy of being received and responded to, a repentance ritual in the sanctuary of the great compassion of Taishang. Only because the repentance master and his fellow worshippers have repented and are equipped with the powers of repentance, of goodness, of the sanctuary, and of the Dao, they may bow to the floor, expect to be received and to have their appeals heard by the Heavenly Worthies and the Perfected Ones who are gathered in the sanctuary of the great compassion of Taishang Laojun who, like the emperor on earth, is the final authority and true power that saves. Thus a constellation of positive resources is marshaled in a collective rescue mission in which the repentance ritual is an essential ingredient to elicit a saving response by the ultimate authority, Taishang Laojun.

The longest single section (no. 5, scrolls 1.13b–24b) of the Daoist text clarifies the dynamics of the repentance. After hearing many questions about life and retribution, the Worthy of Compassion responds quite personally:

> All living beings, every one of them, is a child of the Dao. When a child has sickness and pain, a father and mother love and have compassion for their child. When the sicknesses is gone, the father and mother are relieved and happy. Moreover, when someone has this suffering, then I must cure it.... The questions that you ask really touched my heart. A child faces you but does not speak. I, however, should speak. The compassion that you have for a child is no different than mine. (17a4–8)

Taishang answers with compassion to the cries of a repentant practitioner just as parents respond with love to the sufferings of their children. This is the heart of the Daoist ritual and echoes imagery used in its Buddhist counterpart (T 45.923c.3–14). Although motherly love and the Buddha as loving father are themes that occur in Buddhist writings, they are not as central or powerful in the Buddhist ritual as in the Daoist. Ultimately the Buddhist ritual relies on the mystical power of the vow—an exercise of enlightened mental powers rather than a cosmic and compassionate parent like Taishang.

The Great Compassion of Lord Buddha

The Buddhist *Cibei daochang* repentance ritual has forty sections. The first six sections constitute a complete ritual in themselves (T 45.923a–932a) and reflect the devotional pattern identified by Stevenson: invoking the three refuges, cutting off doubts, repentance, dedication to attaining enlightenment, making vows, and transfer of merits. Vows constitute four or five different sections of the Buddhist text, but they do not appear at the beginning, probably because there was no need to differentiate the Buddhist community from conventional society. (The vinaya did that.) Rather, vows serve other purposes. The first set is for personal enlightenment through successive rebirths (T 45.930–931a). Three lengthy sections (932a28–949b) follow on the theme of karmic retribution (good begets good and evil begets evil) to instill in practitioners fear and remorse for their sins and sympathy and compassion for those suffering in the three lower rebirths. Because the next section of vows seems to be a later addition (949b–950a), these sections on retribution then lead into another devotional liturgy (secs. 11–13, T 45.951b–953a) that follows the basic pattern of praising the three jewels, repentance, and making vows. The third set of vows (952b12–18) lists all manner of beings: gods, kings, ministers, demons, people, monastics, animals, and hungry ghosts. Based on the power of great compassion and wisdom, the power of gods and humans, the power of taking refuge and cutting off doubts, the power of repentance and seeking enlightenment, the power of saving all beings, the power of the compassion of all Buddhas, and so on, vows are then made to save all beings in the six paths of rebirth.

Much of the last third of the Buddhist text (secs. 14–34, T

45.953a–961a9) consists of a series of Buddha devotions (*lifo* 禮佛) that expresses concern for twenty-one different groups of gods, immortals, Brahmā kings, demons, dragons, people, kings, parents in this and previous lives, teachers, elders, monks, nuns, dwellers in various hells, hungry ghosts, and animals. The series focuses on specific groups of beings and ends with its own small set of vows (960c6–13) to save all of these beings by the power of compassion and spiritual power. The ritual ends with sections 35–40 (961a10–967c24), which contain miscellaneous devotions, transfer of merits, and vows. A set of vows (961c25–962a9) is devoted to all who arise from the four kinds of birth and in the six paths of rebirth (i.e., all beings previously mentioned), but in place of the image of a compassionate power, we find Buddhist ideas such as emptiness, merit, concentration, and giving *(dāna)*. The last, very lengthy section of vows (963c11–667a2) ends with personal purification of the six senses to ensure that one never perceives things as evil or wrong but as manifesting the marks of the Buddha. The ritual finishes with an all-inclusive section of worship emphasizing how the vows are inexhaustible (967a3–c23). This philosophical ending contrasts with that of the Daoist text, which calls on divinities to bring about the salvation of all beings.

Unlike the Daoist text, which invokes kinship ties of all beings at the beginning and end of the ritual, the Buddhist repentance ritual emphasizes the variety of beings and their salvation in the middle of the ritual (T 45.953–960), naming twenty-one categories of beings combined with devotion to the Buddha in each case. After listing the beings and displaying devotion, a vow is made to use the power of great compassion to protect and save all beings and cause them to achieve ultimate enlightenment. At first glance, it would seem that the great Buddhas and bodhisattvas are the agents of salvation because they are invoked for each kind of being. The arena for all beings and all actions, however, is the realm of interdependence and emptiness. After the practitioner discards a narrow, self-centered worldview to empathize with those who are suffering and appeal to Buddhist deities, the entire drama is linked to the practitioner's ignorance, the practitioner's repentance, the power of great compassion, and finally the vow to save all and bring all to final enlightenment.

Within the framework of the ritual, it is the practitioner who repeatedly repents through myriad rebirths; the practitioner who does not know about (or care about) the sufferings of beings in other realms; and the practitioner who eventually bows down, takes refuge, and vows that "beings of the four kinds of birth and six paths of rebirth who have committed wrongs may together with me attain purity" (927a3–4). Group culpability and group reform (as a result of compassionate vows) are highlighted. Good karma and merit are not emphasized as agents of salvation, but an array of assisting powers is frequently mentioned. The metaphor is not the impartial balancing of good and bad karma, but bringing the vows to fruition. Thus vows constitute a major force in the Buddhist ritual by appearing in several special sections and as a refrain in many others. The ritual ends by praising the inexhaustibility of vows at the climax.

The vinaya became the institutional code of Buddhism that defined behavior for avoiding evil and cultivating good. Mahāyāna scriptures added social responsibility by creating vows that set forth broad goals, values, and priorities directed toward saving others. The vinaya identified monastic restrictions, but vows defined ideals; the vinaya provided structure, whereas vows gave a direction for spiritual development; the vinaya outlined the formalities of practice, but vows expressed their purpose. Vinaya and vows can coexist, but for the laity the vinaya was largely replaced by vows.[17] In the Buddhist *Cibei daochang* ritual, for example, vows are a supplementary practice for monastics but a primary one for the laity. In both cases, vows made ritual practice more personal, immediate, and effective than institutional religion (Hymes 1996, 50–54).

The repentance ritual successfully fulfilled Emperor Wu's kinship responsibility, and Empress Chi was eventually released from her snake rebirth. But the *Cibei daochang chanfa* takes the practitioner beyond kinship lineages and makes connections with all beings everywhere who are suffering as all of us are fated to do. The text buddhicizes Chinese society by turning all beings into phases in the round of rebirths and ultimately sees them as manifestations of the dharma-realm of emptiness. Accordingly, the sanctuary of great compassion is occupied by beings who share in the same karmic existence, but in the end a traditional Buddhist emphasis is placed on emptiness, true reality, and loss of individuality as everything is swallowed up in the power of the inexhaustible vow. The ritual closes by transcending kinship identities and entering a mystic realm of interrelatedness, emptiness, and the intentionality to save all beings. Although the preface entices the laity with a classic ghost story emphasizing repentance to save a deceased loved one, the ritual itself carries the practitioner out of conventional society and into the dharma-realm of elite Buddhism.

Conclusion

Modern Chinese Buddhists are familiar with the *Cibei daochang chanfa*, (usually under the title *Precious Scroll of the Liang Emperor*), and many temples annually recite the text as part of their preparation for the ghost festival in the seventh lunar month. A folktale claims that the *Precious Scroll of the Liang Emperor* was created by Emperor Wu to save Empress Chi from her rebirth as a snake. Although the Mulian 目蓮 story explaining the Ullambana ritual to feed family ghosts has emerged in a variety of popular dramas (Teiser 1988; Peng and Seaman 1994), the story of Emperor Wu's repentance has not produced any popular plays.[18] It does appear, however, in the *Precious Scroll of the Liang Emperor* (Kamata 1986, 888–912) and has become so popular that the ritual is part of the repertoire of most contemporary Chinese Buddhist temples as a way of easing the suffering of the living and the deceased.[19]

Kinship lay at the heart of everything in traditional China. Misfortune arose not only from individual misdeeds, but from wrongs by family members or neighbors or from deceased relatives in distress. Recovery was also collective. Repentance could relieve the suffering for any and all relatives in visible and invisible worlds as well as bring about individual transformation and salvation. Gregory Schopen (1997, 65) demonstrated that filial piety was "an old, an integral, and a pervasive part of the practice of Indian Buddhism from the earliest periods of which we have any definite knowledge" for both the laity and monastics. What was new for Chinese Buddhists was the notion that individual misdeeds could result in collective punishment and that salvation for the dead was possible if sincere repentance, pleas, and vows were made by the living.

A scholar trained in Buddhist studies will notice numerous Buddhist influences in the Daoist *Cibei daochang* ritual, such as the five lay precepts, the doctrine of karma and rebirth, the Mahāyāna universal compassion for all beings, and Indian individual purification practices. But Buddhism also was transformed in China. Because of the absence of Mādhyamika philosophy and monastic rules in Daoist texts, Erik Zürcher (1980, 143) reasons that interaction did not take place among the competing elites "but rather in lay society where Daoists and Buddhist devotees met, perhaps even as members of one and the same family." Stephen Teiser (1988, 35–42) argues that annual Buddhist and Daoist rituals in the seventh lunar month to liberate relatives from hell share many features and their origins are so obscure that it is impossible to determine which came first. Both Teiser and Zürcher liken Buddhist and Daoist competing elites to two pyramid peaks rising from a common base; they must be examined together as part of a shared religious milieu. What was this common base and how deeply did it influence the heart of Chinese Buddhism?

Kuo Li-ying (1994, 169) asserts that the most effective Buddhist confession is to repent having attachment and to put faith in the true nature of reality, thus freeing us from deluded notions and karma. In the Buddhist *Cibei daochang* ritual, however, repenting before the Buddhas to release ancestors from evil rebirths is not based merely on individualistic or totalistic Indian philosophy, but on Chinese kinship solidarity. The elites who led Buddhist and Daoist *Cibei daochang* repentance rituals may have promoted competing institutions, ontologies, and divine beings (e.g., Taishang versus Buddhas and bodhisattvas), but the rituals themselves have structural similarities. Both Daoist and Chinese Buddhist moral philosophy assumed a collective responsibility and underlying trust in the responsiveness of universal forces to the moral sincerity of individuals.

In the tradition of correlative thinking from the Han dynasty, the formless ultimate was seen as responsive to human morality; exceptional spiritual achievement would naturally manifest itself in external natural wonders. Although the Buddhist repentance ritual avoids theism by invoking the inexhaustible and formless dharma-realm, the miraculous transformation of Empress Chi from a snake into a heavenly being could be seen as a natural response to repentance. Tiantai Buddhism was also based on the idea that when humans are sincere, true reality is responsive (*ganying* 感應; Donner and Stevenson 1993, 74–77, 147–152). Zanning 贊寧 (919–1001) used "spiritual resonance" (*gantong* 感通) when referring to wonder-working monks and declared that "supreme sincerity evokes resonance" (*zhicheng suogan* 至誠所感, T 50.878b.24–25).

The fluidity between the abstract and the concrete in Chinese

and Buddhist thought accommodated elite and common sensibilities; the interchangeability of Buddhist and Daoist divine figures
(Shioiri 1977), however, met the needs of the laity. Indian Buddhist
texts had sufficient analogies describing the Buddha as a loving
parent to warrant the Chinese adopting the Buddha as a savior for
their kinship needs. Although Buddhist philosophy ultimately abandoned such imagery at its highest levels, at the practical level what
counted was the compassion and responsiveness of the Dharma as
embodied in Buddhas and bodhisattvas like Guanyin 觀音 (Avalokiteśvara), Emituofo 阿彌陀佛 (Amitābha), and Dizang 地藏 (Kṣiti-
garbha). But metaphysics and mythology were primarily used as a
backdrop. At the forefront was the fervent belief that a sincere appeal made to these universally compassionate saviors in the proper
way could free relatives from being reborn as ghosts, animals, or
hell-prisoners. As a result, Chinese repentance rituals differ from
the repentance practices found in Indian Buddhism that involve
confessing and rectifying erroneous actions, attitudes, and understanding of the individual. The *Cibei daochang* Daoist and Buddhist
rituals first evoke the kinship responsibilities that humans should
feel toward beings in the three lower rebirths. Humans then sin-
cerely repent their present and past sins so that their pleas for leniency will be heard by the compassionate lords of the universe,
whether Taishang or the Buddha, on behalf of kin suffering in other
realms. Repentance in China, unlike India, was done for the sake of
others and to prompt a response from the compassionate powers of
the universe in proportion to one's sincerity.

Kuo Li-ying (1994, 169) notes that except for the detailed classification of sins and terrifying descriptions of hells, Buddhist repentance rituals do not scrutinize individual sins or faults. Certainly
this is true of group rituals, which are not specific to anyone person
like Indian Buddhist meditation or Catholic confession. But there
may still be great emotion shown—based not on scrutinizing personal actions, but on the need to arouse the gods or Buddhas to compassionate action by displaying sincere concern for the suffering of
family members who are the practioner's personal responsibility.
Chinese repentance did not require the details of one's sins; it
needed to demonstrate the depth of one's sincerity. This echoes the
Confucian intentionality as expressed by the *Great Learning* (*Daxue*
大學): If you want to save others, you must first rectify your mind
and will to manifest true character. With the presumption of guilt,

Liang Emperor Wu's repentance did not seek justice, but mercy. Appeal is not made to laws or to enlightenment, but to a compassionate training site *(cibei daochang)*. Release depends on sincere repentance.

Victor Hori observed at the end of a weeklong Chan retreat that white Americans found meditation had assisted them in their self-understanding and realization. The reaction of ethnic Chinese participants, however, was very different:

> The first woman broke down in tears as she spoke. The week of meditation had made her realize how selfish she was; she wanted, right then and there, to bow down in apology before her family; she wanted to perform some act of deep repentance. The statements from other Chinese people similarly revolved around feelings of shame and repentance. (Hori 1994, 48–49)

After noting the self-absorption of white American practitioners in contrast with the moral self-examination of those who were ethnic Chinese, Hori came to realize how a Buddhist tradition can be used to flavor and decorate existing cultural values rather than transform them. Although repentance and confession of wrongs play a minor role in Indian Buddhism, guilt and a sense of social responsibility are especially important in Chinese culture and gradually infused Buddhism in China until they became prominent features in elite and popular practice.[20]

Kinship responsibilities are the foundation of Chinese culture. Ingrained from youth is the fear of failing to fulfill these responsibilities and causing great suffering to one's family (and oneself if one is haunted or punished after death). Both Buddhist and Daoist *cibei daochang* rituals emphasize family but enlarge their meaning by having practitioners recognize animals, ghosts, and hell-dwellers as relatives, thereby engendering sympathy for all beings. By performing ritual actions to demonstrate profound regret for not serving one's kin adequately and by invoking the aid of universal compassionate powers to relieve the suffering of family members on behalf of the worshipper, the Daoist and Buddhist *cibei daochang* repentance rituals satisfy the deepest needs of Chinese moral life. In the Buddhist case, using repentance to fulfill kinship responsibilities transformed the ritual's narrow Indian emphasis on improving one's own spiritual condition into something much more meaningful to Chinese society. We must therefore conclude that the *cibei daochang* repentance ritual of Emperor Wu represents a clear case of the sinification of Buddhism.

Notes

1. For a general discussion of pre-Han images of ghosts, see Poo 1998 (44–68). In *The Commentary of Zuo* (*Zuochuan* 左傳, ca. 2d cent. BCE), Shenxu reportedly said: "When people have something they are deeply distressed about, their vital energy flames up and takes such shapes [as snakes]" (Poo 1998, 44). There are many stories of those who died unjustly and returned to the world in various animal forms: for example, see the *Yuan hunji* 還魂記 (Tales of vengeful souls), a collection of stories compiled in the sixth century CE (Cohen 1982).

2. Kamata's study (1986) and compilation of contemporary Chinese Buddhist rituals includes 212 pages of repentance texts out of a total of 671. The major research writings on repentance rituals within Chinese Buddhism were done by Shioiri Ryōdō and are listed in his bibliography (Muranaka 1991, 1–6). For an overview in English of Buddhist repentance texts, see M. W. De Visser 1935 (349–409); for the best analysis in a Western language of Indian Buddhist repentance rituals in Chinese translation, see the French study by Kuo (1994).

3. The preface reports that this repentance ritual was composed at the request of Emperor Wu of the Liang in 510 CE, but there is no mention of this text in official secular biographies of Emperor Wu. The first record appears in two ninth-century Japanese Buddhist catalogs: One reports a six-fascicle repentance text by Emperor Wu of the Liang (T 55.1101b3), the second a six-fascicle text of the *Training Site of Compassion (Cibei daochang wen)*, with an attribution to Wu of the Liang (T 55.1106c26). Later editing could have changed these texts into the extant ten-fascicle version that is arranged in terms of the ten stages of a bodhisattva (the name of each stage is listed at the end of each fascicle). Shioiri (1977, 501–504) found the first mention of a ten-fascicle text entitled *Cibei chanfa* attributed to Emperor Wu in a Korean Buddhist bibliography printed in 1090 CE (T 55.1174c.11), but a record of the ghost story with this ten-fascicle text does not appear until the *Summary of Research on Early Buddhist Monarchs (Shishi jigu lüe* 釋氏稽古略), compiled in 1354 (T 49.794c). Shioiri found that the ritual quotes were from numerous Buddhist texts that were extant by the end of the sixth century, so the repentance text could have been compiled in the sixth century based on a request by Emperor Wu. The present organization into ten fascicles accompanied by the ghost story of Empress Chi, however, should probably be placed in the Song 宋 dynasty (960–1279).

4. Today the ten-fascicle ritual attributed to Emperor Wu, popularly known by the name of *Lianghuang baochan*, is regularly performed in Taiwan and by overseas Chinese. For example, Ven. Shih Tszu-kai of Fuhsing Temple, Kao Hsiung, reports that in southern Taiwan the performances are so popular that temples have to check with each other to ensure that their schedules do not conflict and the laity have a chance to attend more than one. Even among the overseas Chinese community in Hawai'i, the ritual was featured at the four main Chinese Buddhist temples in 1998: Three temples performed the ritual (Hsu Yun Temple, Yuk Fut Temple, and Wang Tsick Temple), while Kuan Yin Temple offered lectures on the text every Saturday

during the summer. (The ritual from a previous year at Yut Fut Temple is even available on videotape.) Ven. Heng Sure informed the author (e-mail of 2 December 1998) that Gold Mountain Monastery, San Francisco, and Gold Sage Monastery, San Jose, performed the ritual during the first week of December 1998.

5. In 297 BCE, a Wei general, Xi Wu, pleaded a lawsuit before the otherworldly scribe of the Director of Fate to release a man named Dan who had died in 300 BCE before his appointed time. As a result, when a white dog dug up his grave in 297 BCE, three years after his death, Dan returned to life (Harper 1994).

6. I am indebted to Charles Benn not only for bringing this ritual to my attention and assisting me with other Daoist sources, but also for his enthusiasm for Chinese ghost stories.

7. The lay movements of the sixth century were the probable victims of "persecution" by the Northern Zhou 北周 in 576. The terrible suppression suffered by the folk Buddhist White Lotus movement (*bailianshe* 白蓮社) is so widely known that "White Lotus" is now used to refer to the Chinese mafia! See B. J. Ter Haar 1992 for a thorough study of how folk Buddhism was demonized by the government.

8. According to the *Record of the Three Kingdoms* (*Sanguo zhi* 三國志, ca. 297), Tianshi novices were called "ghost soldiers" (*guizu* 鬼卒) at the beginning of their training, but once they became practitioners they were called "libationers" (Hu 1995, 498–499, 502–503). However, the term "libationers" seems to betray an earlier ritual function that was prohibited in the new Daoist puritanism. "Although the term literally refers to one who sacrifices alcoholic spirits, it does not seem that this was part of the Libationer's function in the Celestial Master church" (Kleeman 1998, 68).

9. The assumption that sickness was caused by wrongdoing, and that good health could be regained through a confession of sins and petitions to the appropriate gods, continued as a central feature of Tianshi Daoism. In a treatise defining correct Daoist behavior in comparison with popular religious practices, Lu Xiujing 陸修靜 (406–477) composed a set of instructions that is very explicit in stating that the confession of wrongs was a primary and necessary healing method. These instructions, *Abridged Codes of Master Lu for the Daoist Community* (*Lu xiansheng Daomen keliie* 陸先生道門科略, HY 1119, Ce 冊 761), are available in an English summary (Nickerson 1994) and translation (Nickerson 1996). Lu states: "In curing illness one does not use acupuncture, moxa, or hot liquid medicines. One only ingests talismans, drinks [talismanic] water, confesses one's sins, corrects one's behavior, and sends a petition—and that is all" (Nickerson 1994, 43).

10. Nickerson (1994, 53) based on *Master Red-Pine's Almanac of Petitions* (*Qingsong zi zhangli* 青松子章歷, HY 615, Ce 冊 335–336, 5.25b8–10). Another selection called "The Great Petition for Lawsuits of the Tomb" (*Da zhong song zhang* 大塚訟章) has also been analyzed and translated by Nickerson (in Bokenkamp 1997, 230–274).

11. *"Taishang"* 太上 is the title of the divine Laozi and is usually found in the combination "Taishang Laojun" 太上老君 (Most High Lord Lao). *"Cibei"* 慈悲 began as a Buddhist term referring not to conventional, limited, ego-centered kindness, but to the great compassion for all beings expressed by someone who is enlightened, namely, the Buddha (Chappell 1997). The phrase *"daochang"* 道場 referred to the place of enlightenment *(bodhimaṇḍa)* of Śākyamuni Buddha under the bodhi tree, but by the mid-Tang it was also used by Daoists and Confucianists to refer to any

place for religious practice and attaining enlightenment. Because of its use in such ritual texts as the *Taishang cibei daochang xijiu jiuyin fachan*, however, the term in recent times has also come to refer to the activities performed at the training sites, namely, "priestly ceremonies for delivering souls from purgatory" (Hu 1995, 560a; Mathews 1994, no. 218, 20).

12. I am indebted to Saitō Enshin (author of *San Tendai Godaizanki* 參天台五臺 山記, Tokyo: Sankibō, 1997) for locating Shangyu for me. Li Hanguang's Daoist master was Sima Chengzhen 司馬承貞 (647–753), who had initiated Emperor Xuanxong in the capital but practiced in the Tiantai mountains. Li may have received the text from Sima as a legacy of the Tiantai Daoist traditions. Attributing Daoist texts to Ge Xuan became a common device for legitimating scriptures in the Lingbao order, a movement that began about 400 CE. See Bokenkamp 1983 and 1997 (373–404) for a discussion of the use of Buddhist texts by the Lingbao.

13. Because the Daoist community did not have a uniform code of behavior like the Buddhist vinaya, the opening vows of the ritual defined the congregation. Vows for the Daoist offered an alternative spirituality to the religious roles of the Confucian state. Membership in the Tianshi Daoist communities was defined by adherence to new codes, scriptures, and a different basis of authority. Organizational structures, procedures, and rules were necessary for the community to perpetuate itself and included the transmission of registers and talismans (*fu* 符). As the Tianshi Daoists branched out and became fragmented, and their ritual practices diffused among the general population, communal rules were replaced by vows made at the beginning of a ritual to reconstitute a religious community for the duration of the practice together, and enable it to continue through time at a spiritual level based on shared intent and commitment.

14. The three jewels (*sanbao* 三寶) in the Daoist tradition symbolize various items, such as the virtues of compassion, frugality, and yielding (*Daodejing* 道德經 no. 67); or the ear, eye, and mouth according to inner alchemy (*Cantong qi* 參同契 of Wei Boyang 魏伯陽). In the rituals of religious Daoism, however, the three jewels usually refer to the Dao, the scriptures, and Daoist teachers (*Daojiao yishu* 道教義樞, fasc. 1).

15. Vows (Skt. *praṇidhāna*) in Buddhism arise in direct connection with defining the core that establishes a bodhisattva, namely, the rise of the determination to seek enlightenment *(bodhicitta).* "*Praṇidhāna* is both the cause and the result of the Thought of Enlightenment. It is of three kinds: that which relates to happy rebirths; that which aims at the good of all beings; and that which is intended to purify the buddha-fields" (Dayal 1970, 65).

16. The English word "kindness" originally did not imply an emotional connection, but the recognition of kinship—being of the same kind or kin to someone else. Repentance in the compassionate sanctuary of Taishang and in Emperor Wu's repentance ritual seems to be based on a similar recognition of kinship that is extended to all beings based on the idea of rebirth. Although great emotion may be part of the ritual, compassion and repentance are set forth as the consequence of seeing our kinship or connection with others, not the cause.

17. For Mahāyāna monastics, vows supplemented the Buddhist vinaya to expand their practice beyond personal purity toward the larger goal of saving others. In the case of lay bodhisattvas, vows established an alternate to the vinaya by provid-

ing a framework of morality and religious values that included the six perfections and the lofty ideal of saving others.

18. I am indebted to Professor Chin-tang Lo, University of Hawai'i, for this information and for providing me with a copy of the *Lianghuang baochan,* which is used in the annual liturgies of the Hsu-yun Temple in Hawai'i.

19. In the folktale, Baozhi has a much bigger role and is recast as a Chan master (Zhigong Chanshi 誌公禪師), which explains why the text is listed in a Japanese catalog of Zen texts (BK 11.252a).

20. For a collection of contemporary Chinese Daoist repentance texts to compare with the Buddhist rituals compiled by Kamata Shigeo, see Ōfuchi Ninji 1983 (463–677). Institutionalized Daoism in contemporary mainland China is largely Quanzhen 全眞 (Ch'üan-chen; Complete Perfection) Daoism, although there are probably more Tianshi priests living with their families in villages. Bartholomew Tsui (1991, 157–166), who has studied Quanzhen temples in Hong Kong, states that the "core of modern Ch'üan-chen rituals is confession."

Chapter 3

Daoxuan's Vision of Jetavana
The Ordination Platform Movement in Medieval Chinese Buddhism

JOHN R. MCRAE

FIRST, A CONFESSION: I used to think of the Vinaya (Lü 律) tradition as little more than a collection of bothersome rules worried over by picayune clerics. Several years ago, however, as I worked to understand the career and teachings of the Chan monk Shenhui 神會 (684–758), I realized that his vocation on the ordination platform was *the* defining element in his life, and that his emphasis on lineage authenticity and extraordinary valuation of sudden enlightenment (*dunwu* 頓悟) were both molded more by his activities on the ordination platform than by any real experience as a "Chan" monk or meditation master. We need to keep in mind, of course, that the vinaya governed the life of all formally ordained monks and nuns, and that it did not represent a separate sectarian tradition within Chinese Buddhism. Shenhui's ordination platform vocation and activities were nevertheless exceptional, and this has led me to examine the nature of the ordination platform as an institution in medieval Chinese Buddhism, part of the results of which are presented here.

In this essay I focus on the visions of the Buddha's ordination platform at Jetavana in India recounted by the great Vinaya authority and historian Daoxuan 道宣 (596–667), and the "ordination platform movement" that emerged in his wake. By discussing these issues I hope to outline an understanding of the Vinaya tradition and medieval Chinese Buddhism in general that begins with at least two basic assertions: (1) the Chinese Vinaya tradition was not limited to the dry explication of monastic regulations, but played an important role in generating rituals of profound religious power by which Chinese Buddhists defined themselves and their religion; and (2) "the Buddha" was for medieval Chinese Buddhists not the humanistic image recreated by modern scholarship, but a magnificent golden deity capable of almost unimaginable feats of wisdom and magic. When approached from this perspective it will soon become apparent that the "ordination platform movement" was a remarkable phenomenon with extensive ramifications for our understanding of medieval Chinese Buddhism.

Daoxuan and the Ordination Platform Movement in Tang China

Daoxuan's Identity within Medieval Chinese Buddhism

Daoxuan is a very important figure in the history of medieval Chinese Buddhism, but he has been largely overlooked in English-language writings. Any well-read student of Chinese Buddhism knows that he compiled the *Continued Lives of Eminent Monks* (*Xu gaoseng zhuan* 續高僧傳, or XGZ), an encyclopedic collection of monastic biographies and analysis that is a major source for Chinese Buddhism of the sixth and seventh centuries. This is a reference work that all scholars of Six Dynasties and Tang Buddhism use, but which has itself attracted very little interest from scholars writing in English.[1] Daoxuan is also the single most important figure in the Chinese Vinaya tradition. Kenneth Ch'en, who devotes less than a page of his history of Chinese Buddhism to this "minor school," describes him as the school's founder. Following a brief summary of the code of discipline for monks and nuns, Ch'en writes:

> In establishing this school Daoxuan wanted to emphasize the fact that Buddhism meant not merely embracing a set of teachings but also strict adherence to monastic discipline, especially as it concerned the ordination regulations. From the available evidence of the period this school did not seem to have a wide following. (1964, 301, with change of romanization by the editor)

Essentially the same interpretation occurs in André Bareau's article on the schools of Hīnayāna *(sic)* Buddhism in the *Encyclopedia of Religion,* which describes the Vinaya school as having been

> established in the mid-seventh century by the eminent monk Daoxuan as a reaction against the doctrinal disputes that preoccupied Chinese Buddhists at the time. He maintained that moral uprightness and strict

monastic discipline were much more necessary for the religious life
than empty intellectual speculations. Consequently, he imposed on his
followers the well-defined rules in the *Sifen lü* [*Four Part Vinaya*], a
Chinese translation of the Vinaya Piṭaka of the Dharmaguptakas made
by Buddhayaśas and Zhu Fonian in 412. Although his school never had
many adherents of its own, it had a clear and lasting influence on Chinese Buddhism. Thanks to the school's activities, the *Sifen lü* became,
and remains, the sole collection of disciplinary rules to be followed
by all Chinese Buddhist monks regardless of their school, including followers of the Mahāyāna. (ER 1987, 2:455, with change of romanization)

The impression one gets from this very small dose of information is
that Daoxuan was a scholar and disciplinarian. Given Ch'en's references to discipline, regulations, and the limited extent of Daoxuan's
following, we might also infer that he was a scholiast interested
only in historical detail and institutional rectitude, the founder of
a generally unsuccessful sectarian entity little given to resonating
with deeper religious issues. How incorrect such an impression
would be!

To be sure, Daoxuan did not regard himself as the founder of a
new school. This is pointed out in the *Encyclopedia of Religion* by
Stanley Weinstein (1987b), who has written a classic article (1973)
defining the characteristics of the Buddhist "schools" established
during the Sui and Tang dynasties. Weinstein indicates it was only
Daoxuan's fourteenth-generation successor, Yuanzhao 元照 (1048–
1116), who accorded him this status. Although the Vinaya school
had become a distinct lineal tradition with effective control of monastic ordinations by Yuanzhao's time, during his own day Daoxuan was effectively codifying practices based on the dominant
Four Part Vinaya on behalf of the entire Chinese Buddhist order.[2]
He never worked to attract lay followers, which would have been
important for any monk with the ambition to create a lasting following.[3] The vinaya was an important branch of learning for all
Buddhist monks; it was not the sort of thing they would declare
allegiance to in place of some doctrinal or practical interpretation
of Buddhism. Daoxuan's influence as a vinaya master should be
gauged by the fact that all subsequent Chinese monks have observed (or have tried, with varying degrees of success, to observe)
the monastic regulations as he defined them. Indeed, one of the motivations for this volume is the shared observation of the vinaya's remarkable durability throughout the history of East Asian Buddhism.

Even a brief look at Daoxuan's biography reveals a complex

and intriguing individual, with widely varied interests in Buddhist studies, a profound dedication to spiritual practice, and a deep personal involvement in supernormal manifestations of the sacred. He was clearly a dedicated teacher of monastic discipline and the prolific author of texts (on ordination ritual, the correct deportment of monks and nuns, and other related topics) that constitute the fundamental guides for East Asian Buddhist monastic discipline. But he was also very interested in meditation practice, and after his first introduction to vinaya studies he had to be admonished by his teacher for wanting to switch immediately to the cultivation of *dhyāna* (concentration meditation) techniques. He was inspired to write several of his works, most notably the *Further Propagation of Wisdom* (*Guang hongming ji* 廣弘明集) but also the *Continued Lives of Eminent Monks,* because he believed himself to be the reincarnation of Sengyou 僧祐 (445–518), compiler of the *Propagation of Wisdom* (*Hongming ji* 弘明集) and *Tripiṭaka Translation Notes* (*Chu sanzang jiji* 出三藏記集). Throughout his entire life, but with an increasing frequency as he grew older, Daoxuan was interested in the role of supernormal experiences, known in Chinese as *"gantong"* 感通, which can be translated as "experiences of *abhijñā*," or "experiences of sensitivity to transcendent penetration," or simply "revelations." Daoxuan filled his *Continued Lives of Eminent Monks* with signs of the divine power of the Buddhist dharma, and he compiled separate anthologies of such experiences in the lives of Buddhist prelates. More importantly, he was himself increasingly given to visitations by divine emissaries, miraculous expressions of transcendent power, and visions of Buddhas and bodhisattvas.

What I find most intriguing is the manner in which Daoxuan's dual attractions to monastic discipline and the supernatural merged at the very end of his life. In Daoxuan's mind the vinaya, and especially the ordination platform and the ceremonies that take place upon it, represented a profound source of religious charisma, the wellspring of an occult power that derives directly from the Buddha Śākyamuni himself. In brief, the ordination platform is an altar centered on a *caitya* (*zhidi* 制底; i.e., a small reliquary stūpa), which represents the Buddha, and the ordination ritual a process that places its celebrants directly in the presence of the Buddha. And although Daoxuan may not have had a large following per se, his establishment of an ordination platform and sponsorship of what must have been a new style of ordination ritual initiated a movement within Chinese Buddhism that continued at least into the

ninth century and was to have a palpable impact on the development of Buddhism in Korea and Japan as well.[4]

Ōchō Enichi (1941 and 1942) points out that there is a natural
connection between Daoxuan's specialization in the vinaya and his
dependence on visions. Ōchō observes that Daoxuan's vinaya writings would have been impossible without a very intimate knowledge of the Indian monastic system, the layout of its buildings, and
its daily operations. The urge to know these details was a very
deeply felt responsibility for Daoxuan, who collected all the materials he could find and learned as much as he could from Xuanzang
玄奘 (ca. 596–664) and others who had traveled to the western regions and south seas, including not only monks but also Buddhist
laymen and traders. Indeed, as Ōchō reads Daoxuan's quotation of
heavenly beings on the original conditions of Indian Buddhism, he
hears the voices of these nameless laymen and traders reporting
their news to Daoxuan.

In the preface to his description of Jetavana Temple, Daoxuan
writes of his awareness that this temple had been the Buddha's residence for twenty-five years and where he preached many of his
scriptures (specifically the four noble truths, the eightfold path,
and the four Āgamas), leading him to search widely through Buddhist literature to learn more about it. Daoxuan does in fact cite
earlier written sources that are now lost, especially the *Temple Revelations* (*Sigao* 寺誥, e.g., T 45.812c13) and the *Sage's Footprints*
(*Shengji ji* 聖跡記, e.g., T 45.812c17) of the Sui-dynasty monk Ling-
you 靈祐 (518–605; see his biography in XGZ, T 50.494–498). The
first of these texts is interesting for its very Daoist title; the latter
was a collection of biographies indebted somehow to Faxian 法顯
(fl. 414). Daoxuan was troubled by the differences in the various
descriptions of Jetavana, until he suddenly realized that it was a divine location (and thus subject to various manifestations), after
which he was able to write down the summary of his knowledge all
at once. Given this description, Ōchō (1941, 30–31) concludes that
the text was written not as an offhand work of fantasy, but rather as
the accumulation of a lifetime of study.

Daoxuan's Vision of the Ordination Platform at Jetavana

As the culmination of years of inquiry into the nature of the Buddha's residence at Jetavana, in the last year of his life Daoxuan had
a series of revelations that he transcribed in the *Jetavana Temple*

of Vaiśālī in Central India Diagram and Sūtra (Zhong Tianzhu She-weiguo Qihuansi tu jing 中天竺舍衛國祇洹寺圖經, hereafter *Jetavana Diagram)* and used as the basis for the description of his own ordination platform in the *Ordination Platform within the Passes Diagram and Sūtra (Guanzhong chuangli jietan tu jing* 關中創立戒壇圖經, hereafter *Ordination Platform Diagram;* see BK 2.102c–d; Murata 1961). Another visionary work by Daoxuan, the *Vinaya Characteristics Revelations (Lüxiang gantong zhuan* 律相感通傳) confirms that he had frequent visions of gods *(deva)* at the end of the second month of 667. The text identifies the god who responded to his request for a description of Jetavana as Huang Qiong 黃瓊.[5] The *Jetavana Diagram* thus represents Daoxuan's transcription of information learned from Huang Qiong:

> I heard the god relate that Zhang Yu 張與, the third son of the Heavenly King of the South, had written a *Jetavana Temple Diagram* in one hundred fascicles, but this had been summarized in heaven, so that what I have produced here is only an abstract of the original.... The sixteenth son of the Heavenly Lord of the North has written a *Temple Record* (*Jingshe ji* 精舍記) in over five hundred fascicles, which exists in that heaven. (Ōchō 1941, 28; T 45.890a23–28)[6]

This is a very Daoist style of textual reception, given the celestial figures and their role in the revelations; what we are witness to here is the explicit creation of a certain type of Buddhist apocrypha.[7] Daoxuan writes that he was able to relate that which was reflected in the "dark mirror" (*yujing* 幽鏡) and explain what he had learned by means of diagrams. Although the celestial originals and Daoxuan's own diagrams are lost, he provides an extensive, if often unclear, explanation in his *Jetavana Diagram*.

Daoxuan asserts (T 45.808a16–b2) that the ordination platform he describes was in existence during the lifetime of Śākyamuni. When the Buddha was about to enter his final nirvāṇa, the pond next to the platform dried up and the roof tiles on top of it flew away, but when Mahākāśyapa held the First Council and Ānanda recounted the Buddha's teachings after the nirvāṇa, the pond filled with water once again and the roof tiles fell back into place.[8] The Council, not incidentally, was held on the ordination platform itself: Kāśyapa had Maudgalyāyana ring the monastery bell to summon the hundred hundred-million monks, both ordinary and sage, from throughout the world, and they all assembled on the platform to pronounce the four acts *(karman)*.[9] After the transgressions of Piṇḍola and Ānanda were excised, Kāśyapa had Ānanda spread the Buddha's robe *(saṅghāṭī)* on the "high seat" and recite the *Bequeathed Teachings Sūtra* (*Yijiao jing* 遺教經).[10] Listening to this, the great bodhisattvas, arhats, devas, *nāgas,* and the eight types of nonhuman beings were all in tears. Next Kāśyapa spread his sitting mat *(niṣīdana)* in front of Ānanda and did obeisance to him, then circumambulated him three times. Brahmā, the great heavenly king, held a treasure-laden canopy over Ānanda's head; Śakra, who presides over the Heaven of the Thirty-Three on top of Mount Sumeru, placed offerings of the seven precious things before him; and the vanquished tempter Māra gave him a ceremonial flywhisk made of the seven precious things. Māra and Śakra stood in service on either side of the arhat while the Four Heavenly Kings stood at the four corners of Ānanda's seat. Thirty-two attendants followed Kāśyapa to kneel behind Ānanda, and Kāśyapa then moved to face him to inquire of the Dharma.

According to Daoxuan, Kāśyapa next placed thirty-eight hundred questions to Ānanda, which he answered exactly as the Buddha had preached before him. After stating that Ānanda's answers with regard to the ordination platform were the same as those contained in the balance of his text, Daoxuan adds that to the north of the platform was a bell tower four hundred feet tall and in the shape of Mount Sumeru. On it were images of nine dragons from whose mouths poured "waters of merit" to anoint the heads of those being ordained (just as the Buddha had been anointed after being born into his final life). Daoxuan states that this scene was precisely like the coronation ceremonies for wheel-turning kings, so those who take the Buddhist precepts for the first time are likened to the Buddha accepting the rank of dharma king. The illumination they experience from the precious pearl (placed on top of the *caitya* in the center of the platform) brings them a pure bliss. When sages receive the precepts a bodhisattva strikes the bell in the tower, and the sound shaking the trichiliocosm causes evil tendencies to cease; when ordinary people take the precepts a monk strikes the bell, and the sound shakes the small chiliocosm.

Although we might be tempted to think of Daoxuan's vision as a quaint occultism irrelevant to the time of the historical Buddha, this would be to disregard the force such creative imaginations had in the mind of medieval Chinese. We will return to this subject presently, but first we must consider the precedents for Daoxuan's ordination platform in both India and China.

Indian and Chinese Precedents for Daoxuan's Ordination Platform

For the first several centuries of the history of Indian Buddhism there is little evidence at all for ordination platforms per se; ordination merely required a clearly demarcated ritual space that was not to be violated during the ceremony. According to Hirakawa 1962, *sangha* unity was of the utmost importance in Indian Buddhism, and ordination a major ritual event, one that all monks of a given *sangha* were required to attend. Because this was inconvenient where there were large numbers of monks, ordinations were usually held in special areas, identified with fixed boundaries and separate from the ordinary limits of the given *sangha*. Here all monks attended the same biweekly *poṣadha* meeting, during which the monastic rules were publically confirmed. A separate boundary (*jie* 界, *sīmā*) was used to establish a smaller area solely for ordinations. Technically, this area and the monks entering it for ordination ceremonies represented a totally different *sangha* from that within the much larger surrounding *sīmā*, a boundary that might vary to include the given monastic compound during most of the year or, during the summer rainy season, an entire neighborhood of monastic establishments. The ordination area was known in Sanskrit as "*sīmā-maṇḍala*" and in Chinese as "*jiechang*" 界場 (boundary area) or "*jietan*" 界壇 (boundary platform) as well as modern homonyms meaning "precept area" 戒場 and "precept platform" 戒壇.[11] These areas could be relatively small: Ordinations done in border regions were sometimes performed by as few as five fully ordained *bhikṣu*. (The optimum standard called for ten.) Daoxuan points out that the ordination platform had to be large enough to hold twenty-one people: three masters and seven witness monks plus eleven ordinands. In any case, in India, although it may have been convenient to mark the outline of the *sīmā-maṇḍala* in some permanent fashion, either by raising its surface off the ground or by means of a stone railing, there was no intrinsic need for a multilevel platform. As far as I know, there are no archaeological remains of ordination platforms in India.[12]

What little evidence there is for ordination platforms in India comes largely from Daoxuan's own text. For example, in the

ninth month of 667 a foreign monk named Śākyamitra saw Daoxuan's ordination platform and (as Daoxuan himself reports in T
45.808c28 ff) was overjoyed that it resembled those used at all Indian monasteries. The same monk also describes a particular example in Uḍḍiyāna (Swāt valley, Pakistan) that was supposedly more
than two hundred paces square (at two steps per pace), about ten
feet tall, and shaped like Mount Sumeru (i.e., hourglass shaped;
Daoxuan mentions a "stone ordination platform in eastern India"
of the same size in T 45.810b23). These dimensions seem unbeliev-
ably large, even if the figure given refers to the overall circumference. (Ōchō and Murata understand the measurement to represent
the length of each side.) Although the Uḍḍiyāna platform was supposedly composed of only one level and Daoxuan's of three, in other
ways the form was similar to that used by Daoxuan, with columns
at the four corners of the second level bearing images of the Four
Heavenly Kings, niches for images of other deities carved into the
wall of the second level, and a stone wall around the entire structure that had lion columns and posts with *garuḍa* birds (*jinchi niao*
金翅鳥) holding dragons in their mouths. Finally, at the four corners
of the uppermost level were stone lions with holes in their backs for
receiving the poles of a canopy.

Given that the Uḍḍiyāna platform is mentioned in neither
Faxian's nor Xuanzang's travel accounts, the veracity of its existence is questionable (see Murata 1961, 3, which cites T 51.858a18
ff and T 51.882b–884b). Ōchō argues, in fact, that Śākyamitra's information about the ordination platform in Uḍḍiyāna was a stimu-
lus for the configuration of Daoxuan's own platform rather than an
after-the-fact validation. He points out that the foreign monk, who
was originally from Sri Lanka and had resided for some time at
Mahābodhi Temple in India before arriving in China in 664–65,
made his pilgrimage to Mount Wutai in the sixth month of 667 to
worship the Bodhisattva Mañjuśrī. While at Mount Wutai Śākyamitra had a two-level rectangular platform about a foot high constructed for his daily religious practice. Although Daoxuan dates
Śākyamitra's comments on ordination platforms near Chang'an 長
安 and in Uḍḍiyāna after the monk's return from Wutai in the ninth
month, Ōchō argues that Daoxuan must have known about Śākyamitra's activities during his prior three years in Chang'an.

The earliest mention of an "ordination platform" in China is
found in an account of a group of nuns who were ordained on a

boat that was designated as such in 358. There had been some discussion beforehand of establishing an ordination platform—best understood in this context as merely a special area demarcated for the purpose—on land, but the idea was abandoned when a vinaya scholar objected. This account is, by the way, the earliest known ordination of nuns in Chinese history (Ōchō 1941, 23–24).[13] According to Daoxuan, the earliest permanent Chinese ordination platform—in the sense of a specially constructed facility that was maintained for use on a regular basis—was established in the early fifth century at Nanlinsi 南林寺 in Jiankang 建康. The individual most closely associated with this platform is the foreign missionary and translator Guṇavarman (367–431), who arrived in Jiankang in 424, only four years after the temple had been established. Guṇavarman, who resided at Qihuansi 祇洹寺 (Jetavana Temple), translated the *Bodhisattva Stage* (*Pusa shanjie jing* 菩薩善戒經, T no. 1582; see the discussion by Nobuyoshi Yamabe in this volume) as well as other vinaya texts and took a special interest in the ordination of nuns. He left instructions to be cremated in Indian fashion on top of the platform, then buried in a stūpa nearby. Daoxuan offers intriguing details about the Nanlinsi ordination platform: When people doubted that bestowing the precepts on top of such a structure was true to the Dharma and scattered flowers about to test him, Guṇavarman's charisma made those on his seat bloom. And when Guṇavarman's body was cremated on top of the platform, a creature resembling a dragon or snake was seen rising up in the smoke from the pyre. Sources contemporaneous with Guṇavarman's career are lacking, but his legacy in medieval Chinese Buddhism was assured by Daoxuan's *Ordination Platform Diagram* and the thirteenth-century *Buddhas and Ancestors Chronicle* (*Fozu tongji* 佛祖通記, T 49.344c24–29), both of which state that the platform he established was the first in China.[14] It was not, however, the only early ordination platform in southern China; Ōchō (1941, 21) notes the existence of another platform established in Sanwu 三吳 during the Southern Qi regime in 483–493.[15]

Although corroborating evidence is lacking, Daoxuan provides an impressive list (T 45.813c27–814a8) of important monks who supposedly established ordination platforms, the best-known of which include Zhu Fatai 竹法汰 (320–381), Zhi Daolin 支道林 (314–366), Daosheng 道生, Huiguan 慧觀, and Sengyou 僧祐 (T 45.812c20 ff).[16] In all, Daoxuan claims over three hundred ordination platforms were established in southern China, which he says accounts for the vitality of Buddhism there over the preceding five or six hundred years. (Of course, many of these may have been simply ritually demarcated spaces or at least far less imposing structures than that described by Daoxuan.) In a statement that modern scholars will find curious, given our assumptions about the Buddhist affinities of northern non-Chinese peoples and the flourishing state of the religion during the Tang, Daoxuan then adds that the three persecutions of Buddhism in the north and the religion's general decline there were due to the fact that the uncultured northern barbarians had not been good Buddhists and had not followed the vinaya: In his mind, it was native Chinese who were the true Buddhists! Daoxuan was therefore establishing his own ordination platform so as to reverse this negative trend and disseminate Buddhism throughout northern China. His interest in founding a movement of religious revitalization is strongly implied throughout the entire text.[17]

Daoxuan's Own Ordination Platform and the Ceremonies of 667

From the eighth to the fourteenth days of the second month of 667, Daoxuan celebrated the establishment of an ordination platform at Jingyesi 淨業寺, outside Chang'an, and he bestowed the Buddhist precepts on twenty-seven monks there (T 45.807a–19a, esp. 816b20 ff).[18] A large number of important monks from several different regions throughout China attended this event; Daoxuan lists thirty-nine of the attendees, which included such figures as Fazang 法藏 (643–712), later to gain prominence as a patriarch of the Huayan 華嚴 school; Hongjing 弘景 (634–712), a vinaya master from Yuquansi 玉泉寺 in Jingzhou 荊州; and Xuanze 玄賾, who worked on several translation projects and later wrote a seminal Northern Chan text.[19] Because of Daoxuan's stature within the Chinese Buddhist community at the time and his success at gathering famous monks from all over China, these events marked the beginning of a trend to establish ordination platforms and hold public ordination ceremonies that lasted at least into the ninth century.

The ordination platform envisioned by Daoxuan was a massive stone affair of three levels (or five including the central *caitya*), a format virtually unknown outside East Asia (Murata 1961; Ōchō 1941, 27–28; T 45.808c28–9a16).[20] A small image of the platform

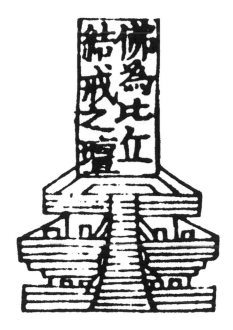

Figure 3.1. Japanese
diagram of Daoxuan's
ordination platform
(T no. 1892.45.813a)

was included in the seventeenth-century Japanese version of Daoxuan's text (reproduced in T 45.813a), but it represents only a small
part of Daoxuan's entire plan for Jetavana and is clearly a simplified
and potentially misleading representation. Nevertheless, because
Daoxuan's own text is so difficult to interpret, it will be useful to
begin with this diminutive image (fig. 3.1).

The three-level structure is made up of three, five, and three
planes per level, with the bottom two levels of equal width and the
top one slightly smaller. These planes may indicate layers of stone;
the middle level seems to consist of the same three planes as the
upper and lower levels, plus two planes beneath the three and of
progressively smaller widths, thus creating the hourglass "Mount
Sumeru" shape characteristic of many Buddhist altar platforms.
The top level is flat, with a deck lower than the three planes that cir-
cumscribe it, suggesting a fence or low wall. The lines on top of the
deck demarcate a rectangular space (depicted as a trapezoid perhaps to impart a sense of depth). Four small rectangles, each at the
front of the two lower levels, probably represent alcoves for images.
(This inference is possible thanks to Daoxuan's description.) In
front of the platform is a stairway leading to the upper level, with
diagonal lines at the tops of the bottom and middle levels indicating

access to the main stairway. Access stairways are not mentioned in Daoxuan's account, so their identification here is speculative.

Daoxuan's description of the ordination platform differs significantly from the Japanese depiction. Here is his initial description of the platform:

> As to the configuration of the ordination platform, its lower two levels are of layered rock, shaped like Sumeru, the king of mountains [i.e., an hourglass shape]. Above and below [or "ascending and descending," *shangxia* 上下] there are placed colored pathways (?, *sedao* 色道), and there are alcoves along all four sides of the body of the platform. Within the alcoves are placed various heavenly kings. On top of each of these two levels are placed stone guardrails, with lions and heavenly kings between the columns underneath the guardrails. At the four corners of the two [lower] levels, tall stone pillars rise up over the platform. Outside of the pillars, on the open ground, are placed images of the Four Heavenly Kings (*si tianwang xiang* 四天王像). [The images] are all made of chiseled stone so as to be long lasting. At the four corners, above the guardrails, are stone *garuḍa* birds, each holding a dragon in its beak. (45.809a5–11)

This description actually applies to the stone platform in Uḍḍīyāna, but Daoxuan states that the structure is identical in form to his own. In any case a far more complex platform than the one depicted in the Japanese woodblock edition is intended, and this is only the beginning!

In Daoxuan's explanation the dimensions of the ordination platform as a whole, as well as its three levels, were scaled to match those of the Buddha's body. For symbolic interpretations Daoxuan uses Indian measurements, but to indicate actual dimensions he doubles these to arrive at Tang-dynasty figures. (Daoxuan frequently expatiates on the symbolic implications of the ordination platform's dimensions, but we will ignore such material here.) According to him the lowest level of the platform was 3 *chi* 尺 (93.3 cm) high, the middle platform 4.5 *chi* (139.95 cm), and the top platform 4 *cun* 寸 (12.44 cm). (One Tang-dynasty *chi* equals 31.1 centimeters; one *cun* is one-tenth of that.) Daoxuan clearly notes the four lions at the four corners of the top level, each with a hole in its back to accept a pole for banners (or, one might suspect, a canopy; 810a27–b1). He also states that the top of the platform is trapezoidal (*cefang* 昃方) and measures 7 *chi* on one side (which side is not stated). All of this is in accord with his description of the ordination platform at Jetavana (T 45.811b7–9). There the lowest level was square and measured 2 *zhang* 丈 9 *chi* 8 *cun* (6.89042 meters) on each side; the middle level (also square) was 2 *zhang* 3 *chi* (6.2933 m). The uppermost level was trapezoidal and measured 7 *chi* (2.177 m) on one side. The top level might seem impossibly small, but as we will see, during the ordination liturgy the ten masters necessary for the ceremony circumambulate the *caitya* at its center and then immediately take up their seats on the second level. At its smallest, the ordination platform must be able to hold twenty-one persons (T 45.810b5–6, 818a9).

Perhaps the most basic difference between Daoxuan's description and the Japanese diagram is that the former posits various sets of steps or stairways on the different levels and a greater number of deities. Actually there are irresoluble contradictions in Daoxuan's account, which refers to different numbers of stairways on the various levels. At one point (810a2) the text even fails the most basic of calculations, referring to two deities each at the head of seven sets of stairs for a total of sixteen! According to Daoxuan, five steps lead from the ground to the top of the lowest level, with two deities on each step. At the four corners of this level are great gods to guard the Buddha's stūpa (809b19–24). On the platform's south face, two stairways lead from the lowest level to the middle level and, on each of the other faces, one stairway (809b24–c1). Similar sets of stairs (two on the south face and one on each of the other faces) lead from the second to the third level. (At one point Daoxuan refers to a north set of stairs on the west face. This would bring the total number of stairways to seven, two on all but one face; see 816b11.) The Four Heavenly Kings grace the corners of the second level (809c1; Daoxuan has perhaps forgotten that these deities also adorn pillars outside the platform structure), and two gods sit on either side of each stairway (809c9).

On the top level sit seven stellar deities (*xingshen* 星神) in alcoves along each of the four sides for a total of 28. In addition, a *caitya* housing relics (*śarīra*) of the Buddha lies at the center of the top level (T 1892, 45.808c4–8 and 810c19–20; T 1899, 45.891a9–12). The *caitya*, which is dome shaped and resembles on overturned pot, and the "priceless pearl" (*wujia baozhu* 無價法珠; *maṇi*, or *maṇiratna*) on top make up the fourth and fifth levels of the ordination platform. Together they symbolize the "five-part Dharmakāya" of the Buddha. The stairs to this level parallel those to the second, but here the low height of the third level indicates that these "stairs" may in fact be gaps in the guardrail marking the boundary of the third level.

The central *caitya* is an important element, and Daoxuan asserts repeatedly that the platform as a whole constituted a stūpa, in effect representing the body of the Buddha himself (T 45.809b7–8, 809c2–3). In the Buddha's original platform, Śakra placed an inverted bowl-shaped reliquary at the center of the top level, and Brahmā put a "priceless pearl" on top of this. After the Buddha's nirvāṇa this pearl disappeared, so Brahmā replaced it with a "bright pearl" (*mingzhu* 明珠), and Śakra added two more pearls. These last two pearls returned to the garden of delight in the Tuṣita heaven after the First Council, so it became the custom not to place pearls on ordination platforms. Daoxuan's platform, however, retains the reliquary.

More than a simple stone structure, the platform includes two lamps, in front, elevated so that their light reaches the top level. Daoxuan specifies that peonies be planted all around and less than 1 *zhang* (3.11 m) from the base, and beyond these eight rows of flowering trees. A path laid with stones (described as a "colored pathway," *sedao*) leads up to the first five steps of the platform; Daoxuan even suggests that this be covered to protect it from rain and wind. Other aspects of the platform can be found in Daoxuan's description of the ordination liturgy that takes place on and around it. His description is tantalizingly detailed and at the same time frustratingly inexact in places; a complete analysis is beyond the scope of the present essay. His liturgical scenario, however, allows us to make the following inferences about the platform's structure: (1) an image of the Buddha is placed in the center of the west face of the platform, on the second level, and probably to the outside of that level. Both masters and ordinands bow to this image at various times throughout the ceremony; (2) on the south face of the second level, and presumably on the inside facing out, are three empty seats for Indian bodhisattva monks who are responsible for making the ordination ceremony possible; and (3) also on the south face of the second level, in the middle, is a single "high seat" and individual places for nine of the ten masters involved in the ceremony (815c23–26). These places are presumably also on the inside of the

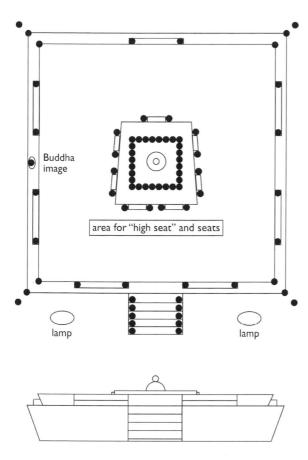

Figure 3.2. Schematic representations of Daoxuan's ordination platform (not to scale). *Top,* bird's-eye view; *bottom,* cross-section view. Drawing by John R. McRae.

second level, that is, just in front of the guardrail around the third level, and face outward.

Figure 3.2 provides a schematic representation of Daoxuan's ordination platform from bird's-eye and cross-section views. The dimensions (height, length, and width) of the three levels are to scale, but those of the trapezoidal third level and the pitch of the first two levels are unknown. The stairways, *caitya,* and deities are only approximations because of contradictions in Daoxuan's reportage. Although lion capitals, posts for banners, and image alcoves are not shown, we should remember that Daoxuan's platform veritably bristled with deities of several varieties. What this limited representation does show, however, is that Daoxuan's design is both architecturally and practically feasible. Even without accounting for minor details (e.g., the width and placement of guardrails), it seems possible that such a structure could have been built and would have been structurally sound. More importantly, the diagrams show that the major ritual celebrants had places on the broad expanse of the second level, and there was enough space for single-file processions on the first level (around the edge of the second level) and the third level (around the central *caitya*).

Ōchō (1941, 36–37) argues that Daoxuan's configuration is based on both Indian and Chinese precedents, and Daoxuan himself notes that the platform he envisioned (and created) is similar to those used in native Chinese contexts. Ōchō suggests that a major impetus for Daoxuan's establishment of his ordination platform was the series of *feng* 封 and *shan* 禪 sacrifices performed on Mount Tai 泰山 by Emperor Gaozong 高宗 (r. 649–683) in early 666. Three platforms were used, two round and one square, and there are some similarities between the square platform and Daoxuan's ordination platform. Daoxuan never refers to the sacrifices in his writings, but he was aware of the altars used (808b24–25). Ōchō goes on to provide several reasons for linking the two events. First, there is the coincidence of the time and place of Daoxuan's ceremonies and certain imperial rites associated with the *feng* and *shan* sacrifices. Second, Daoxuan's platform incorporates images of various protective deities that are similar to the ones used on the imperial altars. Third, his square three-level platform differs from the much larger two-level Uḍḍiyāna platform but resembles one of the imperial platforms. Daoxuan's platform has twelve steps leading up from the south as does the square platform at Mount Tai. An octagonal platform on Moung Song 嵩山 was used in the imperial ceremonies, which reminds Ōchō of a similar platform seen by Ennin 圓仁 (794–864) at Zhulinsi 竹林寺 on Mount Wutai. Fourth, Daoxuan writes that an ordination platform could be made of either stone (as at Uḍḍiyāna) or sand (as in China, where imperial platforms were constructed of earth). Although I do not find all of Ōchō's arguments convincing, it is clear that the notion of the ordination platform as a raised earthen or stone dais is derived from Chinese rather than Indian culture.[21]

In the Wake of Daoxuan

One of the intriguing features of the "ordination platform movement"—if we consider it to be a set of related events propelled by similar forces—is that it continued with precious little concern for Daoxuan's own prescriptions regarding the size and shape of the ordination platform itself. The great pilgrim and translator Yijing 義浄 (635–713, often romanized as I-tsing), who left China in 671 and returned to Luoyang 洛陽 in 695, questioned Daoxuan's configuration of the ordination platform. Yijing had lived at Nālandā for ten years, and he reported that nothing like Daoxuan's ordination platform was used there. In his *Lives of Eminent Monks Who Sought the Dharma* (*Qiufa gaoseng zhuan* 求法高僧傳, T 51.6a15–16; cited in Ōchō 1942, 35–36), written in Sumatra before his return to China, Yijing states: "I recall that a person in the capital [Chang'an] once produced a likeness of Jetavana-ārāma, but it was totally inaccurate." The description of the ordination platform at Nālandā in Yijing's text is very brief, but obviously completely different from Daoxuan's design: Yijing describes a square measuring more than one *zhang* (3.11 m) on each side, covered with layered bricks, and enclosed by a wall a bit more than two feet high. Within the wall is a seat five inches tall and in the middle of it, a small *caitya*.

There is also additional negative evidence in the biographies of pilgrims written by Yijing in Sumatra, prior to his return to China. A monk named Zhen'gu 貞固 established an ordination platform shortly after Daoxuan's death on Mount Xia 峽山, north of Guangdong 廣東. Zhen'gu was a second-generation disciple of Daoxuan, through Zhouxiu 周秀, but he also traveled with Yijing to what is now Sumatra (*Foshi* 佛誓; Ōchō 1942, 33–34; T 51.10b15–11c20, esp. 11a19–21).[22] The text refers to Zhen'gu building a "Chan alcove" behind the ordination platform, where he established a "Vaipulya training center" (*fangdeng daochang* 方等道場) and practiced the Lotus Samādhi. Only an ordination platform of the size visualized by Daoxuan could have been large enough to accommodate such an alcove, which presumably took the place of one of the deity alcoves in the original design. We should also pay attention to this early occurrence of the term "Vaipulya training center," presumably identical with "Vaipulya ordination platform" (*fangdeng jietan*), which is best understood as a place where anyone could gain ordination with a declaration of *bodhicitta* (aspiration for awakening), regardless of impediments (such as crippling injuries) that would have excluded them according to the Indian vinaya.[23]

We should not forget that Yijing was also a vinaya specialist who translated a substantial body of *Mūlasarvāstivāda Vinaya* texts.

Hence it is not surprising that he participated in the construction of a new ordination platform at Shaolinsi 少林寺 on Mount Song 嵩山, outside Luoyang, in 704. In fact an older platform was eliminated in favor of a newly configured one undoubtedly based on Yijing's understanding of the vinaya: The event, which occurred on the seventh day of the fourth month, is described as the "release of the old and demarcation of the new" (*jieqiu jiexin* 解舊結新). The date selected for the dedication of the new platform was a propitious one—just prior to the Buddha's birthday—so more than a hundred prominent monks from Luoyang supposedly practiced at the site for a full month. One indication of the fluidity of lineage loyalties in medieval China is the participation of one of Daoxuan's own students in the ceremonies at Shaolinsi dedicated to the revision of his master's ideas (see Yijing, *Shaolinsi jietan ming* 少林寺戒壇銘, QQT 914.5a–b, 19.12015a).[24]

The construction of the platform at Shaolinsi was only the beginning. In 708 an ordination platform was in place at Shijisi 實際寺 in Chang'an; the famous vinaya specialist Jianzhen 鑑眞 (688–763; J. Ganjin) was ordained here with the influential Hongjing as his master (Ōchō 1942, 41). Then, sometime before his death in 727, the brilliant polymath Yixing 義行 (683–727) and an otherwise unknown vinaya master established an ordination platform at Huishansi 會善寺, also on Mount Song (Ikeda 1988, 107–150). Although we cannot be certain, it is very likely that the platform was built sometime during the years 716–723. We can place Yixing in the area thanks to a text that commemorates the arrival of his esoteric Buddhist master Śubhākarasiṃha (637–735) in Chang'an in 716. The text contains the teachings of Śubhākarasiṃha as addressed to a Northern school Chan monk who resided at Huishansi, Jingxian 景(敬)賢 (d. 723; see McRae 1986, 63–64).[25] Yixing's ordination platform was called the "Five Buddhas' Correct Thought Ordination Platform" (*wufo zheng siwei jietan* 五佛正思惟戒壇), an intriguing title in itself. The exact configuration of this platform is unknown, but Yixing's newly adopted teacher, Śubhākarasiṃha, who had been interested in Mahāyāna scriptures since the early days of his career, once lived at Nālandā. Thus we may assume that the configuration of the platform used by Śubhākarasiṃha and Yixing was similar to Yijing's.[26]

In 724 yet another ordination platform was established, this time by the esoteric master Vajrabodhi (671–741; arrived in

Chang'an in 720) at Guangfusi 廣福寺 in Luoyang, known as the "Sarvāstivāda Stone Ordination Platform" (*yiqieyoubu shijietan* 一切有部石戒壇). Like Yijing, Vajrabodhi had traveled through the south seas on his way to China, and he was trained in the *Mūlasarvāstivāda Vinaya*. Full ordination was bestowed on Vajrabodhi's student Amoghavajra (705–774) at Guangfusi (Ikeda 1988, 124). We also must consider Yinzong 印宗 (627–713), best known for his role in the ordination of Huineng 慧能 (638–713), the legendary "sixth patriarch" of Chan. Yinzong was active in the construction of ordination platforms and the supervision of ordination ceremonies. According to the *Song Lives of Eminent Monks* (*Song gaoseng zhuan* 宋高僧傳, or SGZ), he supposedly began this activity in his native Kuaiji 會稽 after first studying with Hongren 弘忍 (601–674), Huineng's teacher and the traditionally recognized fifth patriarch of Chan. After administering the precepts to great numbers of people there, Yinzong accepted an invitation to the imperial palace, where he constructed a great image of the future Buddha Maitreya.[27] At the emperor's request he continued to establish ordination platforms at various monasteries in the Jiangdong 江東 (east of the Yangzi 揚子 River) or lower Yangzi area. It is of course possible that Yinzong's biography was embellished given his connection with Huineng, but the *Song Lives of Eminent Monks* account seems to be based on an epitaph by a contemporary of Yinzong's from Kuaiji. The sources suggest that Yinzong was initially a *Nirvāṇa Sūtra* specialist who only took up his calling regarding ordination platforms and the bestowal of the precepts after studying with Hongren and Huineng, but it is also possible that the *Platform Sūtra* was given its title on the basis of Yinzong's reputation in these endeavors (see T 50.731b8–26).[28]

We also have information about two monks who, just a few decades after Yinzong, combined both the Chan and vinaya traditions by specializing in bestowing large numbers of bodhisattva ordinations on both the *sangha* and the laity. Xuanyan 玄儼 (675–742) is known to have "bestowed the Dharma" on more than ten thousand people in the area of modern Jiangsu 江蘇 and Zhejiang 浙江, to have led more than one hundred recitations of the *Buddhas' Names Sūtra* (*Foming jing* 佛名經), and to have held more than ten "unrestricted great assemblies" (*wuzhe dahui* 無遮大會). It was said of him that "the realm he had achieved was beyond comparison, and to receive the teachings from him was equivalent to hearing them from the mouth of the Buddha." This claim of religious authority equivalent to the Buddha's is particularly noteworthy because it parallels a similar assertion long made within the meditation tradition. Moreover, Xuanyan's student Dayi 大義 (691–779) supposedly ascended the ordination platform twenty-seven times and had more than thirty thousand "disciples who [had] received the precepts."[29] In this context we should also remember the activities of Jianzhen prior to his travels across the treacherous seas to Japan.[30]

In 743 a new ordination platform was established at Yanxiangsi 延詳寺 on Mount Luofu 羅福山, Guangdong. At about this time, or at least by 744, a platform was established at Fahuasi 法華寺 on Mount Qinwang 秦望山 (Zhejiang). In 750 a "Sweet Dew (ganlu 甘露) Ordination Platform" was established at Donglinsi 東林寺, Huiyuan's 慧遠 (334–416) famous temple on Mount Lu 盧山. In 765 a "Vaipulya [Extensive] Ordination Platform" was established at Da Xingshansi 大興善寺 in Chang'an, and in the same year a system was adopted whereby ten prominent monks and nuns were appointed to serve on a rotating basis as supervisors of ordinations (lintan dade 臨壇大德). In 767 the ordination platform at Huishansi was reestablished (or perhaps rededicated). In 771 ordination platforms were established at the Longxingsi 龍興寺 in Hongzhou 洪州 (Nanchang xian, Jiangxi 江西省南昌縣) and at the Baoyingsi 報應寺 in Fuzhou 撫州 (Linquan xian 臨川縣, Jiangsi). During the years 766–779 platforms appeared at three sites in Sichuan 四川 and one in Zheyang 浙陽 (presumably the northern side of the Zhe River, which empties into Hangzhou Bay 杭州湾). This flurry of activity continued well into the mid-ninth century, with new ordination platforms being established (or reestablished) in and around the capitals and in the provinces (Ōchō 1943, 43–46).

All of this construction took place, of course, in the context of a changing Chinese socioeconomic system. Jacques Gernet (1995) introduces many of the historical sources pertinent to the economics of the ordination platform movement in the Tang, emphasizing the negative long-term impact of the sale of ordinations on both the Chinese state and the Buddhist church. The Tang state used Shenhui and other monks to collect ordination fees during the An Lushan rebellion, and from at least the early years of the ninth century it became profitable for regional authorities to follow the state's example.[31]

Conclusion: The Religious Power of the Ordination Platform

The Motivations and Symbolism of Daoxuan's Ordination Platform

The overall dimensions of the "ordination platform movement" that Daoxuan intiated should now be clear, but what was his motivation? Why did Daoxuan have visions and establish his ordination platform in 667, and what was he trying to achieve? What were the motivations and goals of Yijing, Yixing, and others who followed, not always faithfully, in his footsteps? Although we will not be able answer any of these questions authoritatively, we should be able to make more or less educated guesses.

Ōchō Enichi states that Daoxuan's activities of 667 were inspired by the imperial sacrifices undertaken on Mount Tai the previous year; there is no direct evidence for this, but his argument seems likely enough. Daoxuan undoubtably incorporated Chinese characteristics into the design of his ordination platform, and it seems entirely reasonable that he was inspired by the imperial sacrifices. We might even infer that he was attempting something as significant for the *sangha* and the Buddhist community as the sacrifices were for the imperial family and state. The overall tenor of his actions implies an intended relegitimation of the Chinese Buddhist *sangha*, the reauthentication of the *sangha*'s connections with the Buddha Śākyamuni. Daoxuan might also have wanted to counter any doubts about ordination legitimacy stemming from positions taken by the translator and pilgrim Xuanzang. We know that a monk named Fachong 法沖 (589–665?) objected to Xuanzang's restrictions on lecturing on older translations of Yogācāra texts such as the *Laṅkāvatāra Sūtra*. Fachong grumbled that Xuanzang's own ordination was based on old translations; if Xuanzang objected to their use, Fachong argued, he should laicize and be reordained according to the new translations (T 2060, 666c17–19). We might wonder whether Xuanzang's rather stiff sense of doctrinal correctness also extended to ordination practice itself, setting the stage for Daoxuan's visions and activities of just a few years later.

As we have seen Daoxuan was a distinctly monkish monk, concerned only with the life and vitality of the Buddhist order, and his focus would naturally have been on the *sangha*. But still, what was

he trying to accomplish? Daoxuan clearly sought to locate his ordinations (and reordinations) in the very presence of the Buddha.[32]
Not only did he intend his ordination platform to be an exact copy
of the Buddha's, but he also designed it so that the Buddha is
actually present during each and every ordination. According to
the vinaya regulations the validity of an ordination depends on the
proper ordinations of the officiants; Daoxuan backed this up by
having the Buddha on the ordination platform during the ceremony. Although Yijing and others disagreed with Daoxuan over the
proper configuration of the ordination platform, they seem to have
agreed with him in this crucial point.

How do we know this? In an abstract sense the Buddha exists
on the ordination platform because here the direct lineage of succession from the Buddha (as represented by the ordination) is
preserved. A sense of lineage was developing within the Chan movement at this time, and it is reasonable to note a shared emphasis
among specialists in Chan, vinaya, and, shortly, esoteric Buddhism.
The oldest lineage schemata recorded in Chinese Buddhist literature derive from the *Sarvāstivāda Vinaya* school, and the ideology
of the Chan patriarchate as it developed in the late seventh and
early eighth centuries was based on the same notion of direct, personal transmission as vinaya lineages and monastic ordinations
(McRae 1986, 79–80). This sense of filiation with the Buddha must
have been further enforced with the arrival of Śubhākarasiṃha and
Vajrabodhi, who introduced esoteric rituals involving visualized
identification with the Buddha.

In a more concrete sense the Buddha is present on the ordination platform in the form of relics. As noted above, the ordination
platform described by Daoxuan is an elaborate stūpa structure.[33]
There were five tiers in all: three platform levels, the *caitya* reliquary, and the pearl in the center of the top level. Yijing's ordination platform also had a small *caitya* in the center. In addition to
describing the ordination platform as a stūpa, Daoxuan equates the
five tiers of the platform with the "five-part *dharmakāya*," or the
dharmakāya that is equipped with the five untainted *skandhas* of
morality, meditation, wisdom, emancipation, and the cognition of
emancipation. The term "five-part *dharmakāya*" is both venerable
and widely used, going back to the Āgamas and occurring in a variety of Nikāya and Mahāyāna contexts, both as a description of the
goal of enlightenment and as praise for the Buddha's accomplish-

ment (see BD 2.1288a–c; and Daoxuan in T 45.808c3–7, 810b11–12). Daoxuan is the first writer in Chinese, or perhaps any language, to explicitly link the five pure *skandhas* with the five levels of the stūpa form.[34]

What is so striking about this is that just a few years after Daoxuan's description of the ordination platform, the esoteric Buddhist masters Śubhākarasiṃha and Amoghavajra used the symbolism of the five-part *dharmakāya* to describe the "five-wheeled stūpa" (*wu-lun ta* 五輪塔). One translation by Śubhākarasiṃha, who arrived in Chang'an in 716, states:

> The gates of the three mysteries—the actions of body, speech, and mind—are transformed into the *dharmakāya* and its three mysteries. The five wheels are the five wheels of wisdom; the five wisdoms are made into the five-part [*dharma*]-*kāya*. (T 19.368b14–15)

The same text includes diagrams of the five-wheeled stūpa, which is composed of square, circular, triangular, half-moon, and semicircular shapes that symbolize the five elements of earth, water, fire, wind, and space. According to this text, the *dharmakāya-mudrā* of Mahāvairocana allows one to become complete in the five-part *dharmakāya;* other works equate the five "wheels" of the stūpa with both the five elements and the five wisdoms achieved by the Tathāgata (T 19.371c15–16).[35]

It is unclear how much of this symbolism was known to Daoxuan. A great deal of information was already present in Chinese sources and available before the systematization of the esoteric teachings by Śubhākarasiṃha, Vajrabodhi, and Amoghavajra. (For discussions of esoteric translations by Xuanzang and his contemporaries, see Ōmura 1972b, 207–212, and Osabe 1971, 17 and 38). At this point, we should also note the name of Yixing's ordination platform: "Ordination Platform of the Correct Thought of the Five Buddhas." "Correct thought" was originally one component of the eightfold path, but here it refers to the Buddha's final nirvāṇa. This ordination platform was located on Mount Song, where a former sage had, in the time of the Han or Jin dynasties, planted *śāla* trees, which bloomed three times a season. Because the Buddha himself had entered nirvāṇa under a *śāla* tree, this spot on Mount Song was thought to be uniquely powerful and divine.[36] "Five Buddhas" is not explained in the text describing Yixing's ordination platform, but it is a standard esoteric term referring to both the five Buddhas who reside at the center of the two major maṇḍalas and the five wisdoms they represent. In other words, Yixing's title neatly encapsulates the same fundamental idea present in Daoxuan's mind at the establishment of his own platform: On the ordination platform one is in the direct presence of the Buddha, or in this case, the five Buddhas (see *Mikkyō daijiten*, 2:633c–34a).

Finally, we should note the time at which Daoxuan chose to inaugurate his ordination platform: The ceremonies began on the eighth day of the second month and ended six days later, just before the anniversary of the Buddha's final *parinirvāṇa* as celebrated in East Asia (and the date of Huineng's ordination as related in the *Platform Sūtra*). The timing is not unusual for any important Buddhist ceremony, but in this case it was no doubt selected to link the proceedings as closely as possible with Śākyamuni himself. As for Yijing's platform, it was dedicated on the seventh day of the fourth month. The event was followed by a month of religious practice that presumably began on the following day, the eighth, which is celebrated in East Asia as the anniversary of the Buddha's birth.[37]

About the Ordination Platform Movement

I believe we have marshalled enough data here to use the term "ordination platform movement" without reservation. Its characteristics can now be given as follows:

Daoxuan provided the initial impetus for this movement with his revelation and establishment of an ordination platform in 667. In his mind what was required was the relegitimation of the Chinese Buddhist *saṅgha,* and he set about doing this by devising a framework in which ordinations would be certified by the presence of the Buddha himself.

Subsequent participants in this movement fall into two overlapping categories. Elite monks, especially pilgrims to and missionaries from foreign lands, were the more prominent of the two and received support from the imperial state. Although they may not have perceived the need for the relegitimation of the Buddhist *saṅgha* in Daoxuan's terms, they did take advantage of the new religious format to spread their teachings and solicit the support and participation of their patrons. The second category of participants included monks such as Yinzong who, while no strangers to imperial patronage, became better known for their efforts in bestowing the bodhisattva precepts on large numbers of laypeople. We cannot tell where these monks placed their primary emphasis: on the large numbers of bodhisattva precepts bestowed or on the presumably much smaller numbers of full monastic ordinations they conferred.

Although we do not have detailed information on most of the participants in this movement, it is probable that they derived great advantage from imputing significant religious power to both the ordination platform and its rituals. Those involved may not have accepted Daoxuan's revelations regarding the relationship of the ordination platform to the Buddha's magical realm at Jetavana, but they all partook of similar sorts of belief.

Several ordination platforms seem to have been designed to emphasize the intimate presence of the Buddha. These should be considered along with the fact that the vinaya, Chan, and esoteric traditions from which the participants in this movement derived all emphasized direct lineal succession from the Buddha.

In the last quarter of the eighth century, the movement began to experience numerous changes, namely, the establishment of ordination platforms in provincial cities, increased emphasis on financial gain for the state or provincial ordination platform sponsor, and an upsurge in state control of ordinations.

Notes

1. For an excellent study of Chinese Buddhist hagiography in the "lives of eminent monks" genre, see Kieschnick 1997. Also see Shinohara 1990, 1991a, 1991b, 1994a, and 1994b. The most useful source for Daoxuan is probably Satō Tatsugen 1986 (67–298). There is no single entry for Daoxuan himself in either ER or Hinnells 1991. Most of the dozen or so entries for Daoxuan in ER are citations of the XGZ, but there is no discussion of the importance of the text itself, which was perhaps deemed by the editors as "only" historical and biographical. As Kenneth Ch'en (1964, 192, 248, and 515) points out in his long-useful textbook on Chinese Buddhism, Daoxuan compiled at least two other texts of great historical interest: the *Further Elucidation of Faith* (*Guang hongming ji* 廣弘明記) and *Annals of Buddhist-Daoist Controversy* (*Fodao lunheng* 佛道論衡).

2. Weinstein 1987b points out that the *Four Part Vinaya* had already become universally accepted by the beginning of the Tang. On its Dharmaguptaka background, see Gómez 1987. For further information on the formation of the Chinese Vinaya school, see Satō Tatsugen 1993. Weinstein (1987a, 62–63) points out that the An Lushan rebellion of 755–763 was apparently devastating to the continuation of Vinaya studies: From the time when the "elitist" Faxiang (i.e., Chinese Yogācāra)

school disappeared completely, and Huayan, Chan, and Pure Land continued with a definite "popular" character, no significant works by Vinaya monks survive. There is no evidence that Daoxuan was ever interested in creating a "following," much less a "school," no matter how the term is defined.

3. One of the interesting things Yamazaki (1967, 162–163) observes is that there are no prominent laymen listed anywhere in association with Daoxuan's biography. It was not the case that Daoxuan had no contact with elite society: For example, he was an important figure in the defense of Buddhism at court in 662 (see Weinstein 1987a, 32–33; McRae 1986, 49). Yamazaki is clearly puzzled by Daoxuan's apparent failure to cultivate lay supporters, which can be taken not only as evidence for his lack of interest in founding a following or school, but also as an indication that he lived in a supernatural world populated primarily by monks and spirit bodhisattvas and Buddhas, as we shall see below.

4. For general information on ordination platforms, see BD 1:391a–392b. Yanagida (1985, 394) cites his earlier article (1964) to restate his opinion that the essay on vinaya in XGZ 22 includes the oldest usage of the term *tanchang* 壇場 for "ordination platform." The same usage occurs in the *Lidai fabao ji* 歷代法寶記 (see Yanagida 1967, 154). In his notes, Yanagida (1967, 159) mentions an identical usage in the epitaph (written in 804) for Nanyue Banzhou 南嶽般舟 in fascicle seven of Liu Zongyuan's 柳宗元 literary collection (see Liu 1961, 1:103–105).

5. Huang Qiong was an official during the Latter Han dynasty who is known in Daoist sources as a minister of works (*sikong* 司空). His daughter Jinghua 景華, or Lady Xiechen 協辰夫人, seems better known, however, because she is mentioned in the following Daoist sources: the *Maoshan zhi* 茅山志, 14.1a (HY 304; DZ 9.0193a); the *Yunji qiqian* 雲笈七籤, 115.4b; and the *Lishi zhenxian tidao tongqian houji* 歷世眞仙體道統鑒後集, 4.2a ff. Thanks are due Robert Campany for alerting me to these citations.

6. On Zhang Yu, see Li 1959 (fasc. 91, 2.604) or Kao 1991 (1.1237). The anecdote is not directly relevant here, but it does poke fun at Daoxuan's reputation for displinary strictness.

7. Daoxuan would certainly not have liked his texts to be characterized in this fashion, in part because they were not anonymous but more importantly because of his very strong views on the evils of Buddhist forgeries (see Tokuno 1990, 48–50).

8. Daoxuan's description (T 45.808b2–3) does not otherwise mention a roof; perhaps the tiles were on top of the platform? For convenience, I have rearranged and abbreviated Daoxuan's narrative (see T 45.808a16–b3). The water, incidentally, was white like milk but flavorless; Daoxuan relates this to the *Nirvāṇa Sūtra*'s metaphor of milk and water.

9. In vinaya contexts "karma" refers to any ritual endeavor; I use the form *"karman"* to indicate this special usage. To "pronounce the four acts" is to repent any outstanding transgressions orally, then perform a threefold repentance ritual. See Ryūkoku Daigaku 1972, 2.1461b.

10. Piṇḍola had demonstrated his supernormal powers and was banished from Jambudvīpa by the Buddha; Ānanda had refrained from asking the Buddha to live forever, had stepped on the Buddha's rain cloak, and had persuaded him to allow women to enter the order. For the stories involving Piṇḍola (probably not he of the sixteen arhats, although the identities may have been confused), see BD 4.4334a–35a.

11. The term *"jiechang"* occurs 348 times in the Chinese portion of the *Taishō* canon (vols. 1–55 and 85), including 21 times in the *Four Part Vinaya* and 52 times in Daoxuan's commentary; the term *"jietan"* occurs 400 times in all but not in the *Four Part Vinaya* and only 4 times in Daoxuan's commentary.

12. Indian ordination platforms would be easily overlooked and their remains may have gone unnoticed. Despite elements such as a circumferential fence and lion-shaped canopy supports suspiciously reminiscent of Chinese palace architecture, Daoxuan does provide some evidence (suggests Murata) that the entire structure was clearly that of the Gandhāran style of stūpa. The two-foot-tall ordination platform at Nālandā observed by the pilgrim and translator Yijing 義淨 (635–713), although of only one level, had a small *caitya* in the center. Because this reportage is independent of Daoxuan's (Yijing was at Nālandā around 676–685), Murata infers that in both India and Gandhāra stūpas were used as ordination platforms. There is also evidence for the existence in India up to about the seventh century of *"caitya* halls," which were used for explaining the vinaya regulations and holding *poṣadha* meetings and, no doubt, ordination ceremonies (see Murata 1961, p. 3, which cites a 1925 article by Matsumoto Bunzaburō 松本文三郎 in *Shirin* 史林 9, no. 1). Murata speculates that the custom of holding ordinations in close proximity to stūpas was established through the use of halls such as these, thus facilitating the switch to the use of stūpas as ordination platforms. Unfortunately, Matsumoto's sources are not given.

13. According to the *Lives of Nuns* (*Biqiuni zhuan* 比丘尼傳, T 934c3–35a5) entry for the nun Jingjian 淨撿 (290–359?) of Zhulinsi 竹林寺, while in Yuezhi territory during the years 335–342 the monk Sengjian 僧建 acquired the *Mahāsāṅghika Karmans for Nuns and Precept Text* (*Sengqini jiemo ji jieben* 僧祇尼羯磨及戒本), which he translated in 358 in Luoyang 洛陽. He then asked the foreign monk Dharmagupta (Tanmojieduo 曇摩羯多) to establish an ordination platform, but the Chinese monk Daozhang 道場 criticized this plan on the basis of the *Precepts Background Sūtra* (*Jie yinyuan jing* 戒因緣經), a text that is otherwise unknown. As a result the monks "floated a boat on the Si 泗 [River]," and Jingjian and three others took the ordination on the "same platform." Daoxuan also discusses ordination on a boat in his *Ordination Platform Diagram*, when he says that the monk Huiyi 慧義 of Qihuansi, after discussing the matter with Saṅghavarman, ordained his disciple Huiji 慧基 (412–496) and others on a boat at Caizhou 蔡州. The *Lives of Eminent Monks* entry (T 50.379a) for Huiji mentions that he was ordained in Caizhou at age twenty (i.e., approximately in 421) but does not mention that the ceremony occurred on a boat; Daoxuan must have had some other source.

14. The *Fozu tongji* has Guṇavarman establishing this ordination platform in 434, but other sources state that he died in 431.

15. Although no other evidence is available, Ōchō speculates that this platform was probably established by either Faxian 法獻 or Xuanchang 玄暢, two prominent monks of the time, the former associated with Sanwu and the latter known to have taught the vinaya. Ōchō (1941, 17–18) points out that the *Da Song sengshi lüe* 大宋僧史略 (T no. 2126) by Zanning 贊寧 (919–1001) asserts that Dharmakāla and two other monks active during the years 254–256 of the Wei regime initiated the use of ordination platforms in Luoyang, but no specific platform is mentioned. As a late source, the *Sengshi lüe* cannot be taken as authoritive without corroboration or at least believable detail; Dharmakāla's *Lives of Eminent Monks* entry (T 50.324c15–

25a6; 26b14–c1) describes his translations of vinaya texts but does not mention an ordination platform (see BD 4.3969b–c; 3568c–3569a).

16. Ōchō (1958, 48–52) discusses several of the early figures Daoxuan cites—Zhu Fatai, Zhi Daolin, Zhi Facun (probably Zhu Facun), Zhu Daoyi, and Zhu Daosheng—and the possibility that they established ordination platforms. Ōchō's concludes that there is no evidence, and also no likelihood of the platforms having been established at all. Yanagida (1985, 616 n. 392) refers to Ōchō 1979 (presumably a reprint of Ōchō 1941 and 1942), which he apparently summarizes on p. 405, indicating the innovative nature of Daoxuan's visions, the relevance of platforms in non-Buddhist Chinese contexts, and the impact of esoteric Buddhism with its newly introduced altars. On p. 406, Yanagida points out the significance of Daoxuan referring to his texts as *"jing"* 經 (sūtras), implying they were more than his own creations. See Yanagida 1985 (616 n. 393) on the very specific Daoist antecedents to ordination platforms. Stephen Bokenkamp has also provided me with references to primary sources for these Daoist antecedents, which I have not been able to consider here.

17. Also see Daoxuan's general essay on vinaya masters in the XGZ, in which he refers to the Six Dynasties' establishment of ordination platforms at various locations and their usefulness to "lines of monks like geese" (T 50.621b23), implying an impact on rectifying the religious chaos of the times.

18. The opening date is given in T 45.816b20 and the closing date in 819a9–10. Yanagida (1985, 405) says that two ceremonies were held in the second and fourth months, but the latter is presumably a reference to a ceremony held in Jingzhou 荊州 (see T 45.818c4 ff).

19. No reference should be necessary for Fazang. Hongjing was involved in both the Vinaya and Tiantai traditions (Yanagida 1967, 199–200 and 210 n. 16; Ikeda 1990, 71–113). (I am grateful to Professor Aramaki Noritoshi 荒牧典俊 for providing me with photocopies of Ikeda's work.) Hongjing is mentioned below as the preceptor of Jianzhen (J. Ganjin). On Xuanze, see McRae 1986, 59–60. Also listed (T 45.817a3) is one Chan Master Xingtao 行滔 of Kongguansi 空觀寺 in Chang'an; no figure corresponding to this monk appears in the XGZ or SGZ, but the name is suspiciously identical to the name given to Huineng's father and to the monk who attended Huineng's stūpa in the *Platform Sūtra* (see Komazawa Daigaku 1978, 369).

20. Because subsequent ordination platforms deviate significantly from Daoxuan's configuration or are not described in any detail, it is not of primary importance to reconstruct Daoxuan's precise configuration, which is difficult to follow at several points. Unless otherwise noted, for convenience I have followed Murata's summary. The drawing included in T 45.812–813, and virtually identical to that in Forte 1988 (fig. 1), depicts two ordination platforms (envisioned by Daoxuan to be at Jetavana Temple during the lifetime of the Buddha) that look rather like three-story parking garages, with ramps leading up the front. Obviously, the drawings were done later and without close study of Daoxuan's text.

21. Ōchō also suggests a similarity between the ordination platform's being based on the Buddha's bodily dimensions and the imperial platform's use of ancient standards of length, but the comparison is not compelling. He also errs in stating that the Uḍḍiyāna platform lacked protective deities around its circumference. See Daoxuan's report of Śakyamitra's comments in T 45.808c28–809a16; Ōchō also consults Huixiang's 慧祥 *Gu Qingliang zhuan* 古清凉傳 (T 51.1098c18–1099c13) for its descrip-

tion of Śākyamitra's on Mount Wutai. For an account of the imperial *feng* and *shan* sacrifices, especially those of 666, see Wechsler 1985 (170–194), especially his description of the platforms used (179, 185–186).

22. Ōchō also mentions Wuxing 無行 (see his biography in T 51.921–10a13), who was one of the twenty-seven who received ordination in 667 and the author of an "encomium on *śarīra*" (*sheli zan* 舍利贊) included in Daoxuan's *Ordination Platform Diagram* (T 45.818c4–20). He was also a second-generation disciple of the great Sanlun master Jizang 吉藏 (549–623) and a pilgrim to Sri Lanka, Nālandā, and other parts of India. Ōchō considers Wuxing's travels in terms of a member of Daoxuan's lineage interested in seeing Indian ordination platforms for himself, and he implies that the lack of any testimony on the matter is negative evidence for the accuracy of Daoxuan's description. Ōchō (1942, 34–35) discusses the ordination platform said to have existed or been established in 676 at Zhizhisi 制旨寺 in Guangdong, according to the *Guangxiaosi yifa taji* 光孝寺瘞髮塔記 attributed to Facai 法才 of Faxingsi 法性寺 (QQT 912; see Yanagida 1967, 535–536). According to this text the ordination platform was established by Guṇabhadra during the Song dynasty, and in 502 the Indian Tripiṭaka Master Zhiyao 智藥 planted a single bodhi tree in front of it and erected an inscription. Both foreign masters predicted that a living bodhisattva would come to the spot, a prophecy that was fulfilled by the arrival of Huineng, his answer regarding the moving temple banner, and his ordination by Yinzong. The SGZ includes the story, but with the names changed to Guṇavarman, Paramārtha, and Vinaya Master Zhiguang 智光律師. Ōchō points out that the information on the foreign masters and Zhiguang is specious or unverifiable, but that concerning Yinzong may be accurate. I would add that the accuracy of this text is highly questionable and that it represents an early stage in the creation of the fictional legend of Huineng. Therefore I have not considered it here.

23. Gernet (1995, 334 n. 171) cites the *Da Song sengshi lüe* to the effect that "all that is required [on these ordination platforms] is that [the postulant] has produced the spirit of *bodhi*." This observation harbors important ramifications that Gernet ironically fails to notice (see McRae 1993–1994). Note that Michihata 1970 (108–111) contains a brief discussion of Chinese bodhisattva ordination platforms; see p. 109 for reference to the establishment of the *vaipulya* ordination platform mentioned here. (For a longer treatment, see Michihata 1972, 589–607.)

24. The student mentioned is Mingke 命恪, one of the twenty-seven ordained at Daoxuan's ceremonies in 667 (T 45.817a2; see Ikeda 1988, 122). Ōchō (1942, 37) suggests that this new ordination platform configuration in 704 was related to the *feng* and *shan* activities of Empress Wu on Mount Song in 695.

25. Shiina (1993) points out that a significant number of Northern school monks resided in strong vinaya centers. Incidentally, in 1988 the remains of the ordination platform at Huishansi on Mount Song could still be seen. Unfortunately, the temple was being used as an army training school and was off-limits (Ikeda 1988, 108).

26. Four texts describe this ordination platform. The first, the *Songyue Huishansi jietan bei* 嵩岳會善寺戒壇碑 (*Jinshi cuibian*, fasc. 95), details the platform's reestablishment in 767 by Chengru 乘如 (d. ca. 780–783), a vinaya specialist who had reached Sumatra before relinquishing hope of traveling to India (see Ikeda 1988, 126–136). The event was sponsored by three powerful pro-Buddhist officials, Yuan Cai 元載 (d. 777), Du Hongjian 杜鴻漸 (709–769), and Wang Jin 王縉 (701?–781)

(see Ikeda 1988, 126–128, for brief biographical descriptions of these men). The *Huishansi jietan bei* 會善寺戒壇牌 (*Jinshi cuibian*, fasc. 94, 3.1623a–25d) is the second (and lacunae-filled) text to describe the reestablishment ceremony. It is also by Chengru and contains frequent references to the same officials. The *Xiexiu jietan biao* 謝修戒壇表 (QQT 916.22a–b; 19.12047b) is a memorial written on the same occasion by Chengru. The original stele supposedly included this text and the *Huishansi jietan bei*, plus a response from Emperor Daizong 代宗 (766–799). The fourth text, the *Songyue Huishansi jietan ji* 嵩岳會善寺戒壇記 (QQT 510.5a–b, 11.6571a; Ikeda 1988, 115–117), is a commemoration of the event in 795 written by Lu Zhangyuan 陸長源. Ikeda (1988, 121–125) believes that the establishment of the Huishansi ordination platform implies the eclipse of the platform at Shaolinsi, but he gives no specific evidence for this. These and other related sources for this ordination platform are also discussed by Shiina (1968, 173–185). Another informative epitaph regarding both the vinaya lineage and the establishment of an ordination platform is Yan Zhenqing's 顏眞卿 (709–784) *Fuzhou Baoyingsi Lüzang yuan jietan ji* 撫州寶應寺律藏院戒壇記 (QQT 338.3a–5b, 7.4330a–4331a), written in 771.

27. It is tempting to think that Yinzong's statue-building activities are connected to the efforts by Empress Wu regarding the cult of Maitreya as discussed in Forte 1988.

28. Yinzong was associated primarily with Miaoxisi 妙喜寺 Temple in Kuaiji, and he seems to have had a close relationship with a Wang family of that city (see SGZ, T 50.731b). Two laymen named Wang of Kuaiji (not listed elsewhere in the SGZ) are mentioned in Yinzong's biography, one a magistrate of the city who requested that he establish an ordination platform there and the other the author of his epitaph. Particularly well versed in the *Nirvāṇa Sūtra*, Yinzong began teaching in Chang'an in 670. A few years later he was the subject of an imperial request to take up residence at Jing'aisi 敬愛寺 (Aijingsi 愛敬寺) in Luoyang, but he spurned this to study Chan under Hongren of East Mountain and later met Huineng in Fanyu 番禺 (Guangdong). Based on the profundity of his exchange with Huineng (which the SGZ does not describe), Yinzong went home to Kuaiji, where the prefect Wang Zhou 王冑 asked him to establish an ordination platform. This he did, administering the precepts to great numbers of people (the text says "several thousand/hundreds"). Later he accepted the invitation to the imperial palace and worked on the great image of Maitreya. Yinzong compiled two works, both now lost: a collection probably of Chan tradition stories known as the *Anthology of the Essentials of Mind* (*Xinyao ji* 心要記) and a compendium of statements by Chinese philosophers and Confucian scholars elucidating the three teachings of Buddhadharma. Li Hua's 李華 (d. ca. 766) epitaph for the Tiantai figure Xuanlang 玄朗 (673–754) refers to Chan Master Yinzong as a vinaya specialist (QQT 7.4101a; fasc. 320, p. 1b). (This last citation is drawn from Yanagida 1967, 138. On p. 225, Yanagida holds that the account of Huineng's ordination circulated because of Yinzong's prior reputation rather than vice versa.)

29. On Xuanyan and Dayi, see Yanagida 1967 (255–256) citing the SGZ (T 50.795a27–b8, 800a15–b13). For Xuanyan, also see *Fahuasi jietan yuan bei* 法華寺戒壇院碑 (QQT 335.7a–8a, 7.4292a–94a), which mentions both his establishment of an ordination platform (sometime before 736, judging from context) and his holding of ten unrestricted assemblies (in or after 738).

30. I will not discuss Ganjin's career here except to note the following: He

worked to establish ordination platforms in China before arriving in Japan in 753. Once there he established platforms at Tōdaiji 東大寺 and probably Tōshōdaiji 唐招提寺, in the former case using soil supposedly brought all the way from Nālandā (or perhaps Mount Wutai) for the platform itself. According to Ishida Mizumaro (1986c), Ganjin's only guide for the construction of these platforms was Daoxuan's texts; Ōchō suggests from other evidence that additional models were involved, such as the Chinese examples introduced below. Unfortunately, there does not seem to be any early evidence from Japanese sources about the configuration of the platforms. That only a few of them were established in Japan seems to stem from efforts to limit their number by Japanese clerical authorities—a policy in sharp contrast to that of the Chinese vinaya specialists and one that led to the momentous backlash decades later by the Tendai priest Saichō 最澄 (767–822).

31. The evidence introduced conflicts with Gernet on only one point: He repeatedly (pp. 51–52, 57, 331 n. 122, and 333 n. 157) cites a reference by Emperor Xuanzong 玄宗 on the suspension of official ordinations during the period 713–741. If this did in fact happen, no imperially sponsored ordinations were held at the ordination platforms established at Huishansi by Yixing and in Chang'an by Vajrabodhi in or around the early 720s. Does Xuanzong's comment only apply to certain kinds of imperially sponsored ordinations? I consider these issues briefly in McRae 1993–1994. Concerning the sale of ordination certificates, see T. H. Barrett in this volume. Unfortunately, we do not know much about how these later ordination platforms were configured. The only information we have, on four of them, suggests that they varied in significant ways, including the number of levels, shape, and size (see Ōchō 1942, 51).

32. It is possible that Daoxuan remembered Fachong's remonstration of Xuanzang:

> Tripiṭaka Master Xuanzang did not allow anyone to lecture on the old translations of the sūtras. Fachong said, "You were ordained on the basis of the old sūtras. If you do not allow the dissemination of the old sūtras, you should return to the lay life and then become ordained again on the basis of the newly translated sūtras. Only then will I allow you this interpretation." Upon hearing this, Xuanzang ended his prohibition. (T 50.666c17–19)

Given Xuanzang's famous dedication to accuracy, this anecdote rings true. Exchanges such as this, which implied that Chinese monks were not truly monks because they had not been correctly ordained, may have spurred Daoxuan on to seek the ultimate authority in his visions of the Buddha's ordination platform.

33. After recounting the scriptural sources for some of the features of his platform, Daoxuan writes: "I have just now examined the texts for the characteristics [of the ordination platform], and although they do not use the term 'ordination platform' (jietan), this ordination platform is actually a stūpa of the Buddha" (T 45.809b6–7).

34. This assertion is made based on searches using the printed indexes to the *Taishō* (up through index vol. 19), admittedly a less than perfect resource. Searches using the CBETA electronic texts (http://ccbs.ntu.edu.tw/cbeta/) reveal that *"wufen fashen"* 五分法身 is used three times in the joint commentary by Kumārajīva and his students on the *Vimalakīrti Sūtra* (T 1775) and a few times in texts by Jingying

Huiyuan, Zhiyi 智顗 (538–597), and Jizang. Xuanzang's successor Ci'en Ji 慈恩基 (632–682; often referred to as Kuiji 窺基; see Weinstein 1959) does mention (T 34.727a28, 773c19–20, 812a16) offering incense at a stūpa to attain the fragrance of the five-part *dharmakāya*. In a discussion of stūpas in general, he states that incense represents the cultivation of the five-part *dharmakāya*, but there is no attempt at the symbolic identification used by Daoxuan.

35. In this passage the five wisdoms of the five Buddhas are said to be achieved as part of accomplishing the five-part *dharmakāya*. On the five-wheeled stūpa, see *Mikkyō daijiten*, 1969–1970, 2:650c–651a and 652a–b.

36. The Chinese term used here is *"beiduozi"* 貝多子, which must be equivalent to 貝多羅 given in Nakamura 1975 (1100a). It is a transliteration of *"pattra"* ("leaf," i.e., the leaf of the *tāla* tree). Perhaps there was some confusion here with the twin *śāla* trees that are usually said to have shaded the Buddha at the Nirvāṇa. See Ikeda 1988 (115) and QQT (510.5a, 11.6571a) for information cited. There is no explanation given for the significance of the trees on Mount Song blooming three times a season, but this was certainly an auspicious portent.

37. For the East Asian commemoration of Śākyamuni's birth, enlightenment, and final nirvāṇa, see BD s.v. *kanbutsue* 灌佛會 (1.821c–24b) on 4.8; s.v. *jōdōe* 成道 會 (3.2708a–b) on 12.8; and s.v. *nehan'e* 涅槃會 (5.4149c–50c) on 2.15.

Chapter 4

Buddhist Precepts in a Lawless World

Some Comments on the Linhuai Ordination Scandal

T. H. BARRETT

As RESEARCH INTO the earliest stages of Buddhism unfolds, the central role of the Buddhist monastic *saṅgha* in preserving as oral literature the teachings of the Buddha, the Dharma, has become increasingly apparent. Yet the *saṅgha* as an autonomous body in the most literal sense would not have been able to survive without its own set of ordinances. Despite the natural tendency of earlier scholarship to shun study of the vinaya as a recondite and somewhat sterile area—something roughly equivalent to canon law in the Christian tradition—we are now beginning to realize how important to Buddhism the vinaya was and is and to examine the implications of that realization for the study of Buddhism.

Nor should we stop there, for in East Asia at least Buddhist conceptions of religious law were imported into a cultural area that already possessed well-defined and (by contrast with other ancient societies) relatively secular conceptions of legality that had already brought into being an imperial system more durable than anything encountered by Buddhism in the South Asian heartland. The study of the interaction between the Buddhist vinaya and this non-Buddhist environment constitutes a vast field of research that current scholarship has hardly touched on as yet; in isolating just one particular instance of the function of Buddhist ordination from a non-Buddhist point of view it is possible to do no more than suggest a type of approach that might later prove fruitful. Even so, this very limited study may perhaps serve to show that such interpretation and implementation are not problems for Buddhist studies alone, but have wider implications for anyone interested in the cultural heritage of East Asia.

The Precepts in China: From a Cultural to
a Historical Perspective

For the immediate purposes of this essay, three aspects of the oper-
ation of Buddhist precepts in a non-Buddhist environment may be
discerned. First, the conflict between Buddhist precept and what
one might call secular, or (with reservations) Confucian Chinese,
morality is an obvious one that has long attracted the attention first
of polemicists and latterly of scholars, and is well represented in the
literature on China in Western languages (e.g., Nakamura 1964,
chap. 23). Second, the relationship between Buddhist precept and
state ordinance was a matter of elementary importance to regimes
in both north and south China confronted with the success of Buddhism in the early centuries of the Common Era, and research into
this phenomenon has preoccupied a certain strand in East Asian
scholarship also, again with some resulting publication in Western
languages.[1] But, as we shall see, not only Confucians and (shall we
say) Legalists found the vinaya a problem: Daoists (Taoists), also,
had to confront its religious conceptions of law with sometimes
similar but also quite unrelated ideas of their own. Here modern
scholarship has at last recognized the importance of legal thought
in the formation of Daoist religion.[2] Yet publications on the relationship between the legal aspects of Buddhism and Daoism remain
relatively few, despite all the surviving materials that could throw
light on the interaction between Buddhist and Daoist religious
codes (esp. see Fukunaga 1982; Rao 1991, 103–108; Jan 1986;
Penny 1996).

Of course, a volume on the vinaya as such and its observance
in East Asia is not the right place to carry forward such research.
Although this essay has raised the question of the larger cultural
context in which the vinaya operated in East Asia, all that the
reader is asked to note at this point is that whatever the function of
the vinaya outside the Chinese cultural world, as soon as the Buddhist precepts reached China they became part of a religious environment in which the very term for "precepts" (*jie* 戒) linked them
inevitably with Daoist analogues similarly described. These analogues, termed "precepts of the Dao" (*daojie* 道誡), have so far been
discussed primarily in terms of their relationship to what has been
referred to above as "secular morality."[3] Even so, once one enlarges
one's view of Daoist quasi-legal religious terminology to encompass

terms such as "prohibitions" (*jin* 禁), notions of taboo and talisman tend to become as prominent as any moral meanings. Admittedly these overtones of alien religious meaning may not be at all apparent (or, indeed, all that important) when precepts are discussed within a purely Buddhist context, but at points in the Chinese historical record where the workings of the vinaya appear to break down entirely—from a Buddhist point of view—we might do well to remember their presence.

For it is such a situation that forms the main interest of the case study presented here. Although a comprehensive perspective on the scandal in question might require lengthy explanations concerning its position in the long-term history of the popular Buddhist cult with which it seems to have been associated, too much history (beyond what is necessary to provide the immediate religious background) would certainly distract from the main object of the current exercise, which is simply to remind readers—whose attention is concentrated for much of this volume solely on the Buddhist world—of some of the forces that might have affected the implementation of the vinaya in China, especially in cases where Buddhist norms appear to have become distorted.

As it happens, the Linhuai 臨淮 ordination scandal suits the purpose of a case study extremely well because it is an episode that has already played its part in a number of historiographies. For an example of its appearance in English language scholarship, we may readily cite a standard work that gives a complete summary of the main source on the scandal:

> A revealing memorial by Li Deyu 李德裕 (787–859) dated 824 describes how Wang Zhixing 王智興 (d. 836), the civil governor (*guanchashi* 觀察使) of Xuzhou 徐州 and Sizhou 泗州 (in present-day Jiangsu), acquired great wealth through the sale of ordination certificates in spite of the prohibition against this practice. According to Li, one out of three male adults in Sizhou had taken the tonsure to avoid taxation. He estimated that of more than one hundred monks that he examined daily at a checkpoint at the Yangzi crossing at Suanshan only fourteen had previously served as novices *(shami* 沙彌; *śrāmaṇera)*, the remainder being common people with no previous religious training. The ordination itself was little more than a commercial transaction: upon arrival at the ordination platform that Wang had built, the candidate, whose head had already been shaven, would make a payment of two strings of cash for which he would be issued with an ordination certificate.

Once he had received the certificate, the candidate would return home
without even participating in a religious ceremony. Li Deyu ended
his memorial with a warning that if strong action was not taken to enforce the ban on such activities before the forthcoming celebration of
the Emperor's birthday—no doubt a suitable occasion for promoting ordination—six hundred thousand able-bodied males not only
from Jiangsu but from the area to the south as well would be lost as
taxpayers. (Weinstein 1987a, 60–61, with change of romanization)

This paraphrase of our main source on the episode appears in a
general discussion of the sale of ordination certificates during the
Tang, but its first appearance that I have noticed in the modern historiography of Chinese Buddhism was much earlier, in an article
devoted to the monastic economy of China's middle ages published
in 1934. Here the discussion involves not just ordination certificates
in Tang times, but the far greater struggle on the part of the state to
regulate the numbers of Chinese entering the Buddhist clergy (He
1986, 11). The earliest Japanese mention that I have noticed comes
by contrast some eight years later, in the context of an account of
the history of the ordination platform in East Asia (Ōchō 1979, 40,
44). The source or sources cited in these three contexts, as it happens, are never the same, though in every case the memorial by Li
Deyu given above must represent the report from which the information was ultimately taken. But these three instances by no means
exhaust the number of contexts in which Li's remarks have been
cited: Naturally enough, they may also be found put to some use in
a volume from Taiwan devoted to an evaluation of Li's career (Tang
1973, 107).

To be sure, a biographical approach to understanding this memorial should not be neglected. In the volume in question, Tang
Chengye is content to take Li at face value and assumes that his report reflects the views of an impartial administrator, although materials suggesting devotion to a Daoist master (and hence possible
bias in his reporting of Buddhism) are evaluated as expressing no
more than the polite sentiments normally accorded respectable religious figures (pp. 547–548). Other scholars, however, have noted
that Li had considerable family ties with Daoism, and, most recently, that there are indications of personal devotion on his part
going back a couple of years before the date of this document
(Chen 1980, 37–38; Sunayama 1990).

Bias must, one might think, be imputed to at least one famous Tang worthy in evaluating the Linhuai ordinations. The poet Bai Juyi 白居易 (772–846) took a diametrically opposed view of Wang Zhixing's sponsorship of the ordination platform, lauding him for his support of Buddhism (*Bai Juyi ji* 白居易集, fasc. 69, 1461). Fortunately, however, it is not necessary to choose one's hero and evaluate the evidence based on that choice: The mention of Sizhou in Li's memorial—and particularly that of the Kaiyuansi 開元寺 monastery of Sizhou in Bai's encomium (to which we shall return in due course)—points to a link between the ordination platform and the history of religion in China.[4]

The Perspective of Past History

By the time of the ordination scandal the Kaiyuansi had become the center of a Buddhist cult that was already more than a century old. This cult, which has been studied in some detail by both Makita Tairyō and Chen Zuolong, expanded dramatically during the rest of the ninth century, leading to its conspicuous prominence in sources of the Five Dynasties and Song periods and, despite some vicissitudes, a lasting fame that has endured into our own times. It was devoted to a reputedly miraculous monk from Central Asia named Sengqie 僧伽 (627–710), who is said to have made his home in Sizhou in the late seventh century and to have founded a monastery known as the Puguangwangsi 普光王寺 (later the Kaiyuansi) (Makita 1957, 1–30; Chen 1989, 21–88). It is probably significant that this man was of Sogdian origin; Sizhou occupied a dangerous but important place in Tang international trade routes (just where the canal system joined the less predictable waters of the Huai 淮 River), and Sogdian merchants, the main force in international Asian trade of the time, were probably more than willing to support a compatriot with apparent supernatural powers whose presence hallowed this particular spot.

The location of the monastery may also explain why Sengqie's fame spread not only in China but internationally during the ninth century. His cult is mentioned by several Japanese monks who visited China at the time, and icons associated with him seem to have reached Japan as well. But Sengqie had already attracted the attention of Chinese long before this point—from the emperor on down. A memorial inscription by the writer Li Yong 李邕 (673–742)

datable to some time in the early eighth century gives an account of Sengqie's life that clearly shows he was already regarded as a supernatural figure. A poem wrongly ascribed to Li Bai 李白 (701–763) may also date from the same century. In any case, by the end of the eighth century we may be quite sure that a thriving cult had developed where Sengqie had lived and where his body was preserved in lacquered form.

Further evidence of the cult's prominence may be found in a poem by the famous writer and scourge of Buddhism Han Yu 韓愈 (768–824), written in the year 800. Han put himself forward as the very embodiment of the Confucian morality that found Buddhism utterly offensive and foreign, and indeed line seven of this poem, "Yue 越 [Southern] merchants and Hu 胡 [Sogdian] traders buying deliverance from their own misdeeds," exhibits a fine xenophobia in pointing to continued Central Asian involvement in the cult. But mention of extensive construction work in the poem shows that not only were merchants prepared to support the cult on a lavish scale, but also Sengqie's worshippers were already rebuilding the site to cope with mass demand, presumably from the Chinese population of the area (and not just from alien transients). If the cult was now firmly entrenched in popular belief, one is tempted to wonder whether the fire that made rebuilding necessary at this time—but on a much grander scale—was entirely an accident.

The name of the monk in charge of the construction (and the poem's addressee) is also of interest because in all likelihood he was the abbot in charge immediately before Wang Zhixing took over the patronage of the site. It is a name well known to students of East Asian Buddhism, one shared with the great exegete of the Huayan school Chengguan 澄觀 (738–839). But our Chengguan, in the light of recent research, seems to have pursued an entirely different career, probably as a vinaya master who (like a number of his colleagues in the region) dabbled in versifying with nonclerical friends (Barrett 1992, 71–2, 78–80; Kamata 1992). It is possible that he had some interest in Chan 禪 Buddhism. At about this time a fellow disciple studying under the same vinaya teacher turned to the Chan of Niutou 牛頭 and Caoqi 曹溪—that is, of a complexion probably very similar to that represented in the text of the famous *Platform Sūtra*. The significance of this will be investigated below; for the moment it is more important to explore the final clue to be gleaned from Han's poem concerning Chengguan and his circle—

one that suggests that both the author and addressee were indebted to the patronage of the same man, Zhang Jianfeng 張建封 (735–800).

A Political Perspective

Mention of Zhang necessitates a few words concerning the political history of this period. Switching from Li Yong's inscription to Han Yu's poem, even by way of a putative Li Bai song, may emphasize the continued prosperity of the Sogdian merchant community in China, which by 800 may have had a little more xenophobia to cope with but was well protected by its Uighur patrons. Such an emphasis, however, tends to gloss over the completely changed circumstances in which the Chinese, and especially the Chinese of Sizhou, found themselves. The rebellion of the half-Sogdian An Lushan 安祿山 (d. 757) in 755 was overcome by the Tang dynasty (with Uighur help) but left the government in a severely weakened state. The canal system, on which Sizhou was so strategically located, had always been important to an imperial court in the northwest that could not be sustained without the constant flow of grain tax from more fertile areas. With the loss of a great deal of fertile northern territory to generals in the northeast who owed at best a purely nominal allegiance to the court, supplies from the south were crucial, and the canal system became the jugular vein of the dynasty. According to an edict drafted by Bai Juyi (*Bai Juyi ji*, fasc. 51, 1067), "of all the walled cities of the Huai region, Sizhou is the key, for it controls the transport route." Between Luoyang 洛陽 and the calmer territories south of the Huai, huge armies of doubtful loyalty remained in fact throughout most of the late eighth century, capable at any time of putting a knife against that jugular vein. The central government had to rely on its provincial governors to keep troops loyal, at least along this vital supply line, but even when it was not in open conflict with local warlords trying to defend their independence, its own armies were quite capable of mutinying and threatening Sizhou's canals without a moment's warning (see Twitchett 1979, chaps. 8–9).

In such a world money still talked, but the cultured and humane found their lives less secure than in the happier days of the early eighth century. In 796 Han Yu, soon to be joined by his friends Li Ao 李翱 (772–836) and Meng Jiao 孟郊 (751–814), was on the staff of the ex-chief minister Dong Jin 董晉 (724–799), who had been sent out to take charge of the troops at Bianzhou 汴州. This area was farther up the canal system, at present-day Kaifeng 開封, and notorious for its mutinies. When Dong died in 799, Han was very lucky to be among the party escorting the funeral cortège to Luoyang: The rest of the governor's staff were cut up alive by the local soldiery and eaten. Han was then obliged to seek a job with Zhang Jianfeng, only to lose it in the middle of the next year. Again Han was lucky: Soon after he left for Luoyang (with Li Ao) Zhang died and his troops mutinied. The army was eventually appeased by the recognition of Zhang's son as successor. (In the independent provinces hereditary succession to governorships had become the norm [Hartman 1986, 34–44; Barrett 1992, 66–78].)

What repercussions would all of this have had on Chengguan and his construction work at Sizhou? Very little, perhaps, to start with, especially because court appointment of governors seems to have continued after 800 at a normal rate. Unfortunately, however, apparent normality could (and, in this case, eventually did) mask a situation in which the powers of court appointees counted for less than those of their nominal subordinates. Doubtless Chengguan, who had already lived through enough changes, could see the way things were going: When Li Ao passed through Sizhou again in 809, he made no mention of Chengguan, who probably was no longer there (see Barrett 1992, 37). But it is likely that Chengguan had simply retreated to a safer situation farther south, where he was apparently still alive in 811 (see Barrett 1992, 80 n. 17). Meanwhile Sizhou was coming increasingly under the influence of Li Deyu's target, the eventual governor Wang Zhixing.

A man of humble origins, Wang Zhixing made a considerable impact on the history of his age, despite having to swim against a tide of change that took many men (albeit less daring and ruthless) with it. But in a violent world Wang managed to achieve a reputation for exceptional violence. He astutely kept on the side of the central government while it took in hand all its recalcitrant warlords and reasserted its control in the second decade of the ninth century, but it was Wang's subversive influence that was blamed long after his death when the government collapsed irremediably in the closing agony of Tang rule.[5] He was, it seems, a local man from Xuzhou (the seat of Zhang Jianfeng's governorship) and, according to one rather late source, originally employed as a gate sweeper (*Taiping guangji* 太平廣記, fasc. 138, 992, citing the *Tang-nian bulu* 唐年補錄, a lost tenth-century work; cf. *Jiu Tang shu* 舊唐書, fasc. 156, 4138–4141, which gives him more of a pedigree, but an entirely military one). Judging from anecdotes from the late Tang and thereafter that preserve something of his character, he combined ruthlessness with a certain unexpected intellectual and literary ability and even a somewhat dry sense of humor.[6]

There appears to be nothing in particular in Wang's background that would cause him to take a religious interest in the cult of Sengqie. Two of his subordinates mentioned in our sources bear Sogdian names, but they do not seem to have been his trusted lieutenants at all; rather, he was glad to be rid of them (*Taiping guangji*, fasc. 156, 1123–1124, citing a late-ninth-century source). Economic motives, however, would have been quite another matter. Wang's career took a dramatic turn in 822, leaving him in a position where fiscal independence would have been a matter of concern to him. During the greater part of the preceding two decades the government had reasserted its control over provincial governors who had preserved their independence since the An Lushan rebellion, and in this process Wang Zhixing proved to be an able and unswervingly loyal general. While other military leaders lost their independence, he rose to be deputy governor of the area once under the command of Zhang Jianfeng.

To be the power behind the provincial throne, however, was not the summit of his ambitions. In 822, trading on his indispensability as de facto controller of government supply lines, Wang reacted to a suggestion from his nominal superior, the cultured and well-connected civilian governor Cui Qun 催群 (772–832), that he be transferred away from his local power base by running that unfortunate official out of town. Worse still, to further emphasize his ability to take over the governorship by force with complete impunity, he celebrated this coup by allowing his men to loot the greater part of the government and private commercial traffic then passing through his new domain (*Zizhi tongjian* 資治通鑑, fasc. 242, 7812).

The Economic Perspective

Looting, however, could hardly have commended itself as a viable strategy for long-term survival: If forced to act, the central authorities might do so. Like the 1920s warlords described by David

Faure, Wang may not even have had the means to collect agricultural taxes efficiently (or the incentive to do so in an area of China not known for its productivity), and so other "accessible sources of finance," such as taxes on goods in transit, would have assumed a greater importance (Faure 1989, 17). Because the canal system was Wang's main asset and all traffic stopped in Sizhou to make the transfer between the canal proper and the Huai River, his first move was to levy taxes on all traffic passing this point (*Jiu Tang shu*, fasc. 156, 4140). But Sengqie's relics were surely an important financial asset to him; Chengguan's rebuilding program implies (as we have noted) a considerable number of pilgrims visiting the area.⁷ Taxing pilgrims, however, would probably have been regarded as a highly impious act.

But ordaining them all was quite another matter. Selling blank ordination certificates was, as many scholars have observed, an innovation that can be traced to the time of the An Lushan rebellion, when the government was obliged to raise money rapidly (the collection of agricultural taxes being too slow or too uncertain). If Wang was not particularly interested in agricultural taxes, the revenue lost through the tax exemption conferred by the ordination certificate would have troubled him not one whit, especially if it was not his revenue to start with but was owed to some other provincial governor in the pilgrim's place of origin. Viewed in this light, one can well understand Li Deyu's feelings on the matter.

All that was needed for Wang to get richer quicker, then, was a compliant cleric. Mingyuan 明遠 (765–834), Chengguan's successor, proved to be just the man for the job. According to Bai Juyi, who wrote Mingyuan's epitaph, he succeeded Chengguan in 806 and, to judge from Bai's description of his early career (see *Bai Juyi ji*, fasc. 69, 1460–1462), one may perhaps be able to conjecture why Chengguan preferred not to live out his retirement under the new management. Unlike his cosmopolitan predecessor, Mingyuan was strictly a local man. His master, Lingmu 靈穆, is not known from other sources and is described simply as a vinaya master of Sizhou; there is no record of Mingyuan venturing much farther himself or making further doctrinal studies under any other teachers. Although Bai mentions Mingyuan's lectures, he provides no information that shows him to be any sort of intellectual and concentrates solely on his administrative achievements. Of Mingyuan's first named patron, the local prefect Su Yu 蘇遇, we know very little: By

821 Su had risen to a vice-governorship elsewhere (judging from an inscription unearthed in the eighteenth century), and three years later he was at court and being consulted even by the seasoned politicians there for his mastery of intrigue; otherwise he appears to have been the sort of figure our sources prefer to ignore (see *Jiu Tang shu,* fasc. 173, 4498; *Jinshi cuibian* 金石萃編, fasc. 107, 6a, 7a). At some point, however, Mingyuan is said to have formed a connection with that other local-boy-makes-good, Wang Zhixing. After Wang's seizure of power in 822, Mingyuan was given religious authority over not only Sizhou (a responsibility he had held since 807), but also the entire territory under Wang's control. At some point in the early 820s Wang and Mingyuan started rebuilding the Sizhou monastery. Considerable expansion had taken place under Su's patronage, but the main hall had since been destroyed by fire (again). By this time the monastery is said to have ceased functioning, so we must presume that the fire was accidental.

The Doctrinal Perspective

No full account of Mingyuan's apparent ability to reconcile his aims with those of Wang Zhixing—and maybe also with the secular and religious needs of the common crowd in Sizhou—would be complete without a close examination of the connection between doctrinal texts and historical events. This requires, however, a double effort because it is necessary both to consider the question of ordination as a long-term problem in East Asian Buddhism and to try to detect any textual or doctrinal innovation during Mingyuan's time that might further have encouraged him to take the short step from mass evangelism to mass illegality.

Although the so-called abuse of the institution of ordination in China has, in accordance with the overwhelmingly government-centered bias of our sources, normally been treated as a problem between Buddhism and the state, the entire status of ordination was also an issue within Chinese Buddhism itself. It has recently been suggested that the Chinese tradition before Buddhism was not entirely without any concept of the rival claims of secular and religious authority, but the notion of a corporate group beyond the bounds of normal secular society remained for a long time extremely alien to Chinese ways of thinking.[8] True, religious figures might by virtue of their spiritual powers put some distance between themselves and ordinary human beings, but in Daoism that distance was quite explicitly visualized as a matter of gradation: At the bottom of the ladder stood the young offspring of the Daoist faithful, protected by a simple talisman; at the top stood the master of the whole range of Daoist lore (Schipper 1983). To the extent that the Chinese Buddhist tradition was able to adapt to this model—for example, by making the novitiate a step in its own ladder rather than (as in India) accord it mere transitional status—it did so.[9]

It also attempted to create on the lower rungs of the ladder, at a level comparable to the advanced Daoist believer not officially recognized as a priest, a superior grade of laity with an enhanced Buddhist commitment. This was done through the promotion of the "bodhisattva precepts," Mahāyāna declarations of vows that had clear Indian antecedents but in East Asia generated a new scriptural literature tending in the long run to subvert the efficacy of vinaya-based ordinations (see, e.g., Groner 1990a). Indeed, from the time of the promotion of these vows by the Emperor Wu 武 (r. 502–549) of the Liang 梁 dynasty, they seem to have been used politically as a counterweight to claims of superior status by ordained monks and nuns (Satō Tatsugen 1986, 338). Because the bodhisattva precepts conferred no clerical status, they formed an ideal way to assert mass membership of the larger Buddhist community without entailing any fiscally awkward consequences.

But clearly there existed also a strong pull in the direction of collapsing the lay-clerical distinction altogether. Thus the work of the famous Buddhist scholar Daoxuan 道宣 (596–667) in promoting proper ordination on conspicuous ordination platforms may be seen as answering a number of needs, of which the need for a competitive response to Daoist forms of ordination was not the least important in my view (Barrett 1994). It must surely have also been a response to the Northern Zhou 北周 experience, when the suppression of the clergy was carried out in the name of an alternative model of Buddhism propounded by the onetime monk Wei Yuan-song 衛元嵩 (ca. 567).[10] Daoxuan would have found such a scheme particularly threatening in that it advocated the complete elimination of the binary line between clergy and laity for reasons based on Buddhist doctrine itself. The same notion crops up again (albeit for different doctrinal reasons) in the teachings of the Sect of the Three Levels, suggesting that it was a recurrent concern and not just the reflection of the imperial whim of Emperor Wu of the

Northern Zhou, even if here the notion of an age of decline in which distinctions between clergy and laity had become irrelevant is very much to the fore (Lewis 1990, 216–221). This particular development may be dismissed as sectarian, but it must also be admitted that the awareness of decline, widespread enough in Buddhism even before its East Asian formulation into three stages (let alone the emergence of the sect in question), is frequently connected with a belief that the clergy would one day decline in quality to the point that the laity would have to take on new responsibilities (Nattier 1991, 40, 154).

In China such a development may have gone no further than the eventual emergence of laity-centered Buddhism.[11] But the pressure to abandon a distinct celibate clergy after the manner of Shinran 親鸞 (1173–1262) in Japan cannot have been entirely absent in a society in which even in Tang times the Daoist clergy up to a certain level were recognized as legitimately noncelibate. Indeed, as the Chinese were well aware, Buddhism had established itself in China without the aid of any proper forms of ordination, and though the state obviously found it suited its own interests to involve itself in the certification and regulation of ordination, there is every indication that private ordination and indeed self-ordination continued to flourish alongside the development of state institutions.[12] As Li Deyu makes clear, the main aim of the state was always to curb tax evasion through the pretense of clerical status. Although this practice was undoubtedly a problem, the sharp division drawn by the authorities between fully and officially ordained monk and wily peasant also undoubtedly ignored the existence of genuinely religious individuals who could not meet the formal requirements of the vinaya (Moroto 1990; Gernet 1995, 37–43). Such men and women are hardly given their due in official sources, Buddhist or secular, but do appear in Tang anecdotal literature (e.g., Dudbridge 1988, 32–35).

The clerical elite in the state-supported monasteries may have exhibited a strong reluctance to compromise on the exclusivity of official ordination, but there were also doctrinal grounds for promoting alternatives to full ordination and questioning the absolute value of the clerical status. Moreover, a broader outlook may have been not only more popular but also truer to China's native Buddhist tradition. But were there any specific developments in the general area of Sizhou during Mingyuan's career that might have encouraged a particularly liberal attitude towards ordination? It is difficult to be entirely certain of this, but there are enough clues to suggest that something new was happening.

A Chan Perspective

The doctrinal complexion of the Puguangwang Monastery at this time is difficult to ascertain, but there are indications that Chengguan and his writings were not forgotten in Sizhou even decades after his departure: In a catalogue of works obtained in China in 857 by the Japanese pilgrim Enchin 圓珍 (814–891), we find a letter by Chengguan bound together with a copy of Li Yong's inscription (*Chishō Daishi shōrai mokuroku* 智證大師請來目録, T 55.1107a4–5). These documents may represent souvenirs of a visit to Sizhou to which Enchin's materials relating to Sengqie might also bear witness (Makita 1957). Unfortunately, as noted above, we cannot be sure what Chengguan's doctrinal interests were because we do not have direct evidence of his ideas, only those of one of his associates.

Even so, the change of heart from plain vinaya studies to a combination of vinaya and a form of Chan on the part of Chengguan's fellow disciple mentioned earlier fits into a distinct and very interesting pattern, apparently highly localized in space and time. Monks who specialized in the interpretation of the vinaya seem to have felt fairly free to combine this calling with whatever doctrinal interests were in vogue or took their fancy. A rapid trawl through the vinaya experts represented in the *Song Lives of Eminent Monks* (*Song gaoseng zhuan* 宋高僧傳), for example, reveals adherents of Pure Land and Tiantai 天台, as well as Chan in its various forms. Elsewhere, too, a period of rapprochement between vinaya experts and tantric Buddhism has been noted (Chou 1945, 313, Appendix E). The writings of Bai Juyi, however, confirm that around the year 800 in the region through which the canal system passed, especially around Luoyang, vinaya masters were turning to, or from the start combining their studies with, some variety of Chan.

Thus Zhiru 智如 (749–834), a prominent vinaya master of Luoyang, is described by Bai as having added to his expertise in the vinaya a knowledge of the mind-essentials (*xinyao* 心要) of the *Laṅkāvatāra Sūtra,* a text associated with Northern Chan, though by this time some elements from this tradition had been taken over by the Oxhead (Niutou 牛頭) strand of the movement (*Bai Juyi ji*, fasc. 69, 1462; also see Faure 1988, 135–137; McRae 1983, 201–204). By contrast Ruxin 如信 (750–824) of Luoyang is said by Bai to have combined vinaya expertise with the mind-essentials of the sixth patriarch (*Bai Juyi ji*, fasc. 68, 1428). Bai Juyi is furthermore not the only source to confirm that Chengguan's colleague was in good company: An inscription of 815 relating to a vinaya master named Huihai 慧海 (720–814) of Mount Song 嵩山, not far from Luoyang, specifically states that at the start of the ninth century ("at the end of the Zhenyuan 貞元 period") his interest, too, turned to the *Laṅkāvatāra Sūtra* (Zhou 1992, 2:2004). Further research is needed into the monastic biographies of this period to elucidate this apparent shift, but it would seem at least possible that something had arrived on the scene at this point that piqued the interest of vinaya masters in Chan in general.

As it happens, the one Chan text that declares itself associated with ordination platforms, and which has for some time been recognized as structured to meet the needs of ordination of the Mahāyāna type, is the *Platform Sūtra* attributed to Huineng 慧能 (638–713). Although controversy continues to swirl around its origins, it is at least worth noting that revisionist scholarship has now shifted the first mention of the text to the early ninth century. Hitherto it was thought that a passage in the *Jingde Era Transmission of the Lamp* (T 51.437c–439a) attributed to Huizhong 慧忠 (d. 775) referred to the *Platform Sūtra*, but recently Yanagida Seizan (1990) has argued that the reference is in fact to the *Ordination Platform Diagram* of Daoxuan under an abbreviated title—that is, to the text in which Daoxuan propounds his history of ordination in China. If this specific identification is correct, it would explain the title "*Platform Sūtra*," a famous anomaly among texts self-confessedly composed in China: The title would not mean "sūtra" at all, but "gazetteer," which was the meaning of "*tujing*" 圖經 in Tang times (Luo 1989, 3:668, s.v.). The likelihood that the words of Huineng are not in fact referred to by Huizhong is increased by his use of the epithet "sage" (*sheng* 聖) to qualify the text he describes: During the Tang (and later for that matter) it would have been thought very bad form to use such an epithet for any human being save the emperor, and we can only assume that some text attributed to a Buddha or bodhisattva (Daoxuan claimed revelation as the source of several of his compositions) is intended.

But if we dismiss this passage, we are left for our earliest reference with a funerary inscription written for Ehu Dayi 鵝湖大義 (746–818) by Wei Chuhou 韋處厚 (773–828), now included in the *Quan Tang wen* 全唐文 of 1815 (fasc. 715, 22a). This text contains the famous description of the *Platform Sūtra* as in some sense a transplant illustrating the changes caused by the different environments of the north and south: The source of the metaphor is clear, but its purport is less so (see Needham 1986, 103–110). Moreover, any speculation on Wei's meaning based on the text hitherto cited exclusively in its nineteenth-century form overlooks the fact that at least one earlier version of the text, in a gazetteer of the seventeenth century, reads very differently, locating Huineng rather than his rival Shenhui 神會 (684–758) in the Luoyang area, for example (*Quanshan xianzhi*, fasc. 8, 17a, p. 1107). Earlier gazetteers available only in China go back to the Ming, and clearly they too must be consulted before a conclusion can be reached concerning this witness to the existence of the *Platform Sūtra*.

In some sense, then, any construction that scholars have placed on this source must be regarded as provisional. But one deduction that has been made, its value increased by the newly available second version of the *Platform Sūtra* from Dunhuang 敦煌, concerns not the origins but the conception of the *Platform Sūtra* at this time: All recent commentators are agreed that this source and the Dunhuang texts themselves appear to indicate that in the early ninth century possession of the text as a physical object was taken as proof of membership in the Chan tradition (Yang 1993, 266–270).

How the bearer may have regarded such a text we cannot be entirely sure; in view of what has already been said about overlaps with and reactions against Daoism, it is surely worth raising at this point the possibility that the *Platform Sūtra* was regarded in part as a talisman. But for the moment we should consider first whether the text may have served equally as the functional counterpart to an ordination document and to this question, at any rate, there seems to be an unambiguous answer. Our next, and currently earliest, reliable witness is none other than the famous diarist Ennin 圓仁 (793–864), who lists the *Platform Sūtra* among the texts he brought back from China. We do not know where he purchased this work on his travels, but we do know exactly how he viewed it: Ennin's catalogue is no mere jumble but a careful list with an inter-

nal structure of its own. Chan texts are listed in one place, and the
Platform Sūtra is not among them. It is listed with his ordination
texts (Ono Katsutoshi 1966, 4:589).

We cannot, of course, deduce that Ennin's text came from Sizhou or even from the circles of which Chengguan was once a leading member, though some of its themes (such as repentance) sit
well with what we know of religious life in the Puguangwang si as
described in Tang literature. It is, nonetheless, surely a matter of
some importance that the *Platform Sūtra* or similar materials may
have been known in Sizhou because in doctrinal terms this work
can be read as promoting an attitude toward ordination very different from that favored by government officials like Li Deyu. A recent
study on the trend toward ordination texts of this type concludes
that "the simplicity of some of these ceremonies, especially that
found in the *Platform Sūtra,* suggests that they may, in fact, have
been intended more for lay believers than as a ceremony that
admitted people to any type of religious organization," and "such
changes made the precepts available to virtually anyone and demanded little" (Groner 1990b, 246, 250). To be sure, religious mini-
malism relates in the *Platform Sūtra* to Mahāyāna forms of ordination, not to the vinaya. But it is noteworthy that the only extended
description of a Buddhist ordination that we have from the early
ninth century (albeit in Sichuan) makes clear that Mahāyāna elements were introduced into regular ordinations, thus blurring the
original distinction between the two types (Gregory 1991, 41–43).
We are obviously still not in a position to vindicate unambiguously
Mingyuan's behavior in liberally dispensing full ordinations to all
comers on the basis of any of the materials we have considered,
but perhaps enough has been said to show that such a lapse (if indeed that is the right term) emerged from a climate in which the
maximum possible extension of some form of ordination was seen
as a desirable goal. Li Deyu, naturally, would have disapproved,
but we are now in a better position to understand Bai Juyi's account
of the matter.

Bai's Perspective

On first reading, Bai's epitaph for Mingyuan might be consigned to
the category of examples of groveling flattery that so alienate modern readers from Tang sources. At both the beginning and the end

of the piece it is asserted none too obliquely that Mingyuan must have been an arhat or a bodhisattva. In the final panegyric his buildings are compared to the "magic city" (*huacheng* 化城) of the *Lotus Sūtra*, and he is specifically commended for his diligent practice of the vinaya. If Mingyuan had not been first among monks rich in wisdom, and Wang first among the reverent laity, how could they have carried out this great Buddha-undertaking and resurrected their religion? One imagines that Bai can only have written such sorry stuff in the immediate proximity of Wang's heavily armed henchmen, and it comes as something of a shock to learn that Wang himself had been chosen to write the memorial first but died before he could complete the task.

Our sources tell us that Wang's evil ways lived after him, and it may be that Bai or his relatives remained at the potential mercy of his followers. But once one has discounted the Tang tendency to persiflage, is it possible to redeem Bai's view of Sizhou ordinations? One contemporary scholar better informed than most about the state of the clergy in Tang China does allow a surprisingly lenient interpretation of Mingyuan's actions. Moroto Tatsuo (1990, 319–326), in the most recent extended discussion on the Linhuai ordination scandal, suggests that Wang may have been raising money to build the monastery to shelter travelers rather than serve as a cover for his extortions. This does not entirely square with our other sources on Wang, but Moroto is quite correct in pointing to another source (*Quan Tang wen*, fasc. 745, 15a–21a) that shows Mingyuan as having sponsored Buddhist building in 813 in the Yangzhou 揚州 area, where no pecuniary advantage could accrue to him.

As for the ordinations, Moroto is inclined to believe (following a textual variant, although unfortunately not a strongly supported one) that these were not intended for raw peasants but irregularly ordained monks wishing to rectify their status. His researches illustrate the problems of state interference in religious life, an interference with which eminent clerics were all too happy to collude: One notes, for instance, that the one variety of Chan that had the temerity to countenance irregular ordination at this time was subject to the severest strictures from the contemporary Chan historian Zongmi 宗密 (780–841) (Gregory 1991, 249). Yet if Bai was as compassionate and humane as his writings suggest, could there have been any harm in releasing a certain number of peasants—even unworthy ones—from the relentless exactions of the state?

Conclusion: A Daoist Perspective?

Li Deyu was allowed the first word from among our Tang sources, so perhaps Bai Juyi should be granted the last. But, to repeat my initial point, we are not obliged simply to adopt the different perspectives of contemporaries toward the Linhuai ordination scandal. Much more could, of course, be said about the cultural history of Chinese Buddhism and about the doctrinal history of the ordination ceremony in Tang times, which might bear on our reading of Bai's epitaph and Li's memorial. But if we take into account even some provisional picture of the broader background of the Linhuai scandal—to say nothing the full panorama of its consequences in spreading the Sengqie cult—we may perhaps begin to tackle the problems of interpretation posed at the start of this chapter. Let us remind ourselves that in the short term the consequences may have been everything that Li Deyu claimed, or even a little worse given that Wang's enterprise seems to have spawned a number of imitations (Gernet 1995, 59–60). But granted all of this, Bai's words may also reflect a certain plain truth. To be sure, the cult of Sengqie was a success before Wang and Mingyuan ever began to devote their talents to it. It is not until after their activities, however, that we find reliable sources indicating a transregional proliferation of cult centers, the use of (mass-produced?) icons and other portable items to spread the cult internationally, and a cult center so well known as to become almost proverbial. From the start the cult was well situated and well supported, but if the key to its quite outstanding success by Song times was (to use a phrase not totally anachronistic) mass communication, then what part did the mass ordinations and the mass circulation of ordination certificates emanating from Sizhou play in all of this? Surely we may agree with Li that these ordinations were perfunctory and yet not accuse Bai of hypocrisy in saying that Mingyuan's thirty thousand ordinations (the sum total he actually gives, which may not be too much of an exaggeration) promoted Buddhism.

The case for such an interpretation would be considerably strengthened if it could be shown that the ordination certificates issued represented not simply items of economic value, but in some sense were religious documents as well. For this reason we must return once more to the question of Daoist influence on Buddhist practice first raised at the start of this essay and to the possibility that documents specific to Buddhism might under that influence assume a talismanic status. Were the documents in question Buddhist sūtras there would be no question of this; the collections of miracle tales associated with popular Tang sūtras and the statements of contemporary Chinese Buddhists both affirm that all sūtras bestow some protection on the devotee (for a contemporary example, see Levering 1989, 85). We have noted above, too, that a religious text—the *Platform Sūtra*—could serve as an ordination document. But could an ordination document serve conversely as a religious text? Such a development would be entirely natural in a Daoist context, in which the talisman (*fu* 符) had its origins in the secular form of a contractual document used to establish status (Robinet 1993, 24–25). Is there any evidence that ordination documents were so construed by the populace in China, where the great mass of the people remained open to all forms of religious meaning without drawing the distinctions we ourselves tend to impose?

Yes, as it happens, there is. The evidence has been available for some time though doubtlessly overlooked because it has been presented in relation to an entirely different topic, namely the development of xylographic images of the Buddha. These stamped images from Dunhuang, apparently all dating from the tenth century, are found in many instances on certificates testifying to the bestowal by a monk of precepts—mainly the five or eight precepts of lay Buddhism, but in one case the "Thousand Buddha's Great Precepts," or bodhisattva ordination—on various local inhabitants (Séguy 1979, 119–123). The stamping of a document with the Buddha's image might perhaps be construed as the deliberate sanctification of the secular; secular literature stamped over with sacred text is found in Japan, where such a motive has been suggested for the practice (Bowring 1992, 446–447). But we can be quite sure that these documents represented more than a mere record of having at a certain point assumed a certain status owing to one fact: Five of them (numbers 1, 3, 7, 10, and 12 in the catalogue cited) were bestowed over a span of nearly twenty years on a single individual. Under such circumstances it seems highly likely that these repeated ordination certificates conveyed some immediate, talismanic benefit on the recipient.

This evidence admittedly is both later than the era of Wang Zhixing and does not relate to certificates of full ordination. The case for viewing the certificates that Wang issued as religious thus cannot be proved. It is, indeed, extremely difficult to extract from the sources we have to hand an understanding of events involving the mass of ordinary people; top members of the religious clergy and imperial civil service tend to dominate the production of the texts we use. Stanley Weinstein once remarked in a graduate seminar that "we spend ninety-five percent of our time reading what less than five percent of the population wrote." This essay may have done no more than show how hard it is to get beyond the five percent view, but it should have provided enough material to show that even when dealing with a classic Buddhist topic like the implementation of the vinaya, the views of that hidden ninety-five percent are at least worth bearing in mind.

So, to recapitulate, we have seen that the Linhuai ordination scandal undoubtedly deserves its place in the history of Buddhism and the state in China. For motives that were plainly economic and self-serving, a lawless and violent local boss sold ordinations—which should have been restricted to trained members of the Buddhist clergy—to all those who flocked to his territory to visit a famous site of pilgrimage, whatever their formal training in Buddhism or lack of it. This flouted both clear government regulations and the norms observed by the monastic Buddhist tradition throughout the centuries. At the same time, there are indications that this might not be the full story. The distinction between clergy and laity was one that Buddhism in China did not accept unquestioningly, and there are signs that at the particular time and place of the Linhuai scandal the urge to bring some form of ordination (albeit not one granting access to clerical life) to as many people as possible was unusually prominent—especially among experts on the vinaya who had fallen under the influence of the *Platform Sūtra*.

How the recipients of the Linhuai ordinations perceived the transaction in which they were involved may well have been a similarly ambiguous matter. We may presume that they were moved, like all people of all times and places, by the desire for economic advantage, by the prospect of paying out a sum of money to escape from some of the more demanding exactions of the state. But they came to a particularly holy place to carry out this transaction, and however perfunctory the ceremony in which they were involved, we cannot assume that all or perhaps even most of them regarded the setting as having no significance. In a place whence pilgrims were wont to carry away objects possessed of a certain sanctity—texts, icons, or what have you—even an ordination certificate, even a slightly dubious ordination certificate, might yet have been treated as an object of spiritual as well as secular power.

Indeed, the more we learn about the power of the imperial metaphor in Chinese religion, especially in post-Han China, the more complex we find the relationship between a Chinese sense of religion that read the spirit world as a bureaucracy and a worldly bureaucracy that at times seems tinged with an almost religious sense of its own worth. In this environment, where did the legal institutions of Buddhism fit? An examination of the Linhuai ordination scandal suggests that there is no straightforward answer. But, to return to the assertion made at the start of this essay, all I have hoped to show is that the interpretation and implementation of the vinaya in East Asia is not just a problem for students of Buddhism alone. One trusts, then, that the studies contained in this volume will not be viewed simply as a tribute to one teacher, but as material to be used by all who seek to advance our understanding of East Asian civilization. That is surely the best tribute a scholar can win.

Notes

1. Research in this area has been largely (though by no means exclusively) the preserve of Japanese scholars: The work of Moroto Tatsuo cited below forms a good recent example. Reflections of this scholarship may of course be found in the work of Stanley Weinstein (notably Weinstein 1987a) and also Jacques Gernet (1995).

2. This recognition has been almost entirely due to the exceptional pioneering work of Anna Seidel, which has now been subsumed under more recent scholarship such as Cedzich 1993; see her n. 7 for Seidel's publications.

3. The "precepts of the Tao" (daojie 道誡 written with the speech signifier) are usually discussed in relation to the text studied by Rao (1991, 103–108). But the same term (written as daojie 道戒 minus the speech signifier) occurs in the Baopuzi 抱朴子, a Daoist text in which (to anticipate for a moment) the terms "precept" and "prohibition" (jin 禁) are also compounded together. Unfortunately, this is not the place to explore these matters in detail.

4. The foregoing remarks are simply designed to raise the issue of bias. Sources indicating Li's support for Buddhism also should be considered before any overall judgement is made on his attitudes toward religion. The work of Koichi Shinohara (1991c) on Bai's inscriptions, for example, suggests that we should not associate Bai's personal views too closely with the contents of such writings.

5. Notice Wang's two appearances in Twitchett 1979 (541, 699), first as an exception to the general trend in the 820s, and second as a precedent cited by the rebels whose revolt presaged the final unraveling of Tang authority. The latter reference picks up a theme of the original historiography (Jiu Tang shu 舊唐書, fasc. 162,

4251; fasc. 163, 4271) and beyond (*Jinhuazi* 金華子, fasc. 1, 41) on the climate of violence Wang created.

6. Wang appears as a byword for harshness already in the *Yinhua lu* 凶話録 (fasc. 6, 115). But the *Taiping guangji* (fasc. 200, 1506–1507), drawing on a late-ninth-century source, emphasizes not only the terror with which he was regarded by the educated civil officials of his day, but also his unexpected willingness to defend their preoccupation with writing poetry. The *Taiping guangji* (fasc. 251, 1950) also preserves a sardonic remark Wang is said to have made concerning the court rank conferred on him.

7. The sources deriving from Li Deyu's memorial nowhere mention the Sengqie cult, but the link between Wang's fiscal moves and the pilgrimage center is already made in Hu Sanxing's 胡三省 (1230–1302) commentary on the *Zizhi tongjian* 資治通鑑, fasc. 243, 7840.

8. Gernet 1995 is an excellent survey of the sources from the perspective of relations between Buddhism and state authority. Chan (1991, 94–107) convincingly argues for a Han 漢 dynasty (BCE 206–208 CE) date for the theme of the superiority of the sage over the emperor, establishing the existence of a non-Buddhist Chinese tradition of independence from the state. Zürcher (1959) demonstrates the considerable extent to which acceptance of Buddhism in China amounted to acceptance of the idea of a religious order *(sangha)*.

9. A well-known example of the perpetual novice in mature Chinese Buddhism would be Gao Shami 高沙彌, dharma heir of Yaoshan Weiyan 藥山惟儼 (745–828), whose sayings are found in the *Jingde Era Transmission of the Lamp* (fasc. 14, T 51.315c). Note that the influence of the Buddhist notion of clerical celibacy on the Daoist clergy was picked up quite rapidly by Western scholarship (e.g., Maspero 1981, 390–391). Daoist influence on Buddhist conceptions of the clergy may be less apparent from our sources, but the possibility of such influence must nonetheless be addressed.

10. Kamata (1969, 281–285) sees Wei Yuansong's cooptation of the *Da Zhidu lun* 大智度論 as an important step in stimulating the subsequent development of Sui-Tang Buddhism, for all of Daoxuan's criticism. In view of the suspicion that the *Da Zhidu lun* was composed in Central Asia, one must recognize the possibility that Central Asian Buddhism may have influenced China in muddying the distinction between clergy and laity (note Ogasawara 1961).

11. This took place quite clearly in the Ming, but note the awareness of decline that prompts the remarks of Zhuhong 袾宏 (1535–1615) on the value of the laity quoted by Yü (1981, 140).

12. For early Chinese Buddhism evidence is given by the standard encyclopedia on origins *Shiwu jiyuan* 事物紀原 (fasc. 7, 386–387), whose author was quite well aware of the absence of ordination, though this knowledge is drawn from a Buddhist source. The origins of official ordination are discussed in Moroto 1990 (287–293). Moroto's studies give a comprehensive view of the development of state institutions for the control of Buddhism.

Chapter 5

From the Chinese Vinaya Tradition to Chan Regulations

Continuity and Adaptation

YIFA

CHINESE CHAN hagiographers have viewed the establishment of pure rules (*qinggui* 清規), or Chan monastic codes, as a decisive moment in the history of the Chan tradition, and the codes themselves as declarations of independence from other Buddhist schools, especially the Vinaya (Lü 律). Traditionally, Chan Master Baizhang Huaihai 百丈懷海 (749–814) was thought to have initiated this watershed movement by drawing up a set of innovative monastic rules for his own community, resulting in his commemoration as one of the great patriarchs of Chan along with Bodhidharma and Huineng 慧能 (638–713). This picture, however, has recently been challenged by modern scholars, most notably T. Griffith Foulk (1987 and 1993), who argue that Baizhang's position as the pioneer of the monastic code and the independent Chan monastery is, in fact, a fiction created during the Song dynasty (960–1279). Furthermore, as demonstrated by Morten Schlütter in this volume, the "Vinaya school monasteries" from which Baizhang is supposed to have separated the Chan school turn out to be simply a reference to the hereditary monasteries that constituted the majority of all Buddhist institutions. The earliest Chan monastic codes dating from the Song are still extant. Although scholars have studied this material, little attention has been paid to the question of whether such codes can be understood as declarations of independence by the Chan school.

In this essay I will place Chan regulations in the context of Chinese translations of vinaya literature and commentaries on that literature. When we examine the earliest extant Chan monastic code, the *Pure Rules for Chan Monasteries* (*Chanyuan qinggui* 禪苑清規, 1103), we find that a great deal of its source material and content is based directly on vinaya and on the works of the great vinaya advocate Daoan 道安 (312–385) and the vinaya master Daoxuan 道宣 (596–667). The many textual parallels between vinaya and the *Pure Rules for Chan Monasteries* challenge the widely held belief that Chan monasteries were unique and distinct from those run according to vinaya procedures. In the *Pure Rules for Chan Monasteries* we find not a rhetoric of distinction but an often word-for-word transmission of vinaya rules. Such an appropriation and adaptation of vinaya rules clearly shows that Chan was not a movement born of an innovative declaration of independence. At the same time, however, a close look at the *Pure Rules for Chan Monasteries* brings to light another discovery: its incorporation of Chinese governmental policies and traditional Chinese etiquette based on Confucian ideology, both of which are absent from the vinaya texts. The *Pure Rules for Chan Monasteries* elaborates on certain rules and regulations with respect to the influence of Chinese social and cultural norms. Given these additions, one is compelled to ask if they merely demonstrate the inevitable infiltration of Chinese norms into Chan practices based on Indian vinaya or if the Chan school as represented by the *Pure Rules for Chan Monasteries* was self-consciously calling into question the legitimacy of a purely Indian vinaya by developing a more sinicized one.

Using the earliest extant Chan monastic documents available, we can, through an examination of the differences or similarities that existed between the Chan tradition and monastic procedures based on vinaya regulations, demonstrate both a clear sense of continuity traceable to the original vinaya texts from India and an adaptation to the surrounding Chinese culture. Due to the length of the *Pure Rules for Chan Monasteries,* it is impossible to discuss the entire work in this essay. Instead, I have selected only those portions that will help determine which textual elements may be identified as having been adopted from the vinaya and which reveal traces of Chinese cultural influence.

Because the *Pure Rules for Chan Monasteries* was written for use in public monasteries, it provides us with a wealth of information about monastic life in twelfth-century Song China. The code offers very specific guidelines for itinerant monks, emphasizes the importance of studying under masters at various monasteries, prescribes the proper protocol for attending retreats, and details the procedure for requesting an abbot's instruction. A significant portion of the text is devoted to administrative hierarchy within the monastery, including the duties and powers of monastic officers. An equal amount of attention is given to the proper social deportment of monks of various ranks vis-à-vis one another, especially with regard to decorum at tea ceremonies, chanting rituals, and monastic auctions.

As stated earlier, many Chan practices can be linked to scholar monks who studied vinaya and whose codifications preceded Baizhang. An examination of the works of Vinaya Master Daoxuan reveals that some of the major features of Chan regulations originated in the vinaya scholastic tradition initiated by Daoxuan and were implemented much earlier than has been suspected. But because Daoxuan himself largely preserved practices already codified by the earlier Daoan, through his works we can discern indirectly the number of Chan monastic practices carried out today that can be traced as far back as the fourth century. For instance, the use of the octagonal hammer and its stand, which occupy the center of the *saṅgha* hall (*sengtang* 僧堂) in Chan monasteries, is not a Chan invention but dates from the time of Daoxuan, who, in turn, inherited the practice from Daoan. The striking stand and hammer are described in Daoxuan's *Four Part Vinaya Practice and Service Comments* (*Sifen lü shanfan buque xingshi chao* 四分律刪繁補缺行事鈔), his main commentary on the *Four Part Vinaya*. According to this commentary, during the ceremony of precept instruction, the rector stands at the "place for signaling quietness" (*dajing chu* 打靜處) with the roll-call stick (*chou* 籌) in his left hand and the hammer in his right. The text also provides instruction on how to strike the stand:

> First the rector stands outside the gate, prepares his demeanor, and presses his palms together. He then enters through the side door and approaches the striking position. After standing with his palms closed, he lifts the hammer with his right hand and touches it to the stand silently. He then hits the stand with the hammer once, being careful not to do so too loudly. After this he silently rests the hammer on the stand, holding the handle. Then he presses his palms together and makes the appropriate announcements. If there is a meal offering, a chanting benediction, or a prayer to be made, all must wait until the rector has announced the proper procedure. The hammer cannot be used for any other purposes except to pacify the assembly. (Fasc. 27, T 40.146b16–21)

Thus the method of striking the stand with the hammer in a Chan monastery is very much like that found in the Vinaya tradition. (The *Pure Rules for Chan Monasteries* provides a more detailed description, however [fasc. 6, 217–224; see Yifa 2002, 200–201].) Various verses chanted by Tang- and Song-period Chan monks described in Daoxuan's commentary can also be traced back to Daoan's time. The "verse of five contemplations," chanted by Chan monks before meals up to the present day, has its provenance in Daoxuan's *Four Part Vinaya Practice and Service Comments* (T 40.84a9–12; 40.128b3–129a13).[1] The use of special objects to maintain vigilance during meditation in the *saṅgha* halls and the striking of a signal instrument to summon the assembly are both first depicted in the vinaya.

The *Ten Recitation Vinaya* (fasc. 40, T 23.288c20–289b6), for example, relates the following story of some monks who were unable to meditate without falling asleep. The Buddha allowed them to wash their heads to prevent drowsiness; when this did not succeed, he gave permission to other monks to pour water on them, or nudge them by hand, or cast balls at them. Eventually the Buddha allowed the use of a "meditation stick" (*chanzhang* 禪杖). This stick is held by one of the monks (exactly which monk is not specified) over his head, with one hand on each end. He strikes any monk who falls asleep and returns to his meditation position only when he is sure no one is asleep. Another item approved by the Buddha is the "meditation tablet" (*chanzhen* 禪鎮). A string is run through a hole in the tablet down either side of the head and tied to each ear; a monk falling asleep during meditation will cause the tablet to fall, waking himself up with a start.

Similar objects and practices appear in the *Mahāsāṃghika Vinaya* (fasc. 35, T 22.513a5–b7). Here a junior monk specifically is given charge of the meditation stick. Even if his teacher (*ācārya*) should fall asleep, the monk must wake him, out of respect for the Dharma. First, he shakes the stick in front of the sleeper three times. If this does not rouse him, the sleeper is poked in the knee with the stick. Once a monk is awakened, he must take over the stick duties. During cold weather, the Buddha allowed monks who were shivering and could not properly hold the stick the use of a cloth "meditation ball" (*chanqiu* 禪毬), which is cast in front of the sleeper.

Even the use of four nesting bowls at mealtimes, often thought unique to the Chan monastery, can be found in the vinaya texts. The origin of the four bowls is related in the *Five Part Vinaya* (fasc. 15, T 22.103a23–27). After attaining enlightenment, the Buddha continued to enjoy the happiness of meditation. When five hundred merchants offered the Buddha honey, the Buddha suddenly perceived that all Buddhas in the past had received such offerings in bowls as will all Buddhas in the future. And now, he, too, was receiving food in a bowl. When the four guardian deities divined this thought, each one offered the Buddha a stone bowl that contained natural and pure fragrances. The Buddha accepted all four bowls with equal gratitude. He stacked them on his left palm and with his right hand pressed them into one. The *Four Part Vinaya* (fasc. 39, T 22.848b27–28) states that the Buddha permitted cream, oil, honey, and stone honey to be served in the bowls and ordered them stored "the smallest bowl (*jianci* 鍵瓷) [stacked] inside the second smallest, the second smallest into the third, and the third into the largest bowl."

Ordination seniority as the key factor in determining the order of monks in their various activities is a concept emphasized both in Chan pure rules and in the vinaya. The vinaya explains that when monks did not know how to decide the seniority of members, some suggested that it be based on the caste system, others suggested appearance, still others suggested personal cultivation. The Buddha then told the well-known bird-monkey-elephant story. A bird, a monkey, and an elephant who lived near a tree were arguing one day about which one of them should be considered the senior of the group. The elephant insisted that he could recall that when he was young the top of the tree touched his stomach as he passed over it. The monkey contended that when was young he could bite the top of the tree. Finally the bird announced that long ago he remembered eating a piece of fruit and spitting out the seed from which the tree eventually grew. Thus the bird was regarded as the most senior. By way of analogy, the Buddha proclaimed that those who received full ordination first, who had been at the monastery the longest, should occupy the senior seats (*Five Part Vinaya*, fasc. 17, T 22.121a12–25; *Four Part Vinaya*, fasc. 50, T 22.940a7–27; *Ten Recitation Vinaya*, fasc. 34, T 23.242b15–c13).

The vinaya concept of dividing items or subjects into two categories—pure and impure (or soiled)—was also adopted in the Chan monastic code. According to the *Pure Rules for Chan Monas-*

teries, "pure clothes" (*jingyi* 淨衣), which include the monk's robes, short overshirt (*pianshan* 偏衫; lit., "side clothes"), lined jacket, and vest, should be placed in the front knapsack. "Soiled clothes" (*chuyi* 觸衣) such as the bedsheet, cotton clothes, and undergarments are placed in the rear knapsack. Daoxuan's *Exhortation on Manners and Etiquette for Novices in Training* (*Jiaojie xinxue biqiu xinghu lüyi* 教誡新學比丘行護律儀, T 45.873a24–25) indicates that in the bathroom the "pure pole" and the "soiled pole" are to be used for hanging only corresponding garments. The Chan code notes that the top half of the outside of a bowl is "pure," while the bottom half is "soiled." (According to Daoxuan, "the upper two-thirds of the outside of a bowl is considered 'pure,' the lower third is 'soiled'" [T 45.871b26–27].) The walking stick that a Chan monk takes on his travels is also divided into two parts: The handle of the stick with twigs on it is considered the "soiled end" (*chutou* 觸頭), the tip with no twigs the "pure end" (*jingtou* 淨頭). For the most part, the handle of any object is considered "soiled": In Daoxuan's works the part of the ladle that dips into the water is regarded as "pure," but the handle is "soiled." Stipulations as to which foot must be used first to enter a door or gate in a Chan monastery and rituals and ceremonies such as the auction of a deceased monk's possessions, the offering of food to all sentient beings, and the burning of incense while circumambulating the hall—all of these have clear precedents in the vinaya.

The final section of this essay will focus on Chan regulations in the *Pure Rules for Chan Monasteries* that include elements foreign to the original vinaya texts—elements that, as stated above, incorporated traditional Chinese etiquette. Prevailing Chinese customs exerted a major influence on the composition of Chan Buddhist monastic codes and can themselves be traced in large part to the ancient Confucian scriptures known as the *Book of Rites* (*Lijing* 禮 經), or the *Three Rites* (*Sanli* 三禮): namely, the *Zhouli* 周禮, the *Yili* 儀禮, and the *Liji* 禮記. In adopting many aspects of Confucian governmental protocol, the Buddhist monastery came to resemble the imperial court in miniature with the abbot as emperor, including the design of the abbot's residence and the method of his sermons in the dharma hall. Furthermore, the hierarchical staff of the monastic administration was created in direct imitation of civil and military positions in the Chinese government. The rules of decorum for the highly ritualized monastic tea ceremony have their direct precedents in the literature of Confucianism, and worship of the ancient legendary emperors as national deities in Confucian tradition also found its way into the ceremonies held in Buddhist monasteries. For example, if we examine the layout of buildings in a Buddhist monastery of the Song period, paying special attention to details surrounding the abbot, we see how this is so. The abbot's residency is modeled after the private quarters of the emperor, the original conception of which can be found in the *Book of Rites.* In most monasteries, the abbot's quarters (*fangzhang* 方丈) were built behind the dharma hall, the two bridged by an intermediary chamber known as the *qintang* 寢堂. The abbot gave sermons in the dharma hall on formal occasions but withdrew to receive visitors and give more private sermons in the *qintang* and retired to the rearmost quarters to sleep—an arrangement largely adopted from imperial custom. In the annotation to the *Liji* (see the *Shisan jing zhushu* 十三經注疏, 1982, 1.1362a), the Chinese glyph *qin* 寢 refers to the rear section of an imperial ancestral temple, a meaning clearly explained by the annotation to the *Liji:* "The front part of the [ancestral] shrine is called the '*miao*' 廟; the rear part is called the '*qin.*'" More detailed annotation is given in this commentary (1982, 1.1362a–b): "The *miao* is where deities are received; it is considered a place of honor and therefore it is located in the front. The *qin* is where [the ancestral] clothing is kept; it is considered inferior and therefore it is in the rear. Attached to the east and west sides of the *miao* are two chambers, separated by partitions; the *qin,* however, is just one large room."

From the *Pure Rules for Chan Monasteries* it is evident that the tea ceremony, held on a variety of occasions, was a major component of social life inside the Chinese monastery. The abbot and the prior (*jianyuan* 監院) as the chief of administrators held tea services to commemorate the transfer of duties from old to new administrators or from old to new chief officers. At the commencement and closing of the summer retreat, the abbot, the prior, and the chief seat of the *saṅgha* hall (*shouzuo* 首座) all sponsored tea ceremonies. The abbot was also expected to hold tea services for visiting government officers. Tea services were sponsored by junior monks as well. Even those who were not members of the administrative staff were responsible for holding a tea ceremony for the abbot and administrators. The abbot's dharma heirs and select disciples (*rushi dizi* 入室弟子) sponsored a tea ceremony for the abbot. These ceremonies were indispensable for acquainting members of the assembly with administrators and were so frequent that descriptions of ceremony procedures, down to the most minute details, constitute a central part of the *Pure Rules for Chan Monasteries* and all subsequent monastic codes.

During the Song the tea service became an important part of social life throughout China. It seems clear that the Buddhist community simply adopted a custom predominant in secular society. The development of commerce and industry as well as the growing trend toward urbanization exposed people to a far greater level of material comfort than they had previously known. The drinking of tea was no longer restricted to the aristocracy but became a habit of the common people. Tea was now an indispensable item, as much a daily staple as rice and salt even for the peasant in the countryside. Over time many temples began to grow tea on their estates for their own needs or to sell. Vinaya and Tiantai monastic codes of the later Yuan period contain sections describing tea ceremony protocol, indicating that other schools were eventually affected by the prevailing tea culture and followed practices similar to those found in Chan regulations.

Although Buddhist monasteries adopted the practice of drinking tea from secular society, the Chan tea service undoubtedly wielded its own influence on social customs outside the monastery. Any visitor to a Chan monastery would have been treated to the sweetened drink served in the context of a tea ceremony and would have seen the skillful production of tea on the premises. The monastery helped promote a ritualized conception of tea drinking that ultimately extended beyond its walls, and may have served directly as a major distributor of tea for the Chinese market as well. The extremely meticulous tea service etiquette outlined in monastic regulations—including instructions on where each person should walk, who should bow or speak to whom and when—cannot be found in the original vinaya; it is an invention of Chinese Buddhism that reflects a culture rooted in classical Confucian works, particularly the *Yili*.

The Chan monastic code offers many examples of "humble speech," the ritualized verbal exchanges demanded at auspicious moments between members of the monastery. Characterized by hyperbole and extreme deference, the self-deprecating nature of these expressions can be seen in the following exchanges. An abbot offers

tea to a visiting government official: "We would now like to offer
our low-grade tea (or low-grade sweetened drink) and we will follow all of Official X's instructions." If the official offers a compli-
ment, the abbot is ready with a scripted reply: "This low-grade tea
is merely a token of our sincerity. It is not worthy for you" (fasc. 5,
177–183). At the end of a ceremony sponsored by the prior or chief
seat, the host thanks the abbot: "Today our humble low-grade tea
(or, Today our inferior sweetened drink . . .) has received your grace,
master, for out of kindness you have stooped to receive it; and for
this we are extremely grateful" (fasc. 5, 184–189). Similarly, after a
ceremony sponsored by the assembly, the monastic host expresses
the assembly's gratitude with these words: "Today's tea (or, Today's
sweetened drink . . .) was served specially for X and Y. Although the
tea is of a low grade and the seats are uncomfortable, they came
anyway. For this fact we are extremely grateful." As a show of ap-
preciation to the other guests, the host repeats his expressions of
gratitude: "Today the tea (or sweetened drink) was served especially
for X and Y. I am afraid that this ceremony was not worth bother-
ing you [i.e., the other guests accompanying them]" (fasc. 5, 193–
193).

Such formalized language expressing humility and indebtedness has clear precedents in the Confucian book of protocol, the
Yili, which provides this account of a duke inviting foreign dignita-
ries to a banquet:

> The invitation is extended to them [through envoys] in the following
> form: "Our unworthy Prince has some inferior wine, and, wishing
> your honors to spend a little time with him, he sends me to invite you."
>
> To this [the messengers of the guests] reply: "Our unworthy Prince
> is a feudatory of yours, so let your Prince not incur disgrace by confer-
> ring benefits on us mere messengers. Your servants venture to decline."
>
> The messenger [of the host] then replies: "My unworthy Prince in-
> sists on saying that the wine is of poor quality, and sends me to press
> the invitation on your honors."
>
> To which the [messengers of the] guests reply: "Our unworthy
> Prince is a feudatory of yours, and your Prince should not demean
> himself by showing kindness to mere messengers. Your servants ven-
> ture to persist in declining."
>
> The messenger [of the host] again replies: "My unworthy Prince
> persists in saying the wine is of no quality, and he sends me to urge
> his invitation on you."

> They then answer: "As we have failed to secure permission to decline, dare we do other than accept?"²

From this brief exchange we can discern rules of decorum that will later be standardized in the monastery. Some of these unspoken rules include a depreciation of anything of one's own and observing the pattern of two humble refusals, under the pretense of unworthiness, followed by a seemingly reluctant acquiescence. Highly rhetorical language, so typical of Confucian etiquette, is evident in the *Pure Rules for Chan Monasteries* when, for example, a candidate humbly refuses to accept a proposed abbacy out of respect for the soliciting monastery. Only when the envoys come with a third pressing invitation should the abbot accept the new appointment (fasc. 7, 250–252).

To return to the tea ceremony, members of the *sangha* must show extreme humility when bowing and walking. Once again, we find protocol that mirrors the meticulous courtesies described in the *Yili*. According to the *Pure Rules for Chan Monasteries*, the master of ceremonies (*xing fashi ren* 行法事人; lit., "the person who presides over the service")³ performs the ritual as follows:

> After the midday meal, the bell is struck in front of the *sangha* hall. Everyone is seated and the master of ceremonies stands by the south [left] side of the front gate facing the Holy Monk. With his hands clasped, the master of ceremonies slowly bows and, leaving his position, comes up to the Holy Monk and again bows. Having done this, he stands before the incense burner, bows, opens the incense case, and with his left hand lifts up the incense. Having completed this, he steps back slightly and again bows. Once he has done this he goes to the rear door and bows to the guest of honor. He then turns to the south, approaches the Holy Monk, and bows. Then he turns north and bows to the abbot. He then circumambulates the hall and comes to the first seat from the north [right] side of the rear door. Bending his body, he bows and then moves to the first seat on the south [left] side and, bending his body, bows. If the master of ceremonies then moves to the outside section of the hall, he should bow first to the right-hand section and then to the left, reenter the hall, and approach the Holy Monk. He then bows, returns to his original position, bows, and then remains standing with hands clasped. (Fasc. 5, 184–189)

Here is an excerpt describing an offering of wine to a guest of honor from the chapter "The Banquet" in the *Yili:*

The master of ceremonies walks to where he can wash his cup and stands to the south of the vessel, facing northwest. The guest of honor then descends, and, standing to the west of the westernmost steps, faces east. The master of ceremonies then begs pardon for the undeserved honor of his company, and the guest replies in the proper fashion. Then the master of ceremonies, facing north, washes his hands and, sitting down, takes the drinking cup and washes it. The guest advances slightly and declines the honor [of accepting the drink]. The master of ceremonies, still sitting, places the drinking cup in the basket and, rising, responds with the appropriate words, whereupon the guest returns to his seat. When the master of ceremonies finishes the washing, the guest, with a salute, ascends [the platform] followed by the master of ceremonies. The guest bows in acknowledgment of the washing, and the master of ceremonies, standing at the guest's right side, lays down the drinking cup and responds with a bow. (Steele 1917, 1.125, with slight modifications)

Thus the protocol for the tea ceremony depicted in Buddhist codes reflects the rituals described in Confucian works, which, in turn, stem from carefully prescribed practices carried out by the imperial court and the nobility. In fact, it is possible that a great deal of monastic ritual was adopted directly from the highest levels of Chinese society. Many of the most renowned monks were sponsored by the court or by aristocrats and may have been influenced by their benefactors. At the same time, members of the gentry made social calls or extended visits to monasteries, and their presence may have had an effect on daily monastic life.

In this essay I have attempted to demonstrate that the earliest known records of the Chan monastic code were directly influenced by the vinaya texts, vinaya literature, and the Chinese cultural milieu of the times. These Chan texts, therefore, cannot be said to represent a departure from historical Indian Buddhism any greater than the gradual changes experienced by other contemporary Buddhist schools in China. If one were to isolate any single element of the Chan school that may be considered unique to the tradition, one could perhaps look to the practice of *gong'an* 公案 (J. *kōan*) introspection, which is a later development. In studying the earliest Chan codes, however, I have found no evidence that these regulations distinguish the observances of the Chan tradition from those customarily kept in monasteries governed by vinaya regulations or regulations devised in other Chinese Buddhist schools. In short, this Chan monastic code can in no way be considered a declaration of Chan independence from the vinaya tradition although it offers some rather interesting points for further investigation into the subject of Chan identity vis-à-vis India or China. Thus we are left with a question for future inquiry: To what degree does the *Pure Rules for Chan Monasteries* reflect an attempt at a further sinicization of Buddhism?

Notes

1. The five contemplations are: (1) to ponder the effort necessary to supply this food and to appreciate its origins; (2) to reflect on one's own virtue as insufficient to receive the offering; (3) to protect the mind's integrity, to depart from error, and, as a general principle, to avoid being greedy; (4) to consider the food as medicine and bodily nourishment that prevents emaciation; and (5) to receive this food as necessary for attaining enlightenment.

2. This English translation is from John Steele's *The I-li: Book of Etiquette and Ceremonial*, 1:145. The words in brackets are my own.

3. The master of ceremonies is usually the host of the ceremony. When the abbot sponsors a tea ceremony for the assembly, however, his attendant usually presides as the master of ceremonies.

Chapter 6

Vinaya Monasteries, Public Abbacies, and State Control of Buddhism under the Song (960–1279)

Morten Schlütter

The Buddhist vinaya pictures the monastic community as a largely autonomous, self-regulating body. But nowhere in premodern East Asia was monastic Buddhism truly free of controls imposed by the secular state, even when the Buddhist church exercised considerable political influence. In China, the imperial government always considered the monastic Buddhist community and its activities as properly subject to state supervision. Chinese dynasties actively sought to regulate and control many aspects of the Buddhist church's activities, such as ordination procedures, the building of monasteries, the activities of monks and nuns, and the teachings Buddhism was spreading. The Chinese state was traditionally extremely hostile toward unregulated religious groups and tended to view all religious expression with suspicion (McKnight 1992, 75–79). The fear was that religious groups could disrupt public order, threaten the authority of the state, corrupt people's morals, and even become sources of rebellion. The mainstream Buddhist church was tolerated precisely because of its close ties with the government and its elite's relative aloofness from the populace. Any Buddhist group that appeared deviant was persecuted by the state—and decried by the Buddhist establishment. The state never completely lost its suspicion of even the elite Buddhist church, and from time to time emperors sought to all but eradicate Buddhism from Chinese soil (prior to the Song there were major suppressions in the years 258, 446, 574, 845, 955; see Overmyer 1976, 23). However, government control of Buddhism and other religion was always far from total, and many factors combined to keep much of the growth and development of monastic Buddhism beyond the reach of the state.

During the Song 宋 dynasty (960–1279) monastic Buddhism experienced a tremendous growth but was also more tightly regulated. At first control measures that had existed earlier, such as rules and restrictions concerning ordinations, were further developed and vigorously implemented (Moroto 1990, 233). But the Song government also instituted several innovative ways of controlling monastic Buddhism and concerned itself with aspects of it that had not been previously legislated or directly controlled. These new control measures had a profound and lasting impact on the development of Buddhism in the Song and subsequent dynasties.

In this essay I focus my attention on the new Song system of classifying Buddhist monasteries as either "hereditary" or "public" according to how their abbots were selected. Although the Song monastic classification system has received some attention from scholars (Takao 1975, Chikusa 1982, Huang 1989, Getz 1994), much of it is not well understood, and the profound impact the implementation of the system had on the development of the Chan 禪 school has hitherto gone unnoticed. Furthermore, because hereditary monasteries in the Song were often referred to as "vinaya monasteries," confusion about the meaning of this term has given rise to serious misunderstandings in scholarship concerning both the system of hereditary and public monasteries and the nature and history of the Vinaya school.

The Northern Song System of Registering Monasteries

From its establishment the Song government, like previous imperial governments, saw the primary raison d'être for the Buddhist church to be the supernatural assistance and blessings it could provide to the state and the emperor. Prayers for the long life of the emperor and for the prosperity of the state were important functions of all Buddhist monasteries, and emperors no doubt felt they could accrue merit for themselves and their dynasty through pious acts toward Buddhism. The Song court patronized Buddhism in various ways. Famous monasteries were given money or grants of land, and illustrious monks were invited to court and honored with the bestowal of purple robes. The state was actively engaged in the translation of Buddhist scriptures as well as in the compiling and printing of the Buddhist canon. The imperial family also used the services of Buddhist clergy directly. Specially built monasteries

were charged with taking care of the imperial tombs, and a monastery was even erected on the site of the first Song emperor Taizu's
太祖 (r. 960–976) birthplace (*Song huiyao jigao* 宋會要輯稿, fasc.
200.7879c). But the Song rulers were very aware of the considerable
economic and social power that the Buddhist church wielded and
saw a need to regulate and exercise control over monastic Buddhism. The imperial government was uneasy with the enormous
economic impact the building and maintenance of monasteries
and the upkeep of monks and nuns had on the economy. It was
also concerned about the social and cultural impact of Buddhism
and worried that the Buddhist church could become a threat to the
state's authority or that monasteries might harbor criminals and
insurgents.[1]

Central to the Northern Song (960–1127) policy of tolerating
and even encouraging the growth of monastic Buddhism, while at
the same time seeking to keep it in check, was its policy of granting
name plaques (*e* 額) to a large number of monasteries (Takao 1975,
57–60; Chikusa 1982, 83–110; Huang 1989, 302–305). This policy
had originally been a way of honoring certain important monasteries; in the Tang 唐 (618–906) monasteries with name plaques
enjoyed a high degree of security from officials who wished to
suppress Buddhism, while those that were merely on the list of
approved monasteries did not have the same level of protection.[2]
During the initial stages of the notorious Huichang 會昌 (841–847)
suppression of Buddhism, when the government issued an edict
ordering the dismantling of various types of Buddhist establishments, monasteries with name plaques were explicitly exempted.[3]
Owning a name plaque also became crucial for a monastery during
another vigorous suppression of Buddhism that took place under
the Latter Zhou 後周 (951–960), the regime under which the Song
founder Taizu had served as a general. The Zhou ruler ordered
in 955 that any monastery without an imperially bestowed name
plaque was to be destroyed.[4]

The Song government exploited the positive connotations of
name plaques and used them as a way of registering monasteries
(Chikusa 1982, 101). Beginning with the second Song emperor, Tai-
zong 太宗 (r. 976–997), the imperial government granted name
plaques to monasteries in large numbers. Although the plaque
granting took place throughout the Northern Song (and at a much
reduced scale in the later part of the Song known as the Southern

Song, 1127–1279), it was especially the reigns of Zhenzong 眞宗 (r. 977–1022) and Yingzong 英宗 (r. 1063–1067) that saw large-scale granting of plaques (Chikusa 1982, 109; Huang 1989, 304–305). Usually the main requirement for a plaque was that a monastery's buildings total thirty bays or more (Chikusa 1982, 98–99). This meant that numerous smaller monasteries of primarily local importance could be granted plaques; prior to the Song only especially illustrious or imperially favored monasteries were granted plaques.

It is clear that the Song government's driving motivation in granting plaques was to bring monasteries of any significance under control and supervision. But in spite of the occasional edicts that ordered the destruction of monasteries with no plaques (i.e., those under thirty bays and of no particular significance), plaque-less monasteries seem to have flourished and orders of destruction were rarely, if ever, carried out. The Song government appears to have been fairly unconcerned with smaller monasteries, probably because it was thought that those under thirty bays in general would not be important enough in local life to warrant strong action.[5] It would also seem that the decrees ordering no new monasteries to be built must have been largely ignored because throughout the Northern Song monasteries that qualified for name plaques by having more than thirty bays continued to appear.[6]

The Northern Song government's policy of registering and facilitating control of all monasteries of importance through the granting of plaques was highly successful. Receiving an imperial plaque was perceived as a great honor and could provide security for a monastery in times of persecution. It is not surprising then that those in charge of monasteries petitioned for them with great enthusiasm. Thus the state achieved its goal of facilitating control in a way that secured the cooperation of the clergy, who otherwise may not have felt that government registration was beneficial to them.[7] A large number of monasteries were registered during the Northern Song: One source from about 1059 reports that there were thirty-nine thousand registered Buddhist monasteries in the empire, up from twenty-five thousand fifty years earlier (Chikusa 1982, 89).

Registering monasteries was essential for the state, for without doing so, it could not successfully set down and enforce rules and regulations for them. The registration of monasteries facilitated an entirely new way of regulating Buddhist monasteries that had a profound impact on the further development of Buddhism in China. This was the system of classifying monasteries or, more specifically, their abbacies, into two main groups: hereditary (usually termed "succession" [*jiayi* 甲乙], but also known as "disciple" [*tudi* 徒弟] or "ordained disciple" [*dudi* 度弟]) monasteries and public ("ten directions" [*shifang* 十方]) monasteries (cf. Welch 1967). As I will discuss shortly, a hereditary monastery was associated with a group of monks who held the rights to occupy its abbacy; the monastery and its property in a sense belonged to these monks. Such monasteries could be very large, and many owned land and other property, but in the Song, most were small to medium sized. A hereditary monastery was "private" in the sense that outsiders could not assume any of its offices, and monks from the outside did not have rights to reside there. In contrast, a public monastery was a kind of independent, self-owned institution over which no individual or group of individuals could claim ownership and the abbacy of which supposedly was open to any qualified candidate within certain sectarian restrictions. Any monk with good credentials could be admitted into a public monastery and advance in its various monastic offices. All the largest and most important monasteries in the Song eventually became public monasteries.

Hereditary Monasteries

Hereditary monasteries were recognized by the state as in effect the legal property of the monks or nuns living there. The residents of a hereditary monastery were bound together in a complex lineage relationship and formed a "tonsure family" (cf. Welch 1967, 129–134). Its abbacy was passed down through the tonsure family only and outsiders were excluded. Through its control of the abbacy the tonsure family was able to retain property rights to the monastery and its land because the abbot and his officers were the only ones who could make decisions concerning it. Like the Chan lineages and those developed within other Buddhist groups such as the Tiantai 天台 school, the lineage of a tonsure family was similar to that of a regular family descent group except that it was based on a teacher-disciple relationship. Thus the disciples of one master were regarded as brothers, their master's master was their grandfather, and their master's fellow disciples were their uncles.[8] But unlike the Chan model, the teacher-disciple relationship in a tonsure family was not based on a teacher sanctioning the enlightenment experience or profound insight of a student, but on the tonsure the novice received on entering the Buddhist order. The novice became the personally ordained disciple of the master giving or sponsoring his tonsure and was adopted into the tonsure family of that master. Such personally ordained disciples were usually referred to as *"dudizi"* 度弟子. In this way, all monks and nuns were members of a tonsure family, and for the vast majority their tonsure lineage was what gave them identity and defined the framework of their monastic career. Some monks and nuns went on to gain admission to one of the big public monasteries and perhaps later received a special transmission in the Chan or Tiantai lineages, but even so they remained members of their tonsure family and any disciples they ordained became members of that family.

Hereditary monasteries may have had a long history by the Song, and it is likely that prior to the Song most monasteries were in some sense hereditary.[9] However, it was only in the Song that hereditary monasteries acquired a specific legal status, which recognized the tonsure family's rights to its monastery. This legal status no doubt offered the tonsure families in hereditary monasteries some protection against those who might try to usurp their property. But together with the system of registration, it also greatly facilitated government control and made it possible for the state to set down and enforce rules concerning many aspects of monastic life, including how the abbacy was to be filled.

An important source for the study of Song legislation on monastic Buddhism is the section on Buddhism and Daoism in the Song law compendium the *Classified Legal Articles of the Qingyuan Period* (*Qingyuan tiaofa shilei* 慶元條法事類).[10] The *Classified Legal Articles* is the only extant (though incomplete) Song law manual. Although it dates from the Southern Song, many of the regulations it contains are clearly of long standing, and in the Buddhism and Daoism section some were even long outdated by the Qingyuan period (1195–1200). In this text rules for the passing down of the abbacy in a hereditary monastery are clearly spelled out. For example, when an abbot of a "nonpublic" monastery died or for some reason stepped down, the abbacy passed on to one of his dharma brothers (the other tonsure disciples of his master) according to their order in the lineage, that is, when they were ordained. If there were no dharma brothers available, the abbacy was passed to one of the retiring abbot's disciples or to one of his dharma brothers' disciples, also in accordance with seniority (fasc. 50.476d). In this way, everybody in each generation had a chance, at least theoretically, to succeed to the abbacy, and only when one generation had been exhausted would the abbacy be passed on to the next generation. It seems the abbacy in a hereditary monastery was often held by one person until he passed away, so many members of big tonsure family may not have lived long enough to succeed to the abbacy.[11]

On the other hand, a monk capable of taking over a vacant abbacy may not always have been available from the tonsure family. A note in the *Classified Legal Articles* (fasc. 50, 476d) says that if there is a worthy, well-esteemed monk whom the congregation wants as abbot, they can present him to the authorities to have him first installed to fill the position. This probably refers for the most part to a situation where no one in the tonsure family was ready to take over the abbacy, such as instances when everyone in line for the abbacy was underage. It is also possible that the tonsure family could simply decide to bring an abbot in from outside the group, although it would seem likely that the monks normally in line for the abbacy would protest such a move.[12] The *Classified Legal Articles* further states that only those who were actively involved with the affairs of a hereditary monastery could be appointed to its abbacy (fasc. 50, 476b). Those who had been away from the monastery for more than half a year or who were not actually fulfilling the duties of their positions were not allowed to take over the abbacy even if they were in line for it. The text also asserts that, in most cases, those who had been punished by the law could not succeed to the abbacy (fasc. 50, 477a).

Significantly, a stipulation required the newly selected abbot of a hereditary monastery to be approved by the authorities before he could be installed in the abbacy (fasc. 50.476b). Thus, although the Song state had to recognize the rights of the tonsure family to control the abbacy of its monastery, the government could at least set down very strict rules for how the succession was to take place and who in fact could occupy the abbacy. As we have just seen, by law only those who were actively taking part in the life of a monastery could become its abbots; this rule helped ensure that the governing of the monastery remained a local affair and thus easier to supervise. Because all appointments had to be approved by officials, there were plenty of opportunities in the final instance for local authorities to intervene in various ways and to be sure that no undesirable person occupied an abbacy in their area of jurisdiction.

There are other indications that the state in principle acknowledged that a tonsure family had a legal right to its monastery. An article in the *Classified Legal Articles* concerning the selection of abbots at public monasteries notes that the succession rules must be followed strictly, even at previously hereditary monasteries where "the disciples had agreed to [the] change into public" (fasc. 50.476c). This remark indicates that a tonsure family had to agree to its monastery being changed into a public one and implies that the state recognized that the family had property rights. As will be discussed below, several documented cases of the conversion of hereditary monasteries into public ones further attest to this.

Finally, hereditary monasteries were probably supposed to apply to the government to have their status officially approved.[13] But this seems to have been rarely done—at least there are very few records of such applications. Most likely the understanding was that if a monastery was not categorized as public it was automatically considered hereditary.[14]

Public Monasteries

As noted above, the *Classified Legal Articles* addresses its rules for succession in hereditary monasteries to "all nonpublic" institutions. This suggests that the most important feature of the system of classification, and its main innovation, was the public monastery. In a public monastery the abbacy was not passed down in a tonsure family. In fact, an abbot's own tonsure disciples were not allowed to succeed him to the abbacy, a measure clearly meant to prevent a return to a hereditary system. The abbot of a public monastery was supposed to be the best candidate available, whether he could be found within the walls of the monastery or had to be invited from elsewhere.

Some form of the public abbacy system appears to have existed prior to the Song.[15] But although the Song government did not invent the system of public abbacies, it was only in the Song that public monasteries become an official legal category. The Song government seems very quickly to have become aware of the advantages of having monasteries designated as public and began early on to promote public abbacies as an important part of a national policy toward monastic Buddhism. Unlike the case of hereditary monasteries, where the secular authorities' power over the selection process was limited because the choice of abbot was mainly determined by rules of succession within the tonsure family, the abbacies at public monasteries were wide open to state control.

The *Classified Legal Articles* includes a section of rules concerning the selection of the abbot at a public monastery. According to this text, when the abbacy at a public monastery became vacant, the prefectural authorities were to charge the local Buddhist registry (*Seng zhengsi* 僧正司) with arranging a meeting between the abbots of the other public monasteries (presumably from the whole prefecture). These abbots were to select someone (again, it would seem, from the prefecture) who had been a monk for many years, who was accomplished in conduct and study, and who was held in high esteem by other monks. The choice of the gathered abbots was presented to the prefectural authorities, who would investigate and confirm the appointment if no problems were found. If there was no suitable candidate, perhaps because no one could be found in the prefecture or because the abbots could not agree on anyone, the authorities would select a monk from another area who was held in high regard and who was not known to have committed any crime or to have had other things against him. The *Classified Legal Articles* stresses that this person, once chosen, could not be substituted. Also, as mentioned above, even if the monastery previously had been hereditary, these rules still had to be obeyed (p. 476c). Another source that casts some light on the procedure of appointing a new abbot in a public monastery is the *Pure Rules for Chan Monasteries* (*Chanyuan qinggui* 禪苑清規), compiled by the monk Changlu Zongze 長蘆宗賾 in 1103. Although this code is specifically for public monasteries associated with the Chan school, much of what it contains is derived from the standard vinaya, and later monastic codes of other schools are very similar to it (see Yifa in this volume). The procedures of the *Pure Rules for Chan Monasteries* in general do not seem unique to the Chan school.

Interestingly, the *Pure Rules for Chan Monasteries* does not describe how an abbot was to be selected. However, it does include a detailed outline of the procedure for inviting a new abbot once he had been chosen (fasc. 7, pp. 250–255). This seems to have been a rather complicated affair. From the monastery with a vacant abbacy a group of envoys was chosen to go the monastery where the prospective abbot was residing. They carried with them numerous letters and documents from officials, the monastery itself, Buddhist officials in the area, abbots of other monasteries in the area, lay patrons of the monastery, and retired officials, in addition to letters and reports from the withdrawing abbot to the local authorities in both the area where he had been serving and where the prospective abbot resided (fasc. 7, p. 250). The envoys traveled to the prospective abbot's monastery and lodged there while one of them went to present the various documents to local officials. In the event that the officials refused to let the prospective abbot go, one of the envoys would return to their home district and present the refusal to the officials there. If the officials in the home district wanted the envoys to make a second request they would do so; if not, the envoys would all return home. The authorities in the prospective abbot's area had to agree to his release before the candidate himself could be formally presented with an invitation (fasc. 7, p. 251; cf. Yifa 2002, 212–215). Although much of what is found in the *Pure Rules for Chan Monasteries* is perhaps prescriptive rather than descriptive (i.e., reflecting how its author thought things ought to be done rather than how things were actually done), this section is likely to have been based on Zongze's own personal experience and is hardly an idealized account. It is probable that the process described was common to all public monasteries and not specific to Chan public monasteries.

The most striking aspect of the accounts in both the *Classified Legal Articles* and the *Pure Rules for Chan Monasteries* is the depiction of the very active and central role that the secular authorities played in the selection and invitation of a new abbot. According to the instructions in the *Classified Legal Articles,* the secular authorities were to initiate the search for a new abbot; if there were any problems in finding a candidate, they were to step in and select someone directly. Of course, as with appointments to hereditary monasteries, the authorities always had to approve the choice of a new abbot. The account in the *Pure Rules for Chan Monasteries* nicely complements the one found in the *Classified Legal Articles.* Again it is very clear that the secular authorities played a central role. Among other things, officials in the district of the candidate had the power to refuse to release him; and only after they had decided to do so could the prospective abbot be formally invited to the new post.

Although the *Classified Legal Articles* and the *Pure Rules for Chan Monasteries* depict the secular authorities as having decisive power in the selection of an abbot, members of the Buddhist clergy in both accounts have an important role to play. According to the *Classified Legal Articles,* abbots of other monasteries were actually charged with picking a candidate to present to the authorities, and the statement in the *Pure Rules for Chan Monasteries* that the envoys were to carry with them letters from the abbots in the area of the vacant monastery may be seen as a confirmation of this. The possibility that the person chosen for the abbacy might decline the position is also made explicit in the *Pure Rules for Chan Monasteries* (fasc. 7, 252).

Reading the *Classified Legal Articles* it would seem that the new abbot in most cases was expected to be found within the prefecture; in contrast the *Pure Rules for Chan Monasteries* assumes he will be found in a place outside the jurisdiction of the officials searching for an abbot.[16] According to the *Classified Legal Articles* the selection of the new abbot became the sole responsibility of the officials if he had to be found outside the prefecture, something that is not reflected in the *Pure Rules for Chan Monasteries.* It is possible that the *Classified Legal Articles* stems from a time when public monasteries had become so common that finding an abbot locally was easy. On the other hand, it seems that by the thirteenth century at least half of all registered monasteries were public (cf. Takao 1975, 67), and a number of prefectures must have had several hundred public monasteries: It would hardly have been practicable to gather abbots from all of them for a meeting. The *Classified Legal Articles* is probably reiterating older rules on how the selection of an abbot ought to be done rather than how it was usually done in the late twelfth century. The fact that the *Pure Rules for Chan Monasteries* does not include any information on how the abbot was to be selected is also noteworthy. It may be a recognition by its editor that the clergy had little or no control over most appointments. There is, in fact, much evidence that from early on in the Song the abbot of a public monastery was in many cases appointed directly by secular authorities—without members of the clergy having any formal role in the selection of the candidate. No legislation appears to have existed for this kind of appointment, but it was very widespread. Direct appointment would most often take place at a prefectural level, and in this case the appointing authority was usually the prefect.

But the appointment could also come directly from the court, ultimately deriving its authority from the emperor himself.

The direct appointment of abbots to public monasteries by secular authorities would seem to be a blatant encroachment on the power of the Buddhist church, and one would perhaps expect the clergy to be unhappy with such appointments. But this does not seem to have been normally the case. In biographies of Buddhist monks it is often mentioned that they were appointed to such and such a post by the command of a prefect or through the recommendation of famous literati (which probably then led to an appointment by the prefect). These appointments clearly were seen as evidence of the importance and eminence of a particular monk. Of course, imperial appointments were even more prestigious, and much is made of monks who were appointed to abbacies by imperial command.

The practice of direct appointments to abbacies, whether by the prefect or by imperial command, does not seem to have been a formal category during most of the Song.[17] But in 1103, a special class of monasteries called Chongning 崇寧 (later renamed Tianning Wanshou 天寧萬壽) was established (Chikusa 1982, 95–98). These were Buddhist monasteries set up specifically to pray for the long life of the emperor. Each prefecture was charged with setting up one of these monasteries, although it is not clear whether new monasteries were built or existing ones appropriated. The Chongning monasteries were given various privileges, and it was decreed that the most illustrious monks in the empire were to be appointed to their abbacies (*Luohu yelu* 羅潮野録, Z 2B.15.497b). The abbots for the Chongning monasteries were naturally appointed by imperial command, and it is seems likely that this inspired imperial appointments to the abbacies of other monasteries deemed important to the state. In the late Southern Song, the practice of imperially appointed abbacies seems to have been formalized by classifying the most important public monasteries in the so-called "five mountains" system, in which all abbots were imperially appointed (cf. Imaeda 1970).

Most of the extant biographies of Song-dynasty monks note that their subjects were appointed to at least some of their posts by direct order from secular authorities. For example, every monk in the Song Caodong 曹洞 Chan lineage for whom relevant biographical information can be found is reported to have been appointed to abbacies by influential officials and, for the more illustrious ones, by imperial order. Random sampling of the biographies of monks in other Chan lineages confirms this pervasive tendency. These monks would be moved from monastery to monastery at the will of the politically powerful, and it is clear that the clerical community had little or no direct influence over their appointments.

However, the extant biographical material probably distorts the picture. Relatively few public monasteries would have been considered important enough for the court or powerful officials to take a direct interest. By the late twelfth century there may have been as many as twenty thousand public monasteries in the Song empire. Only a small percentage of these, the largest and most famous, would ever have had their abbots appointed directly by the court or a high official. The monks for whom biographical information is still available were almost all part of the clerical elite and exactly the kind of people who would be appointed to famous monasteries. Virtually nothing is known about the vast majority of monks who served as abbots at the less illustrious public monasteries. It is quite likely that at many of these monasteries, and perhaps also at some of the more prestigious ones, abbots were picked for their posts by a congregation of their peers in a fashion similar to the system outlined in the *Classified Legal Articles*. The notion that this method was the proper one certainly persisted, and a very similar process is described in a Chan code from the Yuan 元 (1279–1368) dynasty (*Qixiu Baizhang qinggui* 勅修百丈清規, T 48.1130b).

But there was yet another way by which a monk could be appointed to the abbacy of a public monastery. At times, secular authorities would demand bribes for, or outright sell, the right to the position. This practice seems to have become increasingly common during the course of the Song. As public monasteries became more numerous, many monks had a chance to be appointed to a public abbacy. This was naturally an attractive opportunity since it was a prestigious position in the clerical world. But there was another aspect of the matter, which seems to have loomed large. Even smaller public monasteries frequently had considerable holdings of land and other property and, without the check of an entrenched tonsure family, abbots at such institutions often took the opportunity to enrich themselves at the expense of the monastery.[18] Unscrupulous officials recognized this and encouraged the trend by demanding bribes to install someone as abbot at a public monastery.[19]

The notion of having to pay for an abbot's position at a public monastery became institutionalized, at least in Fujian 福建, when in 1131 the prefect of Fujian, Zhang Shou 張守 (1084–1145), conferred with the local literati and, as a means of creating revenue, set up a system by which abbacies were auctioned off to the highest bidder. The forty-odd top monasteries in Fujian were exempted (*Song huiyao jigao,* fasc. 134.5240d; Chikusa 1982, 163). It is possible that such a system became common elsewhere. Having to pay either bribes to officials or money to the provincial coffers no doubt further encouraged abbots at public monasteries to exploit their institutions for all they were worth. This exploitation became a problem of such magnitude in the late Song that many public monasteries converted back to the hereditary system, in spite of the severe laws forbidding it (Takao 1975, 65).

Conversion of Hereditary Monasteries into Public Monasteries

Although the Song government's laws stipulated severe punishments for those who tried to convert a public monastery into a hereditary one, it was quite easy to get permission to turn a hereditary monastery into a public one (*Classified Legal Articles,* fasc. 50.476a). Clearly the state had a strong interest in having as many monasteries as possible be public rather than hereditary. Whether the abbot at a public monastery was chosen directly by the court or local authorities, or the abbacy was sold to the highest bidder, or the abbot was selected in a process that heavily involved officials, the state maintained a high level of control. Furthermore, abbots in public monasteries usually held their position for only a few years, and every time a new abbot was selected government officials could make their influence felt.

As we have seen, the Song state in principle recognized the rights of the tonsure family to its monastery, and a rule existed that the tonsure family's agreement was needed to turn a hereditary monastery into a public one. Because such a change in effect meant that the tonsure family lost all rights to its monastery, this seems reasonable enough. Tonsure disciples were excluded from taking over the abbacy of a public monastery from their master or even holding other important monastic office, so the disciples in line for the abbacy of a hereditary monastery would lose both their rights to the abbacy as well as any chance of ever obtaining it (*Shishi yaolan* 釋氏要覽, T 54.302b2–3). Furthermore, monks must have had the right to stay in the monastery of their tonsure family, where they would be fed and could live comfortable lives; no one seems to have had an inalienable right to stay in a public monastery, where life usually was much more strictly regulated.

In an early well-documented instance of a hereditary monastery being turned into a public one, further indications are found that the tonsure family, and especially the younger generation of disciples who had a good chance of succeeding to the abbacy, had to agree to the change. This was the case at Yanqing 延慶 Monastery, which the famous monk of the Tiantai school Siming Zhili 四明知禮 (960–1028), together with Yiwen 異聞, petitioned the court in 1010 to convert into a public monastery dedicated to the Tiantai teachings (Getz 1994, 139–159). Accompanying Zhili and Yiwen's petition was another petition from six of their personally ordained tonsure disciples that voiced the disciples' support for their two masters' plan (*Siming Zunzhe jiaoxing lu* 四明尊者教行録, T 46.909a–910a, 910a–c; Getz 1994, 139–141). Thus the monks most likely to have the opportunity to take over the abbacy of the Yanqing Monastery under the hereditary system agreed to relinquish their rights to it. In light of the remark in the *Classified Legal Articles* cited above, it would seem that the agreement of the students to the conversion not only strengthened the petition but was a legal requirement.[20]

One might well wonder what would persuade especially the younger generation in a tonsure family to give up its monastery and face an uncertain future. In the case of Yanqing Monastery, it seems the sheer charismatic force of someone like Zhili could move tonsure disciples to give up what might otherwise have been theirs. But even Zhili and Yiwen were concerned about their tonsure disciples' willingness to give up their rights. They feared that once the two of them were gone, their tonsure disciples might try to claim back the abbacy, causing Yanqing Monastery to revert to the hereditary system. This is evidenced by an oath Zhili and Yiwen composed and asked their tonsured disciples to take, which stated that the disciples under no circumstances would take over the abbacy after their masters' deaths, even if one of them was the most qualified person that could be found (T 46.907c; Getz 1994, 143–147).

In fact many, and perhaps most, conversions of hereditary monasteries into public ones did not happen voluntarily. The *Classified Legal Articles* includes various laws that show how relatively easy it was for the state to force the conversion of hereditary monasteries. If a monastery was found to harbor criminals, it could be turned into a public institution (fasc. 50.477a). Likewise, if no successor was at hand in a hereditary monastery, it would automatically be converted into a public abbacy, as would a monastery that had become dilapidated and been abandoned (fasc. 50.476a). Furthermore, as was the case with the appointment of abbots to public monasteries, important monasteries would often be converted into public institutions by the government or by high-ranking local officials simply by decree.[21]

Besides pressure from the state and powerful officials on hereditary monasteries to convert to public ones, other forces were at work. In the wars that followed the fall of the Tang, many monasteries were damaged and lost their land holdings; their tonsure families were dispersed. Among the monasteries that continued to operate many must have become almost fully dependent on local lay supporters. These supporters of course had little interest in patronizing a hereditary monastery, and they must at times have been able to force their institution to adopt the system of public abbacies. There is evidence for this in a text by the literatus Yu Jing 余靖 (1000–1064) dated to 1038, which describes the succession of abbots at the Puli 普利 Monastery at Dongshan 洞山. Its abbacy had first been occupied by the "founder" of the Caodong tradition of Chan, Dongshan Liangjie 洞山良介 (807–869). The text implies that at the time of writing the Puli Monastery was a public Chan monastery, although nothing is said about when the conversion took place. According to the text, in the generations after Liangjie the abbacy was passed on from master to disciple, clearly (although this is not stated) in a tonsure relationship. However, during the Five Dynasties period (907–960), which followed the breakdown of the Tang, this system seems to have been disrupted. When the area came under the control of the Southern Tang (937–958) regime, the king ordered a certain monk to take up the abbacy. Later, perhaps at the beginning of the Song, another abbot (it is not clear how he came into the position) wanted his disciple to take over the abbacy after him. The lay supporters of the monastery objected, and another monk was chosen (*Yunzhou Dongshan Puli chanyuan chuanfa ji* 筠州洞山普利禪院傳

法記, fasc. 9.14b–18b, in *Siku quanshu zhenben* 四庫全書珍本 6).
The main forces in converting a monastery from hereditary to public in the Song, aside from those of the state, must thus have been
lay supporters from the local elite and local officials. These groups
gained from having a prestigious monastery in their area, and they
would often have been in a position to apply pressure on hereditary
monasteries to convert.

The efforts to convert monasteries from hereditary to public
were very successful. As mentioned above, by the end of the Northern Song about half of all registered monasteries were public. Although the total number of hereditary monasteries would be much
higher if one were to include unregistered monasteries, which had
proliferated greatly by this time, the proportion of public monasteries to hereditary ones was still remarkably high.

Vinaya Monasteries and Chan Monasteries

In public monasteries the abbacy was supposed to be open to any
competent candidate, but with an important qualification. Most,
and possibly all, public monasteries in the Song had an official association with a particular tradition within Buddhism, and their
abbacies were restricted to lineage holders in that tradition. At first
public monasteries all seem to have been associated with the Chan
tradition, but early in the Song public monasteries associated with
the Tiantai school came into existence and later some public monasteries became affiliated with the Huayan 華嚴 school. In the late
Southern Song, public Tiantai and Huayan monasteries were classified as teaching (*jiao* 教, or *jiang* 講) monasteries. Also in the Southern Song, a further category of public vinaya (*lü* 律) monasteries appeared. These were monasteries associated with the newly emerged
Vinaya school of Buddhism.

One of the most intriguing aspects of the Song system of hereditary and public monasteries is the special connection between the
institution of public monasteries and the Chan school. Not only
were public monasteries in the beginning all affiliated with the
Chan school, but even after public teaching monasteries had become common the system of public abbacies continued to be especially associated with the Chan school. Another important point to
be made here is that the term *"lüsi"* 律寺 (vinaya monastery) originally was a designation for hereditary monasteries and had no con-

nection whatsoever with the later public vinaya monasteries associated with the Vinaya school. These two points are closely related: Because public abbacies began with the Chan school and hereditary monasteries were called "vinaya monasteries," the conversion of a hereditary monastery into a public Chan monastery is often described in Song sources as a change from Vinaya to Chan. This has been almost universally understood to mean that the monastery in question changed its affiliation from the Vinaya school to the Chan school, a serious misinterpretation that obscures the nature of the system of public and hereditary monasteries as well as the history of the Vinaya school.

Several sources attest to the special relationship between the institution of public abbacies and the Chan school on the one hand and the use of "vinaya monastery" for "hereditary monastery" on the other. Consider, for example, an inscription for the Lingfeng 靈峰 Monastery at Mount Dahong 大洪 ("Da Song Suizhou Dahongshan Lingfeng Chansi ji" 大宋隨州大洪山靈峰禪寺記) written by the famous statesman Zhang Shangying 張商英 (1043–1121) in 1102 (*Hubei jinshi zhi* 湖北金石志, fasc. 10.7b–10b, in *Shike shiliao xinbian* 石刻史料新編, 1.16; cf. Ishii Shūdō, 1987, 430–437). Zhang reports that in the fall of 1087 the Lingfeng Monastery was by imperial command changed from Vinaya to Chan, and in 1094 members of the Outer Censorate asked to have the monk Dahong Baoen 大洪報恩 (1058–1111) moved there to take up the abbacy. Then, Zhang says, in 1102 he was asked to write a "Record of [Becoming] a Public Chan Monastery" for the Lingfeng Monastery. Zhang goes on to relate that a disciple of the famous Chan master Mazu 馬祖 (707–786, or 709–788), known as Great Master Ciren Lingji 慈忍靈濟大師, first became abbot of the Lingfeng Monastery during the Yuanhe 元和 period (806–820) of the Tang. After a description of the monastery and its history Zhang states that, after having compared and analyzed Chan and Vinaya, he came to the following conclusion:

Vinaya uses [hereditary] succession *(jiayi)* and Chan uses the public *(shifang)* [system]. That which is called "succession" means that where one generation *(jia)* is coming from, that is where the next generation *(yi)* establishes itself. So [at the time before Lingfeng Monastery became public] they would necessarily say: "We are the sons and grandsons of Ciren [the founder of Lingfeng]." Now that a person [to be the

abbot] is selected publicly the descendants of Ciren have been cut off.
(*Hubei jinshi zhi*, fasc. 10.9b)

Here Zhang Shangyin describes the Lingfeng Monastery's new designation as a public Chan monastery as a change from Vinaya to Chan. He explicitly identifies vinaya monasteries with hereditary succession and Chan monasteries with public abbacies. In explaining how the vinaya system works, Zhang describes how previously those who were abbots at Lingfeng would be the descendants of the monastery's founder, Ciren. But because the monastery had now become public, Ciren's descendants had lost their rights to the abbacy.

First of all, this shows that, as T. Griffith Foulk has already suggested, in the Northern Song the designation "vinaya monastery" did not mean a monastery with an abbacy that was held by members of a Vinaya school.[22] Rather, "vinaya" in this context simply seems to mean "governed by the vinaya." A vinaya monastery is, therefore, an ordinary hereditary monastery.[23] Zhang's statement also shows that even if a monastery had some sort of connection to the Chan lineage through its tonsure family (as was the case with Lingfeng Monastery), it was still a vinaya monastery because the succession to its abbacy was hereditary and stayed within the tonsure family. This statement further drives home the point that "vinaya monastery" in this context has no association whatsoever with a Vinaya school. Another important point to note here is that Zhang Shangyin in the inscription above seems to associate public abbacies exclusively with the Chan school. As we have already seen, and as Zhang must have known, a number of non-Chan public monasteries were in existence at the time he wrote his record of the Lingfeng Monastery in 1102. However, Zhang must have felt that Chan was associated with the system of public monasteries in a special way to write as he did.

Ironically, perhaps the earliest evidence of a special relationship between Chan and public abbacies is found in the 1010 petition referred to earlier by Zhili and Yiwen. In this petition Zhili and Yiwen note that the prefecture already had two monasteries with public abbacies, the Jingde 景德 Monastery at Mount Tiantong 天童 and the Xianju 仙居 Monastery at Mount Damei 大梅. According to them, these institutions were based on the "model of the Buddhist monasteries" in the Jiangnan 江南 (most of modern Anhui and

Jiangxi provinces) and Hunan circuits (*Siming Zunzhe jiaoxing lu*, T 46.909c2–5, 909c26–28; Getz 1994, 139–159). The *Baoqing Siming zhi* 寶慶四明志 reports that the Jingde Monastery received a name plaque in 1007 and the Xianju Monastery had one bestowed in 1008 (*Baoqing Siming zhi*, fasc. 13.18b, in *Song Yuan difang zhi congshu* 8). The monasteries must have become public at this point and been designated Chan, but the *Baoqing Siming zhi* makes no mention of that. However, the *Tiansheng Era Expanded Record of the Lamp* (*Tiansheng guangdeng lu* 天聖廣燈録, Z 2B.8.435c, hereafter *Expanded Record*), a Chan genealogical history first published in 1036, mentions that the Chan master Basheng Qingjian 八聖清簡 (957–1014) late in his life became the abbot at Tiantong. It would seem that Qingjian must have become the abbot at Tiantong very soon after it had become public. At Mount Damei, perhaps the first Chan abbot was Damei Juxu 大梅居煦, who, according to the *Expanded Record* (Z 2B.8.445a), gained his position there in the Xiangfu 祥符 period (1008–1016). All this suggests that Tiantong and Damei around the time of Zhili's petition were in fact public Chan monasteries. In any event, there is ample evidence from later in the Song that both Tiantong and Damei were famous public Chan monasteries, and it seems likely that at the time they received their new plaques they were converted to public Chan monasteries. We should also note that Zhili and Yiwen's petition does not cite any examples of public monasteries devoted to the Tiantai teachings, which suggests that there were none at the time. The 1010 petition leaves the impression that, until then, whatever public monasteries existed had been designated Chan.

The association between Chan and the institution of public abbacies is made further explicit in Yu Jing's previously mentioned text from 1038, which describes the succession of abbots at the Dongshan Puli Monastery:

> In recent times there has been a twofold division of Chan and Vinaya, based on the [selection of] the abbot in residence. In Chan [monasteries] he is chosen according to virtue (*de* 德), in vinaya [monasteries] according to family relationship (*qin* 親) [i.e., tonsure family]. (*Wuxi ji* 武溪集, fasc. 9.14b, in *Siku quanshu zhenben* 6).

Again vinaya monasteries are identified with the hereditary system, and Chan is presented as synonymous with the system of public abbacies. Much additional evidence can be found in Song sources. For example, in an inscription for the Fuyan 福嚴 Monastery, which became public in 1050, it is said several times that disciples agreed to turn their hereditary monastery into a public one, after which authorities were petitioned. The inscription then states that there are not two ways in Buddhism but that Chan and Vinaya are distinguished by the different living arrangements monks have in monasteries. Monasteries where living is communal and where monks are not asked whether they have a "family" connection are called public. Monasteries where monks live in their own rooms and call each other "sons" and "brothers" are called hereditary (*jiayi*) ("Fuyan chanyuan ji" 福嚴禪院記, *Zhiyuan Jiahe zhi* 至元嘉禾志, fasc. 26, 7b–9a, in *Song Yuan difangzhi congshu* 宋元地方志叢書 12).

Even in the late twelfth century, when public monasteries designated Chan were only slightly more numerous than those designated teaching or Vinaya, the tendency to associate Chan with the system of public abbacies continued. A late Song inscription relates how a monastery became public in 1177 and then describes this change as one from Vinaya to Chan ("Jingyan chansi ji" 精嚴禪寺記, *Zhiyuan Jiahe zhi*, fasc. 18.1b, in *Song Yuan difangzhi congshu* 12). It should also be noted that even after public vinaya monasteries appeared, the term "vinaya monastery" continued to be used for hereditary monasteries, so it was necessary to distinguish between public and hereditary vinaya monasteries (e.g., *Baoqing siming zhi*, fasc. 11, 6a–11d, in *Song Yuan difangzhi congshu* 8).

It is safe to conclude that when a Song text mentions that a monastery was changed from Vinaya to Chan, it means that it went from being a monastery with a hereditary abbacy to one that was public and reserved for members of the Chan lineage. However, the granting of a plaque giving a monastery a name that contained the word "Chan monastery" (*Chansi* 禪寺, or *Chanyuan* 禪院) did not necessarily mean that the monastery was converted into a public Chan monastery.[24] Likewise, a monastery designated as a public Chan monastery did not necessarily have the words "Chan monastery" in its official name.

Because public monasteries in the early part of the Song were exclusively associated with the Chan school at the time, no further classification was needed. However, perhaps beginning with Zhili's petition in 1010, public monasteries officially reserved for members of the Tiantai school came into existence. This eventually led to a formal distinction between public Chan monasteries, and public teaching monasteries that were associated with the Tiantai school or the Huayan school that emerged in the eleventh century. A law from 1145 (reformulated in 1154) concerning the taxation of monks has different rates for monks living in hereditary vinaya and public teaching monasteries and those living in public Chan monasteries, making it clear that the distinction by this time had become official (*Song huiyao jigao,* fasc. 127.4998a–c; cited in Eichhorn 1968, 35; cf. Takao 1975, 66–67, and Gernet 1995, 34–35).[25]

However, neither the 1145 or 1154 law nor any earlier source mentions public vinaya monasteries. It seems that this category only appeared in the thirteenth century, and public vinaya monasteries were never very numerous.[26] According to the Japanese founder of the Sōtō Zen 曹洞 school, Dōgen 道元 (1200–1253), who visited China from 1223 to 1227, public vinaya monasteries were associated with a lineage claiming descent from the famous Chinese vinaya master Daoxuan 道宣 (596–667).[27] The Song Vinaya school has not been well studied and it is unclear when it took shape, although it seems that the monk Yuanzhao 元照 (1048–1116) was instrumental in the early stages of its formation (see Getz in this volume). However, it is certain that references to vinaya monasteries in Northern Song sources do not imply the existence a Vinaya school at the time.

Conclusion

Government policies had a profound impact on the shape and development of Buddhism during the Song, when monastic Buddhism experienced a tremendous growth. What especially characterizes the period is the proliferation of monasteries with public abbacies and the great success of the Chan school, which became the dominant school of monastic Buddhism in the Song and later. The rise of Chan can now be understood to a large degree as a result of the Song government's policies, or at least as a development that could not have taken place without these policies. No doubt the Song government had not directly aimed at advancing the Chan school. But because Chan from an early point had a special association with the system of public abbacies and the Song government saw an advantage in having monasteries become public, Chan monasteries flourished. Such policies allowed the Chan school to develop an institutional base and an independent identity that gave further validity to its claim as heir to a special transmission going back all the way to the historical Buddha. This assertion probably contributed to Chan's popularity among the elite and further helped convince the Song government that the proliferation of Chan monasteries was beneficial to the state. In any case, it seems doubtful that Chan could have developed as an independent entity, with its distinct literature and carefully constructed history, if it had not been for the institution of public monasteries.

If the flourishing of the Chan school in the Song can only be fully understood in the context of the state's promotion of public monasteries, then the study of the Vinaya school can only be fruitful if the association of the term "vinaya" with hereditary monasteries is understood. The mention of vinaya monasteries in sources dating to the Song and earlier has long been taken to mean monasteries associated with a Vinaya school, and only T. Griffith Foulk (1993) has suspected the fallacy of this assumption. The evidence, however, clearly shows that the term "vinaya monastery" in Song sources usually refers to hereditary monasteries; only in cases where it is made clear that the institution in question was public can "vinaya monastery" be associated with the Vinaya school.

Notes

1. The regulations the Song government imposed on the Buddhist church and its clergy were also applied to monastic Daoism and were well in line with the rules that existed for the rest of Song society. For in-depth discussion of the social control exercised by the Song state, see McKnight 1992.

2. Thus in 778 an official proposed that all monasteries without plaques be destroyed (*Jiu Tang shu* 舊唐書, fasc. 127.3579; cited in Gernet 1995, 45).

3. See *Nittō guhō junrei kōki* 入唐求法巡禮行記, fasc. 4, year 844, 7th moon, 15th day (in Bai 1992, 446; cited in Weinstein 1987a, 126; cf. Gernet 1995, 45, 304).

4. The Latter Zhou occupied from 951 the area of China that stretched from Peking in the north to the Yangzi River in the south. It is said that during the repression 30,336 monasteries were destroyed and only 2,694 monasteries were spared (Chikusa 1982, 84).

5. According to Hansen (1990, 85), temples for popular gods under the Southern Song were not necessarily considered illegal even if they were not registered. Registration was a final measure of accreditation for a cult. It is possible that the situation for small Buddhist monasteries was similar.

6. These monasteries would, however, usually claim to have been established during earlier dynasties (Chikusa 1982, 100).

7. On the other hand, because the orders to dismantle plaque-less monasteries were seldom carried out, these smaller monasteries could continue their unofficial existence without being subject to government regulations and interference. Such unregulated monasteries seem to have become numerous by the end of the Song (Chikusa 1982, 103).

8. As in a family descent group, the dharma relatives in the tonsure family had inheritance rights to each other's personal property (*Classified Legal Articles*, fasc. 51.487a).

9. The Song system of the abbot as the single head of a monastery did not come into existence until, at the earliest, the end of the Tang. In the Tang and probably earlier, monasteries were governed by the "three supervisors": the dean (*shangzuo* 上座), the abbot (*sizhu* 寺主), and the overseer (*duweina* 都維那). Among these it seems the dean was the most powerful. The abbot system may first have been instituted within the Chan school (Xie et al. 1990, 174; Gernet 1995, 8).

10. See the entry on the *Classified Legal Articles* by W. Eichhorn (in Hervouet, 1978, 180–181). The Buddhism and Daoism section of the *Classified Legal Articles* is reproduced and translated into German in Eichhorn 1968.

11. The proliferation of new monasteries in the Song may have been partly driven by the need to create new opportunities for those who were not likely to receive an abbacy by default, and many of the new monasteries were probably built as branches of existing ones.

12. A note in the *Classified Legal Articles* (fasc. 50.476d) seems to indicate that a class of hereditary monasteries existed where there was no clear concept of an extended tonsure family and where the abbacy primarily was passed from master to disciple. Based on this passage Takao (1975, 74 n. 4) argues that a distinction must be made between *jiayi* (succession) monasteries, where each generation had to be exhausted before the abbacy could be passed on to the next, and *tudi* (disciple) monasteries, where the abbacy passed from master to disciple. I have not found any evidence for this use of terminology.

13. This is indicated in a 1332 inscription for a Daoist temple (*Liangzhe jinshi zhi* 兩浙金石記, fasc. 17.9b–10, in *Shike shiliao xinbian* 石刻史料新編, ser. 1.14; cited in Takao 1975, 63).

14. In the Southern Song another class of monasteries became common: private grave monasteries. These were owned by wealthy families and charged with looking after the family graves. It must be assumed that the abbots of such monasteries commonly were appointed by the family owning them (Chikusa 1982, 111–43; Huang 1989, 241–300).

15. There are indications that some monasteries had a system of public abbacies in the Five Dynasties period (see below), and throughout Chinese history there are reports of monks being appointed directly to monasteries by imperial command. Takao (1975, 61) states that public monasteries did exist in the Tang but does not elaborate. Foulk (1993) states that public monasteries began in the late Tang and were continued on a local level during the Five Dynasties period, but he offers no evidence. Song sources mention at least two monasteries that are said to have attained official public status under the Tang, but both cases can probably be discounted (Getz 1994, 134 n. 17, 154 n. 71).

16. The *Pure Rules for Chan Monasteries* does not specify the administrative level of the officials involved, but it would seem that it must have been prefectural, as in the *Classified Legal Articles*.

17. Ishikawa Shigeo (1988) maintains that from the beginning of the Song there existed a formal category of monasteries whose abbacies were filled only by imperial appointment. This he bases on the *Classified Legal Articles* (fasc. 50.476b), which states that abbacies which in the past had been appointed by imperial order

or proclamation can only be filled by first petitioning the central government; all others go through the prefectural authorities. However, at many monasteries the Song court only occasionally appointed the abbot, indicating that no formal system was in place, at least for most of the Song.

18. Thus the Chan master Zhenjing Kewen 眞浄克文 (1025–1102) is reported to have complained that in his day people would praise an abbot for not appropriating monastic property—as if that were something extraordinary (*Chanlin baoxun* 禪林寶訓, T 48.1021c).

19. The *Songshi* 宋史 (30.10391; cited in Chikusa 1982, 162) tells of an official who, when he became prefect of Fujian in 1077, observed that monks were competing to become abbots at public monasteries and that bribes were common.

20. The Yanqing yuan is in other ways an unusual case. It had originally been turned over to Zhili and Yiwen by its previous abbots, apparently under the condition that it should henceforth be a public monastery devoted to Tiantai teachings (*Siming Zunzhe jiaoxing lu* 四明尊者教行録, T 46.909a; cited in Getz 1994, 139). It is not clear how the previous abbots possessed the power to pass the monastery on to someone who was not in their tonsure family or decide it should be a public monastery.

21. For example, in the *Liangzhe jinshi zhi* (fasc. 10.50b, in *Shike shiliao xinbian*, ser. 1.14) we find a late–Southern Song stele entitled "Chongjian Jingshan Xingsheng wanshou chansi zhiji" 重建徑山興聖萬壽禪寺之記, which records that in 1090 the prefect of Hangzhou changed the monastery at Jingshan into a public institution. There is no mention of anyone having petitioned for this.

22. Foulk (1993, 166) states: "The designation 'Vinaya monastery' in the Northern Sung did not apply to public monasteries and thus does not seem to have had anything to do with membership in a Vinaya lineage as such. The term simply refers to monasteries regulated by the Vinaya, that is, ordinary Buddhist monasteries where no particular precedence was given to Ch'an or T'ien-t'ai monks." Foulk, however, offers no evidence for this.

23. As Foulk (1993, 166) points out, this clearly is the meaning of the statement that Chan monks originally lived in Vinaya monasteries found in the "monastic rules" attributed to Baizhang Huaihai 百丈懷海 (749–814). See the *Jingde chuandeng lu* 景德傳燈録, T 51.251c.

24. Foulk (1987, 94, n. 6) notes that in the Tang, "Chan" in the name of a monastery did not imply any connection with the Chan school. However, this is also true during the Song.

25. Interestingly, monks in Chan monasteries were taxed less than the others. Kenneth Ch'en (1956) suggests, implausibly, that this was because they were thought to engage in productive labor and therefore not considered parasites to the degree other monks were.

26. See the chart in Takao 1975 (67), which shows that public Vinaya monasteries made up only a small fraction of the total.

27. See Dōgen's diary from China, the *Hōkyōki* 寶慶記 (Kodera 1980, 244, translation p. 130). Dōgen describes the division of public monasteries into Chan, teaching, and Vinaya, in addition to the hereditary "disciple" monasteries. He exclusively associates the teaching monasteries with the Tiantai school.

Chapter 7

Popular Religion and Pure Land in Song-Dynasty Tiantai Bodhisattva Precept Ordination Ceremonies

DANIEL A. GETZ

IN THE HISTORY of Chinese Buddhism, the evolution of the bodhisattva precepts—both in their interpretation and conferral—is a
story of ongoing efforts to realize more thoroughly within the cultivation of Buddhist discipline the Mahāyāna teaching of universal
salvation and the corresponding call to a life led for the welfare of
others in the bodhisattva vocation. Although aimed at the liberation
of all beings, this universal vision, in terms of human audience,
meant specifically that the laity as well as monks were summoned
onto the path to Buddhahood. On that path, the reception of the
bodhisattva precepts came to mark one's initiation into the bodhisattva vocation, and the cultivation of the precepts was regarded as
the basic prerequisite for all other activities that would lead one to
Buddhahood.

In light of this Mahāyāna vision, Chinese Buddhists were not
simply confronted with the task of developing a thoroughly Maha-
yāna interpretation of the bodhisattva precepts vis-à-vis other sets
of precepts that were perceived to be inferior (hīnayāna) in orientation; they were also faced with the problem of how to include
laypeople because the conferral and even practice of the precepts
largely remained the province of monastic communities. The inclusion of lay people was not simply a question of recruitment. It was
also a cultic one, requiring the development of rites of conferral
that more adequately addressed the ethical situation, religious outlook, and soteriological needs of laypersons. This process of ritual
inclusion was particularly reflected in a series of ordination rites
produced within the Tiantai 天台 tradition during the period spanning the end of the Tang 唐 dynasty (618–907), the Five Dynasties
五代 era (907–960), and the first century of the Northern Song 北宋

dynasty (960–1127). Although these newer rites were not produced solely, or even primarily, for the purpose of better suiting lay needs, we find in them an unmistakable progression. The rites created in the late Tang and Northern Song introduced a number of elements not found in earlier ceremonies that appear to have stemmed from a wish to address in a more focused way the needs and concerns of a lay audience.

Most prominent among these new aspects were litanies of popular religious deities, prayers for the mundane welfare of society, and an increased emphasis on Pure Land devotion that offered large numbers of lay persons and monks alike a readily accessible path to liberation. These salient characteristics, in fact, reflect transformative currents taking place within Buddhism in the period spanning the late Tang and Northern Song. Among the prevalent trends evident in the Buddhism of this period we find a concerted effort on the part of monastic Buddhism to engage laity from all social strata. Japanese scholarship, in particular, has extensively examined the convergence of lay involvement and a greater interest in Pure Land in the numerous Pure Land societies that appeared throughout the Song (e.g., Ogasawara 1963; Suzuki Chūsei 1974). The implementation of the bodhisattva precepts in the Song, a topic that has received little scholarly attention, can be said just as validly to reflect these same Pure Land and lay devotional trends (Tonegawa 1978). In fact, taking precept ordination rituals as a starting point perhaps offers a better strategy for understanding these developments within Song Buddhism.

The present study examines how the development of bodhisattva precept ordination rituals within the Tiantai tradition reflects the aforementioned lay and Pure Land trends. From its inception, the Tiantai school, which was conceived of as a doctrinal and cultivational blueprint for the bodhisattva vocation, accorded a prominent place to the bodhisattva precepts. Consequently, in the course of centuries the Tiantai tradition time and again attended to developing proper ritual expressions for the conferral of the precepts. This process began with the school's founder, Zhiyi 智顗 (538–597), and was consolidated in the mid-Tang by Zhanran 湛然 (711–782) and his disciple Mingkuang 明曠 (late eighth century), who produced conferral manuals that served as templates for subsequent rituals. Building on these precedents but also forging new directions, a series of rituals emerged in the late Tang, Five Dynasties,

and Northern Song periods that clearly sought to conform more
closely to the practical and spiritual needs of the laity. This process
of accommodation is first strikingly evident in a ceremony traditionally, but spuriously, attributed to Huisi 慧思 (515–577), the
teacher of Zhiyi. The presence of popular religious elements in the
current version of this rite strongly suggests that even if this ceremony had earlier origins it was still evolving in the late ninth or
tenth centuries to meet the needs of lay religiosity. A new approach
to the bodhisattva precepts is further evident in the work of the
Chan 禪 monk Yongming Yanshou 永明延壽 (904–975), who gave
increased significance to the place of Pure Land belief in the context of the bodhisattva precepts. The incorporation of popular religious concerns and Pure Land belief into bodhisattva precept conferral reached its denouement in the Northern Song when the
Tiantai monks Zhili 知禮 (960–1028) and Zunshi 遵式 (964–1032)
and the Vinaya monk Yuanzhao 元照 (1048–1116) composed ceremonies that synthesized previous developments. The discussion
that follows will therefore trace in detail the growth of these later
bodhisattva ordination ceremonies, thereby demonstrating the
Tiantai tradition's ongoing commitment to the thorough engagement of lay persons implicit in the Mahāyāna claim to universality.

Wu Yue Buddhism, Yanshou, and the Bodhisattva Precepts

To understand and highlight properly the changes in the rites
created by Zhili, Zunshi, and Yuanzhao, the innovations that took
place in the Song rites must be examined in light of developments
that had taken place in the region where these rites originated.
Zhili, Zunshi, and Yuanzhao all lived in the area of Mingzhou 明州
(present-day Ningbo 寧波) and Hangzhou 杭州, located in modern
Zhejiang 浙江. During the Five Dynasties period this region comprised the main part of the kingdom of Wu Yue 吳越, a relatively
stable state that actively promoted the welfare of Buddhism. Wu
Yue Buddhism was particularly enriched through the accomplishments of Yongming Yanshou, whose myriad practices included
both Pure Land teachings and the conferral of bodhisattva precepts.
His pivotal contributions in this regard paved the way for the developments that are the focus of this study.

When Yanshou died in 975, the kingdom of Wu Yue, where he
had spent his entire life, had two years previously sent tribute to the

newly established Song dynasty but was yet three years away from being finally annexed into that unified empire. Zanning's 贊寧 (919–1001) *Song Lives of Eminent Monks* (*Song gaoseng zhuan* 宋高僧傳, or SGZ, fasc. 28, T 50.887b) lists Yanshou as a Song-period figure. Properly speaking, however, Yanshou belongs to the Five Dynasties era. Although details of his life are in great dispute, there is little doubt that he was thoroughly a product of Wu Yue and his religious practice is illustrative of changes that were taking place in Chinese Buddhism (see Welter 1993).

By Yanshou's time in the tenth century, Chinese Buddhism had undergone a two-century succession of tribulations. The An Lushan 安禄山 rebellion (755), the Huichang 會昌 suppression (840–846), the general chaos at the end of the Tang and the ensuing Five Dynasties period, and the suppression (955) under the Latter Zhou 後周 emperor Shizong 世宗 (r. 954–959) had severely adverse consequences for Buddhist monasticism and scholasticism. In the various suppressions, the monastic establishment had been criticized for its wealth, inordinate power, corruption, lack of responsibility for society, disregard for the social order, and flagrant violation of the law (Weinstein 1987b, 59–65, 114–150). For subsequent Buddhist monastics, these experiences provided painful lessons on the dire consequences of losing touch with society.

Amidst the generally negative and hostile environment of the Five Dynasties period, the state of Wu Yue offered a notable exception, providing a safe haven for Buddhism. The rulers of Wu Yue were devout Buddhists whose generous patronage made possible a renaissance of Buddhist institutions, scholasticism, and practice. Qian Chu 錢俶 (Prince Zhongyi 忠懿; r. 948–978), the most prominent of the Wu Yue rulers, aspired to realize in his person the ideal Buddhist rulership exemplified by Aśoka and created eighty-four thousand votary stūpas (FT, fasc. 10, T 49.206c). Qian was responsible for building and sponsoring numerous monastic institutions, aiding thereby the Chan, Tiantai, and Vinaya (Lü 律) traditions (Abe 1953; Ogawa 1936, 55–61). For religious guidance, Qian sought out the Chan monk Tiantai Deshao 天台德韶 (891–972), who saw himself as responsible for renewing the spiritual tradition of Zhiyi on Mount Tiantai. Through Deshao, Qian was introduced to the Tiantai monk Xiji 義寂 (919–987), who informed Qian that many Tiantai texts were no longer extant in China.[1] Consequently, the king sent out emissaries to Japan and Korea. This restoration

of texts became a key factor in the renewal of the Tiantai school.
Qian's generous patronage was also extended to Deshao's disciple
Yanshou, who was given the responsibility for building or restoring
a number of Buddhist institutions, among them the Yongmingsi
永明寺—for which he became the first abbot and by which name
he is known (*Jingde chuandeng lu* 景德傳燈録, hereafter JCL, fasc.
26, T 51.421c; also see Abe 1953, 26–27). The dynamic monastic
Buddhism that emerged from the patronage described above was
most certainly acutely aware of the vulnerability of monastic institutions. The historic failings of the monastic establishment in the
Tang impressed those who followed of the need for active engagement with society.

Yanshou's Buddhism was inextricably bound to this environment where secular and monastic Buddhism were in dynamic inter-
play. Although he was a devout Buddhist from childhood, Yanshou
was educated for a civil service career. He consequently spent his
early adulthood as a government official of Wu Yue. It was only
upon being released from his civil post some time after the age of
twenty-eight that he became a monk (JCL, fasc. 26, T 51.421c11–
13). His subsequent activities as a monk paradoxically reflect both
his own personal commitment to monastic separation from society
and his dedication to religious involvement in society. Yanshou's
early biographies in the *Song Lives of Eminent Monks* (fasc. 28)
and the *Jingde Era Transmission of the Lamp* (JCL, fasc. 26) provide the most reliable and unbiased accounts of his life (Welter
1993, 53–63). Significantly, they depict him as being devoted to the
Lotus Sūtra, practicing meditation, administering the bodhisattva
precepts, feeding ghosts and spirits, and releasing living creatures
back into the wild. Pure Land practice, although not mentioned in
these biographical accounts, was clearly an important concern for
Yanshou and is reflected in his various works, including his essays
in the *Myriad Good Deeds Share the Same End* (*Wanshan tonggui ji*
萬善同歸集).

Yanshou's eclectic approach is thus aptly characterized by the
designation "myriad good deeds" (*wanshan* 萬善) that starts the title
of this his most famous work. The myriad good deeds refer to the
wide array of concrete practices in Buddhism standing in contrast
to the exclusive emphasis on meditation demanded by some Chan
practitioners. Yanshou was convinced of the importance and the
efficacy of these miscellaneous practices, and he expended great

effort in trying to synthesize the multitude of disparate practices found in the Chinese Buddhism of his time (Welter 1993, 2). This struggle for a synthesis represented, in part, an attempt to come to terms with the varying demands of monastic and lay religious orientations encountered in Wu Yue Buddhism.

In philosophical terms, Yanshou identified the myriad good deeds or myriad practices (*wanxing* 萬行) with the manifold concrete particulars (*shi* 事) of phenomenal reality. In contrast, contemplative meditation is directed toward the absolute unitary and formless principle (*li* 理). Drawing from the doctrine of nonduality central to Huayan 華嚴 and Tiantai teaching, Yanshou maintained that the concrete particulars and the absolute principle are not separate realities but are ultimately identical (*Wanshan tonggui ji* 1, T 48.958a–c). The bodhisattva dwelling in the realm of the formless principle has the responsibility of immersing himself in this world of particulars, devising multiple methods to address the needs of the myriad sentient beings. The role of the bodhisattva precepts must therefore be considered within the context of these manifold practices of the bodhisattva.

Although the biographical lists of practices might lead one to believe that in Yanshou's mind the conferral of bodhisattva precepts was simply one among a multitude of other practices, his *Bodhisattva Ordination Manual* (*Shou pusajie fa* 受菩薩戒法, Z 2.10.8c–11b), a work that contains his views on the precepts, suggests another interpretation. At the opening of the preface of this work, Yanshou declares that the bodhisattva precepts are the "foundation for generating the myriad good deeds" (Z 2.10.8c3). The precepts and their reception, in other words, are the requisite condition for all other practices. On the basis of this assertion, we can infer that Yanshou accorded special importance to this particular practice because the conferral of the precepts was the quintessential expression of the bodhisattva's responsibility to bring others to liberation; from the perspective of the recipients, however, the reception of the precepts was a requisite condition for proper practice. Upon receiving the precepts other sentient beings gained entrance to the bodhisattva path and could make proper use of the myriad good deeds that Yanshou saw as essential to his own liberation and that of others.

The importance that Yanshou attached to this ceremony might be surmised from the biographical reports noting its frequency as well as the number of participants. The *Jingde Era Transmission of the Lamp* states that Yanshou often bestowed the precepts on monks and laypeople (T 51.42a11). In 974, the year before he died, the assembly for precept ordination on Mount Tiantai was said to number more than ten thousand strong (T 51.42a10). Although this number might be an exaggeration, it clearly expresses Yanshou's wish to cast as wide a net as possible to bring people to this practice.

Another measure of this ceremony's importance can be gathered from Yanshou's composition of the *Bodhisattva Ordination Manual* mentioned above. This work in its original form apparently contained an ordination ceremony for the bodhisattva precepts (BK 5.103b). This fact is suggested both by the title of the text and by the assertion of the last line of the extant edition, which reads: "The conclusion of the Brahmā Net Bodhisattva Precepts Rite" (*Fanwang pusajie yi* 梵網菩薩戒儀, Z 2.10.11b). The text itself, however, contains no ritual instructions. In other words, what survives of this text is either a preface or a postface that serves as a treatise on the precepts dealing with eight topics arranged in question and answer format. The ordination manual is unfortunately no longer extant, but it is possible from this treatise to make several inferences on the nature of Yanshou's ceremony.

Considering his close relationship with Tiantai, Yanshou in all probability consulted all of the available Tiantai manuals for the creation of his rite. However, certain characteristics within his *Bodhisattva Ordination Manual* suggest that Yanshou made particular use of material found in the Tiantai manual traditionally attributed to Huisi, the *Bodhisattva Ordination Rite* (*Shou pusajie yi* 受菩薩戒儀, Z 2.10.1–10, hereafter "Huisi manual"). Modern scholars agree that the work in its present form is not the product of Zhiyi's teacher, Huisi, and that it comes from a later period, but there is great disagreement as to where this text fits into the evolution of Tiantai rites. I have opted here, following Tsuchihashi Shūkō (1980c, 799), to treat the Huisi manual as a transitional work between the Tang-dynasty ordination manuals (i.e., the aforementioned ones attributed to Zhanran and Mingkuang) and the later manuals of Yanshou, Zhili, Zunshi, and Yuanzhao.[2]

Clearly the current recension of the Huisi manual, in emphasizing universal eligibility for the bodhisattva precepts, demonstrates a commitment to engagement with an expansive audience. The opening section of the rite cites the passage from the *Brahmā Net Sūtra* (*Fanwang jing* 梵網經) that declares those wishing to receive the precepts—be they kings, princes, officials, ministers, monks, nuns, gods of the realm of desire, commoners, eunuchs, lustful men and women, various spiritual beings, protective deities, animals, and even Buddhas and bodhisattvas in human guise (*bianhua ren* 變化人)—need but understand the master's words (Z 2.10.1b1–4). Although all sentient beings are potential recipients of the precepts, the rite itself appears particularly addressed to lay aspirants, those in the assembly being addressed in the section dedicated to transference of merit as "good men" (*shan nanzi* 善男子) and "good women" (*shan nüren* 善女人), a standard form of address for laypersons (Z 2.10.4).

The endeavor to reach a wider audience in the Huisi ritual is particularly evident in a litany formula that supplicates indigenous popular deities and spirits (Z 2.10.2a, 8–2b6). This litany, not found in any earlier ordination text, is present in varying forms in Yanshou's manual and in all the Song-period manuals considered below, thus suggesting the transitional role played by the Huisi and Yanshou manuals between the rituals of the mid-Tang and those appearing in the Northern Song. Tsuchihashi (1980c, 799) notes that the addressing of Chinese native deities found in this ritual litany is a common feature of Dunhuang documents dating from the late Tang, Five Dynasties, and early Song periods. The formula starts off rather indistinctively with an address in the first two verses to a standard array of Buddhas, bodhisattvas, and Buddhist protective deities. The third and fourth verses are all the more striking, then, for their entreaty of indigenous Chinese deities that lie outside the list of traditional Indian Buddhist ones. Among these Chinese deities, we find the Magistrate of Mount Tai (*Taishanfu jun* 泰山府君), the Officer of Destiny (*Siming* 司命), the Officer of Records (*Silu* 司録), the Boys of Transgressions and Merit (*Zuifu Tongzi* 罪福童子), the Nether Officials of Good and Evil Deeds (*Shan'e Mingguan* 善惡冥官), the General of the Five Paths (*Wudao Jiangjun* 五道將君), and the Emissary of Contagion (*Xingbing Shizhe* 行病使者) (Z 2.10.2a14–17). The presence of these deities in Huisi's manual reflects the growing preoccupation with the afterlife found throughout Chinese religion from the tenth century on into the Song period (regarding which, see Teiser 1993 and 1994).

The fourth verse of the litany formula addresses Chinese national, local, and ancestral gods. These include the Gods of the Five Peaks (*Wuyue* 五嶽), the Gods of the Four Rivers (*Sidu* 四瀆), city gods (*chenghuang* 城隍), spirits of this world and the next (*youming* 幽冥), spirits on land and water (*shuilu* 水陸), and gods of earth shrines (*shemiao* 舍廟). Although some of these deities, such as the Gods of the Five Peaks and the Gods of the Four Rivers, go back to Han times and before, others are of a more recent provenance. Of particular importance for dating this litany is the presence of the city gods in the assembly of deities addressed. Recent scholars have established that the *chenghuang* originated in the Tang period but became increasingly prominent from the tenth century on through the Song (see Hansen 1993). The growing prominence of these gods responsible for the welfare of rising commercial towns is yet another sign of significant changes that were taking place in Chinese society and religious life. The appearance of these deities in this rite gives witness to the fact that Buddhists were attuned to these changes and were interested in incorporating these new elements into Buddhism.

In contrast to the gods of the previous verse who were overseers of the afterlife, the deities in the fourth verse were guardians of societal well-being, including that of the polity as a whole and the local district. This difference in function also entailed a distinction in audience. Although the functionaries of the afterlife were the focus of a wide and varied constituency in Chinese society, the gods in this fourth verse were more properly the concern of those responsible for the corporate welfare: the emperor, his court, and the official class. The inclusion of these deities here is both an expression of concern for the welfare of the state and a wish on the part of the monastic establishment to more actively recruit members of the official class in Buddhist activities. As we have seen above, cultivation of a positive relationship with the secular order, an important goal of Chinese Buddhism from early on, became a more pressing concern of the Buddhist establishment in the Five Dynasties and Song periods.

The fifth verse addresses a multitude of other sentient beings, including the recipients in the present assembly, departed spirits of recent and distant ancestors, nine levels of spirits (*jiupin lingshen* 九品靈神), deceased beings whose ascent was impeded (*zhipo* 滯魄), deceased beings who died wrongful deaths (*yuanhun* 冤魂), and all unliberated beings (Z 2.10.2b3–5). All of these spiritual entities, like the deities in the previous two verses, are invited to descend on the ritual site and to share in the karmic benefits of the precepts (in addition to witnessing the merit accrued in the reception of the precepts). The sharing of merit serves as a reminder that, notwithstanding the fact that one of the aims of the Huisi litany was to engage laypeople, this ordination rite, being focused on the Mahāyāna bodhisattva ideal, had as its primary goal the welfare and ultimate liberation of all beings.

The concern for all beings prominent in the Huisi rite is equally evident in Yanshou's *Bodhisattva Ordination Manual*. The first question addressed in this work examines the seeming impossibility of ordinary unenlightened people receiving the bodhisattva precepts because these are the domain of such eminent bodhisattvas as Mañjuśrī and Samantabhadra (Z 2.10.8d1–2). In answer to this problem, Yanshou asserts the essential identity between the Buddha, the mind, and sentient beings, thereby deducing that the Buddha precepts that reside in the mind of the Buddha must of necessity also reside in their entirety within the minds of ordinary sentient beings. The second question, then, takes up the problem of why it is necessary to receive the precepts if they are already inherent in the mind—Yanshou's answer being that the mind has been temporarily clouded by delusion (Z 2.10.8d15). This passage of Yanshou's work, which treats themes that were to take on great importance for Song Tiantai, shows a striking resemblance to, and in some cases an exact correspondence with, passages in the second section of the Huisi manual in which the author gives instruction on the nature of the precepts (cf. Z 2.10.8d–9a with Z 2.10.1a–b). This link with the Huisi manual is further strengthened by Yanshou's mention of the "eight superior characteristics" of the bodhisattva precepts (*basheng* 八勝), a category that first gained prominence in the Huisi manual (cf. Z 2.10.10b5 with Z 2.10.1c).

The focus on lay affairs present in the Huisi manual is also apparent in Yanshou's treatise. The general intent of the questions raised by Yanshou has to do with concerns about the ability of those who are deluded to observe the precepts. Although such concerns would be shared by monks and laypeople alike, the possibility of transgression is greatly magnified in worldly life. In stressing the presence of the precepts in the ordinary mind of the sentient being, Yanshou was emphasizing the availability of this path for all. The fourth question in particular addresses the problem of lay obser-

vance, asking whether it would not be better to make gradual progress by means of the eight gates (baguan 八關) or the ten good
acts (shishan 十善), Hīnayāna precepts specifically administered to
laypeople (Z 2.10.9b8). Yanshou emphatically rejects this option
because it would leave the recipient stuck in the cycle of rebirth.
In addressing issues relevant to lay observance, Yanshou's treatise
might well have been setting the stage for a ceremony that, much
like Huisi's rite, was tailored to the religious orientation of laypeople.

The final question of Yanshou's manual considers how Pure
Land practice is related to the bodhisattva precepts (Z 2.10.10d–
11a). In the question, Pure Land practice is cited as one example of
the numerous provisional aids (fangbian 方便) devised by the various Buddhas. Would it not be better, suggests the questioner, simply to entreat people to be reborn in the Pure Land than to have
them break precepts (after having received them), thus blocking
their entrance to the Pure Land? Yanshou in reply shows how the
reception of the precepts guarantees the highest level of rebirth
(shangpin 上品), thereby assuring a vision of the dharma body
(dharmakāya; i.e., truth) and attainment of the first bodhisattva
stage (bhūmi). On the other hand, the lowest level of rebirth is reserved for those who, although they have heard the Mahāyāna
teaching, do not believe in the precepts but simply recite the name
of the Buddha (nianfo 念佛). These people, although they also attain
rebirth in the Pure Land, must wait twelve eons (kalpa) before the
lotus upon which they are reborn opens, and even then they do not
see the Buddha and only gradually come to understand the Hīna-
yana teachings. Yanshou maintains, therefore, that there is a vast
gap between those who have received the precepts and those who
simply recite the Buddha's name. The precepts, then, become a necessary precondition to the practice of recitation if higher spiritual
states are sought.

Yanshou's question suggests that Pure Land practice was indeed prevalent in his audience. Although Yanshou in this section
appears to be critical of exclusive Pure Land practice, he is not denying the importance of rebirth as a soteriological goal. He is simply trying to frame the question correctly, placing the goal of rebirth
in the Pure Land within the more fundamental aspiration to Buddhahood through the bodhisattva path. In the conclusion of this
treatise, he also argues for the necessity of the myriad good deeds,

Pure Land practices being but one (Z 2.10.11a–b). Pure Land belief, although removed from a solitary pedestal, undoubtedly continues to play an important soteriological role.

In light of this discussion, Yanshou's ordination ceremony most certainly inherited the aspiration to rebirth in the Pure Land expressed in the earlier Tiantai manuals of Zhanran and Mingkuang. Considering the final question of his treatise, it is further likely that his rite contained allusions to the practice of reciting the name of the Buddha found in subsequent Song manuals. If this is the case, Yanshou's manual could well have provided an important link between the previous Tiantai ordination ceremonies and those created in the Song by Zhili, Zunshi, and Yuanzhao.

Northern Song Ordination Rites: Zhili, Zunshi, and Yuanzhao

Zhili and Zunshi were still youths when Yanshou died (see FT, fasc. 8, T 49.191c). As students of the Tiantai master Baoyun Yitong 寶雲 義通 (927–988; FT, fasc. 8, T 49.207a), who had trained under Xiji, they undoubtedly were well informed with regard to Yanshou's contributions, and they most certainly absorbed both vision and energy from the highly charged atmosphere of religious practice that Yanshou was responsible for creating. In broader terms, they were heirs to the whole legacy of Wu Yue Buddhism passed on by Deshao, Yanshou, and Xiji. Consequently their adult careers reflected many of the themes found in their Wu Yue predecessors.

Zhili and Zunshi were responsible for the continuity of Wu Yue Buddhism into the Northern Song, but they also left their own unique mark. Carrying forward the renewal of the Tiantai school that had begun with Xiji, both were instrumental in defining the school's distinctive identity in terms of doctrine, practice, and institutions. These contributions increasingly led to a sectarian orientation within Tiantai as well as within other schools as the Song progressed. In this process, although both men were close friends and supported each other in their various enterprises, Zhili is generally credited with the clarification of Tiantai doctrine, while Zunshi is acclaimed for his accomplishments in Tiantai practice. In addition to contributions to Tiantai doctrine and practice proper, we should consider their other activities that reached beyond the confines of the monastic environment. The biographies contain accounts of their establishing Pure Land societies, bestowing the precepts, releasing living creatures, feeding hungry ghosts, praying for rain, and converting deities. These activities either involved the active participation of laypeople or addressed the religious concerns of laypeople.

Given Zhili's and Zunshi's single-minded efforts at defining Tiantai doctrine and practice, this list of miscellaneous activities at first seems incongruous. When it is remembered, however, that the Tiantai school was from Zhiyi's founding inspiration a synthetic enterprise whereby all previous teachings and practices were integrated into a single vision rooted in the bodhisattva vocation, we can say that Zhili and Zunshi were plainly inheriting the mission bequeathed by Zhiyi. More fundamentally, they embraced the bodhisattva vocation as it had been defined by Zhiyi and succeeding teachers. The bodhisattva precept conferral ceremonies that had existed in the Tiantai school from the time of Zhiyi served as one of the primary platforms for articulating the vision of the bodhisattva vocation and for initiating new bodhisattvas, thereby insuring their ultimate liberation. The conferral of the precepts could therefore be considered the bodhisattva act par excellence.

One way that Zhili and Zunshi affirmed their commitment to the Tiantai legacy concerning the bodhisattva vocation was by creating their own ordination manuals, both of which are entitled *Bodhisattva Ordination Rite* (*Shou pusajie yi* 受菩薩戒儀).[3] No explicit evidence of their motivation to produce these rites exists, but one explanation might derive from the problematic nature of the Huisi rite, which represents a significant departure in both form and content from Zhanran's rite. In their attempts to revive Tiantai at the beginning of the Song, Zhili and Zunshi frequently appealed to the textual corpus produced by Zhanran, whose historical authority within Tiantai (given his doctrinal and liturgical articulations of the Tiantai system) is second only to Zhiyi's. Thus, if the Huisi manual or others like it had wide circulation at the beginning of Song—as is suggested by its previously discussed influence on Yanshou—Zhili and Zunshi, who fashioned themselves as doctrinal and ritual heirs to Zhanran's legacy, would have felt an obligation to bring this rite more in line with Zhanran's while at the same time retaining the useful elements of the Huisi rite. Furthermore, if the rite created by Yanshou had gained some popularity, it is possible that Zhili and Zunshi felt the need to create a uniquely Tiantai ritual in contrast to Yanshou's ceremony.

The importance that Zhili and Zunshi attached to these conferral rites (or at least the significance the tradition succeeding these men accorded them) is implied by their being placed at the head of Zhili's and Zunshi's respective collections of works, the *Siming zunzhe jiaoxing lu* 四明尊者教行録 (compiled by Zongxiao 宗曉 [1151–1214] in 1202) and the *Jinyuan ji* 金園集 (compiled by Hui-guan 慧觀 in 1151). Although each of these rites possesses its own distinctive elements, it is clear that both share a common ancestry in the Tiantai tradition of conferral rites as well as a common outlook reflecting some of the emerging religious trends of the Song period. For this reason, these two manuals will be discussed together here as representative of the Tiantai tradition in the early part of the Northern Song. A thorough comparison of the two and a study of which work precedes the other are tasks that lie beyond the scope of this essay and belong to the arena of future research.

Structurally Zhili's and Zunshi's rituals are clearly an improvement on the cluttered and confusing schema found in the Huisi rite. They appear to have restored the relatively simple format of the Zhanran rite. Zunshi took this process of simplification a step further by creating a ritual of ten sections rather than the traditional twelve established by Zhanran, thereby introducing a new structural framework that was later inherited by Yuanzhao. In content and general tenor, Zhili's and Zunshi's rites reflect the inclusive orientation with regard to audience found in the Huisi manual. In this regard, Yanshou's rite, which, as suggested above, was influenced by Huisi's ritual, could well have provided a valuable model for their ceremonies. Both manuals contain considerable evidence that these rites, although intended for monks and lay people alike, were particularly tailored to the needs of the lay community. One indication of this accommodation can be found in the discussion of the ten major precepts in Zhili's rite. Each prohibition is followed by a brief elaboration on the nature of the offense. In the third precept, that banning sexual misconduct, the elaboration is limited to a discussion of offenses related to the married state. Husbands and wives are instructed not to be unfaithful spouses (T 46.861b). Monastic chastity is not mentioned.

Lay religion frequently involves a concern with the benefits that can be accrued in the present life through religious practice. We find this concern addressed by Zunshi, who introduces a new category of "five present benefits" (*wuzhong liyi* 五種利益) into the ordination ceremony. These five benefits precede the discussion of the aforementioned "eight superior characteristics" found in Huisi's rite. Zunshi promises that reception of the precepts will bring about five boons in this current life (*xianshi* 現世): the constant protection of Buddhas and bodhisattvas, an increase in wisdom and discrimination, the joy and respect of other people, the myriad practices, and a calm mind at death, allowing one to be reborn in a Buddha's Pure Land (*fo jingtu* 佛淨土; Z 2.6.109c). These benefits are admittedly spiritual in nature, but they nevertheless offer tangible advantages that would attract clergy and laypeople alike.

As in the Huisi manual, the most conspicuous evidence of concern for broad lay participation in the practices created by Zhili and Zunshi is the role that indigenous deities are given in the rite. Both ceremonies contain litanies that closely resemble the one found in the Huisi ceremony. The litanies call on Buddhas, bodhisattvas, Buddhist protective deities, indigenous deities, and other spiritual beings to witness to the reception of the precepts and to offer their protection. These litanies differ from that in the Huisi rite in that both are situated in clearly demarcated sections concerned with the entreaty to witness and protect.[4] Compared to the five-verse formula in the Huisi rite, the litanies in these rituals are somewhat simplified, being reduced to three verses in Zhili's rite and two in Zunshi's. The indigenous deities addressed in these litanies also differ, with the gods of the afterlife who figured so prominently in the Huisi manual completely absent. Both men seem to focus on national and local deities: the gods of mountains, rivers, provinces (*zhou*), and cities; local earth gods; and monastery guardians. This selection of gods takes on added significance when at the end of the rites—which differs from the conclusions of all previous ceremonies—the gods are entreated through the merit accruing to the reception of the precepts to extend their aid and protection to various aspects of corporate welfare. Such an emphasis is particularly developed in Zunshi's rite.

In the final section of Zunshi's rite, that dedicated to the transfer of merit, the recipients address a number of traditional

Indian Buddhist and Chinese indigenous gods. They express the intention that these deities, through the merit gained from the reception of the precepts, would harmonize wind and rain, assure bountiful harvest, prevent pestilence, send auspicious omens for the nation, and insure permanent tranquility and happiness in the passage of the calendrical intervals and the seasons (Z 2.6.111d6–10). This vow is addressed to Brahmā; Indra; the Four Guardian Devas (Sitian menwang 四天門王); the Twenty-eight Constellations (Ershiba Su 二十八宿); gods of the sun, moon, and stars (*ri yue xingchen* 日月星辰); Lord of the Wind (Fengbo 風伯); Master of the Rain (Yushi 雨師); Lord of Thunder (Leigong 雷公); Mother of Lightning (Dianmu 電母); Gods of the Five Peaks (Wuyue); Gods of the Four Rivers (Sidu)—the Jiang 江 (Yangzi 揚子), He 河 (Yellow), Huai 淮, and Ji 濟 (Jiang He Huai Ji); gods of famous mountains and great rivers (*mingshan dachuan* 名山大川); and all the dragon gods (*longshen* 龍神). The vow continues with the resolve that the merit would accrue to the longevity of the emperor and his princes, the ever increasing majesty and well-being of the imperial consort and her retinue, the successful promotion for ministers and officials, the rectitude and honesty in provincial and prefectural officials, and the goodness and uprightness of functionaries who would accumulate blessings and distribute them for the benefit of all (Z 2.6.111d10–13). The deities addressed here and the concerns for which they were responsible manifestly belonged to the domain of state religion, implying therein the participation of officials in Zunshi's bodhisattva precept rituals. The attendance of official elite at these rituals would have been only natural in light of the close relationships that Zunshi cultivated with officials high and low in the course of his career.[5] His incorporation of this passage into his rite clearly demonstrates a determination to address more forthrightly the worldview and aspirations of this important segment of his audience.

In the continuation of the passage just discussed, we find a set of universal concerns that suggest an audience of laypeople extending beyond the circle of elite officials. The recipients announce their intention that the merit gained will lead the spirits inhabiting the recipients' locale to secure their respective domains and bestow benefits (Z 2.6.111d14–15).[6] The recipients then pray that their ancestors, no matter where they have been reincarnated, will soon reach a Buddha land (*foguo* 佛國) and attain enlightenment and, further, that they will benefit from afar their families and keep them from calamity. This address to local spirits and ancestors was not an isolated instance in Zunshi's career nor was it simply a scheme to enlist more support for himself and his monastery. His career was replete with activities aimed at the conversion of local spirits and their adherents from blood sacrifices as well as the creation of ceremonies attending to the welfare of ancestors and other spirits. All of these accomplishments can be interpreted in terms of the bodhisattva's obligation to work for the good of all beings.[7] By incorporating a prayer for local harmony through the spirits and the hope for ancestral protection of the family into his rite, Zunshi was harnessing universal Chinese religious aspirations that cut across all class lines. In doing so, he was not only fulfilling the bodhisattva obligation to care for the spiritual and material well-being of all, he was astutely appealing to basic sensibilities of lay religion with its penchant for tangible mundane benefits. The obligations of the bodhisattva, proselytizer, and monastery abbot responsible for garnering political, economic, and popular support for his monastery are all seamlessly manifested here.

Interestingly the popular religious concerns discussed above are intermingled in Zunshi's rite with the Buddhist aspiration to rebirth in the Pure Land. The specific nature of this Pure Land in Zunshi's rite, however, is not explicitly identified. In a previously discussed passage, Zunshi promises rebirth in a Buddha's pure land (*fo jingtu* 佛淨土) as a benefit of receiving the precepts (Z 2.6.109c). The ambiguity with regard to the identity of the sought-for realm is reinforced in the just-discussed passage where the recipients pray that their ancestors will be reborn in a Buddha land (Z 2.6.111d16). Following this, the participants go on to make yet another vow in which they pray that all sentient beings on leaving this life will be reborn in the Buddha land, where they would come to understand the doctrine of nonarising (*wusheng ren* 無生忍), attain supernatural powers (*shentong* 神通), and roam through the ten directions making offerings to all Buddhas (Z 2.6.111d17–18). The recipients next proceed to pray that, among other things, all sentient beings will escape from the three undesirable transmigratory realms, will forever leave behind base incarnations, and will reincarnate as human males (Z 2.6.112a1–2).

Considering Zunshi's own personal devotion to Amitābha and his Pure Land, it would seem reasonable to conclude that he is indeed referring to Amitābha's Pure Land here. Such a conclusion would seem to be warranted by the various attainments associated with rebirth (understanding of nonarising, avoidance of undesirable incarnations, attainment of a male body, etc.)—all of these representing standard promises associated with Amitābha's Pure Land. Yet there is also good reason to believe that Zunshi was being intentionally vague. This whole passage, in fact, is an almost verbatim rendering of a section in the Faxiang 法相 patriarch Huizhao's 慧沼 (650–714) bodhisattva ordination rite, in which the goal is rebirth not in Amitābha's Pure Land but in Maitreya's Tuṣita heaven (see Huizhao's *Datang Sanzang fashi chuan Xiyu zhengfazang shou pusa-jie fa* 大唐三藏法師傳西域正法藏受菩薩戒法 in *Quan fa putixin ji* 勸發菩提心集, fasc. 3, T 45.397b18–c1). Later Zhanran adopted Huizhao's wording of this section in his ordination manual while substituting Amitābha's Pure Land for Maitreya's (Z 2.10.8a). Zunshi appears to have been quite aware of Huizhao's rite. Despite his own personal aspiration to Amitābha's Pure Land, he was cognizant of the fact that not all in the audience of those receiving the bodhisattva precepts shared the same aspiration. Steering a course between Huizhao's and Zhanran's rites, Zunshi left the vow sufficiently elastic to include all possible adherents.

In contrast to the ambiguity in Zunshi's rite, Zhili gave pride of place to Amitābha's Pure Land. His rite contains more mentions of the Pure Land than previous ceremonies (including Zunshi's), and, more importantly, his is the first manual to link the Pure Land practice of Buddha mindfulness *(nianfo)* to the reception of the precepts. Zhili's manual exhorts those who have just received the precepts thusly:

> [All of you] present in this great congregation have listened and received this teaching (*fa* 法) [on the precepts]. You must not be negligent in your efforts. You should earnestly realize the impermanence of the world and cultivate the multitude of good works, desiring thereby to adorn the Pure Land. At the end of your life you will certainly attain rebirth. Then you will know that the merit [gained through] recitation of the Buddha's name and reception of the [bodhisattva] precepts (*shoujie* 受戒) is incomprehensible. (T 46.861c12)

This passage reveals that there was a close connection in Zhili's mind between the reception of the bodhisattva precepts and the Pure Land practice of reciting the Buddha's name. Admittedly the term *"nianfo"* has a number of different connotations, the most basic of which refers to a contemplative activity. Yet in light of the practice of daily invocation encouraged in the Pure Land society established by Zhili, the term in this case likely refers to the recitation of Amitābha's name.

The link suggested by the above passage between Pure Land practice and the reception of the bodhisattva precepts finds a correspondence in Zhili's activities. There appears to have been a close relationship between bodhisattva ordination ceremonies convened by Zhili and a *nianfo* society that he established at his monastery, Yanqing yuan 延慶院. According to Zhili's plan, the *nianfo* assemblies were to be held every year on the fifteenth day of the second month and were intended to attract ten thousand participants (see *Jie nianfohui shu* 結念佛會疏, in *Siming jiaoxing lu*, fasc. 1, T 46.862a–c). At the same time, one of Zhili's biographers observes that Zhili convened a bodhisattva precept ceremony every year, also in the second month, that brought together as many as five thousand recipients (ibid., T 46.920a24–25). It is not certain whether these two events are identical or whether they happened in close proximity to each other, although the title of the Pure Land society, the "Assembly for Reciting the Buddha Name and Conferral of the Precepts" (*Nianfo shijie hui* 念佛施戒會, see T 46.857c25), strongly suggests that the two were merged in the same assembly. In any case, the passage cited above and these activities make clear that the bodhisattva precepts and Pure Land practice were inextricably related for Zhili. Furthermore, Zhili in instituting these assemblies demonstrated that he was committed to engaging a wide audience.

Zhili's concerns for the bodhisattva precepts, Pure Land practice, and the inclusion of as many people as possible were inherited by his successors. Zhili's disciples such as Benru 本如 (981–1050; FT, fasc. 12, T 49.214a–c) and Huicai 慧才 (998–1083; FT, fasc. 12, T 49.215b–c) were involved in spreading both the bodhisattva precepts and Pure Land practice among the laity. A biography of a certain layperson relates that he had received the bodhisattva precepts from Benru and portrays this lay adherent as a Pure Land devotee, a practice that might also well have been acquired from Benru.[8] From Huicai ushers a possible line of development that went beyond the confines of the Tiantai school. Huicai's various biographies present him both as a Pure Land devotee and a propagator of the bodhisattva precepts.[9] He is recorded as having administered the bodhisattva precepts to countless clerics and laity, among whom was Yuanzhao (FT, fascs. 12 and 30, T 49.215.7–9, 297b.28–29).

Yuanzhao is renowned in Chinese Buddhist history for his restoration of the Vinaya school (see FT, fasc. 29, T 49.297b–c). This school became one of the three major Buddhist traditions, along with Chan and Tiantai, in the Song period. Its revival was in large part due to Yuanzhao's commentaries on Daoxuan 道宣 (596–667), the founder of the tradition, and his establishment of Vinaya institutions. Despite this seemingly sectarian orientation, Yuanzhao's debt to other traditions must be acknowledged. His Tiantai roots are unmistakable. He trained under the Tiantai master Chuqian 處謙 (1011–1075; FT, fasc. 13, T 49.217c–218a), who had studied with both Zunshi's and Zhili's first-generation disciple Benru. Consequently Yuanzhao's interpretation of the Vinaya tradition reflected a doctrinal orientation heavily influenced by Tiantai. This approach also included the same kind of preoccupation with Pure Land and the bodhisattva precepts that was manifest in the careers of Zhili's and Zunshi's descendants who were Yuanzhao's contemporaries. After receiving the bodhisattva precepts from Huicai, Yuanzhao himself actively promoted them as well as Pure Land belief among both monks and the laity.

Like Zhili and Zunshi before him, Yuanzhao created an ordination ceremony for the conferral of the bodhisattva precepts (*Shou pusajie yi* 受菩薩戒儀 in *Zhiyuan yibian* 芝園遺編, fasc. 2, Z 2.10.268b). In form, his ceremony resembles Zunshi's, which consists of ten parts rather than the traditional twelve found in versions up through Zhili's. In content, Yuanzhao's rite, while not differing significantly from Zhili's and Zunshi's rites in terms of incorporating popular religious concerns, nevertheless surpasses all previous ceremonies in terms of its integration of Pure Land. The number of times "Pure Land" is mentioned in Yuanzhao's text exceeds even that found in Zhili's.

The fifth section of the rite dedicated to repentance is especially prominent in its frequent references to Pure Land. The section opens with the instruction that whoever wishes to receive the precepts must become mindful of all past offenses; failure to lay open these offenses "obstructs the precepts, obstructs the gate to pure land, and obstructs the path to enlightenment." The section proceeds to a reflection on and an expression of repentance for transgressions against the five basic Buddhist precepts. Past transgressions of each precept are recognized as the cause for "falling into birth and death, wandering through the three realms, not being reborn in pure land, and not attaining buddhahood." The recipients, consequently, vow that henceforth they will no longer commit the related offense; they pray that "the purified merit [deriving from newly transformed behavior] be granted universally to all sentient beings and that it adorn the pure land"; and they pledge to seek Buddhahood (Z 2.10.270d–271c). The various allusions to "pure land" in this section are generic, having specific connection with Amitābha, but consideration of Yuanzhao's historical context in which the aspiration to rebirth in Sukhāvatī was widespread leads us to assume that these references must primarily have conjured images of Amitābha's realm in the minds of recipients.

A striking example of the degree to which Yuanzhao incorporated Pure Land belief into the bodhisattva precept ordination ceremony can be found in the sixth section dedicated to inviting ordination masters for conferral of the precepts. Whereas other rites customarily assign the role of preceptor (*heshang* 和上) to Śākyamuni, that of karma master (*jiemo asheli* 羯磨阿闍梨) to Mañjuśrī, and that of instructor (*jiaoshou* 教授) to Maitreya, Yuanzhao offers the option of assigning these three functions to Amitābha and his attendant bodhisattvas Avalokiteśvara and Mahāsthāmaprāpta, respectively. He observes, "In recent times, clerics and lay people alike cultivate the 'pure actions' (*jingye* 淨業; i.e., Pure Land). Because the karmic link to Amitābha has ripened, they frequently invite him [as preceptor]" (Z 2.10.271d). Although Yuanzhao's ceremony is indicative of his proclivity to Amitābha's devotion, it equally illuminates the commonly held connection among Chinese Buddhists in his era between Pure Land devotion and the bodhisattva precepts.

Yuanzhao's integration of Pure Land belief into the rites of bodhisattva ordination at the end of the Northern Song era culminated the long development outlined in this chapter. The merging of the soteriological vision of Pure Land with the bodhisattva vocation and its discipline is a reflection of the changing landscape of Chinese Buddhism in the Song, one in which Buddhism sought to bring ever increasing numbers of laypeople into the Mahāyāna bodhisattva vision through the promise of the Pure Land.

Conclusion

Exploring the development of rituals over time offers lessons in the perpetual tension between continuity and change that is inherent in all religious traditions. The study of bodhisattva precept ordinations within the Tiantai tradition provides a good example of such tension as it existed in Chinese Buddhism during the Tang and Song periods. On the one hand, the rites display a remarkable stability with regard to form and content despite the passage of centuries. On the other hand, however, the fact that new versions of the rites containing innovations were produced time and again throughout the centuries demonstrates that there existed both an institutional freedom to innovate and a flexibility in mental outlook on the part of individual monks to adapt rites to their particular circumstances.

Although the constancy of basic elements in the bodhisattva precept ordination rites of the Tiantai tradition has been acknowledged at various junctures in the preceding discussion, the focus in this essay has been on the aspect of change and adaptation. In particular, the introduction of indigenous religious elements and increased attention to Pure Land have been examined as innovations through which the ordination rites were tailored to the religious needs and orientations of laypeople. These new elements offer a confirmation of changes taking place within Chinese Buddhism in the late Tang and Song, where we find a greater emphasis on lay participation and a greater importance accorded to Pure Land Buddhism. Similarly, these new emphases in Buddhism reflected transformations taking place within the broader context of Chinese religion and society, where we witness an increased attention to popular deities and a growing preoccupation with the afterlife (for an overview, see von Glahn 1993).

From one perspective, these changes within Buddhism can be validly analyzed in terms of the political, social, and economic transformations that were taking place during this period. Such an approach holds great promise for the future study of Buddhism in the Song as increasing use is made of the wealth of recent studies on Song politics, economics, and society. At the same time, however, we cannot lose sight of the inherent motivations and ideals that helped bring about the changes discussed here. To wit, these changes can be understood as deriving from a reappropriation of a religious ideal. The religious fervor and efflorescence in ritual activity, textual study, and interaction with the larger society that characterize the careers of Yanshou, Zhili, Zunshi, and Yuanzhao in the Five Dynasties and the Song are manifestations of a revitalized sense of dedication to the Mahāyāna ideal of the bodhisattva.

Embracing the bodhisattva vocation with renewed vigor, these men were forced to deal creatively with the aforementioned tension between continuity and change. On one side, they keenly felt the bodhisattva vocation's requirement of fidelity to the Dharma and to tradition. Their exegetical contributions, the doctrinal controversies that they engaged in, their codification of rituals, and their efforts in reviving and defining the Tiantai and Vinaya schools can all be understood in this light. At the same time, they were spurred on by the bodhisattva vocation's call to aid all sentient beings. This required them to undertake numerous practices related to the spiritual and physical welfare of other beings and to gear those practices and their message to the disposition and needs of their audience. The multitudinous and seemingly eclectic practices engaged in by these men—the creation of Pure Land societies, the release of living creatures, the feeding of hungry ghosts—all represent responses to this call of the bodhisattva vocation. Among these myriad activities, the conferral and observance of the bodhisattva precepts stands not just as one among many disparate activities but rather as the cornerstone that initiates and orients all the rest. Their creation of new bodhisattva precept ceremonies, then, can be justly interpreted as a bodhisattva act and the innovations introduced into these ceremonies as the bodhisattva's employment of *upaya*, expedient means appropriate to the audience. Viewed in this light, the evolving bodhisattva ordination ceremonies were more than reflections of changes occuring within society; they were the outgrowth of a Buddhist ideal that inspired Buddhism to be not just a reactive institution concerned with conserving its traditions, but an active participant and agent in those changes.

Notes

1. Biographical sources and secondary sources regarding these people are available. For Deshao, see SGZ (fasc. 13, T 50.789a–b); Abe (1953, 19–22); and Ogawa (1936, 54). For Xiji, see FT (fasc. 8, T 49.160c).

2. I am not entertaining the possibility that the Huisi manual and the important changes that it shares with the Song rites are the product of, rather than the model for, those Song rites. For alternative views regarding the dating of this text, see Taira

1955, which argues that the manual was created by Huiwei 慧威; and Tajima Tokuon 田島德音 (BK 5.102), who conjectures that it was produced by someone from the Yuan 元 period (1279–1367) because the recension contained in *Zoku zōkyō* (2.10.4b3–4) mentions the country of Great Yuan (*Da Yuan guo*) 大元國. Due to limitations of space, it was necessary to eliminate from this essay sections that discuss the ordination rituals of Zhanran and Mingkuang.

3. Zhili's ordination manual is included in the *Siming zunzhe jiaoxing lu* 四明尊者教行録 (hereafter *Siming jiaoxing lu*), fasc. 1, T 46.858; Zunshi's manual is found in the *Jinyuan ji* 金園集, fasc. 1, Z 2.6.109a.

4. Compare the litanies in the *Siming jiaoxing lu* 1, T 46.860a, 5–8, and the *Jinyuan ji* 1, Z 2.6.109d, 16–110a3. For Zunshi, the litany appears in the second section dedicated to entreating higher powers to witness and protect the reception of the precepts (Z 2.6.109d–110a). In Zhili's rite, the litany is situated in the third section, which is also an entreaty to witness and protect (T 46.859c–860a).

5. Among the officials whom Zunshi interacted with during his career were Xue Yan 薛顏 (953–1025), the prefect of Hangzhou who was instrumental in bringing Zunshi to Hangzhou; a counselor to the heir apparent Ma Liang 馬亮 for whom Zunshi composed a work on Pure Land practice; and the minister Wang Qinruo 王欽若 (962–1025), who visited Zunshi in Hangzhou and assisted him in getting imperial approval for Tiantai works in the canon. See Zunshi's biography in Qisong's 契嵩 *Tanjin wenji* 鐔津文集, fasc. 12, T 52.714b27–28, 714c16, and 714c18 ff; still other officials are mentioned in 715a21.

6. I am not entirely confident of my reading of this passage. The term *"bailing"* 百靈 (hundred spirits) is preceded by the word *"jinji"* 禁忌 (taboo). Might this refer to spirits considered taboo, that is, non-Buddhist spirits or deities who were the subject of blood sacrifice? Zunshi, in one instance, is recorded as having converted one of these deities to Buddhism, thereby abolishing bloody sacrifice at that deity's temple (*Tanjin wenji*, fasc. 12, T 52.714a17–23).

7. For a narration of some of these activities, see *Tanjin wenji*, fasc. 12, T 52.714a–b. The *Jinyuan ji* includes, for example, the following rituals that Zunshi created to take care of spirits of the dead, hungry ghosts, and other sentient beings: (1) *Xiu Yulanpen fangfa jiumen* 修盂蘭盆方法九門 (in fasc. 1); (2) *Shishi fa* 施食法 (in fasc. 2); and (3) *Fangsheng ciji famen* 放生慈濟法門 (in fasc. 2).

8. See Zuo Shen's 左伸 funerary epigraph by Yuanzhao, the *Taizhou Zuo shi muming* 台州左氏墓銘, in *Zhiyuan ji*, fasc. 2 (Z 2.10.296d–297a) and Zuo's biography in FT, fasc. 28 (T 49.285a).

9. See Huicai's biography written by Yuanzhao, the *Hangzhou Leifeng Guangci fashi xingye ji* 杭州雷峰廣慈法師行業記, in *Zhiyuan ji*, fasc. 1, Z 2.10.292d, and Huicai's biography in FT, fasc. 27, T 49.277b. On his activities in Hangzhou and his Pure Land teachings, see Satō Seijun 1988, 470–475.

Chapter 8

Bodhidharma's Precepts in Japan

WILLIAM M. BODIFORD

PRECEPTS HAVE A rather ambiguous status in Japanese Buddhism. On the one hand, following Saichō 最澄 (767–822) and the acceptance of separate Tendai ordinations in the early ninth century, Japanese Buddhism has been characterized by widespread disregard of the basic monastic norms defined in the vinaya (*ritsu* 律) and transmitted to Japan by Ganjin 鑑眞 (688–763; Ch. Jianzhen) and other Chinese Buddhist teachers. After Saichō received government permission to abandon the ordination procedures of the *Four Part Vinaya* (which Saichō had denounced as being "*hīnayāna*," or "inferior"), the vast majority of Japanese Buddhist monks took monastic vows no more demanding than those asked of laymen and laywomen. Many distinctions between a lay lifestyle and a monastic one were abandoned. The Mahāyāna (superior) bodhisattva precepts followed by Japanese monks nominally apply to every social group in the Buddhist order *(saṅgha)*, but overall these precepts address behaviors of concern mainly to laypeople. Several Mahāyāna precepts in the *Brahmā Net Sūtra* (T 24.1005a–b, 1005c–1006a) stipulate, for example, that one should seek sanctification when appointed to government office and make offerings to the community of monks, indicating that these precepts govern lay, not monastic, affairs. As a result of the establishment of separate Tendai ordinations based on these lay-oriented precepts, most ordained members of the Buddhist order in Japan were freed from having to observe the vinaya rules previously associated with monks and nuns (Groner 2000, 286–303; 1987, 129–159).

It is not surprising then to learn that subsequent Japanese Buddhists openly engaged in affairs that would have been unjustifiable in terms of traditional monastic practice. Wealthy laypersons who

retired from the affairs of the world by taking Buddhist vows continued to reside with their families and servants. Powerful Buddhist
temples employed monastic militias (*sōhei* 僧兵) to intimidate
authorities and destroy rival Buddhist temples. Master teachers
fathered their own disciples to form lineages based on blood ties
(*kechimyaku* 血脈; Tsuji 1947, 2.133–141). Premodern Japanese
literature, especially tales and legends (*setsuwa* 説話), abounds with
depictions of monks who ate meat and engaged in sexual debauch-
ery. Significantly, the moral failings of monks often were depicted
as commonplace and perhaps necessary steps along the Buddhist
path (e.g., Childs 1980).

On the other hand, while precepts declined in status as codes
governing moral behavior, their importance as an abstract concept
grew to an almost absolute degree. Japanese Buddhists began to
distinguish between conventional wording of the precepts (*jikai* 事
戒), to which they assigned secondary importance, and the spiritual
essence (*kaitai* 戒體), or ideal precepts (*rikai* 理戒), which became
equated with Buddhahood itself. Over time, the ordination ceremony, during which a person receives the precepts, came to represent one of the most prominent ritual confirmations of final and
complete salvation. In the context of these ceremonies, Mahāyāna
precepts were no longer seen simply as bodhisattva vows (*seigan* 誓
願) in contrast to the rules of monastic discipline *(vinaya* or *ritsu)*.
Instead they became a category unto themselves. As a result of a
radical transformation in religious value, each of the individual
bodhisattva precepts (*bosatsu kai* 菩薩戒) was (and is) conceived of
as expressing a singular Buddha precept (*bukkai* 佛戒, or *busshō kai*
佛性戒) that transcends all distinctions—whether between so-called
"hīnayāna vinaya" and Mahāyāna precepts, secular life and monastic life, or good and evil.[1] Although the nature of this unified precept is explained differently in various texts and in different schools
of Japanese Buddhism, in general its absolute status rests on certain widely shared assumptions: the Buddha proclaiming the precepts is the ultimate Buddha (e.g., the dharma body of Śākyamuni
according to Tendai 天台, the dharma body of Mahā Vairocana according to tantra, the dharma body of Amitābha according to Pure
Land); each precept of the ultimate Buddha expresses the same unified, all-embracing ultimate reality that is Buddha nature (*busshō*
佛性); and thus the goal of the ordination ceremony is the proper
ritual confirmation of this Buddha nature, cementing the bond

that unites the limited, individual person to the universal, absolute Buddha. Recast in these terms, this precept embodies awakening realized in one's own present body (*sokushin jōbutsu* 即身成佛), in one's own present social circumstances. This view of the precept is summed up in the phrase "Precept is the vehicle of salvation" (*kaijō itchi* 戒乘一致).

Buddhist ordinations based on the doctrine of unity of precepts and salvation can signify less than a withdrawal from secular affairs and imply much more than a preliminary step on the spiritual path. Often ordinations symbolize both the initial acceptance of Buddhism and the spiritual culmination of the path to awakening. This ambiguous symbolism played a major role in the social development of Japanese Zen 禪, especially within the Sōtō Zen 曹洞禪 lineage. Many Japanese Zen rituals rest on the doctrine that the wordless awakening of the Buddhas and patriarchs is conveyed through mysterious Zen precepts (*zenkai* 禪戒) (Kagamishima 1961).[2] Traditionally Japanese Zen leaders believed that these precepts had been transmitted to China by Bodhidharma, the legendary first ancestor of the Chinese Zen (Chan) lineage. They further believed that Bodhidharma's precepts were transmitted to Japan, where they became the basis of the Tendai doctrine of Perfect Sudden Precepts (*endon kai* 圓頓戒) established by Saichō (e.g., *Taikyaku kanwa* 對客閑話 by Manzan Dōhaku 卍山道白 [1636–1714], ESG 20.732b). Surprisingly, these beliefs were based not on the claims of early Japanese Zen pioneers, such as Eisai 榮西 (1141–1215) or Dōgen 道元 (1200–1253), but on the writings of earlier Japanese Tendai leaders. Once new Zen groups began to assert their independence from Tendai, they were able to turn the earlier Tendai association with Bodhidharma to their own advantage, arguing that they alone possessed true access to the awakening conveyed by the precepts because Saichō's Zen lineage had been lost in Japan. Ironically, as Zen leaders explicitly rejected the authority of Tendai, they unconsciously reinterpreted Zen rituals in light of Tendai doctrines.

This essay provides an overview of several Japanese texts that discuss the idea of Bodhidharma's precepts in Japan. In modern times Japanese scholars such as Kagamishima Genryū (1961, 1985) and Ishida Mizumaro (1986a, b, d) have shown that most of the texts discussed below are historically and doctrinally deficient. They present interpretations of the precepts that often contradict one another and rely on creative misquotations of Buddhist scripture. Many medieval Japanese precept texts are of doubtful authorship and uncertain chronology. They describe seemingly historical relationships that have no basis in history. The main thrust of previous scholarship has been to refute the assertions of these texts, deny the historical validity of any role for Bodhidharma in the development of precepts in Japan, and thus maintain a rigid sectarian division between Zen and other forms of Japanese Buddhism (Kawaguchi 1976). Previous scholars, therefore, have examined neither the role that Tendai interpretations of precepts and ordination rituals has played in Zen practice nor the ways in which Japanese monks blended together ideas based on Tendai, Zen, and tantric (*mikkyō* 密教) Buddhism to interpret precepts in ways that transcend commonplace notions of sectarian identity. Below I ignore issues of historical and doctrinal validity and instead present these texts in their own terms in an attempt to rediscover some of the ways that ideas and images of Zen, of precepts, and of Tendai have overlapped in Japanese Buddhism.

Bodhidharma's Precepts in Japanese Tendai

The belief that Bodhidharma's precepts were transmitted to Japan as the precepts of the Tendai school is derived from the *One-Mind Precept Transmission Essays* (*Denjutsu isshin kai mon* 傳述一心戒文, hereafter the *Precept Essays*). This Tendai text was compiled sometime around 834 (more than three hundred years before Eisai was born) by one of Saichō's disciples named Kōjō 光定 (779–858). It is a hastily compiled collection of Kōjō's essays (written in 834) on the history and nature of precepts to be used in sectarian Tendai ordinations and transcripts of Saichō's arguments (from 817 to 823) in favor of replacing the monastic precepts of the *Four Part Vinaya* with exclusive Mahāyāna precepts (Groner 2000, 17–18, 135–136, 292–298). In recent years scholars have carefully distinguished between Kōjō's and Saichō's statements on the precepts. They have criticized traditional Tendai scholarship for naïvely assuming that Kōjō's explanations accurately reflect his master's teachings (esp. Ishida Mizumaro 1986c, 1:269–270, 335 nn. 30–31; 1986d, 117–122). But the extent of Kōjō's influence cannot be understood without acknowledging that Japanese Buddhists traditionally have believed that the entirety of his text revealed Saichō's doctrines. Eisai (*Kōzen gokokuron* 興禪護國論, fasc. 2, p. 49), for example, referred to the *Precept Essays* as if it had been written by Saichō. This haphazard collection of essays was never intended to constitute a well-reasoned theoretical statement on precept doctrine. For this purpose later monks relied on the extensive writings of the Tendai patriarch Annen 安然 (ninth century; Groner 2000, 298; Sueki 1994). Kōjō's essays continued to be studied for their historical information.

Kōjō compiled the *Precept Essays* to clarify the unique character of the new precepts being advocated by Saichō. His preface sets the tone for the work by praising Saichō's solitary genius:

> I have heard that underneath the blue ocean there lies the pearl of the black dragon. The material gods of the three teachings cannot see its substance. The exalted pundits of the other doctrines do not know its color. My great master took it. His name was Saichō, the great meditation master (*zenji* 禪師). A Japanese born in the province of Ōmi 近江, my master had spiritual luminosity (*shōryō* 精靈) for bones and yin and yang for guts. His nature was from Heaven, his wisdom inborn (*jinen* 自然). He comprehended the One Vehicle Doctrine (*ichijō gi* 一乘義) [of the *Lotus Sūtra*] and embraced the One Vehicle Precept (*ichijō kai* 一乘戒).... He ascended Mount Tiantai 天台 [in China], bowed before the image of Great Master Zhiyi 智顗, and thereby inherited the One Mind Precept (*isshin kai* 一心戒). (T 74.634b)

The bulk of the *Precept Essays* concentrates on Saichō's campaign to win government authorization for exclusive Tendai ordinations based on his explanation of the Mahāyāna precepts. Kōjō's summary of these precepts does not appear until the third and final fascicle of the text, which begins with the words: "The One Vehicle Precept is the first sign of good fortune" (T 74.651c). Kōjō's introductory remarks (T 74.652a) next identify the essence of the precept with Vairocana (Rushana 盧舍那) Buddha, the reward-body (*hōjin* 報身) Buddha who assumes the form of many different Śākyamuni (Shaka 釋迦) Buddhas (i.e., response bodies, *ōjin* 應身) as a means of transmitting the precept to the many phenomenal realms where humans—and other creatures—live. Elsewhere in his essay (T 74.656a) Kōjō further identifies this precept as the morality, meditation, and wisdom of the dharma-body (*hosshin* 法身) form of Vairocana (known in this context as Birushana 毘盧遮那) to show that it embodies the self-realized (*jishō* 自證) awakening of all three bodies (or aspects) of Buddhas.[3] Before explaining the full significance of this precept, however, Kōjō first gives a brief history of its earthly transmission.

Kōjō's narrative of the precept's history (T 74.652b) opens with the following assertion: "This precept was bestowed in India for twenty-eight generations. The twenty-eighth generation master, Bodhidharma, took the One Vehicle Precept and traveled to China." Bodhidharma, of course, is the legendary twenty-eighth patriarch of Zen. Kōjō, however, introduces him as a historical figure who transmitted a Tendai precept to China. After quoting from several versions of Bodhidharma's biography, Kōjō then describes (T 74.653b–c) a meeting between Bodhidharma and Huisi 慧思 (515–577), the teacher of Zhiyi 智顗 (538–597), the de facto founder of the Tiantai school. Through this supposed meeting between Bodhidharma and Huisi, for which there is no historical evidence whatsoever, Kōjō has Huisi and Zhiyi inherit their unique Tendai precept by way of Bodhidharma's Zen lineage.[4] Kōjō's account thus suggests the following precept lineage:

> Vairocana Buddha: the spiritual basis of the precepts
> Śākyamuni Buddha: the physical Buddha of our world
> The twenty-eight Zen patriarchs in India
> Bodhidharma: the Zen patriarch who brought the precepts to
>   China
> Huisi: a Tiantai patriarch who met Bodhidharma
> Zhiyi: the de facto founder of Tiantai who was a student of
>   Huisi
> Saichō: a monk who attained the precepts from Zhiyi's image

This lineage is remarkable in many respects, not the least of which is the fact that it differs from all five of the lineage histories that Saichō presented to the court in 819 to document the origins of his teachings (Groner 2000, 255–263). Saichō claimed affiliation to a Zen lineage that derived from Bodhidharma, but it did not include either Huisi or Zhiyi. Saichō also claimed affiliation to a completely separate precept lineage that does not mention Bodhidharma. In Saichō's version of the precept lineage, no Indian sequence of transmission was necessary because both Huisi and Zhiyi had received the precepts during their previous lifetimes directly from Śākyamuni Buddha. Following Zhiyi, moreover, six generations of Chinese Tiantai patriarchs handed down the precepts before reaching

Saichō. Although Kōjō's unified version of a precept lineage that combines Zen and Tendai stands in sharp contrast to Saichō's writings, it is possible that Saichō had acquiesced to Kōjō's version as well. The *Precept Essays* reports (T 74.645b–c) that in the third month of 822—two and a half months before Saichō's death— Kōjō cited the above lineage (i.e., Bodhidharma to Huisi to Zhiyi) in a missive presented to the government on behalf of Saichō's request for an exclusive precept platform. If this account is accurate, it is difficult to believe that Kōjō could have fabricated the precept lineage during Saichō's lifetime without his knowledge.

One can imagine several reasons why Kōjō chose to revise Saichō's precept lineage to give a prominent role to Bodhidharma. First, Saichō and Kōjō saw Bodhidharma as a historical example of a bodhisattva monk (*bosatsu sō* 菩薩僧). This is an important point because Saichō's request for Tendai ordinations had been rejected partially on the grounds that no Buddhist monks had ever been ordained by the bodhisattva precepts alone (Groner 2000, 146–148). In the government's eyes, only ordinations conducted according to the procedures of the *Four Part Vinaya* could properly confer the status of monk. Kōjō quotes Saichō on this point:

> Members of our mountain sect will follow the [*Lotus Sūtra's*] chapter [14] on "Pleasant Activities" (*Anrakugyō bon* 安樂行品) by observing the Mahāyāna precepts (*daijō kai* 大乘戒) while ignoring the Hīnayāna precepts (*shōjō kai* 小乘戒). . . . From beginning to end we shall be ordained only with the bodhisattva precepts, thereby becoming bodhisattva monks who practice the three learnings by holding to the purity that is our intrinsic nature. Without dawdling on roundabout ways, we will proceed directly to where the treasure is and obtain the goal of Buddhahood. How do we know this is possible? . . . The memorial tablet of Master Zuoxi 左溪 states: "During the Liang 梁 and Wei 魏 dynasties there existed a bodhisattva monk named Bodhidharma."[5] (T 74.642b; also see Groner 2000, 146)

This passage suggests that Saichō saw Bodhidharma as a crucial historical precedent for "bodhisattva monks," the new category of Buddhist followers he hoped to found in Japan. In his eyes, Bodhidharma was a role model for future Tendai monks.

The prominent role assigned to Bodhidharma's precepts also enhanced the effectiveness of the many passages in the *Precept Essays* that suggest the existence of a karmic inevitability or divine destiny that demanded the establishment of Tendai precepts in Japan. Kōjō notes (T 74.653c–654a) that the unfolding of this chain of karma began during the former lifetimes of Huisi and Zhiyi when they heard Śākyamuni Buddha preach the *Lotus Sūtra* while standing on Vulture Peak in India. Once reborn in China, Huisi formed a link between Bodhidharma and Zhiyi in China before being reborn yet again in Japan. The *Precept Essays* repeatedly emphasizes (T 74.639b, 645c, 647c, 648a–b, 654b) that the great Japanese cultural hero Prince Shōtoku 聖徳 (547–622)—the legendary founding patron of Buddhism in Japan—was none other than Huisi. Thus, Kōjō argues (T 74.648a, 654a), it is no accident that Shōtoku promoted the *Lotus Sūtra* at court and throughout the land. Just as important, Kōjō proclaims (T 74.645c) that Bodhidharma, like Huisi, had been reborn in Japan. In fact Bodhidharma (in the guise of a beggar) met Huisi (in the guise of Shōtoku) in Japan at Kataoka 片岡, where they exchanged Japanese verse (*waka* 和歌). Shōtoku's attendants were dumbfounded when they discovered that their prince was able to see beyond the beggar's rags to the sage within (T 74.653b).[6] By identifying the precepts with Bodhidharma, and by then showing that Bodhidharma had strong ties to Japan and to Prince Shōtoku, the *Precept Essays* imply that Saichō's new Tendai precepts likewise were hidden in Japan's past, waiting for the fulfillment of longstanding karmic relationships.

Another link between Bodhidharma and the Tendai precepts can be found in Kōjō's account of the legendary meeting between Huisi and Bodhidharma. As recounted in the *Precept Essays*, nothing in their exchange suggests an ordination or precept initiation:

Bodhidharma asked the meditation master *(zenji)* Huisi: "How many years at this tranquil spot have you trained in the Way?"

Meditation Master Huisi replied: "Twenty some years."

Bodhidharma asked: "What miracles (*reigen* 靈験) have you seen? What magical powers (*iriki* 威力) have you acquired?"

Meditation Master Huisi replied: "I haven't seen miracles. I haven't acquired magical powers."

Bodhidharma was quiet for a long time. Then he sighed and said: "It's easy to become fed up with Zen meditation; it's difficult to leave the tainted world. I have chaste relations and have eliminated [retribution caused by] eons of heavy sin (*jūzai* 重罪). Now I associate with pure companions and plant karmic seeds for superior rebirths. Master, you strive so hard. Why do you manifest yourself here, staying at this mountain, instead of filling the ten directions? Your karma here is ended. You should be reborn across the ocean to the east [in Japan]. People in that land lack spiritual aspirations. Their nature is crude and evil. Greed and desire rule their actions. They kill for food. You should proclaim the True Dharma (shōbō 正法; i.e., Buddhism) to them and put a stop to the killing."

Meditation Master Huisi asked Bodhidharma: "Who are you?"

He replied: "I am Empty Sky (kokū 虚空)." The conversation having ended, he turned to the east and left. (T 74.645c–646a, 653b–c)

At first glance it is difficult to know what to make of this conversation. Read within the context of Kōjō's other explanations of the precepts, however, "empty sky" (i.e., space) stands out. This term has a rich history in early Chan literature (e.g., McRae 1986, 155–160, 166, 210–211, 218, 223, 229). The empty sky is infinite, undivided, and limitless. It is, therefore, associated with all-embracing thusness, or Buddha nature. Moreover, just as the sky nurtures all plants, this spiritual thusness nurtures all things and hinders nothing. Early Chinese Zen teachers cultivated the unhindered ability to see not a single thing, which they termed viewing afar and equated with seeing purity (McRae 1986, 172–174, 229–233). Huisi's not seeing miracles, therefore, indicated that he saw the pure emptiness of space quite well. Bodhidharma could only ask how amidst the emptiness did he manage to stay localized in any one spot? This story suggests that, as Bernard Faure (1987, 345) has noted, the emergence of Zen Buddhism was accompanied by the advocacy of a new vision of space "whose homogeneity abolishes the old heterogeneities" associated with previous religious practices.

For Kōjō, Bodhidharma's empty sky was the key to abolishing the traditional Buddhist path and its complex series of spiritual stages. According to Kōjō, realization of empty sky made possible the attainment of Buddhahood in one's very body (sokushin jōbutsu). He explains the theory behind this possibility:

The first meaning (daiichi gi 第一義) is Buddha nature. Buddha nature is Vairocana (Birushana) Buddha. Vairocana Buddha pervades all places.... Because the orthodox doctrines of Tendai lie in the perfect, complete, and real (en jō jitsu 圓成實), they establish the doctrine of attainment of Buddhahood in one's very body.... The orthodox doctrines of Tendai state that because Vairocana (Rushana) Buddha pervades all, therefore the three Buddha [bodies] pervade all and ... each moment (*setsuna* 刹那) pervades all. If one contemplates this way, it is called contemplating defilements (*bonnō* 煩惱), which is contemplation of the dharma body. Contemplating the dharma body is called contemplation of momentariness. It is contemplation of true thusness (*shinnyo* 眞如), of the real appearance of things (*jissō* 實相), of living beings (*shujō* 衆生), of one's own body, of empty sky. (T 74.650b–c)

Kōjō quoted passages from the writings of Zhiyi to extend this metaphor to the Tendai precepts bestowed by Vairocana Buddha:

These are empty-sky immovable precepts (*kokū fudō kai* 虛空不動戒). Moreover, abiding in the intrinsic purity that is one's own mind, being as immobile as Mount Sumeru, is empty-sky immovable meditation (*kokū fudō jō* 虛空不動定). Moreover, because the intrinsic purity that is one's own mind pervades all dharmas, freely and without hindrance, it is empty-sky immovable wisdom (*kokū fudō e* 虛空不動慧). Precepts, meditation, and wisdom of this type are called Vairocana Buddha. (T 74.653a, 656a)

According to Kōjō (T 74.656a–b), this objective Vairocana Buddha (i.e., the reward body known as Rushana) received the precepts from his own subjective self (i.e., his dharma body known as Dainichi 大日 Buddha). These two Buddhas are both the same yet different: the self-authenticated truth (*jishō hō* 自證法) of the dharma-body Buddha is the fundamental precept (*honkai* 本戒), which remains submerged in the empty sky; the reward-body Buddha reveals only the tip of the precept (*matsukai* 末戒), which like the tip of an iceberg only hints at the depth of its own reality (also see Asai 1975, 259). In this way, Bodhidharma's empty sky gave Kōjō an unhindered medium within which to unify Saichō's four teachings of Tendai, tantra, Zen, and Mahāyāna precepts (*en-mitsu-zen-kai* 圓密禪戒). Kōjō, for example, interpreted the tantric ritual of meditation on the syllable "A" (*ajikan* 阿字觀), the seed mantra of Vairocana Buddha, as the appearance of the precepts in the empty sky:

The intrinsic purity that is one's own mind is the A-syllable practice (*ajimon* 阿字門). When one focuses one's mind on the syllable "A," the precepts become the syllable "A." When one focuses one's mind on the real appearance of things, then the precepts are that real appearance.... Because precepts are the same as mind they are the same as the syllable "A." Mind is empty-sky *bodhi* (i.e., empty-sky awakening; *kokū bodai* 虛空菩提). (T 74.656b)

Because the precepts are the same as mind, for Kōjō, insight into the true nature of the precepts was far more important than actually practicing the precepts. He explains (T 74.656b) that this type of insight is salvation: "The Buddha's children of the One Vehicle who understand the One Mind Precept enter the ranks of the Buddhas" (*butsui* 佛位). In this statement, one can detect the beginning of the doctrine of precepts as the vehicle of salvation *(kaijō itchi)*, the unity of precepts, and Buddhahood (Asai 1975, 260–261).

Within the Tendai tradition, Kōjō's version of Bodhidharma's precepts never created much of an impact. His successors found more sophisticated ways to integrate tantric notions of Buddhahood and the precepts. Bodhidharma, of course, never disappeared. The beggar who traded songs with Prince Shōtoku continued to be reborn. His outward form changed, but his precepts remained mostly the same.

Precepts in Medieval Japanese Society

Historically, Japanese Buddhist leaders have exploited the idea of the unity of precepts and salvation in their efforts to win lay support and attract new converts. In the medieval and early modern periods (thirteenth through eighteenth centuries), lay ordination ceremonies played a major role in the popularization and regional propagation of various Buddhist orders (see Dobbins and Groner in this volume). New temple construction was sponsored by regionally powerful leaders who invariably received ordinations at the hands of abbots residing in the new temples. Buddhist monks conducted mass ordination ceremonies that attracted large groups of lay participants who heretofore had rarely enjoyed opportunities to establish direct ties to a religious leader. Precept ceremonies not only provided these laymen and laywomen with spiritual assurances, but also helped cement social bonds among those attending the same ceremony. Buddhist proselytizers used precept ordinations to convert local gods (and their devotees) into ardent supporters of Buddhism. On other occasions the same ordinations exorcised demons or ghosts. Precepts proved especially effective in calming the spirits of the dead—so much so that posthumous ordinations are still a standard feature of the funeral rites performed in many Buddhist sects. Through these various ritual contexts the spiritual power of precepts enabled Buddhist institutions to assume important social roles, which commanded (and continue to command) considerable economic resources (Bodiford 1993).

Rival claims on the religious loyalty and financial support of social groups naturally led to sectarian assertions that true ordination with the Buddha precepts existed only within a single Buddhist lineage. Leaders of new religious groups, such as Zen and Pure Land (both of which splintered off from Tendai), buttressed their sectarian claims by either disavowing their indebtedness to earlier Tendai precept traditions or asserting that they alone maintained the original precept lore that monks within the Tendai school had forgotten. The Pure Land leader Shōgei 聖冏 (1341–1420), for example, took the latter approach. He argued (*Ken jōdo denkai ron* 顯淨土傳戒論, JZ 15.894–895) that only masters of the new Pure Land lineages could properly convey the spiritual essence of the precepts because no Tendai monk other than Hōnen 法然 (1133–1212; Genkū 源空), the founder of the Pure Land school, had properly mastered and taught the arcane secrets of proper ordination ritual. The precepts clearly are the mind transmission (*shinden* 心傳) of the Tendai patriarchs and the legacy of Saichō, declared Shōgei, but they are now transmitted only by Pure Land masters. Just as successive Chinese dynasties had taken the mandate of Heaven from their predecessors, Pure Land initiates had replaced Tendai monks as the proper overseers of the true precept rites.

Zen Claims on Bodhidharma's Precepts

Japanese Zen leaders favored the opposite strategy. To minimize the importance of earlier Tendai traditions they focused attention on Eisai's role in importing a new Zen precept lineage from China. This focus on Eisai no doubt strikes present-day readers as misguided. Modern scholarship reports that Eisai attempted to reform Japanese Tendai monasticism by reintroducing the strict monastic discipline based on careful observance of the precepts of the *Four Part Vinaya* (Ishida Mizumaro 1986a). Eisai cited Tendai writings on Bodhidharma only as evidence of the harmony of Zen and Tendai and did not mention any special precept transmissions (*Kōzen gokokuron,* fasc. 2, p. 49). He repeatedly characterized Zen as promoting strict observance of the *Four Part Vinaya*. He argued that this vinaya-supporting Zen (*furitsu zen* 扶律禪) had once been an important component of Japanese Tendai but was lost until he reintroduced it from China (fasc. 2, pp. 49–53). For medieval Zen monks, however, Eisai's advocacy of the *Four Part Vinaya* left less of an impression than his proclamation of a Zen revival.

Subsequent Japanese Zen monks readily identified Eisai's newly acquired Zen lineage as the introduction of a new precept lineage. Like previous Tendai monks, they saw this precept lineage as separate and distinct from the vinaya. Dōgen, who practiced Zen for eight years under the guidance of one of Eisai's students, wrote that Eisai inherited his Zen lineage on the fifteenth day of the ninth lunar month of 1189 when his Chinese teacher, Xu'an Huaichang 虛庵懷敞, pronounced a transmission formula beginning with the words: "Bodhisattva precepts are to the Zen school the circumstances of the single great affair" (*bosatsukai wa Zenmon no ichi daiji innen nari* 菩薩戒禪門一大事因緣; see the *Ju Rikan kaimyaku* 授理觀戒脉 and the *Ju Kakushin kaimyaku* 授覺心戒脉, DZZ 2.290–291). The phrase "single great affair" (*ichi daiji* 一大事) is a common Zen expression for the importance of attaining awakening. This statement, therefore, clearly connects the certification of Eisai's Zen awakening to his precept ordination. Significantly, neither this expression nor any other identification of the precepts with Zen awakening occurs in Eisai's autobiographical account of his Zen succession (*Kōzen gokokuron*, fasc. 2, pp. 55–56). This discrepancy was "corrected" by the Zen monk Kokan Shiren 虎關師鍊 (1278–1346), who compiled Eisai's hagiography in 1322. Kokan based his account of Eisai's Zen succession closely on Eisai's own record. Without any indication of editorial alteration, however, he inserted the formula repeated by Dōgen into the longer passage quoted from Eisai (*Genko shakusho* 元亨釋書, fasc. 2, DNB 62.76b). Moreover, Kokan omitted all mention of the *Four Part Vinaya*. It was this revisionist account, in which Eisai's Chinese teacher clearly identified Zen awakening with the conveyance of the bodhisattva precepts, that determined Eisai's dominant image until modern times (e.g., see the quote from the *Genkō shakusho* in ESG 20.732a–b).

Kokan spelled out the full implications of Eisai's role in importing a new Zen lineage in another composition, this one devoted to an explanation of precepts. In his preface to the *Zen Precept Procedures* (*Zenkai ki* 禪戒規, ZT 7; Bodiford 1999), Kokan identifies the precepts with Bodhidharma and asserts that their spiritual essence is found in Zen alone because only Zen represents an unbroken lineage dating back to the Buddha in India. His preface begins:

> In ancient times Bodhidharma brought the Buddha mind seal (*bus-shin'in* 佛心印) from south India to China: Pointing directly, a single transmission, fierce and rough. Thus were the bodhisattva precepts granted to the second patriarch and so on to the five houses and seven lineages of Zen. The granting and receiving continued without break. I have seen the precept charts of all other schools [of Buddhism]. None of their lineage names are affiliated. Only our Zen precepts have been handed down from the Buddha Śākyamuni to this day, interlinked without missing a single generation. Therefore, of all precepts, Zen precepts are best.

In the body of the text Kokan extends this argument to Eisai. In the following passage, he states that true precepts can be found in Japan only because Eisai brought them back from China:

> These Vajra precepts (*kongō kai* 金剛戒) were transmitted from the lotus throne across the lotus petals, for one thousand one hundred years, by Śākyamuni Buddha, by twenty-eight Zen patriarchs in India to the West, and by six Zen ancestors in China to the East [and, beginning with the seventh, by]: Nanyue 南嶽, Mazu 馬祖, Baizhang 百丈, Huangbo 黃檗, Linji 臨濟, Xinghua 興化, Nanyuan 南院, Fengxue 風穴, Shoushan 首山, Fenyang 汾陽, Ciming 慈明, Huanglong 黃龍, Huitang 晦堂, Lingyuan 靈源, Wushi 無示, Xinwen 心聞, Xuean 雪奄, and Xu'an [Huaichang]. Only our Eisai made the pilgrimage to Sung China to meet Xu'an, to be ordained with the Buddha mind seal. Xu'an handed over his staff, whisk, as well as the bodhisattva precepts, which constitute the Zen school's single great affair.
>
> Certainly these great precepts do not resemble any of the other varieties. They convey the mind seal of Master Bodhidharma. Therefore, one who is about to be ordained should arouse pure faith.

Kokan's rhetorical stance rests on traditional Zen claims to an exclusive patriarchal lineage, which supposedly conferred a unique legitimacy on Zen masters. Kokan's understanding of the significance of this exclusive Zen lineage, however, seems to have been based on the example of Japanese tantric lineages, not Chinese practices. He automatically identifies affiliation to a Zen lineage with secret initiation into the lore and rituals of precepts. Dōgen's account of Eisai's Zen succession process, as well as his characterization of the bodhisattva precepts as being "the authentic legacy of the Buddhas and ancestors" (*Busso shōden bosatsu kai* 佛祖正傳 菩薩戒, DZZ 2.263), also clearly implies that Zen succession rituals necessarily entailed secret precept initiations. In various lineages of Japanese Zen, especially Sōtō, these two types of initiation were in fact linked. An excellent example of how these two types of initiation functioned together can be seen in the postscript to the *Buddhas and Ancestors Properly Transmitted Bodhisattva Precept Ceremony* (*Busso shōden bosatsu kai sahō* 佛祖正傳菩薩戒作法), which was handed down by members of the Jakuen 寂圓 branch of Sōtō Zen who served as abbots at Eiheiji 永平寺 Monastery from 1333 to 1560 (DZZ 2.270–271; Bodiford 1993, 74–75).

Although both Kokan and Dōgen describe precept initiations as if they occupied a position of central importance in Chinese Zen transmission rituals, all the evidence suggests otherwise. In recent years many Japanese scholars labored to demonstrate links between precepts in Chinese Zen and Japanese Tendai, but even in their most forceful arguments they failed to make a case (Kagamishima 1985b, 141–166). It is true that early Chinese Zen texts, such as the *Platform Sūtra* attributed to Huineng 慧能 (638–713; trans. Yampolsky 1967, 141–148) or the *Five Expedient Means* (*Wu fang-pien* 五方便; trans. McRae 1986, 171–173) of the Northern school, interpret precepts in such abstract terms as the pure mind of awakening. It is also true that Japanese Zen monks such as Dōgen (*Hōkyōki* 寶慶記, DZZ 2.387) and Bassui Tokushō 拔隊得勝 (1327–1387; *Enzan wadei gassui shū* 塩山和泥合水集, fasc. 1, p. 200) cited the example of the novice (*shami* 沙彌) Gao 高, dharma heir of the Chinese Zen teacher Yaoshan Weiyan 藥山惟儼 (745–828), as proof that Chinese Zen monks could reject the rites of full ordination stipulated in the vinaya. As a matter of social practice, however, full ordination in accordance with the vinaya always remained (and still remains) the religious and legal ideal for Chinese monks. Traditional Chinese temple regulations, such as the *Pure Rules for Chan Monasteries* (fasc. 1, pp. 13–39) of 1103, insist on vinaya ordinations as one of the preconditions for residency in state-supported monasteries.

It is not surprising, therefore, that the Chinese Zen monks who came to Japan in the seventeenth century knew nothing of any uniquely Zen precepts or rituals for precept initiations. Japanese Zen monks interpreted this ignorance as evidence that in China during the Ming 明 dynasty (1368–1661), as in earlier Tendai, the secret Zen precept lore had been lost. It helped confirm the Japanese prejudice that true Zen survived only in Japan. The famous Japanese Zen reformer Manzan Dōhaku, for example, wrote that only in Japan has the true essence of Zen, the single great affair of precepts, been preserved (*Tōmon ejoshū* 洞門衣袽集, ESG 20.611a; *Taikyaku kanwa*, ESG 20.732b).

Returning to Kokan, it is worthwhile to quote his description of the Zen precepts at length. He provides a remarkably frank description of Zen precept ideology, explaining doctrines that are only implied in most other Zen ritual texts. The fullness of this text probably results from the fact that Kokan intended his statements to be used as the basis for public lectures addressed to laymen and laywomen who were about to receive an ordination. The private teachings of monks were thus codified for public consumption. Kokan distinguished between the various types of Buddhist precepts, emphasizing the qualitative difference between traditional monastic precepts that concern behavior and Mahāyāna precepts that embody awakening. The purpose of the ordination is not to instill morality but to confirm the inherent awakening naturally possessed by all beings. Thus behavior, either in conformity with or in violation of the precepts, is meaningless. What is important, however, is to have faith in the Zen lineage and faith in the ritual efficacy of the ordination procedure. This ritual alone conferred the status of Buddha and patriarch on participants. The ordination concluded with the presentation of a Zen blood-lineage chart to each participant, which gave the names of all of the Zen patriarchs, beginning with Śākyamuni Buddha and ending with the name of the layperson who had just been ordained. A red line connected all the names together, signifying that the layperson now had a direct link to the Buddha.

According to Kokan, before conducting an ordination the Zen master officiating at the ceremony should explain the precepts:

> There are many varieties of precepts: the 5 and the 8 precepts [for laypeople] and the 250 precepts [for monks according to the *Four Part Vinaya*], as well as the 10 major and 48 minor [bodhisattva precepts of the *Brahmā Net Sūtra*]. Of these, the 5 and the 8 precepts insure rebirth as humans or gods. The 250 lead to realization of the Hīnayāna goal. Only the 10 major and 48 minor bodhisattva precepts lead to accomplishment of the supreme way [i.e., Mahāyāna awakening]. Ordination with Śrāvaka [i.e., *hīnayāna*] precepts can be nullified. But ordination with the bodhisattva precepts can never be revoked. Even if one violates the precepts after ordination one is still the Buddha's child. But one who refrains from both ordination and violation is a non-Buddhist.

Thus a scriptures states: "Just as the scent of champak blossoms, even when withered, smells stronger than that of all other flowers, even precept-violating monks are superior to non-Buddhists." Moreover, the *Brahmā Net Sūtra* [T 24.1004a] states: "Living beings who receive ordination with the precepts enter into the ranks of the Buddhas, attaining the same great awakening. Truly they are the Buddha's children." ...

How can one become a Buddha and [Zen] ancestor? Master Bodhidharma said, "One whose behavior and understanding correspond is called an ancestor." Yet there are many varieties of precepts. ... But ordination with the bodhisattva precepts can never be revoked. How can this be? The 5 and 8 and other Hīnayāna precepts depend on physical ordinations. The bodhisattva precepts, however, are based on mind alone. If mind had a limit, then the bodhisattva precepts would have a limit. But because mind is without limit, the precepts are without limit. ...

Once ordained the efficacy of the precepts can never be lost, even in future lives. Even if one is reborn in hell or as a hungry ghost ultimately the precepts are not revoked. If in a future life one is again ordained with the bodhisattva precepts, it is not called a new ordination. It just allows one's mind of awakening to push aside one's evil mind. Ordination with one precept produces a one-part bodhisattva. Ordination with two precepts creates a two-part bodhisattva, and so forth. Upon ordination with all ten major precepts, one becomes a fully endowed bodhisattva. Thus the precept text states: "You will become a Buddha. I have already become a Buddha." If one always believes in this way then one is fully ordained with the precepts.

These Vajra Jeweled Precepts (*kongō hōkai* 金剛寶戒) are the fundamental basis of all Buddhas, the basis of all bodhisattvas. They are the seeds of Buddha nature. Know that these precepts were not preached for the first time by the Buddha of this age. These have been the original precepts of all Buddhas since long before. Buddhas after Buddhas have chanted these. Thus Vairocana Buddha seated on his lotus throne chanted these jeweled precepts and bestowed them on the thousand million Śākyamuni Buddhas. The thousand million Śākyamuni Buddhas each sat under the tree of awakening, chanting these precepts fortnightly. Thereupon all the bodhisattvas chanted these precepts. All living beings consent to being ordained with these precepts. From the Buddhas and bodhisattvas above down to the most evil low-class beings below, the sagely and the common, Mahāyānists and Hīnayānists, all are included in the great net of these precepts. They are the profound, unobstructed, universal Buddhist teaching. Therefore, the twenty-eight Zen patriarchs of the West in India and the six patriarchs of the East in China each personally handed down these precepts. In China and in Japan all the Zen patriarchs are linked together through this unbroken continuum. One who is about to be ordained should arouse pure faith and uphold this tradition. Faith is the origin of the Way. It is the mother of all virtues. Reflect on this well.

The great bodhisattva precepts handed down in the Zen school are the great precepts of the formless basis of mind. Master Bodhidharma bestowed the Buddha mind seal and the ordination ritual. Thus outside the Zen school there are no precepts, and outside the precepts there is no Zen.

All Buddhas and Zen patriarchs must rely first and foremost on the precept ordination to benefit living creatures. Therefore when Śākyamuni Buddha attained the supreme awakening under the tree of awakening, the first thing he did was to chant these precepts. When Bodhidharma came from the West he used these precepts to transmit the mind seal. Since then these precepts have been handed down from proper heir to proper heir, without missing a single generation. In this way they have been transmitted to me.

Today, in response to the pleas of the four groups [i.e., monks, nuns, laymen, and laywomen], I am about to perform the ordination ceremony. I embody neither understanding nor proper behavior. Embarrassed and ashamed, three times I refused, but in the end I could not avoid giving in to your requests. I will bestow on you the Zen precepts and blood-lineage [chart].

To be ordained with the great precepts of the Zen school is to obtain the True Dharma and precepts of the Buddhas and patriarchs. It is to arouse the precepts of the formless basis of mind, to open the eye perceiving the True Dharma (*shōbō gen* 正法眼), to universally benefit gods and men. How could there be any doubt? How could you fail to arouse pure faith?

Kokan argued that Zen and the precepts are one and the same. The only Zen element in Kokan's explanation of the precepts, however, is his emphasis on the special significance of the Zen lineage. In all other regards his description of this ordination ritual epitomizes the reversal of cause and effect that is characteristic of medieval Tendai doctrines of original awakening (*hongaku hōmon* 本覺法門). Before explaining what this reversal entails, first let us look at the traditional conception of the relationship between precepts and awakening.

Kokan's notion that the awakened awareness realized in Zen naturally corresponds to the awakened behavior described by the precepts is not remarkable in itself. This doctrine is a persistent theme in Mahāyāna Buddhist texts. In the *Vimalakīrti Sūtra*, for example, the awakened vision of the layman Vimalakīrti allows him to observe the spirit of the precepts while violating their letter. He rebukes the monk Upāli—the Buddha's disciple who was foremost in upholding the precepts of the vinaya—for failing to realize that when someone "understands the nature of mind, then no defilement [i.e., sin] exists" (T 14.541b; Watson 1997, 47). Passages such as this imply that only someone who has realized awakening can truly embody the precepts. The formal ordination ritual represents only the first step along the Buddhist path. Ultimately the dualistic categories of good and evil must be transcended so that the precepts are given new spiritual life. True fulfillment of the precepts, therefore, requires the realization of awakening. This view emphasizes the need for human beings to become Buddhas—or what is termed the doctrine of moving "from the seed [i.e., the ordinary human's spiritual potential] to the fruit [of awakening]" (*jūin kōka* 從因向果). Once a person experiences awakening, the physical procedure of ordination with precepts has no ultimate significance.

Medieval Japanese Zen monks sometimes interpreted the precepts in this way. In a sermon of Bassui Tokushō, for example, we find the following exchange:

> Question: If all the doctrines preached by the Buddha can be reduced to the one practice of seeing nature and becoming a Buddha (*kenshō jōbutsu* 見性成佛), then wouldn't observance of the vinaya and precepts be beside the point?

> Answer: In terms of the spiritual essence of the precepts (*kaitai* 戒體), both observance and transgression are the one vehicle of ultimate nature, the nonduality of ideals (*ri* 理) and practices (*ji* 事). But someone who has not yet experienced seeing nature (*kenshō*) drowns in the ocean of passion and intellect, thereby killing the Buddha that is one's own mind (*shinbutsu wo korosu* 心佛を殺す). Of all the types of killing, this is the worst. Therefore, true observance of the precepts is seeing nature and being awakened to the Way. (*Enzan wade gasui shū*, fasc. 1, p. 199; Braverman 1989, 19)

Bassui's answer makes clear that the experience of awakening is all important. Nonetheless, the goal of Zen practice does not excuse moral transgressions.

In the Zen ordination ritual described by Kokan, however, these priorities are reversed. The ordination enacts a process of awakening that occurs in reverse sequence. In what is termed moving "from the fruit [of buddhahood] to the seed [i.e., the ordinary human]" (*jūka kōin* 從果向因), the Buddha awakening embodied in precepts finds human expression through the ordination process.[7] The ritual establishes a homology between the abstract Buddha and patriarchs and the concrete human predicament, allowing faith to replace insight. As in the practices of tantric Buddhism, in which proper ritual actions permit the practitioner to embody fully the characteristics of the Buddha, proper ritual ordination with the precepts allows the ordinary person to assume the mind of awakening regardless of one's behavior. From this perspective, Vimalakīrti's (Jōmyō 浄名) example (T 14.539a) could be cited as proof that even lust and desire constitute the Buddha Way (*in'yoku soku ze dō* 婬欲 即是道; e.g., see *Isshin kongō kaitai ketsu* 一心金剛戒體決, DDZ 4.244).

This ritual process also can be seen in the secret initiation documents (*kirikami* 切紙) that describe the ordination procedures and special precept lore handed down only to fully initiated Zen masters.[8] The document *One Mind Precept Procedure Handed Down by Bodhidharma* (*Daruma sōjō isshin kai giki* 達磨相承一心儀軌; in Furuta 1971, 154–155) is typical of such texts. Traditionally attributed to Eisai, it probably dates from no earlier than the middle of the fifteenth century (Furuta 1971, 153; 1981a). The text begins by describing a procedure for sanctifying water, which is used to consecrate the ordination site as well as the monk being initiated. Once this part of the ritual is complete, the Zen master is instructed to turn to his disciple:

> Anointing his forehead three times with your wand, solemnly address the Three Jewels [i.e., Buddha, dharma, and *saṅgha*], which are the very essence of one's own originally endowed mind, saying:
>
> "Now this disciple of sincere faith requests permission to receive from me the transmission of the One Mind Absolute Precepts (*isshin myōkai* 一心妙戒).[9] These precepts are what Śākyamuni Buddha spent eons searching for. They are the absolute awakening (*myōgo* 妙悟) attained at his training site (*dōjō* 道場). The Dharma Kings [i.e., bodhisattvas] of the past, present, and future conceal these in their topknots; all Buddhas of the ten directions hold these in their svastikas. The sage from India, Bodhidharma, reverently received these precepts from

Śākyamuni Buddha. Through twenty-eight generations of dharma succession, without conveyance, they were conveyed. Without receiving, they were received. Thus did Bodhidharma bestow them on the second patriarch, Huike 慧可. Since then they have been handed down from proper heir to proper heir to me.

"You, reflect well upon [what I am about to say]. These precepts being transmitted to you convert the precepts that are your own mind (*koshin no kai* 己心之戒) into the true, absolute ordination platform (*shin no myō kaidan* 眞ノ妙戒壇). The bodhisattvas of the past, present, and future regard these as their nurturing fathers and mothers. All Buddhas of the ten directions regard these as their training site of permanent residence. Receiving these precepts (*jukai* 受戒; i.e., ordination) is known as receiving the absolute precepts that are one's own mind. Receiving (*ju* 受) is transmission (*den* 傳). Transmission is awakening (*satori* 覺). Living beings awakening their Buddha mind is true ordination.

"The ordination platform [can be conveyed] only by one Buddha to another Buddha (*yui butsu yo butsu* 唯佛與佛). Moreover, abiding in the basis of mind, realizing true awakening, abiding in the real appearance of nature that is one's own mind, these are the true ordination platform. Even if one were to receive endless Mahāyāna and Hīnayāna ordinations while standing on a physical (*so* 麤) ordination platform until the end of one's life, it would not aid liberation, because it lacks even one tenth of the efficacy [of this formless ordination platform]."

. . .

The master alone proclaims: "Now that you properly receive the absolute precepts that are the essence of the Tathāgata (i.e., Buddha), from this day hence you shall be called 'So-and-so Tathāgata.' Now I will explain to you the spiritual essence of the precepts that your own mind has acquired.

"First Precept: Your self-nature in its luminous inconceivability (*jishō ryōmyō* 自性靈妙) eternally abiding in its dharma-ness without giving rise to nihilistic views is known as the precept against killing living creatures. Will you obey this precept from this day forward in your present body and forever? Answer three times, 'I will obey.'" (On Mount Hiei 比叡 "self-nature in its luminous inconceivability" is glossed as the ten dharma realms of matter and mind.)

The above ordination procedures were intended only for advanced disciples who had already completed their Zen training. In this text, as in Kokan's explanation (which seems to address primarily laypeople and novice monks), the ritual actions transfer awakening to the person being ordained. Merely joining the Zen lineage of

Buddhas and patriarchs enables that person to share in their experience of awakening. The objective, visible ordination that occurs at a particular geographical location, symbolized by the physical ordination site, creates a subjective, inner ordination that stands outside of all temporal and geographic boundaries. The inner ordination merely confirms the innate awakening that already exists. Individual precepts do not govern behavior or actions, but describe the spiritual characteristics of Buddha nature. Thus ordination signifies not the beginning of the Buddhist path, but its final culmination. Both Kokan and this initiation text, therefore, present a little-known side of Zen Buddhism in which the approach to salvation depends on proper ritual consecration—not on the individual attainment of a subjective, inner experience *(satori)* as has been popularized in the West.

As radical as these ideas might seem to someone who knows Zen only through the writings of popular authors such as D. T. Suzuki 鈴木大拙 (1870–1966), they have exerted widespread influence on many aspects of Zen ritual. Moreover, although individual details differ, similar ideas can be found in almost any medieval Tendai precept treatise as well as in the precept treatises of other types of Japanese Buddhism.[10] Even a brief passage from a Tendai precept manual, the *One Mind Vajra Precept Essence Secrets* (*Isshin kongō kaitai hiketsu* 一心金剛戒體秘決), reveals significant parallels to the Zen texts cited above. This Tendai initiation text, like its Zen counterparts, interprets the precepts as transcending the need for any other form of Buddhist practice:

> All the Vajra Jeweled Precepts of the Tathāgatas are within your own mind. Believing these words is becoming a Buddha. One must positively know that the Perfect Precept Buddhahood (*enkai jōbutsu* 圓戒 成佛) is attained through faith.... With the Perfect Sudden Precepts *(endon kai)* do not bother with superlative understanding or superlative behavior. Don't engage in mental contemplation (*kannen* 觀念) or seated Zen meditation (*zazen* 坐禪).... Faith is the origin of the Way. It is the mother of all virtues. (fasc. 1, pp. 216–217)

This passage is interesting because it explicitly states an idea that is implied in the ordination texts of medieval Japanese Zen monks: The awakening conveyed by the precepts eliminates any need for Zen practice. The fact that medieval Zen texts could even imply such a position reveals just how profoundly Japanese Zen ritual assumed the values of Tendai doctrines.

Conclusion

The association of Zen and precepts has deep roots. Any form of meditation has natural associations with self-discipline. Without controlling the body, one cannot settle the mind. Without relaxing the demands of the flesh, one cannot free the mind to reflect reality. From the very early days of Japanese Buddhism, terms referring to meditation practice (*zengyō* 禪行) and strict observance of the precepts—what was known as "pure practice" (*jōgyō* 淨行)—commonly appear mixed together. Anyone who engaged in ascetic practices or repentance rituals would be referred to as a meditation master (*zenji* 禪師), regardless of whether he meditated or not (Sonoda 1981; Nei 1980). The new Zen of the Kamakura period (1185–1333) frequently evoked these associations. The Buddhist essayist Mujū Dōgyō 無住道暁 (Ichien 一圓; 1226–1312) titled the essay in which he discusses the beginnings of sectarian Zen practice in Japan "Observing the Vinaya and Sitting in Zen Meditation" (*Jiritsu zazen no koto* 持律坐禪事, *Zōdanshū* 雜談集, pp. 255–258). Likewise, the Japanese military government initially regulated Zen temples through the Office of Zen Vinaya (*Zenritsugata* 禪律方; Collcutt 1981, 118). Eisai's hopes that Zen practice would revive observance of the vinaya were not entirely misplaced.

The Zen precepts that later generations of monks inherited from Eisai, however, owed far more to Japanese Tendai doctrines than to the vinaya. Instead of regulating behavior, the precepts conferred the mind of awakening. The ordination ritual became all important because through ordination alone could one be initiated into the Zen lineage that reached back to the Buddha. For laypeople, therefore, pure faith in this lineage mattered more than either understanding or practice. There are many reasons why Zen ordination rituals were interpreted in light of Tendai doctrines. Saichō's rejection of the traditional rules of monastic discipline had profoundly altered the social status of Buddhist monks in Japan. Zen monks like Eisai who hoped to revive the vinaya ultimately faced a hopeless task. Tendai had occupied a position of doctrinal preeminence for more than three hundred years before the emergence of independent Zen communities. Most early Japanese Zen monks, even those who journeyed to China, had been trained initially in Tendai. Throughout the medieval period Buddhist monks of all persuasions frequently studied together and exchanged secret lore, regardless of lineage affiliations. Under such circumstances it would be more remarkable if Japanese Zen had not been influenced by Tendai doctrines. Most important of all, Zen monks saw Tendai ordination rituals as their own ordination rituals, as Bodhidharma's precepts. However strongly Zen monks believed that their Chinese Zen lineage made them different from other Buddhists in Japan, it in fact made them the same. It was this Zen lineage that linked them to Bodhidharma and through him to Saichō.

Notes

1. For this reason, it is incorrect to identify the Mahāyāna (bodhisattva) precepts used in Japan solely with their wording in the *Brahmā Net Sūtra*, which describes a total of fifty-eight vows (ten major and forty-eight minor). According to Japanese Tendai doctrine, the spiritual essence of Śākyamuni Buddha as expressed in the *Lotus Sūtra* (especially chapter 14, "Pleasant Activities" [*Anrakugyō bon* 安樂 行品]), constitutes the true precept; the *Brahmā Net Sūtra* merely provides it with a liturgical form (Groner 2000, 206–210; Ueda Tenzui 1976, 68).

2. For a convenient list of the principal premodern treatises on Zen precepts, see Shiraishi 1976 (1:349–351). Many important Zen texts concerning precepts unfortunately remain unpublished and are thus difficult to obtain. In this essay my citations will be limited to published materials.

3. In very simple terms the three bodies of the Buddha can be thought of as labels used to distinguish between the Buddha as an object of our experience (i.e., the response body, *nirmāṇakāya*, that appears in our world), Buddhahood as a subjective occurrence (i.e., the reward body, *saṃbhogakāya*, attained by one who becomes a Buddha), and Buddhahood as a religious ideal (i.e., the dharma body, *dharmakāya*, that is beyond all limitations). A commentary on the *Lotus Sūtra*, the *Fahua wenju* 法華文句 (T 34.128a), traditionally attributed to Zhiyi, equates each these three bodies with one another and with particular Buddhas: Śākyamuni Buddha constitutes the response body, Vairocana Buddha as Rushana constitutes the reward body, and Vairocana Buddha as Birushana constitutes the dharma body (Groner 2000, 260–263).

4. Kōjō cites as the basis for the story of Bodhidharma and Huisi an otherwise unknown work entitled the *Record of Seven Generations at the Training Site of the Meditation Master, Monk [Hui]-si on Mount Heng, Heng Province, the Great Tang Nation* (*Da Tangguo Hengzhou Hengshan daochang Shi-si chanshi qidai ji* 大唐國衡州衡 山道場釋思禪師七代記). The passage that Kōjō quotes from this work is also cited in several subsequent Japanese texts, which usually abbreviate the title to *Record of Seven Generations (Qidai ji)*. Seven generations following Huisi would correspond to

the Tiantai patriarchs under whom Saichō studied in China. Perhaps this record was a hagiography of the Tiantai patriarchs compiled by Saichō or his followers in Japan. For an example of this passage in another text, see *Shōtoku taishi denryaku* 聖徳太子傳略 (fasc. 2, ZGR 8A:31a).

5. The memorial inscription cited in this passage is the *Gu Zuoxi dashi bei* 古左溪大師碑 (QQT 7.4101–4102), written by Li Hua 李華 for the Tiantai patriarch Zuoxi Xuanlang 左溪玄朗 (673–754).

6. Sey Nishimura (1985, 308), citing the investigations of Kuranaka Susumu 蔵中進, identifies the earliest source for the story of Bodhidharma and Shōtoku as the *Ihon jōgū taishiden* 異本上宮太子傳 (ca. 771) by Keimei 敬明 (better known as the *Shitennōji taishiden* 四天王寺太子傳 by Kyōmyō), which exists only in manuscript.

7. "From seed to fruit" and "from fruit to seed" originally described the dual directions of spiral movement depicted in the diamond maṇḍala (*kongōkai mandara* 金剛界曼荼羅) used in tantric Buddhist ritual. Eventually, however, these terms were used to characterize broad currents among Tendai practices. Religious cultivation for the purpose of leaving behind one's humanity and becoming a Buddha constitutes the inferior goal of "from seed to fruit"; practices in which Buddha realization is expressed through one's humanity represent the highest teaching of "from fruit to seed" (Shimaji 1933, 177, 499). For an example of how these categories are applied to precepts, see *Isshin kongō kaitai hiketsu* 一心金剛戒體秘決 (fasc. 1, DDZ 4.195).

8. "*Kirikami*" can also be pronounced "*kirigami.*" I use the former spelling to contrast it with the common connotations of the latter one (which has entered the English language as an art term referring to the Japanese craft of cutting paper into ornamental designs) and because it agrees with authoritative Japanese language dictionaries that give the definition "documents" under "*kirikami*" and provide other definitions such as "cut paper" or "cut hair" (切髪) under the pronunciation "*kirigami.*"

9. In this context, the "*myō*" of "*myōkai*" 妙戒 (absolute precepts) refers to something that is inconceivable and beyond all dualistic categories (i.e., *zettai myō* 絶待妙). In other words, it should not be interpreted in a relativistic sense (*sōtai myō* 相待妙) as meaning "marvelous" in contrast to "crude" (*so* 麤). Thus the term "absolute precepts" implies a category of reality unto itself, beyond conceptualization or description, which cannot be compared to the "crude precepts" (*sokai* 麤戒) expressed in words.

10. See, for example, *Keiran jūyōshū* 溪嵐拾葉集 (fasc. 100–103, T 76.835–850) by Kōsō 光宗 (1276–1350); *Isshin kongō kaitai hiketsu* (DDZ 4.193–240) and *Isshin kongō kaitai ketsu* 一心金剛戒體決 (DDZ 4.243–264), both traditionally attributed to Saichō; and *Kongō hōkai shō* 金剛寶戒章 (ZJZ 13.1–35), traditionally attributed to Hōnen.

Chapter 9

Tradition and Innovation

Eison's Self-Ordinations and the Establishment of New Orders of Buddhist Practitioners

PAUL GRONER

THE PRECEPTS ARE often considered a conservative element of Buddhist discipline. They can be used to preserve the status quo and are invoked in arguments against changes in the Buddhist order. At the same time, they can be used by Buddhist reformists who want to show that monastic orders do not adhere to the standards of traditional Buddhism. In many cases, the use of the vinaya has involved both conservative and liberal elements. In this essay, I consider the efforts of Eison 叡尊 (1201–1290) and several of his contemporaries to understand the dynamics of establishing new Buddhist orders. Although their efforts were based on self-ordination, a ritual action that was not permitted according to the vinaya, they carefully followed the vinaya to create the ideal Buddhist order. I examine Eison's biography, noting the ways in which he adapted the vinaya to his needs, before moving on to consider the various groups of Buddhist practitioners that arose around him.

Eison's Biography

Eison's father was Keigen 慶玄 (1164–1252), a scholar monk of Kōfukuji 興福寺 Temple in Nara. Keigen seems to have left no trace of his scholarship, and he was a poor man. (Scholarly monks who were married and poverty-stricken were probably not unusual at this time.) Although Eison never mentions his father's ambiguous status as a monk with a family, this fact must surely have caused Eison to later question the validity of his own ordination lineage from Tōdaiji. Eison's mother was a member of the eminent Fujiwara 藤原 clan, but her family ties do not seem to have helped Eison when he was a young monk. After her death when Eison was

210

only seven, the boy was sent to live with a female shrine attendant (*miko* 御子) associated with Daigoji 醍醐寺 Temple *(Kongō busshi kanjin gakushōki* 金剛佛子叡尊感身學正記, 1, hereafter *Kongō busshi)*. When this woman died, he was sent to live with her elder sister. Through an introduction by the husband of this woman, he was able to study esoteric Buddhism at Daigoji under the monk Eiken 叡賢. He was initiated at age seventeen by Eiken and later ordained according to the rituals of the *Four Part Vinaya* on the ordination platform (*Kaidan* 戒壇) at Tōdaiji 東大寺. Eison does not refer to this ordination in his biography but at one point does mention that he wanted to receive the precepts again (*Kongō busshi*, 9). The date of his Tōdaiji ordination is unknown.

When Eison was twenty-four, he went to Mount Kōya 高野 to study esoteric Buddhism under the Shingon monk Shinkei 眞經, but upon the death of one of his brothers, he returned to Nara to study with monks closer to home. During the next few years, Eison was at Daigoji, Tōdaiji, and Kōfukuji, where he studied not only esoteric Buddhism, but also Hossō 法相 (Yogācāra), *abhidharma,* and logic. (Hossō would prove to be particularly important in the writings of both Kakujō 覺盛 [1193–1249] and Eison on the precepts.) Although Eison practiced assiduously during these years, he was bothered by the nagging doubt that if he did not keep the precepts, his practice would be in vain. Perhaps his father's status as a noncelibate monk contributed to his feelings of impurity. In 1234, he noted the importance placed on the precepts in the *Mahāvairocana Sūtra* (*Dari jing* 大日經), in Yixing's 一行 (673–727) commentary on that scripture (i.e., *Dari jing shu* 大日經疏), and in Kūkai's 空海 (774–835) admonitions to his students (see Kūkai's *Yuikai* 遺誡). In the latter, Kūkai is said to have cautioned his disciples: "Without precepts how can one realize the way of Buddhas? You should rigidly adhere to both the exoteric and esoteric precepts. Be pure and do not violate them. If you purposely violate them, you are not a disciple of the Buddha, nor are you my disciple" (quoted in *Kongō busshi,* 7).

That same winter, Eison received permission from Son'en 尊圓 to join six other monks in observing the precepts at Saidaiji 西大寺 Temple's Hōtōin 寶塔院 (Jeweled Pagoda) Chapel. Son'en had just made large contributions to Saidaiji that seem to have given him the right to decide who could reside there. In 1234 Eison went to live at Saidaiji, which would one day become his headquarters

as he worked to revive the precepts. There he heard some of his
first lectures on the precepts by Kainyo 戒如 and Kakushō 覺證. A
few months later, he began attending lectures at Todaiji on one of
Daoxuan's 道宣 (596–667) main commentaries (the *Sifenlü xingshi
chao* 四分律行事鈔, T no. 1804) on the *Four Part Vinaya*. The lectures, conducted by Enjō 圓晴 (1180–1241) of Kōfukuji, continued
through the spring and fall but only covered the first four fascicles
of the twelve-fascicle commentary. The following year Eison
studied the rest of the text on his own for several months. As a result,
he came to the firm belief that "if a person does not hate impure
items, he does not deserve to be called a disciple of the Buddha; if
he does not follow the precepts of the vinaya, then he ought not be
called a disciple of the Buddha" (*Kongō busshi*, 9). Eison also felt
that he was neither heterodox nor Buddhist because his ordination
had been unsatisfactorily conducted by impure monks: "If the ordination has not been correctly conferred, then adherence to the precepts will be lacking. Although I wished to correctly join the seven
groups of Buddhists, there were no compatriots for this undertak-
ing.... I was unable to avoid feeling that I was a thief of the teaching and feared that I would fall into hell" (*Jisei jukaiki* 自誓受戒記,
SED 337).

Other Japanese monks shared Eison's belief that their ordinations were invalid because they had been performed and
passed down by monks who had broken the required lineage of
pure monks. When Eison heard that Kakujō had discussed self-
ordination, he was overjoyed—here was a way to begin ordination lineages anew. Kakujō seems to have been convinced that
self-ordination was possible while he was preparing for a debate at
Kōfukuji's Jōkiin 常喜院 (Everlasting Happiness) Chapel. There he
reviewed a text by Cien 慈恩 (Ji 基; 632–682), the de facto founder
of the Hossō school, discussing whether the essence of the precepts
should be considered karma in manifested or unmanifested form.

In 1236 Eison went to see Kakujō, probably for the first time,
and was told that several monks had already begun preparing for
the self-ordination ceremonies, which were to take place in a few
months. After Kakujō had encouraged him to participate, Eison began to perform confession rituals. For fourteen days Eison chanted
from memory the list of precepts (*prātimokṣa*) for monks according
to the *Four Part Vinaya*, hoping for an auspicious sign (*kōsō* 好相)
that would encourage him to take part in the self-ordination. At the

time, the use of the *prātimkokṣa* for its power as an incantation had a long history in Japan. Karmic merit derived from observing the precepts, a practice theoretically grounded in the fortnightly assembly, was used to improve the efficacy of a variety of rituals; the mere recitation of the *prātimokṣa* was therefore thought to have considerable power. Two days later, Eison went to see Kakujō, concerned that three monks had already received signs indicating they could proceed with the self-ordination while he had not received any.

Immediately following his meeting with Kakujō, Eison practiced throughout the night in the Buddha hall of Tōdaiji, praying for a sign. The following night in Kaizen'in 戒禪院 (Precepts and Meditative Concentration) Chapel, he received a sign but neglected to record it. On the twenty-eighth day of the seventh moon 1236, while praying in the mid-morning before the image of Vairocana (Birushana 毘盧遮那) in the Buddha hall, Eison opened his eyes and saw two yellow paper flower petals fall. In surprise he looked up and saw three more fall. He immediately remembered passages in the scriptures about heavenly flowers being a message from the Buddha; his doubts about receiving a sign to obtain the precepts ceased. That night he dreamt that his deceased father had presented him with a young and noble girl who was five or six years old and urged Eison to take her for his wife. When he awoke, he rejected this as a bad dream and felt that he had not received a sign. Once again he went before the image of the Buddha to pray. While praying he came to realize that the girl in his dream represented the principle (*ri* 理) that the precepts were the basis of salvation (*gedatsu* 解脫) and that salvation was identical to principle. Finally, in a state of neither sleep nor wakefulness, he thought of his former master (*ajari* 阿闍梨) of esoteric Buddhism and his doubts vanished. (Of course doctrinal considerations played an important role in justifing self-ordination, but because of space limitations they will be considered in a subsequent essay.) On the thirtieth day of the eighth moon, Eison sequestered himself in Kensaku 羂索 (Shackle) Hall at Tōdaiji along with Ugon 有嚴 (1186–1275), Kakujō, and Ensei to perform self-ordinations. The following day they each took lay vows and the vows of novices on the next. Very soon afterward they all took full vows (*Jisei jukaiki*, SED 338). The self-ordinations performed by the Eison and Kakujō were a dramatic break from the tradition espoused by Japanese vinaya masters from Ganjin 鑑眞 (Ch. Jianzhen; 688–763) through Jippan 實範 (1089?–1144) and

Jōkei 貞慶 (1155–1213). None of these vinaya masters would have
allowed the use of self-ordinations to ordain monks. In the next
few paragraphs, the scriptural support advanced by Kakujō for
these ordinations is surveyed.

The first part of Eison's autobiography, *Esoteric Practitioner Eison's Experiences and Studies of the Correct Chronicle* (*Kongō busshi
kanjin gakushōki* 金剛佛師叡尊感身學正記), concerns his lay life; the
second part, events that culminated with his self-ordination. The
third part is called "reviving the Dharma and benefiting sentient
beings" (*kōhō rishō* 興法利生). Eison's self-ordination takes up most
of the pivotal second part, indicating the importance Eison placed
on that event. If his self-ordination had been invalid, the rest of his
life and the movement he founded would have, for him, been rendered invalid. After the self-ordination, Eison and his compatriots
called themselves "bodhisattva *bhikṣu*" (*bosatsu biku* 菩薩比丘), a
term that suggests a new Mahāyāna approach to ordinations. Earlier Nara monks went through a two-step process to obtain such an
appellation: They first were ordained as *bhikṣu* (*biku* 比丘; i.e., full-
fledged monks) at Tōdaiji according to the rules of the *Four Part
Vinaya,* and then they received bodhisattva ordinations. Eison had
accomplished both with a single ordination. Previously, only Tendai
天台 monks had used single (but not self-) ordination for candidates
seeking to become "bodhisattva monks" (*bosatsu sō* 菩薩僧)—a ritual that has its origins in material discussed by Nobuyoshi Yamabe
elsewhere in this volume. Although the Tendai ordination used on
Mount Hiei 比叡 included aspects of self-ordination such as confession, calling upon Buddhas and bodhisattvas to serve as officiants
and witnesses, and a provision for signs from the Buddha, it was essentially a ceremony conducted by an elder of the school in which
the precepts were conferred on the recipient by Buddhas and bodhisattvas. The founder of the Tendai school, Saichō 最澄 (767–822),
seemed to prefer "bodhisattva monks" to "bodhisattva *bhikṣu,*"
though on occasion he did use the latter but only in quotation. Nevertheless the term does appear in later Tendai sources. Kakujō's and
Eison's preference for "bodhisattva *bhikṣu*" probably reflects the
closer association of *"bhikṣu"* with a specific status defined in the
vinaya; "monk" is more ambiguous. In addition, they may have
chosen the term to distance themselves from Tendai practices while
still affirming their Māhayāna status. Although they attempted to
do so, Eison and his compatriots might never have thought of self-

ordination in the first place if Tendai procedures had not laid the groundwork for similar comprehensive ordinations (*tsūju* 通受).

Immediately after the self-ordination, Eison and the others returned to Jōkiin Chapel at Kōfukuji, but their actions met with such disapproval that they soon returned to Tōdaiji. Several weeks later, three of them went to Kōfukuji, "acting as monks within, but as worldly men on the outside" (*Kongō busshi*, 11). "Worldly men" (*seken nin* 世間人) probably indicates that they were not wearing monk's robes. Kakujō continued to dress as a layman until 1243, the year he moved to Tōshōdaiji 唐招大寺 (*Kongō busshi*, 19). Rather than return to Saidaiji, which was in a serious state of disrepair and under the control of Kōfukuji, Eison made Kairyūōji 海龍王寺 Temple his base of operations. Kairyūōji had been founded by Empress Kōmyō 光明 (701–760) in memory of her parents.

Eison's rigid attitude concerning the precepts soon created tension. Kairyūōji had seemed like a good choice at first: Its leaders had been influenced by the revival of the *Four Part Vinaya* precepts at Sennyūji 泉涌寺 by Shunjō 俊芿 (1166–1227), a Tendai monk who had brought the precepts of the *Four Part Vinaya* from China and then propagated them using self-ordination. But the Kairyūōji monks had also adopted certain Chinese monastic customs recently introduced to Japan, including the practice of eating alone at their places or in groups (*betsujiki* 別食). Eison argued that the vinaya required that all monks eat together (*tsūjiki* 通食). Graffiti ridiculing Eison appeared at the temple's gates and even arrows were shot at the monks' quarters (*Kongō busshi*, 12; also see *Four Part Vinaya*, fasc. 14, T 22.658c; Hirakawa 1993–1995, 3:359–365). The extreme reaction of the Kairyūōji monks to Eison's criticisms suggests that reforms by an outside monk threatened the social structure of the monastery. In fact, the rule requiring monks to eat together had been instituted to prevent factions from forming.

In 1238, at Son'en's urging, Eison returned to Saidaiji and made it his home. Once there Eison lost little time in rebuilding the monastery and carrying out the practical aspects of observance of the vinaya. He read the *Golden Light Sūtra* (*Jinguangming jing* 金光明經), one of the scriptures traditionally used to invoke the Four Heavenly Kings (*shi tennō* 四天王) to protect the nation, in Shiōin 四王院 (Four Kings) Chapel, and vowed to continue reciting the text. He built an octagonal five-story pagoda to house a relic of the Buddha that he had brought with him, thereby giving the monastery a base for its spiritual power. The existence of such a pagoda was specified in the monastery's records (*ruki* 流記). Finally, because the monastery's landholdings were being threatened in disputes, Eison had his family and relatives intervene to help Saidaiji (*Kongō busshi*, 13, 14; *Nenpu* 年譜, 121–123).

With the most important buildings finished and the economic base of the monastery stabilized, on the twenty-eighth day of the tenth moon 1238, Eison established the boundaries (*kekkai* 結界) of the area from which the monastery might draw monks for the fortnightly assembly *(fusatsu* 布薩; Skt. *poṣadha;* Pali *uposatha)*. The following day, a fortnightly assembly based on the *Four Part Vinaya* was conducted. Kakujō served as master of ceremonies while Eison announced the landmarks (*shōsō* 唱相) determining the assembly boundaries and Gonjō 嚴貞 (1205–?) acted as rector (*yuina* 維那), with Kyōgen 教玄 and Ugon as members of the order. Eison took great care to list all of the ceremony's participants perhaps to demonstrate that they followed the vinaya in having at least four monks present, the minimum number necessary for a proper order.

At the fortnightly assembly, Kakujō, who also served as the officiant reciting the precepts, was seen shedding tears throughout the entire ceremony. Upon returning to the monks' quarters, Kakujō explained:

> Long ago, when I was nineteen, I participated in my first fortnightly assembly. When asked whether I had purely observed the precepts, although I thought that I actually had not observed them, I chanted the appropriate response [indicating that I had done so]. I deeply feared [the karmic results of] this falsehood, and wondered whether I ever would have the opportunity to perform the fortnightly assembly correctly.... Thus I could not restrain my tears of happiness [that I was able to rectify my past misdeed]. My appreciation of the ceremony is boundless (*Kongō busshi*, 14).

The following day they performed a fortnightly assembly based on the *Brahmā Net Sūtra* (*Kongō busshi*, 14). Conducting assemblies on separate days for the *Four Part Vinaya* and *Brahmā Net Sūtra* precepts dates back to the time of Ganjin (Ishida Mizumaro 1986b, 88–89).

Nara monks criticized not only the strict observance of the precepts by Eison and Kakujō, but also attacked their ordinations on ritual, institutional, and doctrinal grounds. Monasteries influenced by Eison's practices could potentially break away and become independent, which would have economic repercussions for Kōfukuji and Tōdaiji, the temples that had previously controlled or influenced them. In addition these new ordinations threatened to call into question the validity of ordinations conducted at Tōdaiji, undermining its centuries-old claim that its ordinations were valid while those of the Tendai school were not. Yet Eison seems to have been motivated more by a desire to return to the practices of Śākyamuni than to secure financial gain or to establish a new sect. One of Eison's critics contended:

> The seven monasteries of Nara have used the monk's ordination platform at Tōdaiji, as well as the ordination procedure of reading the statement and calling for a vote three times (*byaku shi konma* 白四羯磨) to confer the full precepts so that Mahayana monks can be installed. From the past until now, this procedure has not been broken. Why do you turn against it? ... We fear that the ordination procedure of reading the statement and calling for a vote three times will be rendered invalid. What will become of the ordination platform at Tōdaiji? (*Bosatsukai tsūju kengishō* 菩薩戒通受遣疑抄, ND 69.85a–b; also see *Kongō busshi*, 10)

When compared with the vehement criticisms of Saichō's efforts to establish an ordination platform on Mount Hiei or of Onjōji 園城寺 Temple's to establish an ordination platform independent of Mount Hiei, the reaction of these monks to Kakujō and Eison seems subdued. Their rhetoric was neither particularly bitter or nasty nor was violence or the threat of violence applied except in isolated circumstances (e.g., Eison's expulsion from Kairyūōji for criticizing the practice of eating in separate groups). Later, when Eison established a number of private ordination platforms, opposition to his actions seems to have been muted. Several reasons for this lack of opposition can be suggested. Because many monks were already being ordained outside the official system, the establishment of another ordination procedure was not as threatening as it would have been two centuries earlier. The emerging Pure Land movements seemed to have been much more of a potential threat than Eison's movement. Late in his life Eison enjoyed considerable support from the military government. Finally, many of Kakujō's and Eison's attitudes were conservative and based on the vinaya. Their eventual decision to return to separate ordinations (*betsuju* 別受), the traditional format used at Tōdaiji, might also have reduced friction with other monks.

Eison respected Daoxuan and Ganjin as patriarchs in his tradition. The high regard in which Eison is said to have held Ganjin is evident in his veneration of robes that Ganjin is reported to have given Emperor Shōmu 聖武 (701–756) shortly before the patriarch's death. These robes had been passed down through forty-five generations of the imperial household before they came to Eison, who bestowed them on three of his disciples (*Nenpu*, 197–198). The veracity of this story has not been determined, but it seems unlikely. Whether it is true or not, later Japanese Vinaya school (Risshū 律宗) scholars, such as Shōen 照遠 (1302–1361?), saw little connection between Ganjin's Tōdaiji lineage and Eison's Saidaiji tradition except for their common observance of fortnightly assemblies and the *pravāraṇā* (*jishi* 自恣) ceremony that concluded the rainy season retreat (*Shigyōshō* 資行鈔, T no. 2248, cited in Tokuda 1969, 598).

For several years after the self-ordination of Eison and Kakujō, new monks entering Eison's community seem to have undergone comprehensive ordinations (*Kongō busshi*, 12, 18, 20, 113). For these a single ritual was used to confer all three sets of pure bodhisattva precepts (*sanju jōkai* 三聚浄戒)—those preventing evil, promoting good, and benefiting sentient beings—on the recipient, whether a monastic or a layman. According to the *Yoga Stages* (Xuanzang's translation of the *Yogācārabhūmi; Yuqie shidi lun* 瑜伽師地論, fasc. 40, T 30.511a), the precepts preventing evil are identified with those specified in the vinaya. As a result, a single ritual (the comprehensive ordination) could qualify a person to hold a variety of statuses, from pious lay believer to fully ordained monk or nun. Status in the order would have depended on the person's aspirations and any legal or spiritual obstacles to becoming a monastic. As stated previously, comprehensive ordinations generally confer the three sets of bodhisattva precepts; separate ordinations confer more specific sets, such as the five lay precepts or the full precepts. The term "separate ordination" refers to the use of separate rituals for the various statuses in the Buddhist order (all of which, according to the *Yoga Stages*, used precepts equated with those preventing evil, the first category of the three sets of pure precepts); moreover, a separate ritual was used to confer the bodhisattva precepts (equated with the precepts promoting good and benefiting sentient beings). An ordination in which practitioners with a variety of statuses participate is comprehensive, but one in which only a single type of practitioner participates, such as novices advancing to the status of fully ordained monks, is generally, but not always, a separate ordination. In many cases, the master of ceremonies announced the type of ordination being performed at the beginning of the ritual. Finally, the statuses of participants were much more clearly defined at separate ordinations. As a result, Nara monks frequently criticized Tendai monks by arguing that the comprehensive ordination performed on Mount Hiei could not qualify men as fully ordained monks because the precepts conferred in comprehensive ordinations were too vaguely defined. The self-ordination used by Eison was only one of a variety of comprehensive ordinations. After establishing their order, Eison and Kakujō performed a comprehensive ordination in which an order of monks conferred the precepts on candidates.

Eison and Kakujō do not seem to have encouraged others to emulate their self-ordinations, perhaps because encouraging such rituals could have undermined the institutional structures they were striving to establish. If anyone could take the precepts by himself or herself, the result would be a proliferation of orders, potentially destroying the return to the vinaya that Eison and Kakujō advocated. Instead, Eison and Kakujō conceived of self-ordination primarily as a means to establish a new lineage of monks.

In 1245, nine years after the self-ordination, Kakujō planned to hold a separate ordination in which he would enact the full ordination ceremony *(upasampadā)* of the *Four Part Vinaya* and confer on a group of monks the status of *bhikṣu*. Eison notes that according to the vinaya, Kakujō should have had at least ten years of seniority before serving as a preceptor. If the ordinations were conducted before Kakujō had a full ten years, he would incur an offense requiring confession (Hirakawa 1964, 487, 492). His lack of experience would not, however, invalidate the ordinations conferred. Kakujō defended himself, arguing that the life spans of men were uncertain and that being born in a world where Buddhist teachings could be found was difficult. Thus it was better to go ahead with the ordinations and violate a minor rule. Eison is reported to have been impressed with Kakujō's reply (*Shōdai senzai denki* 招提千歳傳記, DNB 64.247c), and in 1245 they ordained twenty-six monks with the "separate ordination"; Eison received one at the same time (*Kongō busshi,* 20). In subsequent years, even though separate ordinations became more prevalent in Eison's order, comprehensive ordinations were still performed. The circumstances under which they were utilized deserves more study.

Eison felt the need to institute the separate ordination to bring his movement back into line with the ordinations conferred at Tōdaiji. Kakujō's reasons were more complex. He had followed an explanation in the *Yoga Stages* that classified all violations of the bodhisattva precepts (i.e., all precepts conferred in the comprehensive ordination) under the single category known as *"duṣkṛta"* (*osa* 惡作). According to the vinaya, any violation in this relatively minor category could be expiated merely by confessing before another person. Kakujō's return to separate ordinations meant, therefore, that he was returning to a more exact and traditional way of defining the precepts in which violations are expiated according to their various categories. In contrast, Eison had already applied the *Four Part Vinaya*'s classification of the precepts into various grades to the precepts conferred in the comprehensive ordination. The changes in the ordinations conducted by Eison and Kakujō throughout their lives reflect their attempts to reconcile the various sources they used in interpreting the precepts and their deepening understanding of the precepts themselves (Minowa 1999, 387–425).

The rest of Eison's life was primarily devoted to establishing an order that observed the precepts. According to a chronology of his life (*Nenpu*, 199), by the time he died, Eison had 1,226 disciples who had received the full precepts through comprehensive ordinations; approximately 830 had received separate full ordinations (*betsuju gukai* 別受具戒). Some of the members of his order had received both types. He had conferred the precepts for novices (*shami* 沙彌 and *shamini* 沙彌尼) or probationary nuns (*shikishamana* 式叉摩那; *śikṣamāṇā*) on 568 people and the bodhisattva precepts on 90,710 lay and monastic believers. He had built more than 100 temples and chapels, repaired over 590 existing temples, affiliated approximately 1,500 temples with Saidaiji, and established 5 new ordination platforms within the precincts of Saidaiji, Ebaraji 家原寺, Jōjūji 常住寺, Kairyūōji, and Hokkeji 法華寺 temples. Innumerable believers were ordained with the five or eight precepts for laypeople. Eison participated in 10,721 lectures and 41,208 other religious ceremonies, including meditation and chanting. Through his efforts, 1,356 places agreed to ban killing animals.

The exact reckoning and magnitude of these numbers are surprising, but Eison's autobiography often contains precise numbers of people he ordained, probably reflecting the importance of documents attesting to ordinations. Several records listing the names of those who received ordinations survive. The number of affiliated temples is difficult to believe. In some cases, the affiliation was probably not very strong. For example, among the places that agreed to stop killing are many that agreed to do so only on certain days or for a limited period of time. No records concerning the ordination platforms at Jōjūji and Kairyūōji survive (Matsuo 1988, 194).

The Reestablishment of an Order of Nuns during the Kamakura Period

In most Buddhist countries where an order of nuns (bhikṣunī) was established in strict accordance with the vinaya, it eventually disappeared and was rarely reestablished. The vinaya required that an order of nuns already exist before new nuns could be ordained, and nuns often did not have enough standing with the government to inaugurate a new order. No provision is made in the vinaya for establishing a completely new order of nuns once the lineage had been interrupted. An order could only be reestablished by bringing correctly ordained nuns from another place or country. As a result, women in many countries participated in Buddhism as lay patrons and believers (and occasionally as novices) rather than as nuns. The reestablishment of an order of nuns in Japan was, therefore, a remarkable achievement, possible only through unusual historical circumstances and creative interpretations of the vinaya.

The Japanese Tendai tradition might seem a likely candidate for such a revival because it ordained monks with bodhisattva precepts from the *Brahmā Net Sūtra*, a scripture that theoretically permitted men to ordain women (and vice versa) and men and women to perform self-ordinations if an appropriate teacher were not available. Moreover, the sūtra prohibited people from following inferior (*hīnayāna*) teachings and precepts, a rule that could be interpreted as a rejection of the *Four Part Vinaya* and the ordination traditions that it embodied (Andō and Sonoda 1974, 75). However, by the late Heian and Kamakura (ca. twelfth to fourteenth centuries) Tendai

had become a conservative tradition that did little to advance the
cause of nuns. Instead, the seemingly conservative Saidaiji community, who wished to revive the *Four Part Vinaya* precepts, provided
the leadership in restoring an order of nuns.

When Eison and Kakujō claimed that they had received the full
precepts for monks from the Buddha through self-ordination, they
opened the door to interpretations that freed women to make similar
claims. If such declarations could be made by women, they would
be no worse than those made by Eison and Kakujō. Moreover, because Eison and his followers actively proselytized among the laity,
they had a following that would support their efforts. When a move
to reestablish an order of nuns did come, however, it was not accomplished through self-ordinations conducted by women but the
more traditional separate ordinations specified in the vinaya.

Eison helped renovate Hokkeji Temple in Yamato, the most important of the provincial nunneries (*kokubunniji* 國分尼寺), probably in response to requests from a group of former ladies-in-waiting
who wished to lead monastic lives (Hosokawa 1999). On the ninth
day of the fourth moon 1245, he conferred the precepts for female
novices on three women. Before the year was out, he had conferred
them on a total of thirteen women. In 1246 he conducted a fortnightly assembly for female novices. After the rainy season retreat
the following year, he lectured on a list of precepts for nuns according to the *Four Part Vinaya* and conferred the precepts for probationary nuns on eleven women. In 1248 he spoke at the Hokkeji
on two *Brahmā Net Sūtra* commentaries by T'aehyŏn 太賢 (fl. 753),
the *Essentials of the Bodhisattva Precepts* (*Pusa jieben zongyao* 菩薩
戒本宗要, T no. 1906) and the *Commentary on Ancient Traces of
Brahmā Net* (*Fanwangjing gujiji* 梵網經古迹記, T no. 1815), which
were widely used by monks of the Nara schools. A year later he established a precepts platform at the Hokkeji and administered the
full ordination on twelve nuns. According to the vinaya, a candidate
for full ordination as a nun should have undergone two years of
training as a probationary nun. These years are supposed to be cal-
culated according to the number of rainy season retreats a person
has successfully completed, so Eison seems to have been hasty in
conferring the full ordination. However, violation of this rule is
only a minor *(prāyaścittika)* offense and does not invalidate the ordination (Upasak 1975, 234; Hirakawa 1964, 506–513). In addition,
a rule required that women be ordained in both the order of monks

and the order of nuns. Because no properly ordained nuns existed at this time, Eison must have modified the ceremony in some manner (perhaps using a comprehensive ordination), but this aspect of the event is not clear.

Eight days after the full ordination, a fortnightly assembly for nuns was held. In going through the carefully planned process of defining the various stages and practices of female Buddhist renunciants, Eison announced that it "was the first time in Japan that the proper observance for all seven groups [of the Buddhist order] had been established" (*Kongō busshi*, 20–22; also see Hosokawa 1987, 121–22; Matsuo 1988, 193; Wajima 1959, 23). The "seven groups" (*shichishu* 七衆) are comprised of laymen (*ubasoku* 優婆塞), laywomen (*ubai* 優婆夷), male novices, female novices, probationary nuns, monks, and nuns. In his statement, Eison was referring in particular to the proper ordination of women. He probably did not recognize any ordinations of nuns performed before Ganjin as valid; it is possible that he did not believe that even Ganjin had established a valid ordination tradition for women because only three nuns had accompanied him to Japan, instead of the ten required for full ordinations.

The ordinations performed by Eison and his followers are referred to in some documents as "climbing the ordination platform and receiving the precepts" (*tōdan jukai* 登壇受戒). However, the ordination platforms established by Eison were qualitatively different from the court-recognized platforms at Tōdaiji and Mount Hiei. (In the case of Tōshōdaiji, Ganjin intended members of the temple to use the platform for study purposes, not for performing ordinations.) Eison's platform did not have the official status of those established during the Nara and Heian periods; his was a privately established platform, one of the first in Japan. Ordinations for nuns performed on platforms established by Eison did not require the approval of the governmental and the monastic establishment as had been the case with those conducted earlier at Mount Hiei and Tōdaiji (Matsuo 1985, 308). The governmental apparatus regulating Buddhism had become sufficiently lax; several centuries earlier if might have deemed Eison's ordination of nuns an infringement of its rights.

The first group of women to be ordained was led by the nun Jizen 慈善 (1187–?), who had practiced under Tankū 湛空 (1176–1253), a disciple of Hōnen 法然 (1133–1212) and an advocate of the Japanese Tendai doctrine of Perfect Sudden Precepts (*endon kai* 圓頓戒). Unlike the more liberal-minded monks who followed the Perfect Sudden Precepts, Jizen and other would-be nuns were not satisfied with the opportunities offered by Tankū and had turned to Eison and the precepts of the *Four Part Vinaya*. With Eison's support, the order of nuns and novices at the Hokkeji grew rapidly, increasing from 26 in 1249 to 64 in 1259, 79 in 1265, and 119 in 1272. According to a record of ordinations of bodhisattva precepts, by 1280, 183 fully ordained nuns, 48 probationary nuns, and 60 female novices had been ordained. In comparison, 389 monks and 122 male novices were ordained during the same period (*Jubosatsukai deshi kyōmyō* 授菩薩戒弟子交名, SED 359–371). Another document bearing the same title and date lists 138 female novices and 280 male novices (SED 372–379). The reason for this discrepancy is not clear; however, the second document lists the recipients by temple whereas the first does not. The names in the two documents are different. The women listed came from all over Japan, from families of monks as well as the nobility (Hosokawa 1987, 124, 126; Matsuo 1985, 311). Along with increases in the number of male monastic orders, orders of nuns grew as they were established at other temples. In 1285 a full ordination was held for twelve women from Shōbōji 正法寺; ordination in the order of nuns was performed at the Hokkeji and the ordination in the order of monks was performed at Tōshōdaiji (*Shōdai senzai denki*, DNB 64.276c). Thus the vinaya requirement that nuns be ordained in both the order of nuns and the order of monks was met in this instance.

The order of nuns at Chūgūji 中宮寺, a branch temple of Tōshōdaiji, was revived to a large extent by a woman known by her religious name, Shinnyo 信如 (1211–?), who associated with both Kakujō and Eison. Her biography is one of the fuller accounts of a nun of the early medieval period (ca. eleventh to twelfth centuries) and one of the only biographies of a nun found in the biographical collections associated with the Risshū, such as the *Vinaya Cloister Saṅgha Jewel Hagiographies* (*Ritsuon sōbōden* 律苑僧寶傳, 1689, by Eken 慧堅 1649–1704) and the *Tōshōdaiji Millenary Anniversary Hagiographies* (*Shōdai senzai denki*, 1701, by Gichō 義澄). Shinnyo's story sheds important light on one type of nun of the early Kamakura, a woman descended from a family of monks. Widows as well as courtesans and ladies-in-waiting whose services were no longer needed can also be found among female ordinands of the period.

Shinnyo was the daughter of Shōen 璋圓, a scholar monk at Kōfukuji who was one of Jōkei's top disciples. As a young man, Shōen had gone to Yakushiji 藥師寺 in Nara a number of times to further his studies. There he came to know a young woman and had several children by her. Although Shōen seems to have come from a family of high status, he was not able to leave his children much money when he died. In his will, he directed one of his daughters, Shinnyo's sister, to charge a fee to any monk who wished to see a six-part volume of terminology (*rokujō no myō moku* 六帖名目) he had compiled. Those who paid were allowed to read his work for a short period and did not have permission to copy it. Later this text would provide a steady income for Shinnyo (*Shōyoshō* 聖譽鈔, DNB 72.21a).

As a young woman, Shinnyo was under the tutelage of Zeamidabutsu 是阿彌陀佛 of Shōryakuji 正曆寺 at Mount Bodaisan 菩提山, where she studied a text called the *Yūzan* 幽贊 (*Kongō busshi*, 18). According to Nagai Yoshinori (1967), nothing is known of Zeamidabutsu. However, Nagai has identified the *Yūzan* as the *Bore xin jing yuzan* 般若心經幽贊 (T no. 1710), Cien's 慈恩 (632–682) commentary on the *Heart Sūtra* (*Bore xin jing* 般若心經). If this identification is correct, it would reflect a high degree of scholarly attainment on Shinnyo's part; Cien had used his commentary to explain the differences between Mādhyamaka and Yogācāra interpretations of the *Heart Sūtra* (BK 9.84b–c). The subcommentary on Cien's text by Shouqian 守千 (1064–1127) played an important role in the doctrinal justification of self-ordinations. It was used to defend the self-ordinations of Kakujō and Eison well after the fact, so it is possible that Shinnyo may have introduced the text to Kakujō. No conclusive evidence for this thesis, however, has been found.

Shinnyo was devoted to Śākyamuni Buddha and Prince Shōtoku 聖德 (574–622) and performed *nenbutsu* 念佛 (recitations of the Buddha's name) for Śākyamuni as her daily devotion. At some point in her life, she sequestered herself in a pagoda at Chūgūji one week before the anniversary of Prince Shōtoku's death and chanted Śākyamuni's name for eight days and nights. Shōtoku is said to have founded Chūgūji as a nunnery; thus in honor of his mother it is not surprising that Shinnyo later decided to be ordained a nun and revive Chūgūji as a nunnery. Because she believed that nuns were present during Prince Shōtoku's time, she went to see Kakujō to request ordination. Kakujō replied, "The ordination of a full-fledged nun *(bikuni)* is one of the most important events in Buddhism. If I permit you alone [to receive it], people will see it and feel that they should be readily ordained. If this results in a bad state of affairs, then people will criticize it saying 'I permitted it.' Moreover, I find it difficult to authorize a major event in vinaya such as this by myself. If there were some supernatural sign, then I could permit it. You should wait" *(Shōyoshō,* DNB 72.21b–c). Although unmentioned in Eison's autobiography, a meeting in 1243 occurred in which Shinnyo praised Eison and Kakujō and noted that their self-ordination corresponded with unusual dreams that she had experienced *(Kongō busshi,* 18–19). Kakujō was concerned that ordaining nuns would add to the criticism surrounding self-ordination that he and others had received.

Shinnyo fervently prayed that Kakujō would receive a sign that would convince him to ordain her. Shortly afterward, Kakujō had a dream in which he was told, probably by Prince Shōtoku, "The time has already come in Japan when the faculties of those who would become nuns is mature. You should quickly permit nuns to be ordained" *(Shōyoshō,* DNB 72.21c). Shinnyo was approximately twenty-three years old when she went to see Kakujō to obtain an orthodox initiation and ordination. Further objections were advanced and overcome. For example, according to the rules for nuns, a nun could travel and perform certain duties only if another nun accompanied her. To fulfill this need for a companion nun, one of Kakujō's fellow monks suddenly found that he had become a woman. After some discussion, it was decided that "her" precepts had automatically been transformed to those of a nun and that "she" would not need to be ordained anew. After several women had been ordained, the nun reverted to her original sex and the precepts of a monk were automatically restored to the individual *(Shōyoshō,* DNB 72.21c).

Changes in gender are documented in sources concerning nuns, but it is usually a woman who is changed into a man before realizing Buddhahood. Sexual abnormalities are also mentioned in the vinaya in instances where a person is disqualified for ordination. According to the vinaya, a person with serious sexual abnormalities, such as being a eunuch or a hermaphrodite, cannot become a monastic (Hirakawa 1964, 495–504). The validity of the precepts for people with sexual abnormalities became a topic of concern for Kakujō and Eison when they argued that comprehensive ordination conferred the status of a monk on any person for whom there were no obstacles at the time of his ordination. But what of a properly ordained monk who develops sexual abnormalities after his ordination? In keeping with Kakujō's and Eison's argument, he would not lose the precepts. Thus sexual anomalies were considered an obstacle in establishing the precepts but not necessarily in maintaining them (Hirakawa 1993–1995, 1:171–72). In addition, the *Brahmā Net Sūtra* does not discriminate between people with sexual abnormalities and those without (T 24.1004b).

The story of the monk's sexual transformation also appears in the *Tōshōdaiji Millenary Anniversary Hagiographies* but with significant changes. According to this source (DNB 64.268c), during the Kangen 寛元 era (1243–1247), the monk Kyōen 教圓 participated in some of the fortnightly assemblies conducted at the Tōshōdaiji Temple by Kakujō and other monks attempting to revive monastic discipline. Later a god *(ten* 天; *deva)* appeared before him and said, "The order of monks has already been completed [with the reestablishment of a correctly ordained group of monks]; however, there are still no nuns. First, I will make you a nun." The god then disappeared, and Kyōen was immediately transformed into a woman. Kyōen returned to his village and persuaded his elder sister, Shinnyo, to become a nun, thereby establishing the order of nuns. Three weeks later (and following the ordination of more nuns), Kyōen changed back into a man. This story is further elaborated in the *Vinaya Cloister Saṅgha Jewel Hagiographies* (DNB 64.213a): The god is identified as Indra, and just as the monk is changed back into a woman, the room is filled with fragrance.

This second version of Kyōen's transformation focuses on the problem of establishing an order of nuns rather than providing Shinnyo with a companion. It seems to have been formulated to answer the criticism that nuns must be present before new ones can be ordained. If this were the case, however, the narrator would have probably specified that ten nuns (the exact number required for ordinations) were present before the monk was allowed to regain his original form. In addition, Kyōen is identified as Shinnyo's brother, whereas in the *Shōyoshō* his relation to Shinnyo is not defined. Monks turning into nuns is an ironic variation on the more familiar theme of women changing into men to attain spiritual goals. The modern reader may be tempted to attribute these stories to the fertile imaginations of later storytellers. But in his autobiography,

Eison comments on their miraculousness, indicating that such tales were acknowledged as true even by contemporaries (*Kongō busshi*, 23). (Eison does not specifically refer to the story of Kyōen, however.)

Several details of Shinnyo's later life are known. As mentioned earlier, she restored the Chūgūji, the nunnery founded in honor of Princess Anahobe no Hashihito 穴穂部間人 (d. 612), the daughter of Emperor Kinmei 欽明 (510–570) and mother of Prince Shōtoku. Shinnyo probably entered the nunnery around 1262, a time when all that remained of it was a two-story golden (i.e., Buddha) hall (*kondō* 金堂) and a jeweled pagoda (*hōtō* 寶塔). The monk Sōji 惣持 (1233–1312), Eison's nephew, had wished to restore Chūgūji during the Bun'ei era (1264–1275) but could make no progress in doing so. After sequestering himself in the golden hall to pray for guidance, he had a dream in which Prince Shōtoku appeared and told him that because the Chūgūji had originally been a nunnery, it should be restored as one and a nun should serve as its abbess. After talking to Eison, the two of them decided that Shinnyo, who was knowledgeable about the precepts, should go to Chūgūji (*Shōtoku taishi den* 聖徳太子傳, quoted in Hosokawa 1987, 113). Earlier Sōji had assembled a list of precepts for nuns (*Shibunritsu-chū bikuni kaihon* 四分律注比丘尼戒本) based on the *Four Part Vinaya*, which Eison spent three months checking. At the time Daoxuan's commentary on the precepts for nuns (the *Sifen lü biqiuni chao* 四分律比丘尼鈔) had not yet been transmitted to Japan, Sōji therefore compiled a commentary (the *Bikuni-shō kyūfu shigyō roku* 比丘尼鈔糾補資行録) on the precepts for nuns (Mizuno 1964, 7–9; Hosokawa 1989, 142). (Sōji remarked that if an authoritative text were to be found it be used instead of his.) Sōji dedicated this work to his deceased mother and also mentions that it was for the benefit of all sentient beings.

Work to restore Chūgūji began in earnest around 1274. Shinnyo planned to repay the obligation owed to its royal founder by holding memorial services on the anniversary of Shōtoku's mother's death, but she did not know the date. A nun who practiced with Shinnyo dreamt that the date was to be found on an embroidered tapestry sewn shortly after Prince Shōtoku's death known as the "Land of Heavenly Immortality Maṇḍala Tapestry" (*Tenjukoku mandara shūchō* 天壽國曼陀羅繍帳). The tapestry was stored at Hōryūji 法隆寺, a temple founded by Prince Shōtoku, but had long been forgotten. Because the temple's treasury could be opened only by imperial decree, Shinnyo was not permitted to look for it. However, the following year, thieves broke into the treasury, and an inspection of items in the building had to be conducted. As a result, Shinnyo was permitted to search for the tapestry and found it just where the nun had seen it in her dream. Although the piece had been heavily damaged, the date of the princess's death was visible: the twenty-first day of the twelfth moon (*Shōdai senzai denki*, DNB 64.268c). After Chūgūji was reestablished as a nunnery, Shinnyo added punctuation (*katen* 加点) and postfaces (*okugaki* 奥書) to a copy of the *Yoga Stages* treatise in 1282. The difficulty of the text and her interest in it indicate the high level of her scholarship (Hosokawa 1987, 119). Shinnyo refers to herself as a "bodhisattva-precept nun" (*bosatsukai bikuni* 菩薩戒比丘尼) in the colophon and notes that she was seventy-two years old in 1282.

In some ways the restoration of Hokkeji and Chūgūji is similar to Eison's and Kakujō's efforts to reestablish a pure lineage of monks. In both cases, the participants wished to return to patterns of monastic discipline specified in the vinaya. Their devotional activities focused on early figures such as Śākyamuni Buddha and Prince Shōtoku, whom they wished to emulate. When their activities exceeded the rules of the vinaya, they used dreams to legitimate their actions.

Risshū Monks, Nuns, and Japanese Social Structure

According to the vinaya, the order of monks and nuns is like an ocean. Once a person enters it, his or her social class and lay name are lost just as a river entering the ocean loses its name. Once Buddhism enters a country, however, it has to accommodate itself to its host, which results in the continuing influence of lay social structures on monastic orders. When Eison founded an order of nuns or proselytized among the lowest levels of society, he seemed to be following the tradition that Buddhism is available to all. But vinaya teachers in Japan inevitably had to make compromises. In this section, the influence of lay society on the order is investigated in the context of two groups: a set of lay believers who took the eight precepts (*hassaikai* 八齋戒) and the order of nuns.

Ugon, one of the four monks who underwent self-ordination along with Eison, was the founder of a group of lay believers who observed the eight precepts for extended periods of time. Despite his long life, Ugon is remembered in most biographical sources for only two events: participating in the self-ordination mentioned above and traveling to China with Kakunyo 覺如, who spent the years 1246–1248 in China searching for texts on monastic discipline (*Honchō kōsōden* 本朝高僧傳, DNB 63.341c). In the chronology of Eison's life (*Nenpu*, 129, 134), only Kakunyo and Jōshun 定舜 (d. 1244) are mentioned as having traveled to China. The account of Ugon's life in the *Vinaya Cloister Saṅgha Jewel Hagiographies* (DNB 64.117c) is based on the same chronology as Eison's. After investigating these sources, Wajima Yoshio (1959, 29) questions whether Ugon ever went to China and suggests that Eison persuaded Ugon to allow Jōshun to go in his place. However, recently Hosokawa Ryōichi (1987, 8) has demonstrated that Ugon did accompany Kakunyo and Jōshun to China and spent three years there (also see *Kongō busshi*, 19). When Ugon returned, he brought back twenty sets of subcommentaries on Daoxuan's three major commentaries on the vinaya, with each set consisting of seventy-three fascicles. He deposited ten sets each at Tōshōdaiji and Saidaiji. Some of the sets at Saidaiji were deposited there permanently, but others were lent to Eison's disciple Ninshō 忍性 (1217–1303) and other proselytizing monks. (One set remains preserved at Tōshōdaiji [*Shōdai senzai denki*, DNB 64.268b].) These copies helped solve a problem that had long been plaguing the Risshū monks—the lack of authoritative texts (*Hōji ninen shōrai ritsusandaibu haibun jō* 寶治二年將來律三大部配分状, SED 328–329). Ninshō played a major role in urging the others to go to China to find the texts and had apparently intended to travel to China himself until Eison asked him not to go. When Eison heard that the monks were returning from China, he sent Ninshō to Kyushu to await their return.

Later Ugon abandoned the full precepts for unknown reasons. Hosokawa (1987) speculates that he was frustrated because Eison had gained such prominence while his own career languished. Ugon carefully followed the eight precepts and led a number of believers called the "the group observing the eight precepts" (*saikaishu* 齋戒衆) who were associated with Tōshōdaiji. Because the eight precepts are usually kept by lay believers, Ugon's biography is listed among those for laymen in the *Tōshōdaiji Millenary Anniversary Hagiographies* (DNB 64.268b). In *Our Kingdom's Eminent Monks* (*Honchō kōsōden*, DNB 63.341c), however, where his renunciation of the full precepts is not mentioned, he is listed among those pure in the precepts.

The *saikaishu* differed from the vinaya model in one important respect: The former maintained the precepts indefinitely, while the latter (composed of pious lay believers) followed them for a single day in accordance with the vinaya. The eight precepts followed by the *saikaishu* also differed somewhat from those in the vinaya; a few were based on the precepts of the *Brahmā Net Sūtra* and included such provisions as no meat eating and no eating of the five herbs of the onion family—in addition to many of the more traditional rules included in the eight precepts (Minowa 1996, 92–93). The identity of the *saikaishu* is a matter of debate. Recently, Matsuo Kenji challenged Hosokawa's view that they came from villages near the temple; rather, Matsuo contends, they were originally an indistinct entity that in time occupied a specific place in the monastery's hierarchy. He also maintains that the group was established to deal with financial concerns and eventually specialized in certain mortuary functions (Matsuo 1996, 75–77). Ugon built two halls, Saihōin 西方院 (Western Direction) Chapel and Myōkōin 妙香院 (Marvelous Scent) Chapel, for his followers.

At mortuary ceremonies, these pious men carried out some of the more ritually defiling physical tasks while Risshū monks performed the religious rites (Hosokawa 1987, 9–29; Tokuda 1973, 210). Although technically laymen, they were "referred to as low-ranking monks" (*gesō* 下僧). Their close association with monasteries and constant observance of precepts seem to have given them quasi-monastic status. (Even among followers of the vinaya, who tried to bring more precision to the structure of monastic life, ambiguity found its way into their classification system.) Several texts were written to provide guidance for this group, beginning with Eison's *Separate Ordinations with the Eight Precepts Procedures* (*Saibetsuju hakkai sahō* 齋別受八戒作法); Kakujin's 覺深 commentary on Eison's procedures (*Saibetsuju hakkai sahō yōge* 齋別受八戒作法要解, 1686); and Tsūgen's 通玄 expanded commentary on Eison's and Kakujin's procedures (*Saibetsuju hakkai sahō tokudōshō* 齋別受八戒作法得道鈔, 1731). The *saikaishu* took care of many of the fund-raising (*kanjin* 勸進) duties at Tōshōdaiji. They were allowed to live only in certain areas of the monastery and the use of the monastery's eating utensils and bath water (after the monks had finished bathing in it—a clear indication of their inferior status).

Functioning essentially as servants, the *saikaishu* existed for at least four hundred years after Ugon. A similar group was established at the Ryōgon'in 楞嚴院, a hall associated with the precepts platform (*kaidan'in* 戒壇院) at Tōdaiji (Nagamura 1989, 698–699).

Eison and his disciples had to come to terms with the variety of believers whose practices varied from those in the vinaya. Laypersons who lived at home but wore robes and observed the precepts, often called "those who had entered the path" (*nyūdō* 入道), were dubbed "practitioners" (*gyōja* 行者) in Eison's order. Tendai monks who had been ordained with the precepts of the *Brahmā Net Sūtra* were called "those with the appearances of novices" (*gyōdō shami* 形同沙彌) as opposed to others who had received the traditional precepts of the *Four Part Vinaya* for the novice (*hōdō shami* 法同沙彌). These "labels" shifted over time. Late in his life, Eison may have combined bodhisattva precepts from both the *Yoga Stages* treatise and the *Brahmā Net Sūtra* with ordinations based on the *Four Part Vinaya* (Minowa 1996).

The order of nuns also reflected the tension between society and the vinaya. A study by Hosokawa (1999) on the nuns of Hokkeji indicates that many early members of the order were women who probably had known each other when they served at court. One of these women remained a novice; her low monastic status probably reflected her low social status. However, as the order of nuns at Hokkeji and other nunneries affiliated with Saidaiji grew, women from a variety of backgrounds became nuns, and social class may well have ceased to play an important role in the structure of the order. An issue as important as that of social class concerns the question of whether the nuns associated with Saidaiji were respected as independent women or were they so dominated by either their male relatives or the monks in associated temples that they had little autonomy. Evidence for both exists. For example, nuns performed rituals to honor male family members or the monks who had founded their nunnery. Little evidence exists of their performing rituals to commemorate other women. Moreover, many early nuns had been favored members of the court who had since lost the support of powerful male benefactors. On the other hand, some female monastics such as Shinnyo were fine scholars and tried to establish rituals honoring women. Thus determining the standing of nuns at the Saidaiji temples is not a simple matter.

In Sōji's work on behalf of nuns, we see the difficulties nuns faced in becoming autonomous. Sōji played a leading role in activities by nuns to publish works of interest. The *Transformation of Women's Bodies Sūtra* (*Tennyoshin kyō* 轉女身經) concerns the problem of how a woman might obtain the body of a man to become a Buddha. According to many sources, women could not obtain the five spiritual states (including Buddhahood) until they had received male bodies. The vows appended to the published version of the text state:

> This *Transformation of Women's Bodies Sūtra* is a scripture that expresses the ultimate teaching of Mahāyāna; it is a guide for the salvation of women.... Thus in order to both repay the vast favor of worthies and sages as well as to save women from their heavy karmic burdens, the nuns of Hokkeji, along with related [lay]women, have humbly published this text. I hope that it will long be circulated, that nuns and women fervently aspire to [follow] it and vie with each other to uphold it.... I wish that all women be transformed into males, that they be valiant, healthy, intelligent, and wise. All the constant practices (*jōgyō* 常行) are the bodhisattva's path. Strive to achieve the six perfections and arrive at the other shore. (Quoted in Hosokawa 1989, 148)

Nuns seem to have accepted many of the early prejudices about the religious capacities of women and the pollution of female bodies. A female novice named Shinmyō 眞妙 remarked: "I wish that, beginning with my mother and extending to all sentient beings, all women be able to forever abandon their female bodies and quickly realize enlightenment. I hope that this sūtra will enable me to forever abandon my female body, that no bad thoughts arise for successive lifetimes, and that I shall be able to encounter this sūtra again" (Hosokawa 1989, 150).

Much of the rhetoric about women in the work of Eison and his followers echoes traditional Buddhist thinking on the karmic burdens borne by women—burdens that keep them from realizing Buddhahood. Eison and his followers, however, tempered their language with statements to the effect that women are all mothers, therefore, everyone owes them a debt: Buddhist activities should be performed for the salvation of women. Eison's followers sometimes dedicated texts for female monastics to the memories of their mothers. Adherence to the precepts and the use of esoteric rites such as the Mantra of Radiant Light (*kōmyō shingon* 光明眞言) were said to enable women to overcome their karmic defilements

(Nōtomi 1977, 556–561). Thus women were accorded some respect and a certain amount of autonomy.

In evaluating the role of the nuns at Hokkeji, Hosokawa (1987, 146–157) notes that they were cloistered in nunneries and not allowed the same freedoms or opportunities as monks. The rules regarding their behavior were stricter. Many of their activities revolved around services for deceased members of their families, usually males. They prayed that when they died they might receive male bodies and be reborn into the Pure Land. If these women did not feel positive about even their own bodies, how could they have regarded their status as nuns as liberating? Their round of rites focused primarily on the major male figures in Japanese Buddhism—not on other nuns or women. They often did not live autonomous lives but continued to function in ways that suggested continuing ties to their families. A widow might spend most of her time in devotions to ensure the salvation of her husband; a woman who had never married might perform similar devotions for her father.

However, there is evidence, although fragmentary, that suggests that at least some of the nuns practiced in ways similar to monks and held more positive views about their religious roles. Eison conferred the highest esoteric initiation (*denbō kanjō* 傳法灌頂) on sixty-four monks—and six nuns (*Shien shōnin donin gyōhō kechige ki* 思圓上人度人行法結夏記, SED 214). Other sources indicate that nuns continued to receive the highest esoteric initiation after Eison's death. These women were certainly not the passive recipients of salvation ceremonies conducted by men. They may have performed esoteric Buddhist rituals, just as eminent monks did. No clear evidence is available to determine whether nuns conferred high esoteric consecrations on other women, but Matsuo Kenji (1996, 111–116) suggests that just as nuns ordained laywomen so might they have conferred advanced consecrations on other female monastics.

Conclusion

The revival of the traditional set of "hīnayāna" precepts used to ordain monks and nuns by Eison and Kakujō entailed constant tension between the demand to adhere to a collection of rules that reflected Indian society during the centuries following Śākyamuni's death and the demands of medieval Japanese society. On the one hand, both Eison and Kakujō tried to follow the instructions found in the *Four Part Vinaya* concerning such rituals as the establishment of monastic boundaries and fortnightly assemblies. They were willing to follow rules concerning eating meals together even when it meant conflict with other monks. On the other hand, their entire movement was based on a ritual that never would have been permitted in the *Four Part Vinaya:* self-ordination. Also the comprehensive ordinations they used to ordain their followers would never have been countenanced by the vinaya. The structure of Eison's order, with its various types of novices and group of quasi-monastics who followed the eight precepts, does not appear in Indian literature. However, the result was a highly successful movement that spread throughout Japan, winning acceptance from both commoners and the military government. Its attempts to aid the less fortunate revealed a social conscience equal to that of any of the "new Buddhisms" of the Kamakura period.

Note

This essay is part of my ongoing research into efforts within Tendai and Shingon to revive the precepts during the late Heian and Kamakura periods. For a related essay that discusses Eison's efforts to aid the lowest classes of society, the *hinin* 非人, see Groner 2002a. For a related essay that discusses the ordination of nuns during the eighth through tenth centuries, see Groner 2002b.

Chapter 10

Precepts in Japanese Pure Land Buddhism

The Jōdoshū

JAMES C. DOBBINS

PRECEPTS, SUPPOSEDLY the common thread drawing together the Buddhist world, have had a problematic and controversial place in Japanese Buddhism. It is no secret that Japanese have long debated their content, function, and necessity, and that the value ascribed to them in Japan has differed in important ways from their value in other Buddhist countries. In fact, in the eyes of other countries, there may be some question as to whether Japanese follow a legitimate version of the precepts and whether their clergy are properly ordained. Japan's discomfort regarding the precepts has existed from early in its history, and some of its prominent forms of Buddhism emerged with a distinct sense of ambivalence toward them. The Pure Land tradition, for one, exemplifies Japan's attraction-avoidance response to the precepts.

Pure Land Buddhism has a long and complex history in Japan, but the particular school to be examined here is the Jōdoshū 淨土宗, or Pure Land school, which claims the eminent master Hōnen 法然 (Genkū 源空; 1133–1212) as its founder. To be more exact, the school is the Chinzei 鎮西 branch of the Jōdoshū, which is traceable to Hōnen's disciple Benchō 辨長 (1162–1238) and was further developed by such leaders as Ryōchū 良忠 (1199–1287) and Shōgei 聖冏 (1341–1420). This is in contrast to the Seizan 西山 branch of the Jōdoshū, descended from the close disciple of Hōnen named Shōkū 證空 (1177–1247). The Chinzei branch should also be distinguished from two other Pure Land groups, which likewise emerged in the wake of Hōnen's pioneering efforts: the Shinshū 眞宗 (True School), traceable to Shinran 親鸞 (1173–1263); and the Jishū 時宗 (Time School), stemming from Ippen 一遍 (1239–1289). All of these took embryonic form in the Kamakura 鎌倉 period (1185–1333) and

236

gradually assumed a separate identity from the medieval period's prevailing forms of Buddhism.

The Chinzei branch of the Jōdoshū originated somewhat on the periphery of Japan's Buddhist world. It began in Kyūshū 九州, at the western end of Japan, and later expanded eastward into the Kantō 關東 region, where it came to be based particularly at Kōmyōji 光明寺 Temple in Kamakura. In the fifteenth century it grew increasingly prominent and influential when it took over exclusive leadership of Chion'in 知恩院 Temple in Kyoto, the location of Hōnen's grave-site chapel. The branch's fortunes were boosted considerably in the sixteenth and seventeenth centuries when it received special patronage from the great unifier of Japan, Tokugawa Ieyasu 德川家康 (1542–1616), and subsequently from his shogunate government. Today, the Chinzei Jōdoshū is the second largest Pure Land denomination in Japan after the two main branches of Shinran's Shinshū.

Antecedents of Jōdoshū Precepts

All of the aforementioned Pure Land groups arose in Japan after the Buddhist precepts had become an integral part of the established religious order. The precepts that the Jōdoshū adopted were not those of the *Four Part Vinaya,* which temples in the old capital of Nara upheld, but the Mahāyāna (or bodhisattva) precepts, also known as the Perfect Sudden Precepts (*endon kai* 圓頓戒), which Saichō 最澄 (767–822) instituted for ordinations in the Tendai 天台 school (Groner 2000, 107–194). Ample evidence suggests that Saichō's was not a smooth and problem-free system. Many controversies emerged even in Tendai over the precepts' meaning and applicability (Groner 1990a, 251–290). But because Tendai was such an influential form of Buddhism in Japan, its ordination system using the bodhisattva precepts was widely accepted, even though other Buddhist countries did not use them in that way. Hōnen and most of his disciples entered the clergy under the Tendai system. Hence, when the Jōdoshū speaks of the precepts, it is referring to the bodhisattva precepts specifically. It inherited most of the associations and significances, as well as the ambivalences, that Tendai had regarding them.

At the time the Jōdoshū appeared on the scene, Japanese Buddhism was undergoing a crisis over the precepts. The problem was not whether one should follow the *Four Part Vinaya* or the bodhi-sattva precepts, as Saichō had argued. Rather, it was whether any precepts at all should be recognized. There emerged a widespread sense in Japan that the clergy was in a state of moral decay. The types of actions most commonly decried were eating meat, consuming liquor, and indulging in sexual activity and even marriage—all violations of the precepts. Whether the clergy were actually worse than in previous periods or simply the perception of them was worse is not of primary concern here. What is important is that a preoccupation with religious decline seemed to pervade Japan. Violation of the precepts (*hakai* 破戒) was considered a rampant trend within the Buddhist establishment. Outside of the establishment there emerged a burgeoning class of quasi-priests—the *hijiri* 聖 (itinerant monks or recluses)—who acknowledged no set of precepts (*mukai* 無戒), were never fully ordained, or maintained ties to no particular tradition, whether of the *Four Part Vinaya* or the bodhisattva precept variety. These monks broke with tradition by disregarding the precepts, but they nonetheless devoted themselves to religious concerns (Inoue Mitsusada 1975, 215–265). In the context of these events there arose a sense that the precepts had lost their efficacy to lead people to enlightenment, or at least that people had lost their capacity to adhere to them. This assumption was commonly couched in terms of the well-known doctrine of the decline of the Dharma (*mappō* 末法; i.e., decline of Buddhism). According to *mappō*, the world has entered a dark period far removed from Śākyamuni Buddha's time. His teachings can no longer be put into practice because of the deterioration of human spiritual capacity and the disappearance of circumstances and conditions conducive to religious attainment. One of the texts widely read and cited by Buddhist thinkers in the Kamakura period was the *Lamp for the Age of Declining Dharma* (*Mappō tōmyōki* 末法燈明記), a spurious work attributed to Saichō. This text makes it clear that one of the period's conspicuous features is widespread violation of the Buddhist precepts (Matsubara 1978, 180–193). Thus the crisis mentality over the decline of the precepts was inextricably tied to the rise of *mappō* consciousness in Japan.

The precept crisis of the Kamakura period generated two very different responses, sometimes described as the pro-precept (*jiritsu shugi* 持律主義) and the anti-precept (*han jiritsu shugi* 反持律主義)

factions (Furuta 1981d). The pro-precept group was well represented by many religious reformers in temples affiliated with Nara Buddhism. An early example is Jōkei 貞慶 (1155–1213) of Kōfukuji 興福寺 Temple, who made a public vow around 1210 to resuscitate the study and practice of the precepts, specifically those of the *Four Part Vinaya* (see his *Gedatsu Shōnin kairitsu kōgyō gansho* 解脱上人 戒律興行願書 in Kamata and Tanaka 1971, 10–11; Morrell 1987, 7–9). The aspiration to revive the precepts of the *Four Part Vinaya* was further advanced by Shunjō 俊芿 (1166–1227), an eminent vinaya master who brought back vinaya from China after twelve years of study there and introduced the latest Chinese procedures and customs regarding the vinaya and bodhisattva precepts to reform-minded Buddhists in Japan (Etani 1978, 172–173; Ishida Mitsuyuki 1972). The Nara revival movement eventually gave rise to mass ceremonies for administering the precepts to both clerics and lay-people, popularized by Eison 叡尊 (1201–1290) of Saidaiji 西大寺 Temple and his disciple Ninshō 忍性 (1217–1303) of Gokurakuji 極 樂寺 Temple in Kamakura. These ceremonies used not only the *Four Part Vinaya* precepts but also the bodhisattva precepts, depending on the circumstances and the status of those receiving them (see Groner in this volume). The pro-precept faction also included many individuals not directly associated with Nara Buddhism. For instance, the famous Zen 禪 proponent Eisai 榮西 (1141–1215), founder of Kenninji 建仁寺 Monastery in Kyoto, was an early advocate of clerical reform by the *Four Part Vinaya* and a close associate of Shunjō (Bodiford 1993, 168–169; Yanagida 1972, 459–466). Also the intense concern over pure rules (*shingi* 清規) shown by the Zen master Dōgen 道元 (1200–1253) and his institution of ordination procedures into the religious program at Eiheiji 永平寺 Monastery were in many ways an outgrowth of this pro-precept sentiment, though he apparently valued the precepts as an embodiment of enlightenment rather than as moral prescriptions (Bodiford 1993, 169–173). Even Nichiren 日蓮 (1222–1282), by equating acceptance and practice of the five-character "Lotus Sutra" title (*daimoku* 題目) with upholding the precepts, can be construed as a pro-precept advocate, though of a different stripe (see his *Kyōgyōshō gosho* 教行證御書, NSI 2.1488; also Imai 1991, 225–226; Ishii Kyōdō 1972, 373, 378–379).

The anti-precept faction, outside of the ubiquitous *hijiri* tradition, was represented prominently by the exclusive *nembutsu* (*senju nenbutsu* 專修念佛) movement of Pure Land Buddhism. Hence it was associated specifically with Hōnen, who was universally recognized as the author of the exclusive *nembutsu* doctrine. Pure Land Buddhism, even before Hōnen's time, had generated concepts and categories that relegated the precepts to the periphery of its religious path. The time-honored divisions between the Pure Land path (*jōdo mon* 淨土門) and the saintly path (*shōdō mon* 聖道門), between easy practices (*igyō* 易行) and difficult ones (*nangyō* 難行), and between true practices (*shōgyō* 正行) and extraneous ones (*zōgyō* 雜行) became crucial in Pure Land's understanding of the precepts. The category of true practices is defined by the Chinese Pure Land master Shandao 善導 (613–681) in his commentarial treatise *The Contemplation Sūtra's Nonmeditative Practices* (*Guanjing sanshanyi* 觀經散善義, JZ 2.58). Shandao notes that true practices include five activities: reciting scripture (*dokuju* 讀誦), meditation (*kanzatsu* 觀察), worship (*raihai* 禮拜), uttering the name (*shōmyō* 稱名) of Amitābha Buddha (known in Japan as Amida Butsu 阿彌陀佛), and praises and offerings (*sandan kuyō* 讚嘆供養). Of these he deemed uttering Amitābha's name—identified as the *nembutsu*—to be the act that truly ensures enlightenment in Pure Land (*shōjōgō* 正定業) and the other four to be secondary or auxiliary acts (*jogō* 助業). It is this exegetical tradition that Hōnen and his successors inherited, not that of Yongming Yanshou 永明延壽 (904–975) who regarded precepts as central to the Buddhist path and the *nembutsu* as a safety net (see Getz in this volume). Among many Japanese, though, precepts came to be viewed as extraneous practices, appropriate for other forms of Buddhism but not for the Pure Land path, which they considered the only viable form of Buddhism in the age of decline. It is not surprising, then, that Shinran's Shinshū and Ippen's Jishū did not ascribe great importance to the precepts. Shinran characterized himself as "neither priest nor layman" (*hisō hizoku* 非僧非俗; in *Kyōgyōshinshō* 教行信證, SSZ 2.201), repudiated clerical celibacy, married, and begot a family (Dobbins 1989, 21–46). Ippen, for his part, generated entirely new rules for his *hijiri* followers that became the fundamental Jishū regulations (*Jishū seikai* 時宗制誡, in Ōhashi 1971, 299–300). It is in this context that the Jōdoshū, Hōnen's Pure Land school, emerged in Japan. Its view of the precepts, however, was less dismissive than that of the Shinshū and the Jishū.

Hōnen and the Precepts

The starting point for exploring the Jōdoshū's reaction to the precepts is the views of its founder, Hōnen. Though there are a few works on precepts attributed to Hōnen, scholars nowadays consider them to be spurious (Etani 1978, 146). Hence whatever views Hōnen had of precepts have to be culled from other writings and early biographical accounts. In them there is, first of all, one strain of thought clearly subordinating precepts to Pure Land themes. For instance, in Hōnen's *Passages on the Selection of the Nembutsu in the Original Vow* (*Senchakushū* 選擇集, HSZ 315), he says: "There are countless other practices such as alms-giving and upholding the precepts. They can all be subsumed under the term 'extraneous practices.'" If there is a prevailing message in the *Senchakushū*, it is that people should set aside extraneous practices and adhere to one exclusive practice: the *nembutsu*. This is the idea behind Hōnen's statement (*Senchakushū*, HSZ 313), "Master Shandao laid out two types of practice, true and extraneous; one should discard extraneous practices and take refuge in the true practice." Other writings likewise convey this idea (Tsuboi 1961, 281; Etani 1978, 151–153; Ishii Kyōdō 1972, 381–382). In Hōnen's *Twelve Questions and Answers* (*Juni mondō* 十二問答), he specifically cites the *Lamp for the Age of Declining Dharma*'s arguments concerning the precepts:

> The great master Dengyō 傳教 [Saichō] wrote in the *Lamp for the Age of Declining Dharma* that during the age of decline there is no such thing as upholding precepts or violating precepts or even being without precepts. There exists nothing but monks in name only. How then can one debate upholding the precepts or violating them? [Amitābha's] principal vow was made precisely for ordinary unenlightened beings such as ourselves, so we should invoke [Amitābha's] name with all due haste and concern. (HSZ 634)

Hōnen's devaluing of the precepts is a perennial theme in his writings. It is this strand of thought that Shinran inherited, as evidenced in the absence of a precept tradition in the Shinshū.

Within Hōnen's following some monks were clearly radicalized by this depiction of the precepts. They took Hōnen's teachings as an impetus not simply to focus attention on the exclusive practice of the *nembutsu* but also to campaign actively and aggressively against the precepts (Tamura 1959, 70–76). Such wanton disregard for the precepts was commonly known as "violating the precepts without remorse" (*hakai muzan* 破戒無慚). This radical faction of Hōnen's movement stigmatized his teachings in the eyes of the Buddhist establishment, leading eventually to the banishment of Hōnen, Shinran, and other disciples from the capital. During this crisis Jōkei, the precept revivalist of Kōfukuji Temple in Nara, became an outspoken critic of Hōnen. Jōkei is the reputed author of the *Kōfukuji Petition* (*Kōfukuji sōjō* 興福寺奏状, in Kamata and Tanaka 1971, 32–42; Morrell 1987, 75–88), which accuses Hōnen of, among other things, condoning violation of the precepts and thus inflicting harm on the Buddhist order.

Hōnen himself sought to mitigate the provocative implications of his teaching and to rein in his most extreme followers. In 1204 he formulated a code of conduct known as the *Seven Article Pledge* (*Shichikajō kishōmon* 七箇条起請文), which he obliged his followers to observe. The fourth article concerns the precepts specifically:

> Refrain from saying that there is no practice of the precepts in the *nembutsu* path; from avidly encouraging sexual indulgences, liquor, and meat eating; from impulsively calling those who adhere to the vinaya's precepts people of extraneous practice; and from teaching that those who rely on Amitābha's principal vow have no reason to fear committing wrongdoing.
>
> Concerning the above, the precepts are the great foundation of the Buddhist teachings. Though religious practices are diverse, they are all equally intent on the [precepts]. With regard to this, Master Shandao would not look upon a woman whenever he raised his eyes. The upshot of this behavior was to surpass even the regulations of the basic vinaya. If people of pure acts do not conform to the [precepts], then they altogether abandon the teachings bestowed by the *tathāgatas* [buddhas], and they also disregard the ancient traditions of the patriarchs. At the same time, are not they devoid of any grounding? (HSZ 788)

This passage reflects the other dimension of Hōnen's view of the precepts. Though he frequently categorized them as extraneous practice, he clearly did not consider the precepts to be at odds or in conflict with the *nembutsu*. Hōnen in fact tried to demonstrate an affinity between them by linking the two through numerical association. In his *Letter to Those Who Have Ascended the Mountain* [i.e., Mount Hiei 比叡] (*Tozanjō* 登山状, HSZ 427) he writes, "What one should long for deeply in one's heart is to uphold the ten major (*jūjū* 十重) [bodhisattva precepts] and to invoke the ten *nembutsu* (*jūnen* 十念), to adhere to the forty-eight minor (*shijūhachi kyō* 四十八輕) [bodhisattva precepts] and to rely on [Amitābha's] forty-eight vows (*shijūhachi gan* 四十八願)." Far from undermining the *nembutsu,* the precepts, he argues, in fact echo the Pure Land teachings.

Hōnen himself observed the precepts scrupulously, though he declared in all humility that he had not upheld even one of them (*Shōkōbō ni shimesarekeru onkotoba* 聖光房に示されける御詞, HSZ 751). He apparently received the bodhisattva precepts more than once in his life, and early in his career he may have been ordained with the precepts of the *Four Part Vinaya* as well. He administered precepts to countless disciples. He also gave them to lay followers such as Kujō Kanezane 九条兼實 (1149–1207) even when they took them merely as a formality for good fortune or beneficial side effects (Etani 1978, 143–145; Ishii Kyōdō 1972, 403–405). Hōnen's actions therefore reflect a more conventional and positive assessment of the precepts than his portrayal of them as extraneous practices suggests. It is this facet of Hōnen's teachings that the Jōdoshū inherited and preserved.

The Precept Tradition of the Jōdoshū

The three people who instituted a precept tradition in the Jōdoshū were its de facto founder, Benchō; his disciple Ryōchū; and their later successor Shōgei. Together they formalized what was implicit in Hōnen's teachings. From an organizational point of view, they made precept ordination a necessary component in the Jōdoshū's master-disciple lineages. Liturgically, they inherited from Hōnen the so-called *Twelve Part Precept Ceremony* (*Jūnimon kaigi* 十二門戒儀), formally known as the *Bodhisattva Precept Ceremony* (*Ju bosatsu kaigi* 授菩薩戒儀, JZ 15.872–878), the ritual guidelines for conferring the bodhisattva precepts developed by the Chinese Tiantai 天台 patriarch Zhanran 湛然 (711–782) and used ubiquitously in the Tendai school in Japan.[1] Benchō and Ryōchū were scrupulous about administering the precepts to their disciples, but it was Shōgei who initiated the principle that to be recognized as a Jōdoshū priest one would have to receive not only the teachings from the master but also the precepts. Specifically, he argued that it was a long-standing Pure Land tradition to maintain dual lineages between masters and disciples: a teachings lineage (*shūmyaku* 宗脉) and a precept lineage (*kaimyaku* 戒脉) (Ishii Kyōdō 1972, 379–81, 407–409; see Shōgei's *Ken jōdo denkai ron* 顯淨土傳戒論, JZ 15.895–896).

This position made administering precepts the primary mechanism for generating master-disciple lineages in the Jōdoshū. From the standpoint of Buddhism in general, there was nothing strange about this practice because administering precepts has been a standard method of establishing the master-disciple relationship throughout Buddhism's history. What is unusual is that, in contrast to other forms of Pure Land Buddhism in Japan, the Jōdoshū made induction through the precepts one of its mainstream rituals. The Shinshū, in contrast, set aside the precepts and developed its own mechanisms for formalizing master-disciple relationships.[2] The Jōdoshū could have followed this route also because lineages based on Pure Land teachings were established by Benchō. He produced a digest of Pure Land teachings found in the *Handprints Log of Conferral of the Nembutsu in the Latter Age* (*Matsudai nenbutsu jushuin* 末代念佛授手印, JZ 10.1–14), which he personally inscribed and passed on to his closest disciples, who in turn passed it on to their disciples (Matsuo 1988, 209). Such lineages of teachings could have easily provided a mechanism for formal master-disciple ties. Instead, the Jōdoshū opted for a two-track line of descent composed of precept lineages on the one hand and transmission of teachings on the other.

With Benchō, Ryōchū, and Shōgei there was also a gradual reinterpretation of the function of the precepts in the context of the Pure Land path. No longer were the precepts portrayed as extraneous practices. One extreme, however, that they did not go to was to consider the precepts identical to and nondualistically bonded with the *nembutsu* (*nenkai itchi* 念戒一致). Such an interpretation was more characteristic of Shōkū and the Seizan branch of the Jōdoshū than of Benchō and the Chinzei branch (Ishii 1972, 373–375). The Chinzei Jōdoshū, instead, treated the precepts as auxiliary acts to the *nembutsu*. That is, the precepts were presented as enhancing the exclusive practice of the *nembutsu*, not detracting from it. Some passages in Hōnen's writings in fact intimate such an interpretation. For example, in a commentary on the *Immeasurable Life Sūtra* (*Muryōjukyō* 無量壽經; often referred to as the *Larger Pure Land Sūtra)* Hōnen indicates that adherence to anything from the three refuges (*sanki* 三歸) and the five precepts (*gokai* 五戒) for laypeople all the way up to the full set of precepts (*gusoku kai* 具足戒) for monks and nuns specified in the *Four Part Vinaya*, as well as the ten major and forty-eight minor bodhisattva precepts and the three categories of pure precepts (*sanjujōkai* 三聚淨戒) of bodhisattvas, is an act leading to birth in the Pure Land (*Muryōjukyō shaku* 無量壽經釋; HSZ 93). Though he did not explicitly apply the category of auxiliary acts to the precepts here, he did include them in the larger scheme of the Pure Land path, as was customary in earlier Pure Land thought. Benchō, however, unambiguously described adherence to the precepts as an auxiliary act, and Shōgei furthered the argument, saying:

> Even though we speak of extraneous practices, there are a few ancillary practices (*kengyō* 兼行) that are recognized in our school. Why should we despise them? Furthermore, in the context of differentiating true (*shō* 正) from extraneous (*zō* 雜) and auxiliary (*jo* 助) from true [practices], none of these few ancillary exercises should be seen as extraneous. (*Ken jōdo denkai ron*, JZ 15.896)

With this type of argument, Shōgei challenged the stereotyping of precepts as extraneous practices common in Pure Land circles. Without countermanding Hōnen's ideas, Shōgei essentially set up a twofold view of the precepts in the Jōdoshū. When the precepts are followed separately from the *nembutsu*, they constitute extraneous practices. But if observed in conjunction with the *nembutsu* so that they lead to a greater realization of Amitābha's vow, the precepts function as auxiliary acts in the Pure Land path (Tsuboi 1961, 283–284; Hamada 1967, 304–307). In this way the early organizers of the Jōdoshū provided the doctrinal underpinnings for the perpetuation of precepts in the school.

The Pure Land Fortnightly Assembly Ceremony

With Shōgei the precepts assumed a prominent institutional role in the Jōdoshū, but they did not necessarily coalesce smoothly with Pure Land teachings. Now and then reactions against them would erupt among Jōdoshū adherents. These reactions did not take the form of the anti-precept iconoclasm that rocked Hōnen's movement, nor did they result in the total rejection of the precepts as found in Shinran's Shinshū tradition. But they did give rise to a unique rendition of the precepts in the form of a ritual manual entitled the *Pure Land Fortnightly Assembly Ceremony* (*Jōdo fusatsu shiki* 淨土布薩式, HSZ 1058–1088). This work—attributed to Hōnen but traceable more to Shōgei and his contemporaries, and thus probably composed in the late 1300s or early 1400s (Ikawa 1975, 47–48)—presents in liturgical format an explanation of the precepts interpolated with Pure Land themes. Rather than describe procedures for a fortnightly assembly *(fusatsu* 布薩; Skt., *poṣadha;* Pali *uposatha)*, it is structurally more similar to the *Twelve Part Precept Ceremony,* the standard liturgical text for administering the bodhisattva precepts (Ikawa 1960, 27–29). But from the beginning the *Pure Land Fortnightly Assembly Ceremony* (HSZ 1065–1066) depicts itself as transmitting a distinctive Pure Land lineage of the precepts handed down from Śākyamuni Buddha to the Bodhisattva Mañjuśrī; from Mañjuśrī, who purportedly resided on Mount Wutai 五台 in China, to the three Pure Land patriarchs of China, Tanluan 曇鸞 (476–542?), Daochuo 道綽 (562–645), and Shandao; and finally from Shandao to Hōnen in a dream.

What is most interesting about the *Pure Land Fortnightly Assembly Ceremony* is how the precepts are interpreted to fit the Jōdoshū's assumptions and circumstances. For instance, in the liturgical section explaining the ten major bodhisattva precepts, the injunction against sexual activity and marriage by priests is qualified substantially, no doubt to adapt it to alternative views of the priesthood. The discussion of this precept (HSZ 1072–1073), while enumerating all the obstructions and disadvantages of physical desire and attachment, goes on to indicate that in certain situations a priest could have a wife and children, just as a bodhisattva might have them whenever such a position serves the larger goal of bringing sentient beings to enlightenment. This same idea is reinforced indirectly later in the text (HSZ 1080) where it states that, if people are incapable of upholding all ten major precepts, they should at least observe the four most important ones: (1) not to kill; (2) not to steal; (4) not to lie; and (10) not to slander the three jewels (*sanbō* 三寶; i.e., the Buddha, the Buddhist teachings, and the Buddhist order). The fact that the injunction against sexual activity (i.e., the third precept) is omitted from this final list suggests that the Jōdoshū found the clerical vow of celibacy problematic. This strategy was not unique to the *Pure Land Fortnightly Assembly Ceremony,* for in the version of the *Twelve Part Precept Ceremony* (i.e., the so-called

Kurodani kohon 黒谷古本, ZJZ 12.5) used by the Jōdoshū until mid-Tokugawa times the third major precept omits the term "sexual desire" (*in* 婬) altogether. Instead, it equivocates by framing the vow as an "injunction against practicing desires without compassion" (*fu muji gyōyoku kai* 不無慈行欲戒). The implication is that such desires can be practiced if compassion is present in them. Rationalizations against the vow of celibacy reflect substantial openness to the marriage of clergy and thus an ongoing tension in the Jōdoshū with this item in the traditional precepts.

Partisans of the *Pure Land Fortnightly Assembly Ceremony* version of the precepts were always a minority in the Jōdoshū, primarily because the work was fairly late in appearing and circulated only in restricted circles. Though the origins of the text are obscure, scholars now think that its proponents were based principally at Kōmyōji Temple in Kamakura. This temple was established in the 1240s by Ryōchū, the foremost leader and popularizer of the Chinzei branch of the Jōdoshū during its formative period, and it emerged as one of the premier institutions of the school. Ordinations based on the *Pure Land Fortnightly Assembly Ceremony* were apparently conducted at the temple over successive generations and produced a master-disciple lineage organized around the text. But these ceremonies were generally performed in private and were perpetuated as a secret ordination reserved for an elite few. They were portrayed as the highest form of Pure Land ordination one could receive. During the fifteenth, sixteenth, and seventeenth centuries, the Kōmyōji extended its influence first to Chion'in Temple in Kyoto, the location of Hōnen's grave-site chapel; and later to the Zōjōji 増上寺 in present-day Tokyo, the leading Jōdoshū temple connected with the Tokugawa shogunate (1600–1867). With this expansion, certain priests from those temples underwent the *Pure Land Fortnightly Assembly Ceremony* ordination. As Japan entered the Tokugawa period, several priests began campaigning for the adoption of the *Pure Land Fortnightly Assembly Ceremony* as the Jōdoshū standard because other precept ceremonies in use did not reflect distinctive Pure Land values (Suzuki Ryōshun 1982, 106–109; Ikawa 1975, 45–48).

A debate emerged in which advocates of the *Pure Land Fortnightly Assembly Ceremony* were countered by other priests from both the Chinzei and Seizan branches of the Jōdoshū who criticized the work as a spurious composition wrongly ascribed to Hōnen.

One of the leading critics was the scholar-priest Nanso 南楚 (1592–1671), who denounced, among other things, the interpolation of *yin-yang* 陰陽 thought and ideas from the *Laozi* 老子 into the concluding section of the text; he saw them as undermining the strict meaning of the precepts and inviting physical indulgences (*Fusatsu shiki benshō* 布薩式辨正, ZJZ 13.348–350; Sanda 1975, 757–765). His arguments and those of like-minded priests essentially stalled the drive to disseminate the *Pure Land Fortnightly Assembly Ceremony* throughout the school, thereby preserving the traditional ordination procedures of the bodhisattva precepts as the norm. Nonetheless, the *Pure Land Fortnightly Assembly Ceremony* was popular enough that it persisted in certain circles throughout the Meiji 明治 period (1868–1912), though a movement spearheaded by the eminent Jōdoshū activist and reformer Fukuda Gyōkai 福田行海 (1806–1888) finally led to its discontinuation in 1912 (Etani 1978, 191–193; Ishii Kyōdō 1972, 418–421, 428–429).

Precepts Revival in the Tokugawa Period

Though there was some momentum in favor of the *Pure Land Fortnightly Assembly Ceremony* at the beginning of Tokugawa times, what eclipsed it ultimately was the wider precepts revival that pervaded Buddhism as a whole during this period. Reforms were initiated in most schools to place greater emphasis on the precepts and to study their content and significance. It is difficult to say what provoked this outpouring of concern for the precepts. Sectarian sources often claim that it was a reaction to the decadence of the clergy. Zen scholars sometimes cite the arrival of Yinyuan Longqi 隱元隆琦 (Ingen Ryūki; 1592–1673), the famed master from China who introduced from the mainland procedures for mass ordination ceremonies that included lay precepts, the monastic precepts of the *Four Part Vinaya*, and bodhisattva precepts. Even a few members of the Shinshū, which had rejected the precepts throughout its history, argued for the recognition of the bodhisattva precepts (Ishii Kyōdō 1972, 410). This preoccupation with precepts thus extended to virtually every Buddhist school during the seventeenth and eighteenth centuries, and the Jōdoshū was no exception. Precepts rose to ever greater prominence in the thought and religious life of the Jōdoshū, and the earlier Pure Land critique of them as extraneous practices faded from discourse.

Two noteworthy developments in the context of this precept revival were the efflorescence of the world-abandoning (*shasei* 捨世) movement, exemplified by Ninchō 忍澂 (1645–1711) and his Hōnen'in 法然院 Temple in Kyoto, and the rise of the Pure Land Vinaya (Jōdo Ritsu 淨土律) movement, organized by Reitan 靈潭 (1676–1734) at his Shōrin'an 照臨庵 hermitage also in Kyoto. The world-abandoning ideal was not specifically inspired by Tokugawa precepts reform but rather had its origins in earlier traditions of *nembutsu* practice. The goal was to dedicate oneself to exclusive and intense *nembutsu* practice in a monastic setting, while maintaining a strict and religiously pure lifestyle. This philosophy, needless to say, coalesced well with the precepts and prompted Ninchō to institute monastic rules at the Hōnen'in based on the vinaya (Itō 1958, 31–49; Itō 1964, 1–3; Etani 1978, 182–183; Ishii Kyōdō 1972, 412–414). Reitan, by contrast, concentrated more directly on the issue of precepts per se and explicitly advocated adherence to them as fundamental to clerical practice of the *nembutsu* (Itō 1964, 1–4; *Ryakudenshū* 略傳集, JZ 18.480–82; Etani 1978, 182–183; Ishii Kyōdō 1972, 414–418). To this day his tradition is kept alive by the Jōdoshū nun Kondō Tesshō 近藤徹称, head resident and Reitan's dharma heir at the Shōrin'an in Kyoto.

What is striking about these two Tokugawa movements is that, though they considered the bodhisattva precepts to be primary, they both adopted a conciliatory attitude toward the *Four Part Vinaya* precepts. This constituted a new trend in the Jōdoshū. Prior to that time, the school recognized only the bodhisattva precepts inherited from the Tendai tradition. One impetus for the interest in the *Four Part Vinaya* no doubt came from the Tendai school itself, where reform-minded monks such as Myōryū 妙立 (1637–1690) and Reikū 靈空 (1653–1739) pressed for the use of *Four Part Vinaya* ordinations in addition to the regular Tendai bodhisattva ordinations (Etani 1978, 180–182; Ishii Kyōdō 1972, 411–412). Ninchō argued that, although the Pure Land teachings were derived from Hōnen, the precepts, properly speaking, were traceable back to Shandao in China, and his precepts no doubt included those of the *Four Part Vinaya* (Ishii Kyōdō 1972, 365, 367–368). Reitan, for his part, actually underwent ordination in the full set of precepts for a monk as specified in the *Four Part Vinaya* (*Ryakudenshū*, JZ 18.481). Though the viewpoints and activities of these two movements were not necessarily widespread in the school during this period, they nonetheless

made a strong impression on the Jōdoshū clergy. They fostered
serious consideration of the precepts among them and countered
sectarian tendencies favoring *Pure Land Fortnightly Assembly Ceremony* ordinations.

Alongside proponents of the *Pure Land Fortnightly Assembly
Ceremony*, world-abandoning monasticism, and the Pure Land Vinaya Ritsu movement, many mainstream clerics in the Jōdoshū
were likewise stimulated to explore and promote the traditional
bodhisattva precepts. A succession of Jōdoshū priests in the Tokugawa period wrote treatises on them and reasserted their primacy
as the fundamental precepts of the school (Etani 1978, 186–187).
One development resulting from their efforts was that the version
of the ordination ceremony in use at that time, commonly known
as the *Old Kurodani Text* (*Kurodani kohon* 黒谷古本, ZJZ 12.1–6),
was replaced by the *New-Text Precept Ceremony* (*Shinpon kaigi* 新本
戒儀, ZJZ 12.9–14). A manuscript of the *Old Kurodani Text* survives
in Shōgei's own handwriting, so it must have been in widespread
use by the late fourteenth century. There is some evidence that it
may go back to the time of Hōnen himself, for a version of the ceremony used by Hōnen's senior disciple Shinkū 信空 (1146–1228) is
almost identical to it. Nonetheless, in content the *Old Kurodani Text*
differs in crucial ways from texts used in Tendai and other Japanese
Buddhist schools. For one thing, the ten major bodhisattva precepts
are written in variant language from that found in other versions,
including the third precept, which, as framed, could be construed
as condoning the marriage of priests. In the mid-Tokugawa period,
another version of the ordination procedures, the so-called *New-
Text Precept Ceremony,* came to light, which contained language
very close to that found in the ceremonies of other schools. This
new text was in fact quite old, having been preserved in the treasure
storehouse of Nison'in 二尊院 Temple in Kyoto, where Hōnen had
once resided and was briefly interred. Hōnen himself is said to be
its author, though it is impossible to verify such a claim. Even so
the work can definitely be traced back to the Kamakura period.
The discovery of this text gave the Jōdoshū an alternative that was
just as venerable as the Kurodani one yet closer to those used by
other schools. It was quickly disseminated throughout the Jōdoshū
and from mid-Tokugawa times on became the standard for ordination ceremonies. This shift was significant because it aligned the

Jōdoshū more closely with the precept traditions of other Japanese Buddhist schools. The new version continues down to the present as the basis for the Jōdoshū's precept ceremony (Etani 1972; 1978, 234–236).

Precepts in Modern Times

In the Jōdoshū today there are two forms of precept ceremonies conducted, one for clerics and the other for laypeople. Originally, the precepts were administered primarily to the clergy, but sometime during the Tokugawa period they were popularized among the common people as well. The early "ordinations" of laypeople were apparently a one-day affair, though the actual content of the proceedings and the motivations of the ordinands are not entirely known (JD 2.199, s.v. *jukai* 授戒 and *jukaie* 授戒會).[3] Lay precept ceremonies today last for seven days. The first six days function as a religious retreat including worship services, *nembutsu* chanting, sūtra recitation, and lectures on the three refuges, the five precepts for laypeople, the three categories of pure precepts *(sanjujōkai)* of bodhisattvas, the ten major precepts (*jūjūkinkai* 十重禁戒) of bodhisattvas, and the twelve parts of the precept ceremony (*jūnimon kaigi* 十二門戒儀). On the seventh day the precepts are formally administered to the participants. The ceremony is ordinarily performed before a scroll painting known as the Three Holy Ones Administering the Precepts (*jukai sanshō zu* 授戒三聖圖), which depicts Śākyamuni Buddha flanked by the bodhisattvas Mañjuśrī and Maitreya. They fulfill the roles of the three ordination masters required for the ordination procedures specified in the *Four Part Vinaya*. Needless to say, this ritual does not serve the same purpose for laypeople as it does for the clergy. The lay ceremony is frequently called "administering the precepts to establish a karmic bond" (*kechien jukai* 結縁授戒). The implication here is that through this event recipients of the precepts form a karmic link that leads them to enlightenment in Amitābha's Pure Land. The ordination ceremony for the clergy is similar in sequence and procedure. The most visible difference is that the seven-day initiation is integrated into a longer retreat for the clergy known as preparatory practice (*kegyō* 加行). In significance, however, the ordination of the clergy marks their induction into the ranks of formally recognized

teachers of the Jōdoshū. Hence the precept ceremony is the mechanism by which they become part of the school's official lineage
(Fujii 1979, 64–66; Shiio 1931, 99–124).

In light of these ceremonies and in the context of their historical evolution, what then is the role of the precepts in the Jōdoshū,
and what meaning do they have for its adherents? For one thing,
they provide the cohesion of a religious transmission from master
to disciple over successive generations, which is crucial to the identity and perpetuation of the Jōdoshū as a sectarian body. Precepts
have exerted this same cohesive effect throughout Buddhist history
on other sectarian groups, and to the extent that these groups have
the precepts in common, the groundwork exists for a shared, pan-
Buddhist identity between them. But that function, crucial as it
may be from an institutional standpoint, does not address whether
the actual content of the precepts is important to the Jōdoshū. Do
the specific injunctions in the bodhisattva precepts represent normative rules of behavior for Jōdoshū adherents? That question is
far more complex.

When perceived as extraneous practices, precepts, it would
seem, do not have direct relevance or application to the Pure Land
path. But the Jōdoshū, as shown earlier, adopted a different interpretation, construing the precepts to be auxiliary acts that work in
tandem with the *nembutsu*. When one upholds the moral imperatives of the bodhisattva precepts, those virtuous acts augment
and enhance the boundless saving power already inherent in the
nembutsu. Hence ethical action does have a soteriological value
but only in conjunction with the *nembutsu*. By contrast, the *nembutsu* constitutes both necessary and sufficient cause for birth in
the Pure Land. Its efficacy is not dependent on other acts. Thus
while acknowledging the primacy of the *nembutsu*, the Jōdoshū
affirms the value of the precepts. It would be a mistake, however,
to assume that the Jōdoshū expects its adherents to observe the
precepts without fail. There is adequate evidence that certain
injunctions—the rule of celibacy, for instance—were never stringently observed even among the clergy. Moreover, there is some
question as to whether Jōdoshū adherents actually believe they can
follow the precepts unerringly. Some doctrinal scholars depict the
precepts as valuable simply because they awaken in one an awareness of human failings and inadequacies, thus leading one to the
superior practice of the *nembutsu* (Etani 1978, 149–151).

In the end, the meaning of the precepts in the Jōdoshū lies not in successful observance of them in every detail, but in the adherent's commitment to them as an ideal. That is, their symbolic value is just as important as their moral value. This understanding of the precepts is frequently couched in terms of the age-old Buddhist division between ideal (*ri* 理) and specific (*ji* 事), categories that the Jōdoshū inherited from other Buddhist schools. Viewed as specific, the precepts (*jikai* 事戒) constitute a collection of rules and injunctions which, when followed scrupulously, yield a lifestyle wherein one desists from evil and cultivates good. Viewed as ideal, however, the precepts (*rikai* 理戒) represent a palpable expression of the impalpable Buddhist absolute, convergent with the *nembutsu*.[4] When analyzing the precepts in this way, the Jōdoshū considers it possible to uphold them as ideal without necessarily upholding them as specific. Needless to say, such an interpretation is prey to cynical and self-serving manipulation if used as an excuse for not doing good. But the important point is that the Jōdoshū values an inner assent to the precepts as much as an outward performance of them. From this point of view, the precept ceremony represents not simply a commission to do good but rather an occasion for acknowledging one's karmic bond to universal powers working to bring sentient beings to enlightenment. The ritual event of receiving the precepts therefore contains meaning over and above one's actual capacity to obey them. Through such doctrinal analyses, the Jōdoshū has attempted to bring harmony to seemingly diverging aspects of its tradition: the *nembutsu* path on the one hand and the precepts on the other.

Notes

I would like to thank Professor Fukuhara Ryūzen 福原隆善 of Bukkyō 佛教 University in Kyoto and the Venerable Kondō Tesshō 近藤徹称, head resident of the Shōrin'an 照臨庵 in Kyoto, for meeting with me during the preparation of this essay to discuss the precepts in the Jōdoshū.

1. The Jōdoshū recognized this Zhanran version as its authoritative text for ordination ceremonies rather than the versions by Zhili, Zunshi, and Yuanchao (described by Getz in this volume), even though their versions integrated Pure Land themes and motifs into the ceremony.

2. The Shinshū is commonly depicted as devoid of master-disciple lineages based on Shinran's comment, "I, Shinran, do not have even one disciple" (*Tannishō* 嘆異抄, SSZ 2.776). But it is clear that there were lineages from the earliest period, as reflected in such lineage charts as the *Shinran Shōnin monryo kyōmyōchō* 親鸞聖

人門侶交名帳 (in Yamada 1979, 351–380). Though there were apparently no uniform ceremonies formalizing the master-disciple tie, religious objects such as inscribed texts or portraits of the master were frequently passed on to disciples as tokens of the relationship, and disciples would frequently receive new clerical names from the master. Shinran, for instance, received the name Shakkū 綽空 from Hōnen, had him inscribe a copy of his *Senchakushū* for Shinran, and was allowed to make a portrait of Hōnen (*Kyōgyōshinshō*, SSZ 2.202). The Shinshū subsequently developed its own tonsure (*tokudo* 得度) procedure for ordination, but it never adopted the precepts as part of the ordination (Matsuo 1988, 226–227).

3. These ceremonies may have been similar to those described in Bodiford 1993 (179–184).

4. The analysis of precepts from the perspective of specific *(ji)* and ideal *(ri)* has precedents in Tendai. The bodhisattva precepts in the *Brahmā Net Sūtra* are identified as precepts with form *(jikai)*; the attitudes and views promoted by the *Lotus Sūtra* are identified as precepts without form *(rikai;* Groner 2000, 206–210). For a Jōdoshū exegesis of precepts using the categories of *ji* and *ri,* see Inoue Tokujō 1908 (438). Jōdoshū doctrine shares the Tendai view that *"jikai"* refers to the specific injunctions of the bodhisattva precepts. Likewise, it defines *"rikai"* as the essence of the precepts (*kaitai* 戒體), which once received is never lost (*ittoku fushitsu* 一得不失) and constitutes the seed of Buddhahood (*jōbutsu no shuji* 成佛の種子). But the Jōdoshū understanding differs in other ways from the Tendai view of *rikai.* Specifically, it does not posit a link between *rikai* and the *Lotus Sūtra.* If *rikai* is identified with any teaching, it is with the *nembutsu* as the *nembutsu* precepts (*nenbutsu kai* 念佛戒).

Chapter 11

The Debate over Meat Eating in Japanese Buddhism

RICHARD M. JAFFE

THE DISTINCTIVENESS of contemporary Japanese Buddhist practice with regard to the major precepts—as several essays in this volume demonstrate—is well known among scholars and practitioners of Buddhism. One important element of this distinctiveness is that apart from monastic and temple settings, most Japanese clerics do not refrain from eating meat, fish, fowl, and other flesh foods.[1] Those who have spent any length of time with Japanese Buddhist clergy in Japan or outside of Japan will have no doubt seen them eat meat and fish. The general acceptance of meat eating in Japanese Buddhism today, however, belies the contentious debate over meat eating that sporadically took place in Japan from the start of the seventeenth century until the full-fledged outbreak of overseas wars in the 1930s. Current defenses of clerical meat eating are rooted in arguments defending the practice that began during the Tokugawa (1603–1867) era and continued through the Meiji (1868–1912), Taishō (1912–1926), and Shōwa (1926–1989) periods. Additionally, tolerance of clerical meat eating in Japan was fostered by changing attitudes toward meat consumption that occurred with the reopening of Japan to the Euro-American powers and by changing views of human biology over the course of the nineteenth and twentieth centuries. Ultimately, clerical meat eating came to be viewed as a necessity if the Buddhist clergy were to contribute to the Japanese effort to create a modern imperial nation-state on par with the Euro-American powers.

The discussion of meat eating by the clergy frequently accompanied arguments concerning fornication and clerical marriage and, as a result, was known, at least as early as the eighteenth century, as the "eating-meat-marriage" (*nikujiki saitai* 肉食妻帯) problem. The association between the consumption of foods considered to be aphrodisiacs (meat, garlic, onions, leeks, and scallions) with illicit sexual activity by the clergy was a long-running one in Japan. For example, the "Regulations for Monks and Nuns" (*Sōniryō* 僧尼令) in the *Yōrō Era Law Codes* (*Yōrō ritsuryō* 養老律令) of 757 contained an article banning the consumption of meat, alcoholic drink, and smelly herbs. As noted by Ishida Mizumaro (1995, 8–13), the provision was probably intended to help curb sexual transgressions by monastics, because these foods were believed to heighten sexual desire. Over the course of premodern Japanese history complaints against the Buddhist clergy for their profligate behavior frequently included claims that the clergy were eating forbidden foods. For example, Miyoshi Kiyoyuki 三善清行, a tenth-century critic of the Buddhist clergy, wrote, "All of them keep wives and children in their homes; they eat fish and meat (*kuchi ni seisen o kurau* 口に腥膻を啖らふ). Their appearance resembles monks, but in their hearts they are like butchers" (*Miyoshi Kiyoyuki iken fūji* 三善清行意見封事, 914, cited in Kuroda 1980, 250). To be sure, Miyoshi's criticisms were far from isolated (e.g., Ishida Mizumaro 1995, 97–98).

In addition to the more general attacks on clerical meat eating and fornication, there were also criticisms directed specifically at clerics belonging to the Jōdo Shinshū 淨土眞宗 school of Pure Land Buddhism. Citing the precedent of their founder, Shinran 親鸞 (1173–1263), Shinshū clerics openly took wives, practiced patrilineal inheritance, and even in their training halls (*dōjō* 道場) consumed foods usually avoided by the Buddhist clergy. According to James Dobbins (1989, 91), the Shinshū leader Zonkaku 存覺 (1290–1373) riposted that because Jōdo Shinshū practitioners were allowed to engage in these activities in their daily lives, they were quite free to do so in their training halls. Similarly, Dobbins (1989, 153) notes that despite the growing similarity between the late-medieval Honganji 本願寺 Temple and other Buddhist temples, Shinshū clerics alone "ate fish and meat, and they even served it to guests inside the Honganji."

An extensive literature concerning meat eating (specifically by clerics) did not emerge in Japan until after the start of the seventeenth century. The stigmatization of meat eating by successive shoguns; the increased prominence of non-Buddhist intellectual factions as Confucian scholars, Nativists, and Shintō Revivalists; and, toward the end of the Tokugawa period, the growing body of knowledge about the dietary habits of the Europeans—all contributed to an unprecedented level of public debate concerning meat consumption. One historian of Japanese food customs, Kamo Gi'ichi, has observed:

> Prior to the Tokugawa period we can say that edicts prohibiting meat eating were frequently promulgated, but there was no general debate about that practice. With the advent of the Tokugawa period, however, meat eating was opposed because it was considered polluting (*kegare*) and, at the same time, the exclusionary attitude toward foreigners who made meat part of their everyday diet grew in strength. Probably in no other period was the issue of meat eating as rancorously debated as in the Tokugawa. (Kamo 1976, 196; also see Harada 1993, 257)

Kamo's comments apply not only to the general public in the debate over meat consumption but the Buddhist clergy as well. In particular, scholar-clerics of the Jōdo Shinshū denomination—reacting to partisan attacks by clerics affiliated with the rival Pure Land Jōdoshū 淨土宗 and the Ōbakushū 黃檗宗 branch of Zen as well as by such nativists as Hirata Atsutane 平田篤胤 (1776–1843) in the later Tokugawa—produced a sizeable body of literature that staunchly defended the clerical consumption of meat and fish, clerical marriage, and patrilineal inheritance even in temple settings (Jaffe 2001, 36–42). Over the course of the Tokugawa period, Jōdo Shinshū clerics such as Saigin 西吟 (1665–1663), Chikū 智空 (1634–1718), Erin 慧琳 (1715–1789), Hōrin 法霖 (1693–1741), and others produced an apologetic genre defending their practices. In these tracts, many of which were given similar-sounding titles such as *Defense of Meat Eating and Clerical Marriage* (*Nikujiki saitai ben* 肉食妻帯辨) and *Defense of Eating Meat and Clerical Marriage* (*Jikiniku saitai ben* 食肉妻帯辨), the authors devoted considerable attention to rebutting arguments that meat eating by the clergy should be prohibited. (For a description of this genre of Buddhist literature, see Ishikawa Rikizan 1996; Jaffe 2001, 36–57.)

A look at an early, often reproduced, and mimicked example of Tokugawa-period Jōdo Shinshū apologetical literature of this genre reveals several of the arguments employed by the Shinshū clergy in the defense of clerical meat eating. The *Defense of Meat Eating and Clerical Marriage* (hereafter *Defense*) by the aforementioned Chikū, the second head scholar (*nōke* 能化) of the Shinshū seminary at Nishi Honganji 西本願寺, provided a template for the Jōdo Shinshū defense. The work was based on lectures given by Chikū at least partially in response to attacks from clerics of other denominations. Specifically, Chikū's effort to defend Jōdo Shinshū appears to have been stimulated by lectures on the *Śūraṅgama Sūtra* (*Shoulengyan jing* 首楞嚴經, T no. 945) that were delivered in 1669 by Tetsugen Dōkō 鐵眼道光 (1630–1682), who had converted to Ōbakushū Zen after first being a Jōdo Shinshū cleric and student of Chikū's teacher, Saigin (Baroni 1994; Jaffe 2001, 38–42). As later described by the Shinshū cleric Erin, the strife between the Shinshū clergy and Tetsugen began when the latter delivered a series of talks in Edo as part of his effort to raise funds for printing in Japan a copy of the Ming-dynasty edition of the Buddhist canon. While lecturing on the *Śūraṅgama Sūtra*, a text that stresses the importance of maintaining the monastic precepts, Tetsugen apparently enraged Shinshū clerics in the audience, who then entered into a debate with the speaker over his interpretation of the text. When a local Edo cleric, Kūsei 空誓 (d. 1692), was bested by Tetsugen in debate, Chikū was sent to Edo to challenge Tetsugen (*Shakunan Shinshū sōgi* 釋難眞宗僧儀, SZS 59.349; Baroni 1994, 196–197).

Although Erin does not record exactly the sort of charges brought by Tetsugen against the Shinshū clergy, a text attributed to Tetsugen, the *Absentminded Conversation with Bats* (*Kōmori bōdanki* 蝙蝠忘談記, reprinted in Ishikawa Rikizan 1996), gives us a sense of the complaints leveled by Shinshū opponents and the heated nature of the rhetoric in these Tokugawa-period anti-Shinshū polemics.[2] In this text, Tetsugen (or someone writing in his name) equates the Shinshū clerics' continued sexual relations and meat eating after ordination with the commission of the five grave offenses (*go gyakuzai* 五逆罪) of Buddhism.[3] In particular, the text argues that although these men have the appearance of "people who have left home" (*shukke* 出家), their meat eating and fornicating are destroying the order of monks *(saṅgha)*. Because of their deception, the author compares them to bats (*kōmori* 蝙蝠)— that is, animals that are neither fully rodents nor birds—thus alluding to a passage in the *Buddha's Canon of Morality Sūtra* (*Fozang jing* 佛藏經, T 15.788c) where Śākyamuni compares monks who violate the precepts to bats.

In the *Defense*, Chikū begins with feigned puzzlement over the current state of the Buddhist denominations in Japan. Noting that the Shinshū clergy do not follow the same protocols of behavior as other Buddhist denominations, Chikū expresses amazement that rather than being punished by the deities who protect Buddhism, the Shinshū denominations have prospered far more than any other Buddhist school:

> If one looks at the *Nirvāṇa Sūtra* (*Niepan jing* 涅槃經), the *Brahmā Net Sūtra*, or the *Laṅkāvatāra Sūtra* (*Lengqie jing* 楞伽經), one will see that these sūtras all enjoin those who are ordained to give up the four acts of taking life, stealing, licentiousness, and lying. Therefore one would expect one who has been ordained to refrain from eating meat and marriage. Two-thirds of the people of Japan, however, now follow the school of our founder [Shinran] and those who request deliverance to the Pure Land are numerous. What does the god Brahmā (Bonnō 梵王) do about this? Is the god Śakra (Taishaku 帝釋; Indra) blind? They vowed in the presence of the Buddha [to punish such transgressors], so why do they not censure these things? Why did the kings and great ministers not split the head of Shinran into seven pieces and drive him to another cosmos? I grew angry and resentful that not even the four great heavenly kings (*shi ten daiō* 四天大王; gods of the four directions) understood that this teaching had spread to two-thirds of Japan and that many sentient beings had been led astray. (*Defense,* 293b)

Chikū details the sorry state of venerable Buddhist temples and monasteries before launching into an extensive defense of the Shinshū practices of meat eating and clerical marriage. His arguments in favor of allowing the Buddhist clergy to eat meat—a category in which he includes seafood—focus on the inconsistency of the teachings regarding meat eating in the canonical literature and records concerning the consumption of meat, fowl, and various forms of seafood by illustrious clerics of the past (Jaffe 2001, 42–53). Chikū was clearly aware of the differing attitudes toward meat eating in the vinaya literature and some of the Mahāyāna sūtras seminal for the Buddhist cultures of East Asia.

Poring over the Buddhist canon, Chikū uncovered numerous examples of monks and nuns eating various animal foods for both medicinal and strictly culinary purposes. For example, he cites passages in the *Four Part Vinaya* (e.g., fasc. 42, T 22.872b) where Śākyamuni permits eating meat that is pure in three ways: It must not come from an animal one has seen being killed, an animal one has heard being killed, or an animal suspected to have been killed specifically for one's consumption (*Defense,* 298b; for an overview of restrictions on meat eating in Buddhist scriptures, see Shimoda 1997; Ruegg 1980). Chikū refers to other passages in the *Four Part Vinaya* where Śākyamuni allowed sick monks to consume such foods as the rendered fat of five animals (fasc. 10, T 22.627b) or raw ox meat and blood (fasc. 42, T 22.868b) to cure their illnesses (*Defense*, 297a–298b). After citing these and other sources, Chikū concludes that because the prohibition against meat eating was not in effect during Śākyamuni's lifetime, such great disciples as Śāriputra (Sharihotsu 舍利弗), Maudgalyāyana (Mokuren 目連), and Gautamī (Kyōdonmi 憍曇彌) all ate meat: "If this is the case, when Buddha was alive, his disciples all ate meat, so there is no reason to censure so severely our patriarch [Shinran] for having eaten meat" (*Defense*, 298b).

True, Chikū admits, Śākyamuni does proscribe meat eating in the *Nirvāṇa Sūtra* (T no. 374), but in the same sūtra he also proscibes many other activities that the clergy of Chiku's day freely performed. For example, he forbids ownership of eight varieties of impure things (*hasshu fujō motsu* 八種不淨物), such as domestic animals, servants, gold, land, orchards, and grains (e.g., fasc. 6, T 12.402b, etc.). Chikū writes that this selective obedience is the height of hypocrisy:

> If we read the *Nirvāṇa Sūtra*, there are passages that anyone would take issue with today. It says that people of the future who possess the eight impure things are not my disciples, but are companions of [the evil] god Māra (Tenma 天魔) [e.g., fasc. 7, T 12.404a].... I do not know about India, and I have not examined China, but today there is not a single priest in Japan who follows these proscriptions. Because the disciplinarians (*risshi* 律師) and *saṅgha* supervisors (*sōzu* 僧都) of various temples and monasteries, to the contrary, accept retainer's stipends, own fields, and build residences, even the highest-ranking individuals possess the eight impure things. They all violate the prohibitions of the Buddha, therefore they are not disciples of the Buddha, they are Māra's companions. (*Defense*, 298b–299b)

Chikū lambasted the selective way in which the critics of Shinshū practice chose particular proscriptions to obey while ignoring many others and cited numerous examples of clerics in both China and Japan who he claims, based on traditional sources, had eaten meat and married. To demonstrate that Shinshū clerics were following illustrious precedents, Chikū mentions, for example, the founder of the Hossō lineage, Cien Ji 慈恩基 (often referred to as Kuiji 窺基 632–682); the sixth ancestor of the Chinese Zen lineage Huineng 慧能 (639–713); and the famous Chinese Zen monks Zhutou 猪頭 (also known as Panshan Baoji 盤山寶積; n.d.) and Xianzi 蜆 子 (n.d.; *Defense,* 301a; 302a–b).[4] He also poked fun at what he saw as widespread violation of the ban against clerical meat eating and marriage by clerics of the non-Shinshū denominations. He notes that despite the proliferation of so-called "ordination platform pillars" (*kaidan seki* 戒壇石) outside Zen temples inscribed with the phrase "It is not permitted to enter this temple gate with pungents or liquor" (*fukyo kunshu nyū sanmon* 不許葷酒入山門), clerics continued to consume these very foods within the temple. Chikū's comments indicate that he interprets the obscure term "pungents" (*kun* 葷) to include not just smelly or spicy herbs (its usual meaning) but also meat. He goes on to say, however, that the clergy have found all sorts of clever ways to ignore the ban. Raising one particular "culinary" practice as an example, Chikū writes:

> When one visits temples one sees that a small amount of seaweed *(wakame)* is put into a bowl. Saying that they will "season it with liquor (saké)," they pour in liquor and drink heavily from their soup bowls. At first it was done in the above fashion, but then clerics said, "The seaweed is no good, it's stale" and drank just the liquor. They thus violate the prohibition against entering the temple with liquor, meat, or the five smelly herbs (*goshin* 五辛).[5] (*Defense,* 299b)

Having provided numerous examples of inconsistencies within the Buddhist canon with regard to meat eating and clerical marriage, Chikū concluded that Śākyamuni had not preached absolute rules banning either practice. Rather, the acts of prohibiting or allowing meat and marriage are "clever devices and expedient means created because sentient beings have a multiplicity of spiritual dispositions. In any case, to lead even one person to the Buddhist teaching, sometimes it is permitted and sometimes it is forbidden" (*Defense,* 304b). Because of the flexibility in the teaching, it is an error to pronounce either forbidding or allowing meat and marriage as being absolutely correct and condemn the opposite behavior as absolutely wrong (*Defense,* 305a).

Based on this principle, Chikū defends Shinran and his successors' departure from the customary, although frequently ignored, strictures forbidding meat eating and marriage by the Japanese

Buddhist clergy. He asserts that Shinran, whether eating meat or marrying, was not motivated by sensual desire. Rather his actions must be viewed as expedient means *(hōben* 方便; *upāya)* performed to rescue suffering sentient beings trapped in the "mud of the five defilements" (*gojoku* 五濁; *Defense*, 307b).[6] Chikū concludes:

> [Shinran's] eyes were only fixed on rescuing sentient beings, and he paid no attention to what he wore or consumed, to which people ate meat, etc., or which people married, etc. The expedient means used by the bodhisattva to benefit and convert sentient beings are all just like this. Therefore, when we investigate the examples, proofs, and principles, we see that there is no special reason to condemn our patriarch for meat eating and marriage in that way [as clerics from other denominations do]. (*Defense*, 308b)

Apologia like Chikū's *Defense* were copied, and new ones (e.g., the *Defense of Meat Eating and Clerical Marriage, Shokuniku taisai ben* 食肉帶妻辨, by Hōrin) were produced throughout the Tokugawa period, indicating the ongoing interest within Shinshū circles in this genre. Spurred on by anti-Buddhist attacks like Hirata Atsutane's scathing *Humorous Words after Meditation* (*Shutsujō shōgo* 出定笑語, posthumously published in 1849), Shinshū clerics continued to defend their practices. Fearing retribution from government authorities for their exceptional behavior, however, Shinshū leaders warned their clergy to avoid red-light districts and such activities as fishing and hunting (Jaffe 2001, 52–53). The creation of a sizeable body of Shinshū literature devoted to defending clerical meat consumption and marriage helped reify these practices as ongoing "problems" that religious reformers and government leaders would try to resolve at the start of the Meiji period.

Debating Meat Eating after the Tokugawa Period

Meat eating became a more prominent issue for the Buddhist clergy, regardless of denominational affiliation, in the early Meiji period. Official state policy, the dissolution of old status laws, and changes in attitudes regarding the enforcement of protocols among the Buddhist clergy raised the issues of meat and marriage to prominence in both the secular and Buddhist world. Following the upsurge in violence directed at Buddhist institutions and clergy (*haibutsu kishaku* 癈佛毀釋) from approximately 1868 to 1871 (Ketelaar 1990), new government policies catalyzed the debate over the appropriateness of clerical meat eating that far exceeded in scope the much more limited Tokugawa-period discussion. The Tokugawa debate had focused on the Shinshū clergy; post-Tokugawa literature and legal maneuvering engaged Buddhist clerics of all denominations (Jaffe 2001, 58–113).

Advocates of meat eating ranged from pro-Westernization intellectuals like Fukuzawa Yukichi 福澤諭吉 (1834–1901) to the highest level of the Meiji regime. Most prominently, perhaps, the court announced in February 1872 that from that time on meat was to be served to the emperor at the imperial palace. According to the announcement, beef and lamb (regularly) as well as pork, venison, and rabbit (occasionally) would now be part of the imperial menu (Edamatsu 1983–1986, 1:540). In addition, French cuisine replaced Japanese-style meals at official state functions (Harada 1993, 17). In a similar vein, by the early Meiji the Japanese navy had begun serving bread and meat to its sailors to prevent malnutrition, despite protests from within the ranks against such unfamiliar foods (Harada 1993, 22).

Meat eating was so prominent in the early Meiji period that the practice became both a symbol of Westernization and "progress" and the target of social critics who lampooned the spread of foreign customs among the upper and middle classes. In *Aguranabe* 安愚樂鍋, his playful 1871 fictional depiction of dinnertime discussions taking place among patrons of a beef restaurant in Tokyo, Kanagaki Robun 假名垣魯文 (1829–1894) sarcastically remarked, "Samurai, farmer, artisan or trader; oldster, youngster, boy or girl; clever or stupid; poor or elite; you won't get civilized if you don't eat meat!" John Mertz, in his forthcoming study of Kanagaki's novel, has observed that eating meat, particularly beef, became a "synecdoche for all things Western." Demonstrating that even the Buddhas had been swept up by the zeitgeist, another acerbic observer of the Meiji social scene, Kawanabe Kyōsai 河鍋暁齋 (1831–1889), produced a painting of Fudō Myōō 不動明王 (Acalanātha), the popular, fierce manifestation of Dainichi 大日 (Mahāvairocana) Buddha, comically entitled "The Civilizing of Fudō Myōō" (*Fudō Myōō kaika* 不動明王開化). Fudō is shown reading the influential *Shinbun zasshi* 新聞雜誌, the very paper in which it was announced that meat would be eaten at court. In the foreground, an acolyte, Seitaka Dōji 制吒迦童子 (Ceṭaka), uses his sword to prepare meat for Fudō's meal. In the

Figure 11.1. The Civilizing of Fudō Myōō (*Fudō Myōō kaika*) by Kawanabe Kyōsai. Image number 5 in the series "Kyōsai's Amusing Drawings" (*Kyōsai rakuga*), 1874. Courtesy of the Kawanabe Kyōsai Memorial Museum.

background, another acolyte, Kongara Dōji 矜羯羅童子 (Kiṅkara), cleverly makes use of the nimbus of flames surrounding Fudō to heat the pot and a bottle of *saké* (Oikawa 1998, 112–114).

The government action that triggered the debate over meat eating, clerical marriage, and other practices formerly deemed improper for the Buddhist clergy was the adoption of what became known as the "Meat and Marriage *(nikujiki saitai)* Law." Promulgated on 31 May 1872 by the Grand Council of State (Dajōkan 太政官), the decriminalization measure read: "From now on Buddhist clerics shall be free to eat meat, marry, grow their hair, and so on. Furthermore, they are permitted to wear ordinary clothing when not engaged in religious activities" (Jaffe 2001, 72). Arguments in favor of decriminalizing these practices had been circulating in some Buddhist circles prior to the passage of the new law. Previously Ōtori Sessō 鴻雪爪 (1814–1904), the Sōtō Zen 曹洞禪 cleric who served in the Ministry of Doctrine (Kyōbushō 教部省) and was instrumental in drafting and passing the regulation legalizing meat and marriage, complained in a petition to the government that Buddhist leaders were enforcing protocols that ran counter to human nature, thus vitiating the clergy. Although not specific in its recommendations, the petition did urge the government to have these leaders remember that clerics were human beings and needed to be instructed more kindly (Yasumaru 1988, 30). Ōtori was able to act on his own recommendations when he was appointed to the Ministry of Doctrine.

Soon after the promulgation of this law, some clerics began clamoring for acceptance of the new standards and more active engagement of the clergy in national affairs. Ugawa Shōchō 宇川照澄, a Tendai 天台 cleric and head of Senkōji 千光寺 Temple in Ōzonemura 大曽根村 (Ibaraki prefecture), petitioned the government, urging that all Buddhist clerics be ordered to act in accordance with the decriminalization measure by eating meat, marrying, and wearing nonclerical clothing. Ugawa's argument in favor of meat eating was straightforward. Like Fukuzawa Yukichi and members of the government who viewed the practice as essential for a strong, virile populace, Ugawa wrote that by eating meat, the clergy would become more vigorous, enabling them to contribute more fully to the great task of serving the nation. In a time of national crisis (as the early Meiji period was deemed to be), it was inappropriate for the clergy to waste their time arguing over small points of morality. They needed instead to devote themselves fully to strengthening Japan (Ugawa 1949, 222).

Although the exact import of the new measure was vague—was it actually a recommendation to engage in the listed activities or simply a decriminalization of them—the negative reaction of the high-ranking clergy of almost every Buddhist denomination was vigorous and swift. One point of contention, of course, was the portion of the law allowing the clergy to eat meat openly without incurring any penalties from the state. Clerics from Jōdoshū, Sōtō, Shingon 眞言, and Tendai criticized the attempt to legitimize meat eating for the clergy. The high-ranking Jōdoshū cleric Fukuda Gyōkai 福田行誡 (1809–1888), an ardent opponent of the decriminalization law, condemned meat eating in a 1876 tract:

When the cleric leaves his home and takes the tonsure he follows the
example of the Buddha entering Mount Daṇḍaloka (Dandoku Sen 檀特
山) [where Śākyamuni supposedly practiced austerities]. By not eating
meat he obeys the proscription set forth at the assembly in Laṅkā
(Ryōga) [where Śākyamuni supposedly preached] and manifests the
great compassion of a bodhisattva. This is the behavior of a member
of the Buddhist clergy. Chapter 31 of the *Great Perfect Wisdom Treatise*
(*Dazhidu lun* 大智度論 [T no. 1509]) says that "upholding the precepts
shall be your inner essence; the tonsure and robes shall be your outward appearance." (Fukuda Gyōkai 1942, 177)

Similarly, in a letter to the Sōtō clergy of Miyagi prefecture
written in 1875, the Sōtō Zen cleric Nishiari Bokusan 西有穆山
(1821–1910) wrote:

Eating meat and marrying are matters dealt with in the vinaya (*ritsu*
律) and have nothing to do with the government. Although since 1872
the decision concerning these matters has been entrusted to each individual, and the former restrictions have been lifted, one should reflect
on the fact that eating meat causes the killing of sentient beings; marriage is the cause of confused action (*wakugyō* 惑行). (Nishiari 1875, 2)

In a text that appears to answer each point in the defense of
meat eating by Chikū and other Jōdo Shinshū clerics, the Shingon
cleric Ueda Shōhen 上田照遍 (1828–1907) grounded his arguments
for vegetarianism on a traditional periodization of Śākyamuni's
teachings. The ban on meat eating in the *Brahmā Net Sūtra*, which
Ueda saw as having been delivered at the beginning of the Buddha's
ministry, "was a prohibition based on principle. It was a teaching
that was unchanging in the past, present, and future." According to
Ueda, the Buddha did allow meat eating by clergy who followed inferior *(hīnayāna)* doctrines and, for a time, by bodhisattvas who followed the superior (Mahāyāna) teaching. But late Mahāyāna texts
such as the *Nirvāṇa Sūtra*, which set forth the Buddha's final injunctions to the order *(saṅgha)*, completely ended those allowances.
After Śākyamuni's death it was no longer permissible for a Buddhist
cleric—regardless of doctrinal orientation—to eat meat, even if he
or she were ill. Ueda urged students of esoteric Buddhism in particular to cure any illnesses with incantations *(ju* 呪; *dhāraṇī)* rather
than meat, which, as Chikū had noted, vinaya texts allowed for medicinal purposes. Ueda, like many critics of meat eating and clerical

marriage, commented that such licentious behavior by Buddhist clerics would make the laity reticent to believe the clergy when they preached about Buddhism (Ueda 1982, 228–229).

By 1878, when it was clarified that the intention of the decriminalization measure was not to supplant denominational regulations but rather to end government interference in Buddhist affairs, the leaders of many denominations notified their clergy that they were to obey the rules prohibiting meat eating and clerical marriage stringently. Typical of these notices was the one issued by the leaders of the Nichiren 日蓮 denomination, which reminded the clergy that

> the basis of Buddhism is achieving awakening and liberation from attachments. Therefore, there is no abandoning of one's obligations and entering the unconditioned unless one takes the tonsure, dons Buddhist robes, ceases sexual relations, and stops eating meat. That which is the most difficult to abandon is abandoned; that which is the most difficult to endure is endured. The names for "home dwellers" (*zaike* 在家; i.e., the laity) and "home leavers" (*shukke*, i.e., the clergy) are different from each other; their actions are also distinguished from each other. Furthermore, [one must practice the bodhisattva ideal of] upwardly seeking unlimited awakening while downwardly benefiting the living beings of the nine realms. We should call those who transcend the masses, rise above the secular, impartially abandon conventional emotions, and earnestly avoid sullying their reputation "Buddhist monks" (*sō* 僧). ("Nichirenshū rokuji" 日蓮宗録事 1878, 2–3)

The various negative responses to the decriminalization of clerical meat eating cited above did not represent a significant departure from the sort of argument marshaled by Tetsugen against the Jōdo Shinshū clergy approximately two hundred years earlier. Meat eating involved the taking of an animal's life and was therefore uncompassionate. Ever since the *Nirvāṇa Sūtra* and the *Śūraṅgama Sūtra* were preached, the eating of meat had been proscribed for the Buddhist clergy and this rule could not be modified.

Although the anti–meat eating arguments remained relatively constant over the course of the Tokugawa and early Meiji periods, by the mid-Meiji arguments in favor of meat eating underwent considerable change. Reflecting new conceptions of human biology, nutrition, and evolution, advocates portrayed meat eating as essential for the creation of a vigorous, engaged Buddhist clergy that could contribute to the development of Japan as a modern nation capable of competing in the international arena with the Euro-American powers. Most significantly, several of the proponents of meat eating argued that the new understanding of human biology placed contemporary Buddhists in a better position to assess meat eating, no matter what the canonical texts seemed to advocate.

Writing a brief tract favoring consumption of meat in 1898, the Buddhist intellectual Inoue Enryō 井上圓了 (1858–1919) clearly reflected the shifting intellectual landscape upon which social Darwinism, the Euro-American colonialism, and Japan's increasingly ambitious international aspirations had left their marks. Noting that "survival of the fittest" (yūshō reppai jakuniku kyōshoku 優勝劣敗弱肉強食; lit., "the superior win, the inferior lose; the weak are food for the strong") had long been the operative principle in the West (seiyō 西洋), Inoue contended that this sort of cutthroat thinking had found its way to the Orient (tōyō 東洋). The question of clerical meat eating and marriage could no longer be considered solely in terms of Buddhist doctrine. Rather, Inoue urged Buddhists to consider how, in the context of the Darwinian struggle for survival, they might contribute to policies that benefited the nation-state (kokka 國家). According to Inoue, the growing dissatisfaction with the established practices of Buddhism among the young clergy reflected the sense among the majority of the Japanese that world-abnegating Buddhism was ineffectual in a world marked by international competition (Inoue 1898, 25). The only way to enhance Buddhism's power and influence in the world, concluded Inoue, was "to advance the state of the nation and bring about Japan's victory in the international struggle. That victory, will cause not only the Orient, of course, but also even the West to revere the light of the sun of Buddhism." To bring this about, Buddhists must eliminate their religion's world-renouncing tendencies and create a new Buddhism with a secular flavor (konzoku shūfū 混俗宗風). First and foremost, this entailed allowing the clergy to eat meat and marry (Inoue 1898, 27).

Another advocate of meat consumption and marriage, the Nichiren cleric Tanabe Zenchi 田邊善知 (1901, 8–13), cited the importance of expedient means: A Buddhist cleric might eat meat or have relations with a woman to help sentient beings. Tanabe also defended meat and marriage from the perspective that the Lotus Sūtra is the ultimate teaching of Buddhism and that "the core meaning of the Mahāyāna *Lotus Sūtra* is found in the doctrine about accepting the marvelous dharma (*myōhō* 妙法), not in the doctrine prohibiting meat and wives" (Tanabe 1901, 24). Tanabe recognized, however, the problem posed by meat eating for Buddhists, which seemingly contradicts the fundamental Mahāyāna emphasis on the perfection of compassion (*jihi enman* 慈悲圓満). Although there was no way around the fact that eating meat involved taking life, according to Tanabe:

> it is not the fundamental purport of Mahāyāna Buddhism that out of pity for such lower animals as birds, beasts, and water dwellers we should pay no heed to the vicissitudes of human kind. Nor is it the fundamental purport of Mahāyāna Buddhism that for the sake of one person we should sacrifice rule over the realm (*tenka* 天下). Rather, the main purport of Mahāyāna Buddhism is that for the sake of the world we kill one person. The main purport of Mahāyāna Buddhism is that for the sake of advanced human beings we kill lower animals. The main purport of Mahāyāna Buddhism is that for the sake great compassion we sacrifice lesser compassion. Planning to slaughter birds and beasts to nourish our bodies and extend our lives is the essence of abandoning lesser compassion and adopting great compassion. We cannot escape the fact that those who, failing to grasp the main purport of Mahāyāna Buddhism, recklessly are carried away by their notion of compassion and thereby advocate the prohibition of meat eating, mistakenly misappropriate the notion of compassion. Those who misunderstand things in this way should not be spoken of simultaneously with Mahāyāna Buddhism. (Tanabe 1901, 24–25)

Underlying this argument was the late-nineteenth-century belief, prevalent in Japan, that meat was essential for vigor. Like Tanabe, almost every other Buddhist proponent of meat eating held that without the protein derived from meat and fish, one could not become an active, effective proselytizer of Buddhism (Tanabe 1901, 26–27; for a similar argument, see Suzuki Daisetsu 1970).

In addition Tanabe saw the cleric's freedom to eat meat and to marry as a fundamentally endowed right that could not be infringed on by the leaders of the Buddhist denominations. Denying the clergy these rights was to fail to treat them as human beings, who after all have certain needs:

> Even if one is a cleric (*sōryo* 僧侶), one is not apart from the human world. One is a blood relative of human kind. To exist in the world as

a human being entails that demanding those things necessary for survival is an "innate right" (*tenpu no kenri* 天賦の權利) that others are not permitted to violate. To deny only the Buddhist clergy meat eating and marriage is clearly a suppression of human rights (*jinken* 人權) and is a practice that follows the old evils of the feudal period. (Tanabe 1901, 4–5)

From the beginning of the twentieth century onward, those who addressed the meat and marriage problem began to focus their attention on the numerous thorny practical issues associated with the growing presence of women in temples: temple inheritance, succession, and finances. Although article-length treatments on the meat-eating problem continued to appear in the Buddhist press during the 1920s, their number was far outstripped by those discussing clerical marriage. Titles of works from the mid-Meiji period also reflect this shift: *Reforming Clerical Lifestyles, or How to Keep a Wife and Become a Buddha* (*Sōfū kakushin ron, ichimei Chikusai jōbutsu gi* 僧風革新論・一名畜妻成佛義, 1899) by Nakazato Nisshō 中里日勝; *On Clerical Families* (*Sōryo kazoku ron* 僧侶家族論, 1917) by Kuriyama Taion 栗山泰音 (1860–1937). However, Furukawa Taigo 古川碓悟, the author of *On Clerical Marriage* (*Sōryo saitai ron* 僧侶妻帶論, 1938), did not completely ignore clerical meat eating in his work. Instead he relegated an extended discussion of it to an appendix that constitutes approximately 15 percent of his book. He posited the relative insignificance of the meat-eating issue as his reason for doing so (Furukawa 1938, 5).

As Brian Victoria has observed, Furukawa was a staunch supporter of Japanese expansion in Asia and envisioned the creation of a new, activist Mahāyāna Buddhism that would further Japanese imperial ambitions (Victoria 1997, 91–93; 103–105). Written on the eve of Japan's wars of overseas aggression, Furukawa's treatise reflected growing Buddhist support for and involvement in the war effort. Since the Meiji period the Buddhist clergy had been subject to conscription, and as full-fledged hostilities began on the Asian continent, clerics were drawn into military service. With Japan moving rapidly toward a state of total war, many clerics and temple resources were mobilized. This had serious implications for temple wives, who were still not recognized by leaders of many denominations, and for the male clerics who were now serving as soldiers.

At the heart of Furukawa's defense was his vision of a "new

Mahāyāna Buddhism" (*Shin Daijō Bukkyō* 新大乘佛教) that did not lack an understanding of "cosmic evolution" (*uchū shinka* 宇宙進化) and was not tainted with fear of the decline of the Buddhist dharma (*mappō* 末法). If Buddhism shed its world-abnegating tendencies and infused itself with a spirit that "actively, expansively, and hopefully believed in the perpetual development of the cosmos and human life that is identical with the dharma nature of true thusness," the new Mahāyāna Buddhism would thrive. An ardent supporter of the Japanese state and its expansion in Asia, Furukawa found the fundamental purpose of clerical activity in working for the imperial cause. By embracing the principles of the new Mahāyāna Buddhism and engaging fully in the world, the clergy would be able to "guard and maintain the prosperity of the imperial throne," thus supporting the national polity (*kokutai* 國體) that was the very pinnacle of cosmic evolution (Furukawa 1938, 44).

Because even after the government decriminalization of meat eating and clerical marriage clerics who engaged in such activities were censured as "precept-breaking monks" (*hakai sō* 破戒僧), it was important to mount a cogent defense of these actions. The emphasis on compassion in both the so-called lesser *(hīnayāna)* and greater (Mahāyāna) forms of Buddhism, according to Furukawa, must be reconsidered in light of a more accurate understanding of human biology. Humans by nature need the nutrients found in meat, and although strict vegetarianism is not an impossibility, it is highly impractical for all but a small fraction of people. Lack of biological knowledge was but one reason for Buddhism's misdirected advocacy of vegetarianism. Developing points briefly expressed by proponents of meat eating such as Ugawa Shōchō and Tanabe Zenchi, Furukawa wrote that, at least in part, vegetarianism was promoted by Mahāyāna Buddhists because they lacked "an evolutionary conception of human existence" (*shinkaronteki jinseikan* 進化論的人生觀; Furukawa 1938, 62–63). Even more importantly, Buddhists made meat eating taboo because they mistakenly accepted the absolute equality of different species, an idea that Furukawa believed was grounded in pessimistic Buddhist ideas of transmigration through the six courses of rebirth (*rokudō rinne* 六道輪廻) and, ultimately, the doctrine that the triple world (*sangai* 三界) is marked by suffering. Furukawa held that Buddhism at least partially had moved beyond this kind of world rejection with the Mahāyāna doctrine of the identity between the afflictions and awakening (*bonnō soku bodai* 煩悩即菩提) and the identity of saṃsāra and nirvāṇa (*shōji soku nehan* 生死即涅槃). He urged Japanese Buddhists to reject the negative emphasis on suffering and transmigration—holdovers from a time even prior to Śākyamuni's awakening—and adopt an "evolutionary" understanding of the cosmos. The universe was able to witness the manifestation of true thusness only through humanity. Because of their unique capacity for self-awareness, humans stand at the pinnacle of the chain of being. Thus "for the sake of the development of human existence, it is natural that [humans] can freely utilize all things—inanimate, vegetable, and animal" (Furukawa 1938, 66–67). In advocating his new understanding of Mahāyāna Buddhism, Furukawa stated: "Having seen that from the perspective of the aforementioned New Mahāyāna … humanity is the ultimate fruition of the cosmos, the attitude towards animals must be human-centered. So long as it does not injure the human spirit, one can freely use them and it absolutely is not a transgression to eat their meat" (p. 67). This was the reason most religions (Furukawa cites Shintō, Confucianism, and Christianity, specifically) allowed humans to use animals for food.

Employing an argument reminiscent of Tanabe's differentiation of "greater" and "lesser" types of compassion, Furukawa concluded that the acts of sacrifice and being sacrificed are fundamental to the universal order:

> For better or worse, the world truly is a sacrificial order (or a mutual assistance order). The inorganic is the victim of the organic, plants are the victims of animals, animals are the victims of humans, lesser life forms are the victim of greater life forms. Because they forever are destined to strive for development, those that in the least bit attempt to go backward truly become seclusionists who do nothing other than bring about individual and national self-extinction. Both the self-extinction of lesser Buddhism and Indian Mahāyāna Buddhism's reaching a decadence from which it could not be roused resulted from this principle. If Buddhist clerics aim even a little bit for the flourishing of the national polity *(kokutai)* and the development of humanity, they resolutely must shed the corpse of the passive thought of the Buddhism of India and, must, when circumstances require, openly nourish their body and mind through eating meat and press on with their duty. (Furukawa 1938, 68)

This duty, as Furukawa saw it, was spelled out clearly in his 1937 book in which he described the new Mahāyāna Buddhism in detail. In that work, Furukawa called on his fellow clerics to join the legitimate struggle against the Chinese in Manchuria and "to participate in this rarest of holy enterprises" (Victoria 1997, 92).

Conclusions

> "You haven't had any meat in a long time have you?" Suzuki said to him.
> "No, Roshi, not in two years. No animal food. No dairy or eggs."
> "That's very good," Suzuki said, as the waitress walked up. "You order first."
> "I'll take a grilled cheese sandwich." It was the best he could do with that menu.
> "Hamburger please," said Suzuki, "with double meat."
> The food arrived and they each took a bite. "How is it?" asked Suzuki.
> "Not bad."
> "I don't like mine," Suzuki said, "let's trade. With that he picked up Bob's sandwich and replaced it with the double-meat hamburger. "Um, good. This is good. I like grilled cheese." (Chadwick 1999, 299–300)

Despite the fact that some members of the Japanese Buddhist clergy have throughout the centuries undoubtedly consumed meat, from time to time circumstances external and internal to the Buddhist world stimulated increased debate over the legitimacy of the practice. Changing attitudes toward meat eating in society at large, shifts in state policy regarding meat consumption, and changes in the Buddhist world itself catalyzed an ongoing discussion concerning the merits of meat eating among the clergy. In particular, during the Tokugawa period and, even more so, the post-Tokugawa period Buddhist clerics weighed in on the appropriateness of meat eating. During that time, the debate changed from an argument over Shinshū exceptionalism with regard to meat eating to a pan-denominational discussion among clerics anxious to recoup Buddhism's importance in a newly formed nation-state whose leaders held growing international and imperial aspirations. As the context for the debate shifted, so did the various rationales for permitting the Buddhist clergy to eat meat, fish, and other previously proscribed foods.

Today when asked to explain their departure from the strict vegetarianism that is part of clerical life in other Buddhist countries within the Chinese cultural sphere of influence, Japanese clerics no longer argue that meat eating is necessary for health or that clerics need to eat meat to better serve the nation. When pressed, some defend their meat eating as a manifestation of expedient means or a general expression of their nonattachment to the precepts. In writing about the final injunctions of Śākyamuni to his disciples as recorded in the *Final Admonitions Sūtra* (*Yijiao jing* 遺教經, T 381), Sōtō cleric Andō Yoshinori 安藤義則 mentions the departure of Japanese monastics from standard clerical behavior in other Buddhist countries, particularly Sri Lanka and Thailand: "Japanese clerics, meanwhile, are sure to feel a prick of conscience when they recall the precepts about eating meat, marrying or drinking alcoholic beverages." After invoking the dangers of an overly rigid adherence to these rules, Andō concludes: "Nevertheless, we must be careful to avoid an overly literal 'the precepts for the sake of the precepts' attitude" (Andō 1994, 14). Similarly, David Chadwick, the biographer of the Sōtō Zen teacher Suzuki Shunryū 鈴木俊隆 (1904–1971), who taught in San Francisco from 1959 until his death, considers the exchange quoted above as an illustration of how Suzuki would "use a meal to make a point that Buddhism wasn't the captive of any trips, especially food trips." (Chadwick 1999, 299). In other denominations where meat eating is tolerated, for example the Pure Land schools, there is no longer even the expectation that clerics will follow the precepts to the letter or that such strict adherence is even humanly possible (see Dobbins' essay in this volume).

Arguments justifying meat eating are infrequent today. To a large extent, the Tokugawa- and Meiji-period debates over Buddhist clerics eating flesh food appear to have been settled or, at the very least, dwindled to insignificance. The problem was resolved not through an express acknowledgment by the leaders of various denominations that meat eating was acceptable for the clergy, but because the practice eventually became so commonplace and accepted by the laity that debate was no longer necessary. Clerical marriage, however, continues to pose numerous doctrinal, moral, and practical problems for the clergy and temple wives, whose valuable contributions to temple life are frequently unacknowledged. As a result, unlike meat eating, clerical marriage remains a much discussed and studied topic in denominational headquarters, study centers, and temples (Jaffe 2001, 228–241). Meat eating is occasionally mentioned alongside clerical marriage as a sign of the gap between practice and doctrine in many of the non-Shinshū Buddhist denominations, but in Japan, at least, it merits little comment. A survey conducted by the Sōtō Headquarters (Sōtōshū Shūmuchō

曹洞宗宗務庁) in the late 1980s concerning the religious attitudes of Sōtō parishioners provides a case in point. To track opinion toward some of the changes wrought initially by the 1872 decriminalization regulation mentioned above, parishioners were asked how they felt about local temple clerics marrying, growing their hair, and abandoning clerical garb. The surveyors did not deem it necessary to include a question concerning the eating of meat (Odawara 1993, 91–95).

Notes

1. Philip Kapleau (1982, 27–28), for example, observes that the majority of Zen clerics he met in Japan in the 1950s ate meat outside the monastery even while undergoing monastic training. They were frequently aided in the process by the laity, who treated them to meat and fish at special celebrations. Nonomura (1996, 154–159) describes the daily diet at Eiheiji 永平寺, one of the principal Sōtō Zen training monasteries, as less than absolutely vegetarian. The premade roux used in preparing the occasionally served curry and cream stew contains animal fat. In defense of this small departure from strictly vegetarian fare, Nonomura mentions the allowance in the vinaya and in Theravāda Buddhism for eating meat that is pure in three ways.

2. Baroni 1995 (198–99) provides a brief description of the text and voices doubts about Tetsugen's authorship. Ishikawa Rikizan (1996) does not question Tetsugen's authorship of the work. Regardless of its provenance, the *Kōmori bōdanki* relates the sorts of attacks leveled against the Shinshū clergy by their opponents during the Edo period. Ishikawa later provides a detailed survey of the Shinshū literature defending clergy eating meat and marriage (2000).

3. The five grave offenses are matricide, patricide, killing an arhat, causing a Buddha to bleed, or causing a schism in the Buddhist order *(sangha)*.

4. Chikū relies on a variety of biographical sources and paintings for information about the meat eating of these monks. Cien Ji was nicknamed the "Three Vehicle Dharma Master" *(sanjo hōshi* 三乗法師) because he upheld the existence of the doctrines of three separate vehicles (i.e., methods of salvation). Later some wag stated that the three vehicles referred to three carts: one in front containing Buddha images, sūtras, and *śāstras;* one in the middle on which he rode; and one behind containing meat and wine, and women. Huineng, according to Chikū, ate meat once while traveling. Zhutou (J. Chotō) and Jianzi (J. Kensu) are often depicted in Japanese paintings as either holding up the head of a boar (as a hunter might) or using a fishing net for shrimp and eels, respectively. For Chikū's descriptions of these individuals, see *Defense*, 302a–b.

5. There are numerous possible interpretations as to the precise identity of the five smelly herbs. One list found in Japanese texts consists of leeks, onions, garlic, shallots, and ginger.

6. The five defilements consist of (1) the epoch experiencing more wars, epidemics, and famines; (2) false views becoming more widespread; (3) spiritual afflictions *(kleśa)* growing stronger; (4) people becoming weaker, becoming more ignorant, and suffering greater pain; and (5) life spans becoming shorter.

Bibliography

Abbreviations

BD   *Bukkyō daijiten* 佛教大辭典. 10 vols. Edited by Mochizuki Shinkō 望月信亨. Sekai Seiten Kankō Kyōkai, 1933–1936, 1958–1963.

BK   *Bussho kaisetsu daijiten* 佛書解説大辭典. 15 vols. Edited by Ono Genmyō 小野玄妙. Tokyo: Daitō Shuppan, 1933–1936, 1974, 1988.

DDZ   *Dengyō daishi zenshū* 傳教大師全集. 5 vols. Edited by Hieizan Senshuin nai Eizan Gakuin 比叡山専修院内叡山學院. Tokyo: Tendaishū Shūten Kankōkai, 1912.

DNB   *Dai Nihon Bukkyō zensho* 大日本佛教全書. 100 vols. Edited by Bussho Kankōkai 佛書刊行會, 1912–1922. Revised by Suzuki Gakujutsu Zaidan 鈴木学術財団. Tokyo: Kōdansha, 1972–1975.

DZ   *Daozang* 道臧. 1,120 vols. Edited by Hanfenlou 涵芬搜. Shanghai: Shangwu Yinshu Guan, 1924–1926.

DZZ   *Dōgen zenji zenshū* 道元禪師全集. 2 vols. Edited by Ōkubo Dōshū 大久保道舟. Tokyo: Chikuma Shobō, 1969–1970.

ER   *Encyclopedia of Religion*. 16 vols. Edited by Mircea Eliade. New York: Macmillan, 1987.

ESG   *Eihei shōbō genzō shūsho taisei* 永平正法眼藏蒐書大成. 25 vols. Edited by Dai Honzan Eiheijinai Eihei Shōbō Genzō Shūsho Taisei Kankōkai 大本山永平寺内永平正法眼藏蒐書大成刊行会. Tokyo: Taishūkan, 1974–1982.

FT   *Fozu tongji* 佛祖通記. Compiled by Zhipan 志盤 in 1258–1269. T 2035.

HSZ   *Shōwa shinshū Hōnen Shōnin zenshū* 昭和新修法然上人全集. Edited by Ishii Kyōdō 石井教道. 1955. Reprint. Kyoto: Heirakuji Shoten, 1974.

HY   Harvard-Yenching serial numbers for Taoist literature. See *Combined Indices to the Authors and Titles of Books in Two Collec-*

tions of Taoist Literature. Edited by Weng Tu-chien 翁獨健. Harvard-Yenching Institute Sinological Index Series, no. 25. Beijing: Yanjing University, 1925.

JCL   *Jingde chuandeng lu* 景德傳燈録. Compiled by Daoyuan 道原, 1004. T 2076.

JD   *Jōdoshū daijiten* 浄土宗大辞典. 4 vols. Edited by Jōdoshū Daijiten Hensan Iinkai 浄土宗大辞典編纂委員会. Tokyo: Sankibō, 1974–1982.

JZ   *Jōdoshū zensho* 浄土宗全書. 20 vols. Edited by Jōdoshū Shūten Kankōkai 浄土宗宗典刊行會. Tokyo: Jōdoshū Shūten Kankōkai, 1907–1914.

ND   *Nihon daizōkyō* 日本大藏經. 100 vols. Edited by Nakano Tatsue 中野達慧 et al., 1914–1922. Revised by Suzuki Gakujutsu Zaidan 鈴木学術財団. Tokyo: Kōdansha, 1973–1978.

NSI   *Shōwa teihon Nichiren Shōnin ibun* 昭和定本日蓮聖人遺文. 3 vols. Edited by Risshō Daigaku Shūgaku Kenkyūjo 立正大学宗学研究. Minobu, Japan: Sōhonzan Minobu Kuonji, 1953.

Peking   *Eiin Pekinban Chibetto Daizōkyō* 影印北京版西藏大藏經. 169 vols. Peking edition of the Tibetan Tripiṭaka, reprinted under the supervision of Ōtani University, Kyoto. Kyoto: Tibetan Tripiṭaka Research Institute, 1956–1962.

Pelliot   Pelliot serial numbers, Collection of Dunhuang Manuscripts, held in the Bibliothèque Nationale, Paris. See *Catalogue des manuscrits chinois de Touen-houang, fonds Pelliot chinois.* 5 vols. Établi par Jacques Gernet et Wu Chi-yu, avec la collaboration de Marie-Rose Séguy et Hélène Vetch, sous la direction de Marie-Roberte Guignard. Paris: Bibliothèque Nationale, 1970–1995.

QQT   *Qinding quan Tangwen* 欽定全唐文. 1,000 fasc. Edited by Tung Kao 薫誥 et al. 1814. Reprinted in 20 vols. Taipei: Huai-wen Shu-chü, 1961.

SED   *Saidaiji Eison denki shūsei* 西大寺叡尊傳記集成. Edited by Nara Kokuritsu Bunkazai Kenkyūjo 奈良国立文化財研究所. Kyoto: Hōzōkan, 1977.

SGZ   *Song gaoseng zhuan* 宋高僧傳. Compiled by Zanning 贊寧 (919–1002). T 2061.

SSZ   *Shinshū shōgyō zensho* 眞宗聖教全書. 5 vols. Edited by Shinshū Shōgyō Zensho Hensanjo 眞宗聖教全書編纂所. Kyoto: Kōkyō Shoin, 1940–1941.

Stein   Stein serial numbers, Collection of Dunhuang Manuscripts, held in the British Museum, London. See Lione Giles. *Descriptive Catalogue of the Chinese Manuscripts from Tunhuang in the British Museum.* London: British Museum, 1957.

SZS   *Shinshū zensho* 眞宗全書. Edited by Tsumaki Jikiryō 妻木直良.
        Tokyo: Zōkyō Shoin, 1913–1916.

T   *Taishō shinshū daizōkyō* 大正新脩大藏經. 100 vols. Edited by Taka-
        kusu Junjirō 高楠順次朗 and Watanabe Kaikyoku 渡邊海旭.
        Tokyo: Daizōkyōkai, 1924–1935.

Vin   *The Vinaya piṭakam*. 5 vols. Edited by Hermann Oldenberg. Lon-
        don: Pali Text Society, 1879–1883.

XGZ   *Xu gaoseng zhuan* 續高僧傳. Compiled by Daoxuan 道宣 (596–667).
        T 2060.

Z   *Dainippon zoku zōkyō* 大日本續藏經. 750 vols. in 150 cases. Edited
        by Maeda Eun 前田慧雲 and Nakano Tatsue 中野達慧. Kyoto:
        Zōkyō Shoin, 1905–1912.

ZGR   *Zoku gunsho ruijū* 續群書類從. 19 vols. Compiled by Hanawa Hoki-
        noichi 塙保己一 and Hanawa Tadatomi 塙忠寶. 1903. Reprint
        Tokyo: Zoku Gunsho Ruijū Kanseikai, 1929.

ZJZ   *Zoku Jōdoshū zensho* 續淨土宗全書. 19 vols. Edited by Shūsho
        Hozonkai 宗書保存會. 1915. Reprinted and edited by Jōdoshū
        Shūten Kankōkai 淨土宗宗典刊行會. Tokyo: Sankibō Bus-
        shorin, 1972–1974.

ZT   *Zengaku taikei* 禪學大系. 8 vols. Edited by Zengaku Taikei Hensan-
        kyoku 禪學大系編纂局. Tokyo: Ikkatsusha, 1913.

Primary Sources

Aṣṭasāsasrikā prajñā-pāramitā. Edited by Rājendralāla Mitra. Calcutta: Bap-
tist Mission Press, 1988.

Bai Juyi ji 白居易集. Bai Juyi 白居易 (772–846). Beijing: Zhonghua Shuju,
1979.

Bodhisattva prātimokṣa sūtra. See "Bodhisattva Prātimokṣa Sūtra." Edited
by Nalinaksha Dutt. *Indian Historical Quarterly* 7, no. 2 (1931):
259–286.

Bodhisattva Stage. See (1) *Pusa dichi jing* 菩薩地持經, T no. 1581; (2) *Bodhisattvabhūmi*, Sanskrit text edited by Wogihara 1971; (3) *Pusa shanjie jing* 菩薩善戒經, T nos. 1582–1583.

Brahmā Net Sūtra. See *Fanwang jing* 梵網經, T no. 1484.

Classified Legal Articles. See *Qingyuan tiaofa shilei* 慶元條法事類. Ca. 1195–
1200. Reprint. Taipei: Xinwenfeng Chubanshe, 1976.

Dari jing shu 大日經疏. See *Da piluzhena chengfo jing shu* 大毘盧遮那成佛經
疏, T no. 1796.

Defense of Meat Eating and Wives. Chikū 智空. See *Nikujiki saitai ben* 肉食妻
帶辨, SZS 59:293–318.

Enzan wadei gassuishū 塩山和泥合水集. Bassui Tokushō 拔隊得勝 (1327–
1387). In *Chūsei Zenke no shisō* 中世禪家の思想, edited by Ichikawa Hakugen 市川白弦, Iriya Yoshitaka 入矢義高, and Yanagida

Seizan 柳田聖山. Nihon Shisō Taikei 日本思想大系, vol. 16. Tokyo: Iwanami Shoten, 1972.

Five Part Vinaya (Mahīśāsaka Vinaya). See *Wufen lü* 五分律, T nos. 1421–1424.

Four Part Vinaya (Dharmaguptaka Vinaya). See *Sifen lü* 四分律, T. no. 1428.

Golden Light Sūtra. See *Jinguangming zuishengwang jing* 金光明最勝王經, T no. 665.

Jetavana Diagram. Daoxuan 道宣 (596–667). See *Zhong Tianzhu Sheweiguo Qihuan si tu jing* 中天竺舍衛國祇洹寺圖經, T no. 1899.

Jingde Era Transmission of the Lamp. Daoyuan 道原. See *Jingde chuandeng lu* 景德傳燈録, T no. 2076.

Jinhuazi 金華子. Liu Chongyuan 劉崇遠 (10th century). Shanghai: Zhonghua Shuju, 1958.

Jinshi cuibian 金石萃編. Compiled by Wang Chang 王昶 in 1805. Shanghai: Saoye Shanfang, 1921.

Jiu Tang shu 舊唐書. Compiled by Liu Xu 劉昫 in 945. Beijing: Zhonghua Shuju, 1975.

Kongō busshi. Eison 叡尊 (1201–1290). See *Kongō busshi Eison kanjin gakushōki* 金剛佛子叡尊感身學正記. In SED, pp. 1–63.

Kōzen gokokuron 興禪護國論. Eisai 榮西 (1141–1215) in 1198. In *Chūsei Zenke no shisō* 中世禪家の思想, edited by Ichikawa Hakugen 市川白弦, Iriya Yoshitaka 入矢義高, and Yanagida Seizan 柳田聖山. Nihon Shisō Taikei 日本思想大系, vol. 16. Tokyo: Iwanami Shoten, 1972.

Lijing zhengyi 禮經正義. Annotated by Zheng Xuan 鄭玄 (127–100 BCE) and Kong Yingda 孔穎達 (574–648). In *Shisan jing zhushu* 十三經注疏. Reprint of 1815 edition, based on a Song-dynasty edition. Taipei: Dahua Shuju, 1982.

Lotus Sūtra. See *Miaofa lianhua jing* 妙法蓮華經, T no. 262.

Mahāsāṃghika Vinaya. See *Mahesengqi lü* 摩訶僧祇律, T nos. 1425–1427.

Mahāvairocana Sūtra (Dari jing 大日經). See *Da piluzhena chengfo shenbian jiachi jing* 大毘盧遮那成佛神變加持經, T no. 848.

Mūlasarvāstivāda Vinaya. See *Genben shuoyiqieyoubu lü* 根本説一切有部律, T nos. 1442–1459.

Myriad Good Deeds Share the Same End. Yongming Yanshou 永明延壽 (904–975). See *Wanshan tonggui ji* 萬善同歸集, T no. 2017.

"Nichirenshū rokuji" 日蓮宗録事. 1898. *Meikyō shinshi* 明教新誌 596:2–3.

Nittō guhō junrei kōki 入唐求法巡禮行記. Ennin 圓仁 (794–864). Edited by Bai Huawen 白化文 et al. *Ru Tang qiufa xunli xingji xiaozhu* 入唐求法巡禮行記校註. Shijiazhuang: Huashan Wenyi Chubanshe, 1992.

One Mind Vajra Precept Essence Secrets. Eisai (1141–1215). See *Isshin kongō kaitai hiketsu* 一心金剛戒體秘決. Matsugaoka Bunko 松ヶ岡文庫 manuscript (ca. 1492–1500). In Furuta 1971, pp. 154–156.

Ordination Platform Diagram. Daoxuan 道宣 (596–667). See *Guanzhong chuangli jietan tu jing* 關中創立戒壇圖經, T no. 1892.

Nenpu 年譜. Compiled by Jikō 慈光 in 1688–1703. See *Saidai chokushi Kōshō bosatsu gyōjitsu nenpu* 西大勅諡興正菩薩行實年譜. In SED, pp. 107–267.

Platform Sūtra. See *Liuzu tan jing* 六祖壇經, T nos. 2007–2008.

Pure Rules for Chan Monasteries. Compiled by Changlu Zongze 長蘆宗賾 in 1103. See *Chanyuan qinggui* 禪苑清規. Edited by Kagamishima Genryū 鏡島元隆 et al. *Yakuchū Zennen shingi* 訳註禪苑清規. Tokyo: Sōtōshū Shūmuchō, 1972.

Quanshan xianzhi 銓山縣志. 1683. *Zhongguo fangzhi congshu* 中國方志叢書, series 3.3 (Jiangxi), no. 908.

Quan Tang wen 全唐文. Compiled by Dong Gao 董誥 in 1818. Palace edition.

Shakunan Shinshū sōgi 釋難眞宗僧儀. 1760. Erin 慧琳 (1715–1789). SZS 59:340–350.

Shike shiliao xinban 石刻史料新編. Series 1. Taipei: Xinwenfeng Chubanshe, 1982.

Shiwu jiyuan 事物紀原. Compiled by Gao Cheng 高承 during 1078–1085. Beijing: Zhonghua Shuju, 1989.

Shokuniku taisai ben 食肉帶妻辨. Hōrin 法霖 (1693–1741). (copied 1821). Shidō Bunko Meiji Bukkyōshi Hensanjo 斯道文庫明治佛教史編纂所. Catalog no. 1–201 *Wachū* 和中 34.

Śikṣāsamuccaya. Edited by Cecil Bendall in 1897–1902. Reprint. Delhi: Motilal Banarsidass, 1992.

Siku quanshu zhenben 四庫全書珍本. Taipei: Taiwan Shangwu Yinshuguan, 1976.

Song huiyao jigao 宋會要輯稿. Taipei: Xinwenfeng Chubanshe, 1976.

Song Lives of Eminent Monks. Compiled by Zanning 贊寧 (919–1002). See *Song gaoseng zhuan* 宋高僧傳, T no. 2061.

Songshi 宋史. Beijing: Zhonghua Shuju, 1977.

Song Yuan difang zhi congshu 宋元地方志叢書. Taipei: Dahua Shuju, 1987.

Suvarṇabhāsottama-sūtra. Edited by Johannes Nobel. Leipzig: Otto Harrassowitz, 1937.

Taiping guangji 太平廣記. Compiled by Li Fang 李昉 during 977–978. Beijing: Zhonghua Shuju, 1961.

Ten Recitation Vinaya (Sarvāstivāda Vinaya). See *Shisong lü* 十誦律, T nos. 1435–1437.

Tōshōdaiji Millenary Anniversary Hagiographies. Compiled by Gichō 義澄 in 1701. See *Shōdai senzai denki* 招提千歲傳記. DNB, vol. 64.

Upāli's Questions Sūtra on Determining [the Meaning] of Vinaya. See *Upāli paripṛcchā vinaya viniścaya-sūtra* (section 24 of the *Mahā ratnakūṭa* collection). Edited by Pierre Python. *Vinaya-Viniścaya-*

Upāli-Paripṛcchā: Enquête d'Upāli pour une exégèse de la Discipine. Paris: Adrien-Maisonneuve, 1973.

Vimalakīrti Sūtra. See *Weimojie suoshuo jing* 維摩詰所説經, T no. 475.

Vinaya Characteristics Revelations. See *Lüxiang gantong zhuan* 律相感通傳, T no. 1898.

Vinaya Cloister Saṅgha Jewel Hagiographies. Compiled by Eken 慧堅 in 1689. See *Ritsuon sōbōden* 律苑僧寶傳. DNB, vol. 64.

Yili zhushu 儀禮注疏. Annotated by Zheng Xuan 鄭玄 (127–100 BCE) and Jia Gongyan 賈公彥 (Tang dynasty). In *Shisan jing zhushu* 十三經注疏. Reprint of 1815 edition, based on a Song-dynasty edition. Taipei: Dahua Shuju, 1982.

Yinhua lu 因話録. Zhao Lin 趙璘 (9th century). Shanghai: Shanghai Guji Chubanshe, 1979.

Yogācārabhūmi. See *Yujiashi dilun* 瑜伽師地論, T no. 1579.

Yuikai 遺誡. Kūkai 空海 (774–835). In *Kōbō daishi chosaku zenshū* 弘法大師著作全集, edited by Katsumata Shunkyō 勝又俊教, 2:164–166. Tokyo: Sankibō Busshorin, 1970.

Zhizhai shulu jieti 直齋書録解題. Chen Zhensun 陳振孫 (13th century). Shanghai: Shanghai Guji Chubanshe, 1987.

Zizhi tongjian 資治通鑑. Compiled by Sima Guang 司馬光 during 1067–1084. Beijing: Zhonghua Shuju, 1956.

Zōdanshū 雜談集. Mujū Dōgyō 無住道暁 (Ichien 一圓; 1226–1312). Edited by Yamada Shōzen 山田昭全 and Miki Sumito 三木紀人. Chūsei no Bungaku 中世の文学, vol. 1, no. 3. Tokyo: Miyai Shoten, 1973.

Secondary Sources

Abe Chōichi 阿部肇一. 1953. "Goetsu Chūi ō no Bukkyōsaku ni kansuru ichi kōsatsu" 呉越忠懿王の仏教策に関する一考察. *Komazawa shigaku* 駒沢史学 2:19–30.

Andō Toshio 安藤俊雄 and Sonoda Koyū 薗田香融. 1974. *Saichō* 最澄. Nihon Shisō Taikei 日本思想大系, vol. 4. Tokyo: Iwanami Shoten.

Andō, Yoshinori. 1994. "The World of the Yuikyogyo." *Zen Quarterly* 6, no. 2:10–14.

Asai Endō 浅井円道. 1975. *Jōko Nihon Tendai honmon shisōshi* 上古日本天台本門思想史. Kyoto: Heirakuji Shoten.

Baroni, Helen J. 1994. "Bottled Anger: Episodes in Ōbaku Conflict in the Tokugawa Period." *Japanese Journal of Religious Studies* 21, nos. 2–3:191–210.

Barrett, T. H. 1992. *Li Ao: Buddhist, Taoist or Neo-Confucian?* Oxford: Oxford University Press.

———. 1994. Review of *The Cavern-Mystery Transmission: A Taoist Ordination Rite of A.D. 711* by Charles Benn. *Bulletin of the School of Oriental and African Studies* 47, no. 2:414–415.

————. 1996. *Taoism Under the T'ang: Religion & Empire during the Golden Age of Chinese History.* London: Wellsweep.

Bell, Catherine. 1992. *Ritual Theory, Ritual Practice.* New York: Oxford University Press.

Benn, Charles. 1977. "Taoism as Ideology in the Reign of Emperor Hsüan-tsang (712–755)." Ph.D. diss., University of Michigan.

————. 1991. *The Cavern-Mystery Transmission: A Taoist Ordination Rite of A.D. 711.* Honolulu: University of Hawai'i Press.

————. 1998. "Daoist Ordinations and Retreats in Medieval China." Unpublished manuscript.

Bodiford, William M. 1991. "Dharma Transmission in Sōtō Zen: Manzan Dōhaku's Reform Movement." *Monumenta Nipponica* 46, no. 4: 423–451.

————. 1993. *Sōtō Zen in Medieval Japan.* Honolulu: University of Hawai'i Press.

————. trans. 1999. "Kokan Shiren's 'Zen Precept Procedures.'" In *Religions of Japan in Practice,* edited by George J. Tanabe Jr., 98–108. Princeton, N.J.: Princeton University Press.

————. trans. 2000. "Emptiness and Dust: Zen Dharma Transmission Rituals." In *Tantra in Practice,* edited by David Gordon White, 299–307. Princeton, N.J.: Princeton University Press.

Bokenkamp, Stephen R. 1983. "Sources of the Ling-pao Scriptures." In *Tantric and Taoist Studies in Honour of R. A. Stein,* edited by Michel Strickmann, 2:434–485. *Mélanges chinoises et bouddhiques,* no. 21. Brussels: Institute Belge des Hautes Études Chinoises.

————, ed. 1997. *Early Daoist Scriptures.* Berkeley: University of California Press.

Bowring, Richard. 1992. "The *Ise monogatari:* A Short Cultural History." *Harvard Journal of Asiatic Studies* 52, no. 2:401–480.

Braverman, Arthur, trans. 1989. *Mud and Water: A Collection of Talks by the Zen Master Bassui.* San Francisco: North Point Press.

Buswell, Robert E., Jr., ed. 1990. *Chinese Buddhist Apocrypha.* Honolulu: University of Hawai'i Press.

Cedzich, Angelika. 1993. "Ghosts and Demons, Law and Order: Grave Quelling Texts and Early Taoist Liturgy." *Taoist Resources* 4, no. 2:23–33.

Chadwick, David. 1999. *Crooked Cucumber: The Life and Zen Teaching of Shunryu Suzuki.* New York: Broadway Books.

Chan, Alan. 1991. *Two Visions of the Way.* Albany: State University of New York Press.

Chappell, David W. 1990. "Formless Repentance in Comparative Perspective." In *Fo Kuang Shan Report of International Conference on Ch'an Buddhism,* 251–267. Tashu, Kaohsiung, Taiwan: Fo Kuang Publishers.

———. 1991. "Stories in Buddhist Repentance Liturgies." In *Tendai shisō to Higashi Ajia bunka no kenkyū: Shioiri Ryōdō sensei tsuitō ronbunshū* 天台思想と東アジア文化の研究、塩入良道先生追悼論文集, edited by Muranaka Yūsei 村中祐生, 65–76. Tokyo: Sankibō.

———. 1995. Introduction to *Divine Emptiness and Historical Fullness: A Buddhist-Jewish-Christian Conversation with Masao Abe*, edited by Christopher Ives, 4–21. Valley Forge, Penn.: Trinity Press International.

———. 1997. "Buddhist Compassion (ci-bei 慈悲) and Zhiyi's Moho Zhiguan 摩訶止觀." In *Tendai daishi kenkyū* 天台大師研究, 1–23. Kyoto: Tendai Gakkai.

Ch'en, Kenneth. 1956. "The Sale of Monk Certificates during the Sung Dynasty: A Factor in the Decline of Buddhism in China." *Harvard Theological Review* 49:307–327.

———. 1964. *Buddhism in China: A Historical Survey*. Princeton, N.J.: Princeton University Press.

Chen Yinke 陳寅恪. 1980. "Li Deyu biansi nianyue ji guizang chuanshuo bianzheng" 李德裕貶死年月及歸葬傳説辨證. Reprinted in *Jinmingguan conggao erbian* 金明館叢稿二編, 8–51. Shanghai: Shanghai Guji Chubanshe.

Chen Zuolong 陳祚龍. 1989. *Dunhuangxue sance xinji* 敦煌學散策新集. Taipei: Xinwenfeng.

Chikusa Masaaki 竺沙雅章. 1982. *Chūgoku Bukkyō shakaishi kenkyū* 中国仏教社会史研究. Kyoto: Dōhōsha.

Childs, Margaret H. 1980. "'Chigo Monogatari': Love Stories or Buddhist Sermons?" *Monumenta Nipponica* 35:127–151.

Chou I-liang. 1945. "Tantrism in China." *Harvard Journal of Asiatic Studies* 8:241–332.

Cohen, Alvin P. 1982. *Tales of Vengeful Souls: A Sixth-Century Collection of Chinese Avenging Ghost Stories*. Taipei: Ricci Institute.

Collcutt, Martin. 1981. *Five Mountains: The Rinzai Zen Monastic Institution in Medieval Japan*. Cambridge, Mass.: Harvard University Press.

Dayal, Har. 1970. *The Bodhisattva Doctrine in Buddhist Sanskrit Literature*. 1932. Reprint, Delhi: Motilal Banarsidass.

de Groot, J. J. M. 1893. *Le Code du Mahāyāna en Chine: Son influence sur la vie monacale et sur le monde laïque*. Amsterdam: Johannes Müller.

Demiéville, Paul. 1954. "La Yogācārabhūmi de Saṅgharakṣa." *Bulletin de l'École Française d'Extrême-Orient* 44, no. 2:339–436.

de Visser, M. W. 1935. *Ancient Buddhism in Japan*. Vol. 1. Leiden: E. J. Brill.

Dobbins, James C. 1989. *Jōdo Shinshū: Shin Buddhism in Medieval Japan*. Bloomington: Indiana University Press.

Donner, Neal, and Daniel Stevenson. 1993. *The Great Calming and Contemplation: A Study and Annotated Translation of the First Chapter of Chih-i's* Mo-ho chih-kuan. Kuroda Institute Classics of East Asian Buddhism. Honolulu: University of Hawai'i Press.

Dudbridge, Glen. 1988. "Three Fables of Paradise Lost." *Bulletin of the British Association for Chinese Studies,* 27–36.

Dutt, Nalinaksha. 1931. "Bodhisattva Prātimokṣa Sūtra." *Indian Historical Quarterly* 7, no. 2:259–286.

Eberhard, Wolfram. 1967. *Guilt and Sin in Traditional China.* Berkeley: University of California Press.

Eckel, M. David. 1997. "A Buddhist Approach to Repentance." In *Repentance: A Comparative Perspective,* edited by Amitai Etzioni and David W. Carney. New York: Rowman & Littlefield.

Edamatsu Shigeyuki 枝松茂之 et al., eds. 1983–1986. *Meiji nyūsu jiten* 明治ニュース事典. 9 vols. Tokyo: Mainichi Komunikēshonzu Shuppanbu.

Eichhorn, W. 1968. *Beitrag zur Rechtlichen Stellung des Buddhismus und Taoismus im Sung-Staat.* Monographies du Toung Pao, vol. 7. Leiden: E. J. Brill.

Etani Ryūkai 惠谷隆戒. 1972. "Enkai sōsho: Kaisetsu" 圓戒叢書、解説. In ZJZ 12:1–14.

———. 1978. *Endonkai gairon* 円頓戒概論. 1937. Rev. (*kaitei* 改訂) ed. Tokyo: Daitō Shuppansha.

Faure, Bernard. 1986. "Bodhidharma as Textual and Religious Paradigm." *History of Religions* 25, no. 3:187–198.

———. 1987. "Space and Place in Chinese Religious Traditions." *History of Religions* 26, no. 4:337–356.

———. 1988. *La volonté d'orthodoxie dans le bouddhisme chinois.* Paris: Centre National de la Recherche Scientifique.

———. 1989. *The Rural Economy of Pre-Liberation China.* Hong Kong: Oxford University Press.

———. 1991. *The Rhetoric of Immediacy: A Cultural Critique of Chan/Zen Buddhism.* Princeton, N.J.: Princeton University Press.

———. 1993. *Chan Insights and Oversights: An Epistemological Critique of the Chan Tradition.* Princeton, N.J.: Princeton University Press.

———. 1996. *Visions of Power: Imagining Medieval Japanese Buddhism.* Translated by Phyllis Brooks. Princeton, N.J.: Princeton University Press.

Faure, David. 1989. *The Rural Economy of Pre-Liberation China.* Hong Kong: Oxford University, Press.

Forte, Antonino. 1988. *Mingtang and Buddhist Utopias in the History of the*

Astronomical Clock: The Tower, Statue and Armillary Sphere Constructed by Empress Wu. Rome: Istituto Italiano per il Medio ed Estremo Oriente.

Foulk, T. Griffith. 1987. "The 'Ch'an School' and Its Place in the Buddhist Monastic Tradition." Ph.D. diss., University of Michigan.

———. 1993. "Myth, Ritual, and Monastic Practice in Sung Ch'an Buddhism." In *Religion and Society in T'ang and Sung China,* edited by Patricia Buckley Ebrey and Peter N. Gregory, 147–208. Honolulu: University of Hawai'i Press.

Fu, Charles Wei-hsun, and Sandra A. Wawrytko. 1994. *Buddhist Behavioral Codes and the Modern World: An International Symposium.* Westport, Conn.: Greenwood Press.

Fujii Masao 藤井正雄, ed. 1979. *Jōdoshū* 浄土宗. Nihon Bukkyō Kiso Kōza 日本仏教基礎講座, vol. 4. Tokyo: Yūzankaku.

Fujita Kōkan 藤田光寬. 1983. "Byaṅ chub bzaṅ po cho 'bosatsu ritsugi giki' ni tsuite" Byaṅ chub bzaṅ po 著「菩薩律儀儀軌」について. *Mikkyō bunka* 密教文化 141:87–100.

Fukuda Gyōei 福田尭穎. 1954. *Tendaigaku gairon* 天台学概論. Tokyo: Bun'ichi Shuppan.

Fukuda Gyōkai 福田行誡. 1942. *Sessō tōmon* 雪窓答問. 1876; corrected by Ōuchi Seiran 大内青巒 in 1887. Reprinted in *Gyōkai shōnin zenshū* 行誡上人全集, edited by Mochizuki Shindō 望月信道, 161–182. Tokyo: Daitō Shuppansha.

Fukui Kōjun 福井康順. 1955. *Tōyō shisō no kenkyū* 東洋思想の研究. Tokyo: Risōsha.

Fukunaga Mitsuji 福永光司. 1982. "Dōkyō ni okeru tenjin kōrin jukai" 道教における天神降臨授誡. In *Chūgoku chūsei no shūkyō to bunka* 中國中世の宗教と文化, 1–46. Kyoto: Kyōto Daigaku Jinbun Kagaku Kenkyūjo.

Funayama Tōru 船山徹. 1995. "Rikuchō jidai ni okeru bosatsukai no juyō katei" 六朝時代における菩薩戒の受容過程. *Tōhō gakuhō* 東方學報 67:1–135.

Furukawa Taigo 古川碓悟. 1938. *Sōryo saitai ron* 僧侶妻帯論. Tokyo: Chūō Bukkyōsha.

Furuta Shōkin 古田紹欽. 1971. *Nihon Bukkyō shisōshi* 日本仏教思想史. Tokyo: Kadokawa Shoten.

———. 1981a. "Daruma sōjō isshinkai giki o megutte" 達磨相承一心儀軌をめぐって. In *Daijō Bukkyō kara mikkyō e: Katsumata Shukyō hakase koki kinen ronshū* 大乗仏教から密教へ、勝又俊教博士古稀記念論集, edited by Katsumata Shunkyō Hakase Koki Kinen Ronshū Kankōkai 勝又俊教博士古稀記念論文集刊行会, 1197–1206. Tokyo: Shunjūsha.

———. 1981b. "Dōgen in okeru jikai jiritsu shisō no tenkai" 道元における持

戒持律思想の展開. 1964. Reprinted in *Nihon Bukkyō shisōshi* 日本仏教思想史, 279–301. Furuta Shōkin Chosakushū 古田紹欽著作集, vol. 1. Tokyo: Kōdansha.

———. 1981c. "Eisai ni okeru jikai jiritsu shisō no igi" 栄西における持戒持律思想の意義. 1964. Reprinted in *Nihon Bukkyō shisōshi*, 259–279. Furuta Shōkin Chosakushū, vol. 1. Tokyo: Kōdansha.

———. 1981d. "Kamakura Bukkyō ni okeru jikai jiritsu shugi to han jikai jiritsu shugi: Hōnen no baai" 鎌倉仏教における持戒持律主義と反持戒持律主義・法然の場合. 1958. Reprinted in *Nihon Bukkyō shisōshi*, 243–258. Furuta Shōkin Chosakushū, vol. 1. Tokyo: Kōdansha.

———. 1988. *Nihon Zenshūshi no sho mondai* 日本禅宗史の諸問題. Tokyo: Daitō Shuppan.

Gernet, Jacques. 1995. *Buddhism in Chinese Society: An Economic History from the Fifth to the Tenth Centuries.* Translated by Franciscus Verellen. 1956. Reprint, New York: Columbia University Press.

Getz, Daniel A., Jr. 1994. "Siming Zhili and Tiantai Pure Land in the Song Dynasty." Ph.D. diss., Yale University.

Gómez, Luis O. 1987. "Sarvāstivāda." In ER, 13:78b.

Gregory, Peter N. 1991. *Tsung-mi and the Sinification of Buddhism.* Princeton, N.J.: Princeton University Press.

Groner, Paul. 1987. "Annen, Tankei, Henjō, and Monastic Discipline in the Tendai School: The Background of the 'Futsū jubosatsukai kōshaku.'" *Japanese Journal of Religious Studies* 14, nos. 2–3:129–159.

———. 1989. "The Lotus Sūtra and Saichō's Interpretation of the Realization of Buddhahood within This Very Body." In *The Lotus Sūtra in Japanese Culture,* edited by George Tanabe Jr. and Willa Jane Tanabe, 53–74. Honolulu: University of Hawai'i Press.

———. 1990a. "The Fan-wang ching and Monastic Discipline in Japanese Tendai: A Study of Annen's 'Futsū jubosatsukai kōshaku.'" In *Chinese Buddhist Apocrypha,* edited by Robert E. Buswell Jr., 251–290. Honolulu: University of Hawai'i Press.

———. 1990b. "The Ordination Ritual in the Platform Sūtra Within the Context of the East Asian Buddhist Vinaya Tradition." In *Fo Kuang Shan Report of International Conference on Ch'an Buddhism,* 220–250. Kaohsiung: Fo Kuang.

———. 1992. "Shortening the Path: The Interpretation of the Realization of Buddhahood in This Very Existence in the Early Tendai School." In *Paths to Liberation: Mārga and Its Transformations in Buddhist Thought,* edited by Robert Buswell and Robert Gimello, 439–374. Honolulu: University of Hawai'i Press.

———. 1995. "A Medieval Japanese Reading of the Mo-ho chi-kuan: Placing the Kankō ruijū in Historical Context." *Japanese Journal of Religious Studies* 22, nos. 1–2:49–81.

———. 2000. *Saichō: The Establishment of the Japanese Tendai School.* 1984. Reprint, Honolulu: University of Hawai'i Press.

———. 2002a. "The Relics and Images of Eison." In *Living Images: Japanese Buddhist Icons in Context,* edited by Robert H. Sharf and Elizabeth Horton Sharf, 114–150, 230–239. Stanford, Calif.: Stanford University Press.

———. 2002b. "Vicissitudes in the Ordinations of Japanese 'Nuns' during the Eighth through Tenth Centuries." In *Engendering Faith: Women and Buddhsim in Premodern Japan,* edited by Barbara Ruch, 65–108. Ann Arbor: University of Michigan, Center for Japanese Studies Publications.

Haar, B. J. Ter. 1992. *The White Lotus Teachings in Chinese Religious History.* Leiden: E. J. Brill.

Hamada Kōsei 浜田耕生. 1967. "Nihon no Jōdokyō ni okeru kai ni tsuite" 日本の浄土教における戒について. In *Bukkyō ni okeru kai no mondai* 仏教における戒の問題, edited by Nihon Bukkyō Gakkai 日本仏教学会, 297–314. Kyoto: Heirakuji Shoten.

Hansen, Valerie. 1990. *Changing the Gods in Medieval China, 1127–1276.* Princeton, N.J.: Princeton University Press.

———. 1993. "Gods on Walls." In *Religion and Society in T'ang and Sung China,* edited by Patricia Buckley Ebrey and Peter N. Gregory, 75–114. Honolulu: University of Hawai'i Press.

Harada Nobuo 原田信男. 1993. *Rekishi no naka no kome to niku* 歴史の中の米と肉. Tokyo: Heibonsha.

Harper, Donald. 1994. "Resurrection in Warring States Popular Religion." *Taoist Resources* 5, no. 2:13–28.

Harrison, Paul. 1990. *The Samādhi of Direct Encounter with the Buddhas of the Present.* Tokyo: The International Institute for Buddhist Studies.

Hartman, Charles. 1986. *Han Yü and the T'ang Search for Unity.* Princeton, N.J.: Princeton University Press.

He Ziquan 何茲全. 1986. "Zhonggu shidai Zhongguo Fojiao siyuan" 中古時代中國佛教寺院. 1936. In *Wushinianlai Han-Tang Fojiao siyuan jingji yanjiu* 五十年來漢唐佛教寺院經濟研究, 1–54. Beijing: Beijing Shifan Daxue Chubanshe.

Hervouet, Yves, ed. 1978. *A Sung Bibliography.* Hong Kong: The Chinese University Press.

Hinnells, John R., ed. 1991. *Who's Who of World Religions.* London: Macmillan Press.

Hirakawa Akira 平川彰. 1962. "Kaidan no gen'i" 戒壇の原意. *Indogaku Bukkyōgaku kenkyū* 印度學佛教學研究 10, no. 2:680–700.

———. 1964. *Genshi Bukkyō no kenkyū: Kyōdan soshiki no genkei* 原始仏教
の研究、教団組織の原型. Tokyo: Shunjūsha.

———. 1970. *Ritsuzō no kenkyū* 律蔵の研究. Tokyo: Sankibō Busshorin.

———. 1989. *Shoki Daijō Bukkyō no kenkyū* 初期大乗仏教の研究. 1968. Reprinted as vols. 3–4 of Hirakawa Akira Chosakushū 平川彰著作集.
Tokyo: Shunjūsha.

———. 1990a. "Daijōkai to bosatsu kaikyō" 大乗戒と菩薩戒経. 1960. Reprinted in *Jōdo shisō to daijōkai* 浄土思想と大乗戒, 253–245. Hirakawa Akira Chosakushū, vol. 7. Tokyo: Shunjūsha.

———. 1990b. "Shoki Daijō Bukkyō no kaigaku toshite no jūzendō" 初期
大乗仏教の戒学としての十善道. 1968. Reprinted in *Jōdo shisō to
daijōkai*, 201–238. Hirakawa Akira Chosakushū, vol. 7. Tokyo:
Shunjūsha.

———. 1993–1995. *Nihyaku gojukkai no kenkyū* 二百五十戒の研究. 4 vols.
Hirakawa Akira Chosakushū, vols. 14–17. Tokyo: Shunjūsha.

Hori, Victor. 1994. "Sweet-and-sour Buddhism." *Tricycle* 4, no. 1:48–52.

Horizawa Somon 堀沢祖門. 1984. "Kōsōgyō no hanashi" 好相行の話. 1979.
Reprinted in *Gudō henreki: Jūninen rōzan soshite sono go* 求道遍
歴：十二年籠山、そしてその後, 70–86. Kyoto: Hōzōkan.

———. 1994. "Gyō ni ikiru (1): Kōsōgyō no taiken" 行に生きる (1)：好相行
の体験. *Hakuju* 柏樹 9:6–11.

Hosokawa Ryōichi 細川涼一. 1987. *Chūsei no Risshū jiin to minshū* 中世の
律宗寺院と民衆. Tokyo: Yoshikawa Kōbunkan.

———. 1989. "Ōken to niji: Chūsei josei to shari shinkō" 王権と尼寺、中世
女性と舎利信仰. In *Onna no chūsei* 女の中世, edited by Hosokawa
Ryōichi, 124–160. Tokyo: Editā Skūru Shuppanbu.

———. 1999. *Kanjin gakushōki: Saidaiji Eison no jiden* 感身学正記、西大寺
叡尊の自伝. Tokyo: Heibonsha.

Hsu Li-ch'iang 徐立強. 1998. "A Preliminary Study of the Liang Emperor's
Repentance Ritual." *Zhonghua Foxue yanjiu* 中國佛學研究 *(Chung-
Hwa Buddhist Studies)* 2:177–206.

Hu Fuchen 胡孚琛, ed. 1995. *Zhonghua Daojiao dacidian* 中華道教大辭典.
Beijing: Zhongguo Shehui Kexue Chubanshe.

Huang Minzhi 黃敏枝. 1989. *Songdai Fojiao shehui jingjishi lunji* 宋代佛教社
會經濟史論集. Taipei: Xuesheng shuju.

Hymes, Robert. 1996. "Personal Relations and Bureaucratic Hierarchy
in Chinese Religion: Evidence from the Song Dynasty." In *Unruly
Gods: Divinity and Society in China*, edited by Meir Shahar and
Robert P. Weller, 37–69. Honolulu: University of Hawai'i Press.

Ikawa Jōkei 井川定慶. 1960. "Jōdo fusatsu shiki no kentō" 浄土布薩式の検
討. *Bukkyō Daigaku kenkyū kiyō* 佛教大学研究紀要 38:17–36.

———. 1975. "Jōdo fusatsu kai ni tsuite" 浄土布薩戒について. *Bukkyō ronsō*
仏教論叢 19:45–48.

Ikeda Shūjō 池田宗譲. 1988. "Ichigyō zenji sōken Sūgaku Kaizenji kaidan
    (1): Kaizenji kaidanshi" 一行禪師創建崇岳会善寺戒壇（一），会善寺
    戒壇史. *Sankō bunka kenkyūjo nenpō* 三康文化研究所年報 21:107–
    150.

———. 1990. "Ichigyō zenji sōken Sūgaku Kaizenji kaidan (2): Ichigyō no
    Rikkei (Kōkei no jiseki to kai shisō)" 一行禪師創建崇岳会善寺戒壇
    （二），一行の律系（弘景の事蹟と戒思想）. *Sankō bunka kenkyūjo
    nenpō* 三康文化研究所年報 23:71–113.

Imaeda Aishin 今枝愛真. 1970. *Chūsei Zenshi no kenkyū* 中世禅史の研究.
    Tokyo: Tōkyō Daigaku Shuppankai.

Imai Masaharu 今井雅晴. 1991. *Kamakura shin Bukkyō no kenkyū* 鎌倉新仏
    教の研究. Tokyo: Yoshikawa Kōbunkan.

Inagaki Hisao. 1998. *Nāgārjuna's Discourse on the Ten Stages (Daśabhūmika-
    vibhāṣā)*. Kyoto: Ryūkoku Gakkai.

Inoue Enryō 井上円了. 1898. "Nikujiki saitairon" 肉食妻帯論. *Zenshū* 禪宗
    35:25–29.

Inoue Mitsusada 井上光貞. 1971. "Eizon, Ninshō and the Saidai-ji Order,"
    Acta Asiatica 20:77–103.

———. 1975. *Nihon Jōdokyō seiritsushi no kenkyū* 日本浄土教成立史の研究.
    1956. Rev. (*shintei* 新訂) ed. Tokyo: Yamakawa Shuppansha.

Inoue Tokujō 井上徳定. 1908. *Jukai kōzetsu mozōroku* 授戒講説摸象録.
    Kyoto: Shūsuisha.

Ishida Mitsuyuki 石田充之, ed. 1972. *Shunjō Risshi: Kamakura Bukkyō no
    seiritsu* 俊芿律師、鎌倉仏教成立の研究. Kyoto: Hōzōkan.

Ishida Mizumaro 石田瑞麿. 1986a. "Eisai: Sono Zen to kai to no kankei."
    1962. Reprinted in *Nihon Bukkyō shisō kenkyū* 日本仏教思想研究,
    2:294–316. Kyoto: Hōzōkan.

———. 1986b. "Ganjin ni okeru fusatsu no igi" 鑑眞における布薩の意義.
    1968. Reprinted in *Nihon Bukkyō shisō kenkyū*, 2:80–90. Kyoto:
    Hōzōkan.

———. 1986c. *Nihon Bukkyō ni okeru kairitsu no kenkyū* 日本仏教における
    戒律の研究. 1963. Reprinted in *Nihon Bukkyō shisō kenkyū*, vol. 1.
    Kyoto: Hōzōkan.

———. 1986d. "Saichō to deshi Kōjō" 最澄と弟子光定. 1959. Reprinted in
    Nihon Bukkyō shisō kenkyū, 2:117–122. Kyoto: Hōzōkan.

———. 1995. *Nyobon* 女犯. Tokyo: Chikuma Shobō.

Ishii Kyōdō 石井教道. 1972. *Jōdo no kyōgi to sono kyōdan* 淨土の教義と其教
    團. 1929. Rev. and enl. (*kaitei zōho* 改訂増補) 1931 ed. Reprint,
    Kyoto: Fuzanbō.

Ishii Shūdō 石井修道. 1987. *Sōdai Zenshūshi no kenkyū: Chūgoku Sōtō-
    shū to Dōgen Zen* 宋代禅宗史の研究・中国曹洞宗と道元禅. Tokyo:
    Daitō Shuppansha.

Ishikawa Rikizan 石川力山. 1996. "Naikan Bunko shozō shiryō no kenkyū

(2): 'Kōmori bōdanki'—'Jōkōki' ni tsuite" 内館文庫所蔵史料の研究
(2)：「蝙蝠忘談記」・「攘攘記」について. *Komazawa Daigaku Bukkyō
Gakubu kenkyū kiyō* 駒沢大學佛教學部研究記要 54:57–146.

———. 2000. "Kinsei Bukkyō ni okeru nikujiki saitai ron" 近世佛教におけ
る肉食妻帶論. In *Chūsei no Bukkyō to shakai* 中世の佛教と社会,
edited by Ōsumi Kazuo 大隅和雄, 184–207. Tokyo: Yoshikawa
Kōbunkan.

Ishikawa Shigeo 石川重雄. 1988. "Sōdai chokusa jūjisei shōkō" 宋代勅差住
持制小考. In *Sōdai no seiji to shakai* 宋代の政治と社会, edited by
Sōdaishi Kenkyūkai, 65–104. Tokyo: Gyūkō Shoin.

Itō Shintetsu 伊藤真徹. 1958. "Jōdoshū Shaseiha no jiritsusei to shakaisei"
浄土宗捨世派の自律性と社会性. *Bukkyō daigaku kenkyū kiyō* 佛教大
学研究紀要 35:31–49.

———. 1964. "Tokugawa jidai ni okeru Jōdoshū shinkō kakushin undō"
徳川時代における浄土宗信仰革新運動. *Bukkyō daigaku kenkyū kiyō*
佛教大学研究紀要 46:1–16.

Jaffe, Richard M. 2001. *Neither Monk nor Layman: Clerical Marriage in Modern Japanese Buddhism.* Princeton, N.J.: Princeton University Press.

Jan Yü-hua. 1986. "Cultural Borrowing and Religious Identity: A Case
Study of the Taoist Religious Codes." *Chinese Studies/Hanxue
yanjiu* 4, no. 1:281–294.

Kagamishima Genryū 鏡島元隆. 1961. "Zenkai shisō no tenkai" 禪戒思想の
展開. 1939. Reprinted in *Dōgen zenji to sono monryū* 道元禅師とそ
の門流, 149–173. Tokyo: Seishin Shobō.

———. 1985a. "Endonkai to Eisai-Dōgen" 円頓戒と栄西・道元. 1962. Reprinted in *Dōgen zenji to sono shūhen* 道元禅師とその周辺, 23–34.
Tokyo: Daitō Shuppansha.

———. 1985b. "Endonkai to Zenkai" 円頓戒と禅戒. 1973. Reprinted in
Dōgen zenji to sono shūhen, 141–156. Tokyo: Daitō Shuppansha.

———. 1985c. "Zenkai no seiritsu to endonkai" 禅戒の成立と円頓戒. 1967.
Reprinted as "Endonkai to Busso shōden bosatsukai" 円頓戒と佛
祖正伝菩薩戒, in *Dōgen zenji to sono shūhen*, 157–166. Tokyo:
Daitō Shuppansha.

Kamata Shigeo 鎌田茂雄. 1969. *Chūgoku Bukkyō shisōshi kenkyū* 中国佛教
思想史研究. Tokyo: Shunjūsha.

———. 1986. *Chūgoku Bukkyō girei* 中国仏教儀礼. Tokyo: Daizō Shuppan.

———. 1992. "Futari no Chōkan" 二人の澄觀. *Indogaku Bukkyōgaku kenkyū*
印度學佛教學研究 41, no. 1:89–96.

Kamata Shigeo and Tanaka Hisao 田中久夫, ed. 1971. *Kamakura kyū Bukkyō* 鎌倉舊佛教. Nihon Shisō Taikei 日本思想大系, vol. 15. Tokyo:
Iwanami Shoten.

Kamo Gi'ichi 加茂儀一. 1976. *Nihon chikusan shi: Shokuniku-nyūraku hen*
日本畜産史：食肉・乳酪編. Tokyo: Hōsei Daigaku Shuppan Kyoku.

Kao Kuang 高光 et al. 1991. *Wen-pai tui-chao ch'üan-i 'T'ai-p'ing kuang chi'* 文白對照全譯「太平廣記」. Tienjin: T'ien-chin Ku-chi Ch'u-pan-she.

Kapleau, Philip. 1982. *To Cherish All Life: A Buddhist Case for Becoming Vegetarian.* San Francisco: Harper & Row.

Kawaguchi Kōfū 川口高風. 1976. "Sōtōshū no kairitsu kenkyū shiryō to kenkyū dōkō" 曹洞宗の戒律研究資料と研究動向. *Zen kenkyūjo kiyō* 禪研究所記要 6–7:93–115.

Ketelaar, James E. 1990. *Of Heretics and Martyrs in Meiji Japan.* Princeton, N.J.: Princeton University Press.

Kieschnick, John. 1997. *The Eminent Monk: Buddhist Ideals in Medieval Chinese Hagiography.* Kuroda Institute Studies in East Asian Buddhism, no. 10. Honolulu: University of Hawai'i Press.

Kleeman, Terry F. 1998. *Great Perfection: Religion and Ethnicity in a Chinese Millennial Kingdom.* Honolulu: University of Hawai'i Press.

Kodera, Takashi James. 1980. *Dōgen's Formative Years in China: A Historical Study and Annotated Translation of the Hōkyō-ki.* London: Routledge and Kegan Paul.

Komazawa Daigaku Zenshūshi Kenkyūkai 駒沢大学禅宗史研究会, ed. 1978. *Enō kenkyū* 慧能研究. Tokyo: Taishūkan Shoten.

Kuo, Li-ying. 1994. *Confession et contrition dans le bouddhisme chinois de V^e au Xe siècle.* Paris: L'École Française d'Extrême-Orient.

Kuriyama Taion 栗山泰音. 1917. *Sōryo kazoku ron* 僧侶家族論. Tokyo: Ōju Gedō.

Kuroda Toshio 黒田俊雄. 1980. "Chūsei jisha seiryoku ron" 中世寺社勢力論. In *Chūsei* 中世, vol. 2. Iwanami Kōza: Nihon Rekishi 岩波講座・日本歴史 6:245–295. Tokyo: Iwanami Shoten.

Lagerway, John. 1981. *Wu-shang pi-yao: Somme Taoiste du VIe siècle.* Paris: L'École Française d'Extrême-Orient.

Levering, Miriam. 1989. "Scripture and Its Reception: A Buddhist Case." In *Rethinking Scripture,* edited by Miriam Levering, 58–101. Albany: State University of New York Press.

Lewis, Mark Edward. 1990. "The Suppression of the Three Stages Sect: Apocrypha as a Political Issue." In *Chinese Buddhist Apocrypha,* edited by Robert Buswell Jr., 207–238. Honolulu: University of Hawai'i Press.

Li Fang 李昉 et al. 1959. *Taiping guangji* 太平廣記. Beijing: Renmin Wenxue Chubanshe.

Liu Zongyuan 柳宗元. 1961. *Liu Hedong ji* 柳河東記. Beijing: Zhonghua Shuju.

Luo Zhufeng 羅竹風, ed. 1989. *Hanyu dacidian* 漢語大詞典. 10 vols. Shanghai: Hanyu Dacidian Chubanshe.

Makita Tairyō 牧田諦亮. 1957. *Chūgoku kinsei Bukkyōshi kenkyū* 中國近世佛教史研究. Kyoto: Heirakuji Shoten.

Maspero, Henri. 1981. *Taoism and Chinese Religion.* Translated by Frank A. Kierman Jr. Amherst: University of Massachusetts Press.

Mathews, R. H. 1944. *Chinese-English Dictionary.* Rev. American ed. Cambridge, Mass.: Harvard University Press.

Matsubara Yūzen 松原祐善. 1978. *Mappō tōmyōki no kenkyū* 末法燈明記の研究. Kyoto: Hōzōkan.

Matsuo Kenji 松尾剛次. 1985. "Kansō to tonseisō: Kamakura shin Bukkyō no seiritsu to Nihon jukaisei" 官僧と遁世僧、鎌倉新仏教の成立と日本授戒制. *Shigaku zasshi* 史学雑誌 94:3.

———. 1988. *Kamakura shin Bukkyō no seiritsu: Nyūmon girei to soshi shinwa* 鎌倉新仏教の成立、入門儀礼と祖師神話. Tokyo: Yoshikawa Kōbunkan.

———. 1996. *Kyūsai no shisō: Eison kyōdan to Kamakura shin Bukkyō* 救済の思想、叡尊教団と鎌倉新仏教. Tokyo: Kadokawa Shoten.

McKnight, Brian E. 1981. *The Quality of Mercy: Amnesties and Traditional Chinese Justice.* Honolulu: University of Hawai'i Press.

———. 1992. *Law and Order in Sung China.* Cambridge: Cambridge University Press.

McRae, John. 1983. "The Ox-head School of Chinese Ch'an Buddhism." In *Studies in Ch'an and Hua-yen,* edited by Robert M. Gimello and Peter N. Gregory, 169–252. Honolulu: University of Hawai'i Press.

———. 1986. *The Northern School and the Formation of Early Ch'an Buddhism.* Honolulu: University of Hawai'i Press.

———. 1993–1994. "Yanagida Seizan's Landmark Works on Chinese Ch'an." *Cahiers d'Extrême-Asie* 7:51–103.

Mertz, John. Forthcoming. *Novel Japan: Spaces of Nationhood in Early Meiji Narrative, 1870–1888.* Ann Arbor: University of Michigan Press.

Michihata Ryōshū 道端良秀. 1970. *Chūgoku Bukkyōshi no kenkyū* 中国仏教史の研究. Kyoto: Hōzōkan.

———. 1972. "Chūgoku Bukkyō to Daijō kaidan" 中国仏教と大乗戒壇. *Satō hakase koki kinen Bukkyō shisō ronshū* 佐藤博士古希記念仏教思想論集, 589–607. Tokyo: Sankibō.

Mikkyō daijiten 密教大辭典. 1969–1970 (1931–1938). 6 vols. Rev. ed. Tokyo: Mikkyō Daijiten Hensankai.

Min Zhiting 閔智亭 and Li Yangzheng 李養正, eds. 1994. *Daojiao dacidian* 道教大辭典. Beijing: Huaxia Chubanshe.

Minowa Kenryō 蓑輪顕量. 1996. "Eison kyōdan ni okeru kōseiin no kaisō" 叡尊教団における構成員の階層. *Shūkyō kenkyū* 宗教研究 309:75–98.

———. 1999. *Chūsei shoki Nanto kairitsu fukkō no kenkyū* 中世初期南都戒律復興の研究. Kyoto: Hōzōkan.

Mizuno Kōgen 水野弘元. 1964. "Kanazawa bunko shozō no kairitsu kankei no bunken ni tsuite" 金沢文庫所蔵の戒律関係の文献について. *Kanazawa bunko kenkyū* 金沢文庫研究 10, no. 2:7–9.

Mochizuki Shinkō 望月信亨. 1946. *Bukkyō kyōten seiritsu shiron* 佛教經典成立史論. Kyoto: Hōzōkan.

Mori Shōji 森章司, ed. 1993. *Kairitsu no sekai* 戒律の世界. Tokyo: Hokushindō.

Moroto Tatsuo 諸戸立雄. 1990. *Chūgoku Bukkyō seidoshi no kenkyū* 中国仏教制度史の研究. Tokyo: Hirakawa Shuppansha.

Morrell, Robert E. 1987. *Early Kamakura Buddhism: A Minority Report*. Berkeley, Calif.: Asian Humanities Press.

Muranaka Yushō 村中祐生, ed. 1991. *Tendai shisō to Higashi Ajia bunka no kenkyū: Shioiri Ryōdō Sensei tsuitō ronbunshū* 天台思想と東アジア文化の研究：塩入良道先生追悼論文集. Tokyo: Sankibō Busshorin.

Murata Jirō 村田次郎. 1961. "Kaidan shōkō" 戒壇小考. *Bukkyō geijutsu* 仏教芸術 50 (December):1–16.

Nagai Yoshinori 永井義憲. 1967. *Nihon Bukkyō bungaku kenkyū* 日本佛教文學研究. Tokyo: Tōshima Shobō.

Nagamura Makoto 永村眞. 1989. *Chūsei Tōdaiji no soshiki to keiei* 中世東大寺の組織と経営. Tokyo: Hanawa Shoten.

Naitō Tatsuo 内藤龍雄. 1962. "Bosatsu zenkaikyō ni okeru ni san no mondai" 菩薩善戒経における二三の問題. *Indogaku Bukkyōgaku kenkyū* 印度學佛教學研究 10, no. 1:130–131.

Nakamura, Hajime 中村元. 1964. *Ways of Thinking of Eastern Peoples*. Honolulu: East-West Center Press.

———. 1975. *Bukkyōgo daijiten* 佛教語大辞典. 3 vols. Tokyo: Tōkyō Shoseki.

Nakazato Nisshō 中里日勝. 1899. *Sōfū kakushin ron, ichimei Chikusai jōbutsu gi* 僧風革新論・一名畜妻成佛義. Tokyo: Banjudō.

Nattier, Jan. 1991. *Once Upon a Future Time*. Berkeley, Calif.: Asian Humanities Press.

Needham, Joseph. 1986. *Science and Civilization in China*. Vol. 1. Cambridge: Cambridge University Press.

Nei Kiyoshi 根井浄. 1980. "Nihon kodai no zenji ni tsuite" 日本古代の禅師について. *Bukkyō shigaku kenkyū* 佛教史学研究 22, no. 2:13–56.

Nickerson, Peter. 1994. "Shamans, Demons, Diviners, and Taoists: Conflict and Assimilation in Medieval Chinese Ritual Practice (c. A.D. 100–1000)." *Taoist Resources* 5, no. 1:41–66.

———. 1996. "Abridged Code of Master Lu for the Daoist Community." In *Religions of China in Practice*, edited by Donald S. Lopez Jr., 347–359. Princeton, N.J.: Princeton University Press.

———. 1997. "The Great Petition for Sepulchral Plaints." In *Early Daoist Scriptures*, edited by Stephen R. Bokenkamp, 230–274. Berkeley: University of California Press.

Nishiari Bokusan 西有穆山. 1875. "Sōtōshū rokuji" 曹洞宗録事. *Meikyō shinshi* 明教新誌 150:1–2.

Nishimura, Sey. 1985. "The Prince and the Pauper: The Dynamics of a Shōtoku Legend." *Monumenta Nipponica* 40, no. 3:299–310.

Nonomura Kaoru 野々村馨. 1996. *Kū neru suwaru: Eiheiji shugyō ki* 食う寝る坐る：永平寺修行記. Tokyo: Shinchōsha.

Nōtomi Jōten 納富常天. 1977. "Nanto Bukkyō ni okeru nyonin ōjō shisō ni tsuite" 南都仏教における女人往生思想について. *Indogaku Bukkyōgaku kenkyū* 印度學佛教學研究 12, no. 2:556–561.

Ōchō Enichi 横超慧日. 1941. "Kaidan ni tsuite" 戒壇について. *Shina Bukkyō shigaku* 支那佛教史學 5, no. 1:15–41.

———. 1942. "Kaidan ni tsuite (chū 中)." *Shina Bukkyō shigaku* 5, no. 2:32–56.

———. 1958. *Chūgoku Bukkyō no kenkyū* 中国仏教の研究. Kyoto: Hōzōkan.

———. 1979. "Kaidan ni tsuite" 戒壇について. 1941–1942. Reprinted in *Chūgoku Bukkyō no kenkyū, dai-san* 中国仏教の研究・第三, 1–74. Kyoto: Hōzōkan.

Odawara Toshihito 小田原利仁, ed. 1993. *Toshi danshinto no shukyō ishiki* 都市団信徒の宗教意識. Tokyo: Sōtōshū Shūmuchō.

Ōfuchi Ninji 大淵忍爾. 1983. *Chūgokujin no shūkyō girei: Bukkyō Dōkyō minkan shinkō* 中国人の宗教儀礼、仏教、道教民間信仰. Tokyo: Fukutake Shoten.

Ogasawara Senshū 小笠原宣秀. 1961. "Toroban monjo ni arawaretaru giransō no mondai" 吐魯番文書に現れたる偽濫僧の問題. *Indogaku Bukkyōgaku kenkyū* 印度學佛教學研究 9, no. 2:205–211.

———. 1963. *Chūgoku kinsei Jōdokyōshi no kenkyū* 中国近世浄土教史の研究. Kyoto: Hyakkaen.

Ogawa Kan'ichi 小川貫弌. 1936. "Senshi Goetsukoku no Bukkyō ni tsuite" 錢氏呉越國の仏教について. *Ryūkoku shidan* 龍谷史談 18:45–65.

———. 1968. "Sō, Gen, Min, Shin ni okeru kyōdan no kōzō" 宋元明清に於ける教団の構造. In *Bukkyō kyōdan no kenkyū* 佛教教團の研究, edited by Yoshimura Shūki 芳村修基, 283–321. Kyoto: Hyakkaen.

Ōhashi Shunnō 大橋俊雄, ed. 1971. *Hōnen-Ippen* 法然・一遍. Nihon Shisō Taikei 日本思想大系, vol. 10. Tokyo: Iwanami Shoten.

———. 1973. *Jishū no seiritsu to tenkai* 時宗の成立と展開. Tokyo: Yoshikawa Kōbunkan.

Oikawa Shigeru 及川茂. 1998. *Saigo no ukiyoe shi: Kawanabe Gyōsai to hankotsu no bigaku* 最後の浮世絵師・河鍋暁斎と反骨の美学. Tokyo: Hōsō Shuppan Kyōkai.

Okimoto Katsumi 沖本克巳. 1972. "Bodhisattva Prātimokṣa." *Indogaku Bukkyōgaku kenkyū* 印度學佛教學研究 21, no. 1:130–131.

———. 1973. "Bosatsu zenkaikyō ni tsuite" 菩薩善戒経について. *Indogaku Bukkyōgaku kenkyū* 印度學佛教學研究 22, no. 1:373–378.

Omaru Shinji 小丸真司. 1984. "Hanju sanmai kyō to kanbutsu sanmai" 般舟三昧経と観仏三昧. *Indogaku Bukkyōgaku kenkyū* 印度學佛教學研究 32, no. 2:378–381.

———. 1985. "Kanmuryōjukyō to shōmyō shisō" 觀無量壽經と稱名思想.
    In *Hirakawa Akira hakushi koki kinen ronshū Bukkyō shisō no sho
    mondai* 平川彰博士古希記念論集：仏教思想の諸問題，　427–442.
    Tokyo: Shunjūsha.

Ōmura Seigai 大村西崖. 1972a. *Shina bijutsushi chōso hen* 支那美術史彫塑
    篇. 1917. Reprint, Tokyo: Kokusho Kankōkai.

———. 1972b. *Mikkyō hattatsu shi* 密教発達史. 1919. Reprint, Tokyo: Ko-
    kusho Kankōkai.

Ōno Hōdō 大野法道. 1954. *Daijō kaikyō no kenkyū* 大乘戒經の研究. Tokyo:
    Risōsha.

Ono Katsutoshi 小野勝年. 1966. *Nittō guhō junrei kōki no kenkyū* 入唐求法
    巡禮行記の研究. Tokyo: Suzuki Gakujutsu Zaidan.

Osabe Kazuo 長部和雄. 1971. *Tōdai mikkyōshi zakkō* 唐代密教史雑考. Kobe:
    Kōbe Shōka Daigaku Gakujutsu Kenkyūkai.

Overmyer, Daniel L. 1976. *Folk Buddhist Religion: Dissenting Sects in
    Late Traditional China*. Cambridge, Mass.: Harvard University Press.

Pagel, Ulrich. 1995. *The Bodhisattvapiṭaka: Its Doctines, Practices and Their
    Position in Mahāyāna Literature*. Buddhica Britannica Series Con-
    tinua, vol. 5. Tring, England: The Institute of Buddhist Studies.

Peng, Fei, and Gary Seaman. 1994. *Chinese Mulian Plays: Resources for
    Studies of Ritual and Performance*. Los Angeles: Ethnographics
    Press, University of Southern California.

Penkower, Linda. 1993. "T'ien-t'ai during the Tang Dynasty: Chan-jan and
    the Sinification of Buddhism." Ph.D. diss., Columbia University.

Penny, Benjamin. 1996. "Buddhism and Taoism in the 180 Precepts Spoken
    by Lord Lao." *Taoist Resources* 6, no. 2:1–16.

Peterson, Charles A. 1973. "The Restoration Completed: Emperor Hsien-
    tsung and the Provinces." In *Perspectives on the T'ang*, edited by A.
    F. Wright and D. C. Twitchett, 151–191. New Haven, Conn.: Yale
    University Press.

Poo, Mu-chou. 1998. *In Search of Personal Welfare: A View of Ancient Chi-
    nese Religion*. Albany: State University of New York Press.

Pulleyblank, E. G. 1952. "A Sogdian Colony in Inner Mongolia." *T'oung Pao*
    41:319–352.

Python, Pierre. 1973. *Vinaya-Viniścaya-Upāli-Paripṛcchā: Enquête d'Upāli
    pour une exégèse de la Discipline*. Paris: Adrien-Maisonneuve.

Rao Zongyi 饒宗頤. 1991. *Laozi Xiang'er zhu jiaozheng* 老子想爾注校證.
    Shanghai: Shanghai Guji Chubanshe.

Reis-Habito, Maria. 1993. *Die Dhāranī des grosen Erbarmens des Bodhi-
    sattva Avalokiteśvara mit tausend Handen und Augen*. Nettetal:
    Steyler Verlag.

Ren Jiyu 任繼愈, ed. 1991. *Daozang tiyao* 道臧提要. Beijing: Chinese Acad-
    emy of Social Science, New China Bookstore.

Robinet, Isabelle. 1993. *Taoist Meditation*. Albany: State University of New York Press.

Ruegg, David S. 1980. "Ahiṃsā and Vegetarianism in the History of Buddhism." In *Buddhist Studies in Honor of Walpola Rahula*, edited by Ṣomaratna Bālasūriya and Walpola Rahula, 234–241. London: Gordon Fraser.

Ryūkoku Daigaku 龍谷大学, ed. 1972. *Bukkyō daijii* 佛教大辭彙. 1914. 7 vols. Reprint, Tokyo: Fuzanbō.

Sanda Zenshin 三田全信. 1975. "Kongōhōkai to Jōdo fusatsu no ronshū: Kaisetsu" 金剛宝戒と浄土布薩の論集・解説. In *Jōdoshū tenseki kenkyū* 浄土宗典籍研究, edited by Sankibō Busshorin 山喜房佛書林, 755–765. Tokyo: Sankibō Busshorin.

Satō Seijun 佐藤成順. 1988. "Hokusō jidai no Kōshū no Jōdokyōsha" 北宋時代の杭州の浄土教者. In *Chūgoku no Bukkyō to bunka: Kamata Shigeo hakushi kanreki kinen ronshū* 中国の仏教と文化、鎌田茂雄博士還暦記念論集, 457–482. Tokyo: Daizō Shuppan.

Satō Tatsugen 佐藤達玄. 1986. *Chūgoku Bukkyō ni okeru kairitsu no kenkyū* 中国仏教に於ける戒律の研究. Tokyo: Mokujisha.

———. 1993. "Shibun risshū no keisei to tenkai" 四分律宗の形成と展開. 1973. Reprinted in *Kairitsu no sekai* 戒律の世界, edited by Mori Shōji 森章司, 511–529. Tokyo: Hokushindō.

Satō Tetsuei 佐藤哲英. 1961. *Tendai daishi no kenkyū* 天台大師の研究. Kyoto: Hyakkaen.

Schipper, K. M. 1975. *Concordance du Tao-tsang: Titres des Ouvrages*. Paris: L'École Française d'Extrême-Orient.

———. 1983. "Tonkō monjo ni mieru Dōshi no hōi kaitei ni tsuite" 敦煌文書に見える道士の法位階梯について. In *Tonkō to Chūgoku Dōkyō* 敦煌と中國道教, edited by Kanaoka Shōkō 金岡照光, Ikeda On 池田温, and Fukui Fumimasa 福井文雅, Kōza Tonkō 講座敦煌 5:325–345. Tokyo: Daitō Shuppansha.

Schopen, Gregory. 1995. "Deaths, Funerals, and the Division of Property in a Monastic Code." In *Buddhism in Practice*, edited by Donald S. Lopez, 473–502. Princeton, N.J.: Princeton University Press.

———. 1997. *Bones, Stones, and Buddhist Monks: Collected Papers on the Archaeology, Epigraphy, and Texts of Monastic Buddhism in India*. Studies in the Buddhist Traditions. Honolulu: University of Hawai'i Press.

———. 2000. *Daijō Bukkyō kōki jidai Indo no sōin seikatsu* 大乗仏教興起時代インドの僧院生活. Tokyo: Shunjūsha.

Séguy, Marie-Rose. 1979. "Images xylographiques conservées dans les collections de Touen-houang de la Bibliothèque nationale." In *Contribution aux Etudes sur Touen-houang*, edited by Michel Soymié, 119–133. Geneva and Paris: Librarie Droz.

Shih, Robert. 1968. *Biographies des moines éminents (Kao seng tchouan) de Houei-kiao*. Louvain: Institut Orientaliste.

Shih Ta-rui 釋大睿. 1998. "Zhongguo Fojiao zaoqi chanzui sixiang zhi xing-cheng yu fazhan" 中國佛教早期懺罪思想之形成與發展. *Zhonghua Foxue yanjiu* 中國佛學研究 *(Chung-Hwa Buddhist Studies)* 2:313–338.

Shiina Kōyū 椎名宏雄. 1968. "Sūzan ni okeru Hokushū Zen no tenkai" 嵩山に於ける北宗禅の展開. *Shūgaku kenkyū* 宗学研究 10:173–185.

———. 1993. "Hokushū Zen ni okeru kairitsu no mondai" 北宗禅に於ける戒律の問題. 1969. Reprinted in *Kairitsu no sekai* 戒律の世界, edited by Mori Shōji 森章司, 533–550. Tokyo: Hokushindō.

Shiio Benkyō 椎尾辨匡. 1931. *Jukai kōwa* 授戒講話. Tokyo: Kōdōkaku.

Shimaji Daitō 島地大等. 1933. *Nihon Bukkyō kyōgakushi* 日本佛教教學史. Tokyo: Meiji Shoin.

Shimoda Masahiro 下田正弘. 1997. *Nehangyō no kenkyū: Daijō kyōten no kenkyū hōhō shiron* 涅槃経の研究：大乗経典の研究方法試論. Tokyo: Shunjūsha.

Shinohara, Koichi. 1990. "Daoxuan's Collection of Miracle Stories about Supernatural Monks *(Shenseng gantong lu)*: An Analysis of Its Sources." *Zhonghua Foxue xuebao* 中華佛學學報 *(Chung-Hwa Buddhist Journal)* 3:319–379.

———. 1991a. "The 'Ji shenzhou sanbao gantong lu': Exploratory Notes." In *Kalyana Mitta: Professor Hajime Nakamura Felicitation Volume*, edited by V. N. Jha, 203–224. Delhi: Sri Satguru Publications.

———. 1991b. "The 'Ruijing lu': An Analysis of Its Sources." *Journal of the International Association for Buddhist Studies* 14, no. 1:73–154.

———. 1991c. "'Structure' and 'Communitas' in Po Chü-yi's Tomb Inscription." *Zhonghua Foxue xuebao* 中國佛學學報 *(Chung-Hwa Buddhist Journal)* 4:379–448.

———. 1994a. "Two Sources of Chinese Buddhist Biographies: Stupa Inscriptions and Miracle Stories." 1988. In *Monks and Magicians: Religious Biographies in Asia*, edited by Phyllis Granoff and Koichi Shinohara, 119–128. Reprint, Delhi: Motilal Banarsidass.

———. 1994b. "'Biographies of Eminent Monks' in a Comparative Perspective: The Function of the Holy in Medieval Chinese Buddhism." *Zhonghua Foxue xuebao* 中國佛學學報 7:477–500.

Shioiri Ryōdō 塩入良道. 1961. "Bunsennō Shō Shiryō no 'Jōjūshi jōgyō hōmon' ni tsuite 文宣王蕭子良の「淨住小淨行法門」について. *Taishō daigaku kenkyū kiyō* 大正大学研究記要 46:43–96.

———. 1964. "Chūgoku Bukkyō ni okeru raisan to butsumyō kyōten" 中国仏教に於ける礼懺と仏名経典. In *Bukkyō shisōshi ronshū: Yūki kyōju shōju kinen* 仏教思想史論集、結城教授頌寿記念, 569–590. Tokyo: Daizō Shuppan.

———. 1977. "'Jihi dōjō senpo' no seiritsu"「慈悲道場懺法」の成立. In *Dōkyō kenkyū ronshū: Dōkyō no shisō to bunka; Yoshioka hakase kanreki kinen* 道教研究論集、道教の思想と文化、吉岡博士還暦記念, edited by Makio Ryōkai 牧男良海, Yasui Kōzan 安井香山, et al., 501–521. Tokyo: Kokusho Kankōkai.

Shiraishi Hōryū 白石芳留. 1976. *Zenshū hennenshi* 禪宗編年史. 2 vols. 1937. Reprint, Osaka: Tōhōkai.

Shirato Waka 白土わか. 1969. "Bonmōkyō kenkyū josetsu" 梵網経研究序説. *Ōtani daigaku kenkyū nenpō* 大谷大学研究年報 22:105–153.

Shizutani Masao 静谷正雄. 1974. *Shoki Daijō Bukkyō no seiritsu katei* 初期大乗仏教の成立過程. Kyoto: Hyakkaen.

Sonoda Kōyū 薗田香融. 1981. "Kodai Bukkyō ni okeru sanrin shugyō to sono igi: Toku ni Jinenchishū o megutte" 古代仏教における山林修行とその意義、特に自然智宗をめぐって. 1957. Reprinted in *Heian Bukkyō no kenkyū* 平安佛教の研究, 27–57. Kyoto: Hōzōkan.

Soper, Alexander C. 1958. "Northern Liang and Northern Wei in Kansu." *Artibus Asiae* 21, no. 2:131–164.

———. 1959. "Literary Evidence for Early Buddhist Art in China." *Artibus Asiae Supplementum* 19:1–296.

Steele, John, trans. 1966. *The I-li: Book of Etiquette and Ceremonial.* 1917. London. Reprint, Taipei: Ch'eng-wen Publishing.

Stevenson, Daniel B. 1987. "The T'ien-t'ai Four Forms of Samādhi and Late North-South Dynasties, Sui, and Early T'ang Buddhist Devotionalism." 2 vols. Ph.D. diss., Columbia University.

Strickmann, Michel. 1990. "The 'Consecration Sūtra': A Buddhist Book of Spells." In *Chinese Buddhist Apocrypha*, edited by Robert Buswell, 75–118. Honolulu: University of Hawai'i Press.

Sueki Fumihiko 末木文美士. 1994. "Annen: The Philosopher Who Japanized Buddhism." *Acta Asiatica* 66:69–86.

Sunayama Minoru 砂山稔. 1990. *Zui-Tō Dōkyō shisōshi kenkyū* 隋唐道教思想史研究. Tokyo: Hirakawa Shuppansha.

Suwa Gijun 諏訪義純. 1971. "Tonkō bon Shukke-nin ju bosatsukai hō ichi jo ichi ni tsuite: Chigi jutsu Kanjō ki Bosatsukai gisho to sono kanren o chūshin to shite" 敦煌本「出家人受菩薩戒法」一序一について：智顗述灌頂記「菩薩戒義疏」とその関連を中心として. *Zen kenkyūjo kiyō* 禅研究所紀要 1:55–63.

———. 1972a. "Ryō Tenkan jūhachi nen chokusha Shukkenin ju bosatsukai hō maki daiichi shiron" 梁天監十八年勅写「出家人受菩薩戒法巻第一」史論. In *Tonkō koshakyō* 敦煌古写経, edited by Nogami Shunjō 野上俊静, 2:85–92. Kyoto: Ōtani Daigaku Tōyōgaku Kenkyūshitsu.

———. 1972b. "Tendaisho no seishi ni tsuite: Perio bon 'Shukkenin ju bosatsukai hō maki daiichi' kara" 天台疏の制旨について：ペリオ

本「出家人受菩薩戒法卷第一」から. *Indogaku Bukkyōgaku kenkyū* 印度學佛教學研究 21, no. 1:348–350.

Suzuki Chūsei 鈴木中正. 1974. *Chūgoku ni okeru kakumei to shūkyō* 中国史における革命と宗教. Tokyo: Tōkyō Daigaku Shuppankai.

Suzuki Daisetsu 鈴木大拙. 1970. "Beikoku tsūshin (sōryo no nikujiki ni tsukite)" 米穀通信（僧侶の肉食に就きて）. 1900. Reprinted in *Suzuki Daisetsu zenshū* 鈴木大拙全集, 27:415–418. Tokyo: Iwanami Shoten.

Suzuki Ryōshun 鈴木靈俊. 1982. "Jōdo fusatsu kai no ichi kōsatsu: Fumyaku yori mita kaikei" 浄土布薩戒の一考察、譜脈より見た戒系. *Bukkyō ronsō* 仏教論叢 26:106–109.

Taira Ryōshō 平了照. 1955. "Den-Eshi bon 'Jubosatsukaigi' ni tsuite" 伝慧思本授菩薩戒儀について. *Taishō daigaku kenkyū kiyō* 大正大学研究記要 40:1–36.

Takao Giken 高雄義堅. 1975. *Sōdai Bukkyōshi no kenkyū* 宋代仏教史の研究. Kyoto: Hyakkaen.

Tamura Enchō 田村圓澄. 1959. *Nihon Bukkyō shisōshi kenkyū: Jōdokyō hen* 日本仏教思想史研究、浄土教篇. Kyoto: Heirakuji Shoten.

Tanabe Zenchi 田邊善知. 1901. *Nihon Bukkyō nikujiki saitai ron* 日本佛教肉食妻帶論. Tokyo: Sugino Iheiei.

Tang Chengye 湯承業. 1973. *Li Deyu yanjiu* 李德裕研究. Taibei: Jiaxin Shuini Gongsi Wenhua Jijin Hui.

Tatz, Mark. 1986. *Asanga's Chapter on Ethics: With the Commentary of Tsong-kha-pa, "The Basic Path to Awakening," The Complete Bodhisattva.* Lewiston, N. Y.: The Edwin Mellen Press.

Teiser, Stephen F. 1988. *The Ghost Festival in Medieval China.* Princeton, N.J.: Princeton University Press.

———. 1993. "The Growth of Purgatory." In *Religion and Society in T'ang and Sung China*, edited by Patricia Buckley Ebrey and Peter N. Gregory, 115–146. Honolulu: University of Hawai'i Press.

———. 1994. *The* Scripture of the Ten Kings *and the Making of Purgatory in Medieval Chinese Buddhism.* Kuroda Institute Studies in East Asian Buddhism, no. 9. Honolulu: University of Hawai'i Press.

Tokuda Myōhon 徳田明本. 1969. *Risshū gairon* 律宗概論. Kyoto: Hyakkaen.

———. 1973. *Tōshōdaiji* 唐招提寺. Tokyo: Gakuseisha.

Tokuno, Kyoko. 1990. "The Evaluation of Indigenous Scriptures in Chinese Buddhist Bibliographical Catalogues." In *Chinese Buddhist Apocrypha*, edited by Robert E. Buswell Jr., 31–74. Honolulu: University of Hawai'i Press.

Tonegawa Kōgyō 利根川浩行. 1978. "Shimei Chirei no *Jubosatsukaigi*" 四明知礼の授菩薩戒儀. *Indogaku Bukkyōgaku kenkyū* 印度學佛教學研究 27, no. 1:303–305.

Tsai, Kathryn Ann, trans. 1994. *Lives of the Nuns: Biographies of Chinese*

    Buddhist Nuns from the Fourth to Sixth Centuries. Honolulu: University of Hawai'i Press.

Tsuboi Shun'ei 坪井俊映. 1961. "Nenbutsu to kai ni tsuite: Toku ni Hōnen no baai" 念仏と戒について、特に法然の場合. *Indogaku Bukkyōgaku kenkyū* 印度學佛教學研究 9, no. 1:281–284.

Tsuchihashi, Shūkō 土橋秀高. 1980a. "Jukai girei no hensen" 受戒儀礼の変遷. 1968. Reprinted in *Kairitsu no kenkyū* 戒律の研究, 281–363. Kyoto: Nagata Bunshōdō.

———. 1980b. "Perio-bon 'Shukkenin jubosatsukaihō' ni tsuite" ペリオ本「出家人受菩薩戒法」について. 1968. Reprinted in *Kairitsu no kenkyū*, 832–886. Kyoto: Nagata Bunshōdō.

———. 1980c. "Tonkōbon 'Jubosatsukaigi' kō" 敦煌本「受菩薩戒儀」考. 1960. Reprinted in *Kairitsu no kenkyū*, 792–805. Kyoto: Nagata Bunshōdō.

Tsui, Bartholomew. 1991. *Taoist Tradition and Change: The Story of the Complete Perfection Sect in Hong Kong.* Hong Kong: Christian Study Centre on Chinese Religion and Culture.

Tsuji Zennosuke 辻善之助. 1947. *Nihon Bukkyōshi* 日本佛教史. 10 vols. Tokyo: Iwanami Shoten.

Tsukamoto Zenryū 塚本善隆. 1975. *Chūgoku kindai Bukkyōshi no shomondai* 中国近代仏教史の諸問題. *Tsukamoto Zenryū chosaku shū* 塚本善隆著作集, vol. 5. Tokyo: Daitō Shuppansha.

Turner, Karen. 1990. "Sage Kings and Laws in the Chinese and Greek Traditions." In *Heritage of China: Contemporary Perspectives on Chinese Civilization*, edited by Paul S. Ropp, 86–111. Berkeley: University of California Press.

Twitchett, Denis. 1957. "The Monasteries and China's Economy in Medieval Times." *Bulletin of the School of Oriental and African Studies* 18, no. 2:526–549.

———, ed. 1979. *The Cambridge History of China.* Vol. 3. Cambridge: Cambridge University Press

Ueda Shōhen 上田照遍. 1982. *Shakumon yuitei tekagami sōhiron* 釋門遺弟手鏡僧非論. 1879. Reprinted in *Meiji Bukkyō Shisō Shiryō Shūsei* 明治佛教思想集成, edited by Meiji Bukkyō Shisō Shiryō Shūsei Henshū Iinkai 明治佛教思想集成編集委員会, 7:228–232. Tokyo: Dōbōsha Shuppan.

Ueda Tenzui 上田天瑞. 1976. *Kairitsu no shisō to rekishi* 戒律の思想と歴史. Wakayama prefecture, Japan: Mikkyō Bunka Kenkyūjo.

Ugawa Shōchō 宇川照澄. 1949. *Kyōbu Goshōsho* 教部御省書. 1872. Reprinted in *Meiji Bukkyōshi no mondai* 明治佛教史の問題, edited by Tsuji Zennosuke 辻善之助, 219–227. Tokyo: Ritsubun Shoin.

Upasak, Chandrika Singh. 1975. *Dictionary of Early Buddhist Monastic Terms.* Varanasi: Bharati Prakashan.

Ushiba Shingen 牛場眞玄. 1971. "Denjutsu isshin kaimon no seiritsu ni tsuite no utagai" 伝述一心戒文の成立についての疑. *Nanto Bukkyō* 南都佛教 26:54–77.

Victoria, Brian D. A. 1997. *Zen at War*. New York: John Weatherhill.

von Glahn, Richard. 1993. Review of *Changing Gods in Medieval China, 1127–1276*, by Valerie Hansen. *Harvard Journal of Asiatic Studies*. 53:616–642.

Wajima Yoshio 輪島芳男. 1959. *Eison-Ninshō* 叡尊・忍性. Tokyo: Yoshikawa Kōbunkan.

Watanabe Baiyū 渡邊楳雄. 1920a. "Sakana wa kutte warui ka" 魚は食って惡いか. *Daiichigi* 第一義 24, no. 1:76–85.

———. 1920b. "Sakana wa koroshite warui ka (sesshū kai no hihan)" 魚は殺して惡いか（殺生戒の批判）. *Daiichigi* 24, no. 2:41–46.

Watson, Burton, trans. 1997. *The Vimalakirti Sutra*. New York: Columbia University Press.

Wechsler, Howard J. 1985. *Offerings of Jade and Silk: Ritual and Symbol in the Legitimation of the T'ang Dynasty*. New Haven, Conn.: Yale University Press.

Weinstein, Stanley. 1959. "A Biographical Study of Tz'u-en." *Monumenta Nipponica* 15, nos. 1–2:119–149.

———. 1973. "Imperial Patronage in the Formation of T'ang Buddhism." In *Perspectives on the T'ang*, edited by Arthur F. Wright and Denis Twitchett, 265–306. New Haven, Conn.: Yale University Press.

———. 1987a. *Buddhism under the T'ang*. New York: Cambridge University Press.

———. 1987b. "The Schools of Chinese Buddhism." In ER, 2:486.

Welch, Holmes. 1967. *The Practice of Chinese Buddhism, 1900–1950*. Cambridge, Mass.: Harvard University Press.

Welter, Albert. 1993. *The Meaning of Myriad Good Deeds: A Study of Yung-ming Yen-shou and the 'Wan-shan t'ung-kuei chi.'* New York: Peter Lang.

Wogihara Unrai, ed. 1971. *Bodhisattvabhūmi: A Statement of Whole Course of the Bodhisattva (Being Fifteenth Section of Yogācārabhūmi)*. 1936. Reprint, Tokyo: Sankibō Busshorin.

Wright, Arthur F. 1990. "Biography and Hagiography: Hui-chiao's *Lives of Eminent Monks*." 1954. Reprinted in *Studies in Chinese Buddhism*, edited by Robert M. Somers, 73–111. New Haven, Conn.: Yale University Press.

Xiang Da 向達. 1957. *Tangdai Chang'an yu Xiyu wenming* 唐代長安与西域文明. Beijing: Sanlian Shudian.

Xie Zhongguang 谢重光 and Bai Wengu 白文固. 1990. *Zhongguo sengguan zhidu shi* 中国僧官制度史. Qinghai: Qinghai Renmin Chubanshe.

Yamabe Nobuyoshi 山部能宜. 1999a. "An Examination of the Mural Paintings of Toyok Cave 20 in Conjunction with the Origin of the *Ami-tayus Visualization Sutra*." *Orientations* 30, no. 4:38–44.

———. 1999b. "The Sūtra on the Ocean-like Samādhi of the Visualization of the Buddha: The Interfusion of the Chinese and Indian Cultures in Central Asia as Reflected in a Fifth Century Apocryphal Sūtra." Ph.D. diss., Yale University.

———. 2000. "'Bonmōkyō' ni okeru kōsōgyō no kenkyū: toku ni zenkan kyōten to no kanrensei ni chakumoku shite" 「梵網経」における好相行の研究、特に禅観経典との関連性に着目して. In *Hokuchō Zui-Tō Chūgoku Bukkyō shisōshi* 北朝隋唐中国仏教思想史, edited by Aramaki Noritoshi 荒牧典俊, 205–269. Kyoto: Hōzōkan.

———. 2001. "External World: An Approach to Environmental Problems from a Buddhist Perspective." *The Eastern Buddhist* 33, no. 1:128–143

Yamada Bunshō 山田文昭. 1979. *Shinshūshi no kenkyū* 眞宗史の研究. 1934. Reprint, Kyoto: Hōzōkan.

Yamazaki Hiroshi 山崎宏. 1967. "Tō no Saimyōji Dōsen to kantsū" 唐の西明寺道宣と感通. In *Zui-Tō Bukkyō no kenkyū* 隋唐仏教の研究, 159–186. Kyoto: Hōzōkan.

Yampolsky, Philip B. 1967. *The Platform Sutra of the Sixth Patriarch.* New York: Columbia University Press.

Yanagida Seizan 柳田聖山. 1964. "Daijō kaikyō toshite no 'Rokuso dankyō'" 大乗戒経としての「六祖壇経」. *Indogaku Bukkyōgaku kenkyū* 印度學佛教學研究 23, no. 2:1–31.

———. 1967. *Shoki Zenshū shisho no kenkyū* 初期禅宗史書の研究. Kyoto: Hōzōkan.

———. 1972. "Eisai to Kōzen gokokuron no kadai" 栄西と興禅護国論の課題. In *Chūsei zenka no shisō* 中世禪家の思想, edited by Ichikawa Hakugen 市川白弦, Iriya Yoshitaka 入矢義高, and Yanagida Seizan 柳田聖山, Nihon Shisō Taikei 日本思想大系, 16:439–486. Tokyo: Iwanami Shoten.

———. 1976. *Shoki no zenshi II: Rekidai hōbō ki* 初期の禅史 II・歴代法寶記. Tokyo: Chikuma Shobō.

———. 1985. "Goroku no rekishi: Zen bunken no seiritsu shiteki kenkyū" 語録の歴史・禅文献の成立史的研究. *Tōhō gakuhō* 東方学報 57:211–663.

———. 1990. "Tanyu yu tanjing" 壇語與壇經. In *Foguangshan guoji Chanxue huiyi shilu* 佛光山國際禪學會議實録, edited by Foguangshan, 41–48. Gaoxiong: Foguangshan Chubanshe.

Yang Zengwen 楊曾文. 1993. *Dunhuang xinben Liuzu tanjing* 敦煌新本六祖壇經. Shanghai: Shanghai Guji Chubanshe.

Yasumaru Yoshio 安丸良夫 and Miyachi Masato 宮地正人, eds. 1988. *Shūkyō to kokka* 宗教と国家. Tokyo: Iwanami Shoten.

Yifa. 1996. "The Rules of Purity for the Chan Monastery: An Annotated Translation and Study of the *Chanyuan qinggui.* " Ph.D. diss., Yale University.

———. 2002. *The Origins of Buddhist Monastic Codes in China: An Annotated Translation of the* Chanyuan qinggui. Kuroda Institute Classics in East Asian Buddhism. Honolulu: University of Hawaiʻi Press.

Yoshida Fumio 吉田文夫. 1972. "Nanto Bukkyō no fukkō" 南都仏教の復興. In *Kamakura Bukkyō 3: Chihō bushi to daimoku* 鎌倉仏教3：地方武士と題目, edited by Nakamura Hajime 中村元, Kasahara Kazuo 笠原一男, and Kanaoka Shūyū 金岡秀友, Ajia Bukkyōshi: Nihonhen アジア仏教史・日本編, 5:167–220. Tokyo: Kōsei Shuppansha.

Yoshioka, Yoshitoyo 吉岡義豊. 1983. *Dōkyō to Bukkyō* 道教と仏教. 1970. 3 vols. Reprint, Tokyo: Kokusho Kankōkai.

Yü Chün-fang. 1981. *The Renewal of Buddhism in China.* New York: Columbia University Press.

Zhou Shaoliang 周紹良. 1992. *Tangdai muzhi huibian* 唐代墓誌彙編. Shanghai: Shanghai Guji Chubanshe.

Zhuang Weifeng 莊威風. 1985. *Zhongguo difangzhi lianhe mulu* 中國地方志聯合目録. Beijing: Zhonghua Shuju.

Zürcher, Erik. 1959. *The Buddhist Conquest of China: The Spread and Adaptation of Buddhism in Early Medieval China.* 2 vols. Leiden: E. J. Brill.

———. 1980. "Buddhist Influence on Early Taoism." *T'oung Pao* 66:84–147.

———. 1982. "Prince Moonlight: Messianism and Eschatology in Early Medieval Buddhism." *T'oung Pao* 68:1–75.

Contributors

T. H. Barrett received his Ph.D. from Yale University in 1979. He is professor at the School of Oriental and African Studies, University of London, and author of *Li Ao: Buddhist, Taoist or Neo-Confucian?* (Oxford: Oxford University Press, 1992) and *Taoism Under the T'ang: Religion & Empire during the Golden Age of Chinese History* (London: Wellsweep, 1996).

William M. Bodiford received his Ph.D. from Yale University in 1989. He is associate professor at the University of California, Los Angeles, and author of *Sōtō Zen in Medieval Japan* (Honolulu: University of Hawai'i Press, 1994).

David W. Chappell received his Ph.D. from Yale University in 1976. He is professor at Soka University of America, California, and professor emeritus at the University of Hawai'i. He has edited several books, including *T'ien-t'ai Buddhism: An Outline of the Fourfold Teachings* (Tokyo: Daiichi Shobo, 1983), *Buddhist and Taoist Practice in Medieval Chinese Society* (Honolulu: University of Hawai'i Press, 1987), and *Buddhist Peacework: Creating Cultures of Peace* (Somerville, Mass.: Wisdom Publications, 1999). He served as founding editor (1981–1995) of the academic journal *Buddhist-Christian Studies*.

James C. Dobbins received his Ph.D. from Yale University in 1984. He is professor at Oberlin College, Oberlin, Ohio, and author of *Jōdo Shinshū: Shin Buddhism in Medieval Japan* (1989; reprinted Honolulu: University of Hawai'i Press, 2002) and *Letters of the Nun Eshinni: Images of Pure Land Buddhism in Medieval Japan* (Honolulu: University of Hawai'i Press, in press). He edited "The Legacy of Kuroda Toshio," a special issue of *The Japanese Journal of Religious Studies,* 1996.

Daniel A. Getz received his Ph.D. from Yale University in 1994. He is associate professor at Bradley University in Peoria, Illinois. He served as coeditor of *Buddhism in the Sung* (Honolulu: University of Hawai'i Press, 2000) and is the author of several studies on Buddhism and Pure Land in China.

PAUL GRONER received his Ph.D. from Yale University in 1979. He is professor at the University of Virginia, Charlottesville, and author of *Saichō: The Establishment of the Japanese Tendai School* (1984; reprinted Honolulu: University of Hawai'i Press, 2000) and *Ryōgen and Mount Hiei: Japanese Tendai in the Tenth Century* (Honolulu: University of Hawai'i Press, 2002).

RICHARD M. JAFFE received his Ph.D. from Yale University in 1995. He is assistant professor of Buddhist Studies in the Department of Religion, Duke University, and author of *Neither Monk nor Layman: Clerical Marriage in Modern Japanese Buddhism* (Princeton, N.J.: Princeton University Press, 2001) as well as other studies of Buddhist modernism.

JOHN R. MCRAE received his Ph.D. from Yale University in 1983. He is associate professor at Indiana University, Bloomington, and author of *The Northern School of Chinese Ch'an Buddhism* (Honolulu: University of Hawai'i Press, 1986) and *Seeing Through Zen* (Berkeley: University of California Press, 2003).

MORTEN SCHLÜTTER received his Ph.D. from Yale University in 1998. He has taught at Victoria University, New Zealand; the University of Wisconsin, Madison; the University of California, Los Angeles; and Yale University. He is the author of "Silent Illumination, Kung-an Introspection, and the Competition for Lay Patronage in Sung-Dynasty Ch'an" (in *Buddhism in the Sung*, edited by Peter N. Gregory and Daniel Getz, Honolulu: University of Hawai'i Press, 1999) and "'Before the Empty Eon' versus 'A Dog has no Buddha-nature': Kung-an Use in the Ts'ao-tung Tradition and Ta-hui's Kung-an Introspection Ch'an" (in *The Kōan: Texts and Contexts in Zen Buddhism*, edited by Steven Heine and Dale S. Wright, New York: Oxford University Press, 2000).

NOBUYOSHI YAMABE 山部能宜 received his Ph.D. from Yale University in 1999. He is professor at Tokyo University of Agriculture and has written numerous articles, including "External World: An Approach to Environmental Problems from a Buddhist Perspective" and "An Examination of the Mural Paintings of Toyok Cave 20 in Conjunction with the Origin of the *Amitayus Visualization Sutra.*"

YIFA 依法 received her Ph.D. from Yale University in 1996. She is a Buddhist nun, professor at Hsi Lai University, California, and author of *The Origins of Buddhist Monastic Codes in China: An Annotated Translation of the Chanyuan qinggui* (Honolulu: University of Hawai'i Press, 2002).

Index

Kuroda Institute
Studies in East Asian Buddhism

Printed in the United States
By Bookmasters